HETEROSEXUAL HISTORIES

Heterosexual Histories

Edited by

Rebecca L. Davis *and* Michele Mitchell

NEW YORK UNIVERSITY PRESS

New York

NEW YORK UNIVERSITY PRESS
New York
www.nyupress.org

References to Internet websites (URLs) were accurate at the time of writing. Neither the author nor New York University Press is responsible for URLs that may have expired or changed since the manuscript was prepared.

Library of Congress Cataloging-in-Publication Data
Names: Davis, Rebecca L., editor. | Mitchell, Michele, 1965–   editor.
Title: Heterosexual histories / edited by Rebecca L. Davis and Michele Mitchell.
Description: New York: New York University Press, 2021. |
Series: Nyu series in social and cultural analysis |
Includes bibliographical references and index.
Identifiers: LCCN 2020015866 (print) | LCCN 2020015867 (ebook) |
ISBN 9781479878079 (cloth) | ISBN 9781479802289 (paperback) |
ISBN 9781479897902 (ebook) | ISBN 9781479852284 (ebook)
Subjects: LCSH: Heterosexuality—History.
Classification: LCC HQ23 .H538 2021 (print) | LCC HQ23 (ebook) | DDC 306.76/609—dc23
LC record available at https://lccn.loc.gov/2020015866
LC ebook record available at https://lccn.loc.gov/2020015867

New York University Press books are printed on acid-free paper, and their binding materials are chosen for strength and durability. We strive to use environmentally responsible suppliers and materials to the greatest extent possible in publishing our books.

Manufactured in the United States of America

10 9 8 7 6 5 4 3 2 1

Also available as an ebook

CONTENTS

Introduction, or, *Why* Do the History of Heterosexuality?

REBECCA L. DAVIS AND MICHELE MITCHELL

Josephine A. Jackson (1865–1945) was an exceptional woman. Born in the last year of the American Civil War and raised on a farm in Iowa, she became a medical doctor and nationally renowned health expert. When Jackson was given a diagnosis of tuberculosis and told she had three days to live, she later recalled that she took a train from Chicago to Pasadena and thrived for another forty years. Her first book, *Outwitting Our Nerves: A Primer of Psychotherapy* (1922), a general interpretation of psychotherapy for lay readers, was widely praised as "the best book on psychotherapy."[1] It and her next book, *Guiding Your Life with Psychology as a Key* (1937), went through multiple printings. Jackson's advice column ran in local newspapers from Nebraska to Texas during the 1920s and 1930s.

We might also remember Jackson for teaching Americans the meaning of heterosexuality. Loosely translating Freudian psychology for the masses, she instructed her readers both that different-sex sexual attraction was called "heterosexuality" and that heterosexuality was normal. This understanding marked a decisive shift; as Jonathan Ned Katz shows in his book on the origins and history of "heterosexuality," early twentieth-century dictionaries defined heterosexuality as a "morbid" sexual interest in the opposite sex.[2] In a column dated April 21, 1930, which ran adjacent to the comics, Jackson advised a young man who worried that he was more interested in boys than in girls. Jackson implored him to make sure that the "unfolding of the love instinct" was not arrested, as Freud would have it, in any of its immature early stages and thus susceptible to "become ensnared in the wild tangle of a perversion." His sexual instincts, Jackson advised, should culminate in "heterosexual love *or attraction between the sexes.*"[3] Jackson relayed not simply a new type of desiring subject but a class of desiring subjects.

When other contemporaneous physicians and mental health experts discussed sexual matters in their syndicated columns, however, they did not necessarily use the words "heterosexual" or "heterosexuality." More specifically, the politics of respectability complicate any linear narrative of heterosexuality's emergence and adoption.[4] Black writers and the publishers of black-owned periodicals may have been especially keen to distance themselves from heterosexuality's associations with deviance. For example, during the 1910s and 1920s, the *Chicago Defender* featured what was reportedly the first newspaper health column in the United States by a doctor of African descent. That doctor, A. Wilberforce Williams (1865–1940), was a leading physician in Chicago, and he did not hesitate to broach intimate matters in print. Williams's frank discussion of venereal disease even led to his expulsion from a medical society.[5] The fact that Williams was willing to address masturbation, that he advocated teaching children "sex hygiene," that he urged adult men who still had their foreskins to be circumcised, and that he pointedly associated venereal disease with those who had "sow[ed] wild oats" before marriage as well as "male profligates and female prostitutes" raised hackles among some readers of the *Defender* as well.[6] Still, there was a silence of sorts within Williams's columns: he did not explicitly name different-sex attraction, identity, pairing, or practice as "heterosexual." In leading black newspapers such as the *Chicago Defender*—but also the *New York Amsterdam News*, the *Pittsburgh Courier*, and the *Baltimore Afro-American*—the word "heterosexual" did not, it seems, appear until after 1930.[7] By 1925, Williams had received so many queries about venereal disease and the like that he was keen to "get away from the sex questions," yet he was either unaware of the term "heterosexuality" or purposefully avoided using it when answering those questions. Why would this prominent black doctor *not* use a term for sexual desire, practice, and identity that we now accept as commonplace?[8]

The academic theories of sexual identity that historians often associate with sexual "modernity," ideas that medical experts like Josephine A. Jackson adopted and taught in syndicated newspaper columns printed throughout the United States, shaped the broader culture gradually and unevenly.[9] Indeed, as much as A. Wilberforce Williams prided himself on eschewing "mock modesty" when it came to discussing sexual matters, it is a figure such as Jackson who reveals the intentional efforts through which Americans came to recognize heterosexuality as a name for psychologically "normal" desires.[10] Jackson's story fundamentally disturbs narratives that mark a clean transition from a "Victorian" nineteenth-century sexual regime to a twentieth-century sexual modernity or sexual liberalism as well.[11] Those narratives work only if we presume that the white, educated middle classes created a mainstream culture that others had not yet embraced, rather than a particular source of sexual identity making amid a far more varied array of desires, behaviors, and intimate bonds. Jackson's career serves for us not as evidence of the inevitable ascendancy of a medical model of heterosexuality but rather as a demonstration of the effort required to convince Americans of that model's existence and importance.

Locating a more complex and critical history of what we now think of as heterosexuality is the aim of this volume of original essays, which investigates what it means to trace a history of heterosexuality in North America across four centuries. Our aim is both historical and historiographical. Each chapter represents an investigation into ideas about gender, sexuality, and difference in North America. Such investigation challenges us to set aside presumptions of heterosexuality's timelessness or familiarity.[12] Instead, we concur with the historian Daniel Wickberg that heterosexuality "has been a historically specific creation," even as we challenge his assertion that no history of heterosexuality exists prior to the word's invention.[13] Heterosexuality has a history, and that history is intrinsically bound up with the history of the relatively recent idea of the sexually normal. The social conditions of people's lives, the gendered and raced class relations that determine the opportunities and obstacles for people understood as men and women, and the bodily experiences of sexual desires and fertility's consequences, among other aspects of human existence, all profoundly shaped what it means to live a gendered life and engage in sundry sexual acts. The essays gathered in this volume seek to explore the history of the idea of heterosexuality as well as the lived experiences of different-sex desires, bodies, practices, reproductive capacities, relationships, and politics.[14] We are keen to trouble easy, prevalent assumptions that *the* story of "heterosexuality" can be reduced to—or solely represented by—the experiences of majority population, suburban, male-female married reproductive couples. Such couples certainly came to embody heteronormativity, yet there are both social and political consequences of privileging narrow conceptions of sexually "normal" people.

We are aware that many readers might already wonder, "Hasn't heterosexuality always existed in some fashion?" As a partial response, we underscore a question posed by Jeffrey Weeks in *Sexuality and Its Discontents*: "If the gay identity is of recent provenance, what of the heterosexual identity?"[15] Our aim is to trace the emergence of a heterosexual identity as much as we are trying to trace a history of heterosexuality as a concept. We presume that heterosexuality is historical, as are all forms of sexuality, all gender roles, and all hierarchies of power—just as prevailing notions of race are historical *and* constructed. To be analytically useful, "heterosexuality" must refer not simply to social arrangements that presume women's economic dependence on men, men's prerogatives under patriarchy, reproductive sex, or ostensibly universal notions of a gender binary.[16] These historical contingencies are why insisting on heterosexuality's ubiquity can be problematic. The gender theorist Monique Wittig argued against historical nuance when she wrote in the early 1990s that heterosexuality has been embedded within the Western mind since Plato: "to live in society is to live in heterosexuality. . . . Heterosexuality is always already within all mental categories. It has sneaked into dialectical thought (or thought of differences) as its main category."[17] Randolph Trumbach's study of changing gender norms in eighteenth-century London similarly insists that heterosexuality existed for centuries before it had a name: "How can the human race otherwise have continued to exist?" Trumbach conflates human reproduction with heterosexuality and mistakes gender-based communities (the "exclusive male heterosexual majority") for heterosexual social or political identification.[18] The male-female household unit remained an economic necessity for most people, but that class relation coexisted with an array of relationships among men and women.

Historical work about the newness of the idea of the "normal" further challenges us to revisit the history of "heteronormativity" and of presumptions that heterosexual desires or relationships have deep historical links to ideas of the normal. "Heteronormativity" describes ways of assuming, seeing, and knowing; it articulates something that is both an ideal and presumed to be natural. Yet heteronormativity is historical: the privileges of heterosexuality depended on the modern concept of heterosexuality as normal. The literary scholar Karma Lochrie explains that the late-medieval and early modern European people she studies would have found the concept of the sexually normal incomprehensible. She can locate ideas of neither "heterosexuality" nor "heteronormativity" in medieval sources.[19] Ruth Mazo Karras similarly notes in her history of "unmarriages" in the Middle Ages that while "sexual unions between men and women were a dominant social form in medieval Europe," those relationships existed alongside "a variety of pair bonds," which included celibacy and same-sex unions. Karras's intention to "analyze pair bonds without privileging marriage, while still recognizing that medieval people did, in fact, privilege marriage," well captures our goal of studying the history of heterosexual privilege while attending to its historical specificity. If the essays herein do not, as Karras puts it, explicitly explore "elements that fell by the wayside" as opposite-sex pair bonds and activity assumed normalcy in North America, many of the authors do carefully consider how what we now think of as "race" informed that process.[20] Often invisible to those who experience the privileges of the sexual practice, heteronormativity serves as a historically specific exclusionary boundary and form of discipline on the lives of those who fail to meet its particularistic guidelines and expectations.

The association between heterosexuality and "the normal" (and thus the deployment of heteronormativity's incredible cultural and political power) may have occurred much later than historians have long assumed.[21] In *Normality: A Critical Genealogy* (2017), the historian Peter Cryle and the cultural theorist Elizabeth Stephens demonstrate that the idea of "the normal" was not fully realized in Europe and North America until the conclusion of World War II.[22] Much new scholarship questions the historicity of the very idea of norms and "the normal."[23] More controversially, in a special issue of the feminist journal *differences*, scholars interrogated the centrality of "antinormativity" to queer theory.[24] This wave of provocative scholarship challenges us to question not only how normality shapes modern sexuality but also the extent to which queer theory relies on notions of deviance, normality's binary opposite. We thus need to examine critically the histories of heterosexuality and the historiographical uses of heteronormativity.

The intertwined histories of heterosexuality and heteronormativity reveal systems of meaning-making and of privilege. Lochrie explains that scholars often conflate this concept of heteronormativity (hetero-sexuality as a regnant norm) with the more limited idea of heterosexu-ality (different-sex erotic ideal). As Lochrie writes, "Heterosexuality is rarely used in its strictly technical meaning of desire for the opposite sex without invoking all of its cultural appurtenances, including the sexual act of intercourse, the social and legal rights of marriage, ideas of domesticity, doctrines of procreation, concepts of parenting and child rearing, legal definitions of privacy, and even scientific concepts of animal behavior."[25] The theorists Lauren Berlant and Michael Warner define heteronormativity as "the institutions, structures of understand-ing, and practical orientations that make heterosexuality seem not only coherent—that is, organized as a sexuality—but also privileged." Berlant and Warner associate heteronormativity with their concept of "national heterosexuality," which they define as "the mechanism by which a core national culture can be imagined as a sanitized space of sentimental feel-ing and immaculate behavior, a space of pure citizenship." Such a "famil-ial" model hides the "structural racism and other systemic inequalities" that constitute its origins and that sustain it.[26] This approach provides more of an opening for historically variable heterosexuality, a product of human actions and culture, not a preexisting condition.

Historically specific, heterosexuality has changed over time, and its meanings can shift according to context. The "modern" reconceptual-ization of sexuality as a discrete and particularly important aspect of individuality changed the stakes in possessing and benefiting from a heterosexual disposition or family organization. Even so, heterosexual-ity's modes and effects are various. Heterosexuality in its modern form anxiously reiterates its asserted privilege within an array of legal and so-cial rights, not to mention its associations with psychologically "normal" health. Yet many people who engage in practices and/or form relation-ships that meet all other basic criteria of "heterosexual" do not enjoy that privilege because of their race, class, ability, nationality, citizenship, or religion. To be sure, heterosexuality is a culturally understood idea about what is "natural," "normal," or some combination of the two con-cepts, but it is far from universally defined, applied, or valued.

Our goal is not to reify heterosexuality or claim a special place for it, intellectually or politically. As David Halperin has written about his his-tory of homosexuality, "I wish to avoid the implication that by analyzing the triumphalism of a modern discursive category I am in any way participating in that triumphalism."[27] Rather, we have encouraged the authors in this anthology to subject heterosexuality to careful scrutiny as a means to reveal its inseparability from hierarchies of power; its intersections with ideals of race, class, and gender; and, as several of these essays demonstrate, its utility as a weapon against marginalized groups. In this introduction and in the essays that follow, we seek to explain how and why heterosexuality became a known *thing* in the United States—and to establish that seemingly long-standing terms emerged in our vernacular far later than many readers might realize. We do not take a heterosexual identity as a timeless given, then. We endeavor as well to interrogate the imprint of heteronormativity on same-sex desires both before and after the word "heterosexual" existed and the consequences of those definitions, norms, and values in North American history.

We hardly seek to entrench what Marjorie Garber terms "a binary opposition between homosexual and heterosexual" herein. As much as there is no exploration of the concepts and histories of asexuality or pansexuality in this anthology, we certainly recognize that individuals can go through the course of their lives without feeling (or acting on) sexual attraction to others and that sexuality can be fluid. It is worth noting that some scholars—Garber included—have maintained that bisexuality is "not just another sexual orientation but rather a sexuality that undoes sexual orientation as a category, a sexuality that threatens and challenges . . . easy binaries."[28] We do not necessarily seek to *undo* sexual categories, but we certainly seek to *unsettle* "heterosexuality" and its history. In the remaining pages of this introduction, we offer a brief overview of the ways that historians and theorists have defined both heterosexuality and heteronormativity, we consider how "race" has been invoked in terms of both heterosexuality and heterosexism, and we preview the essays in this volume to highlight how each one addresses these and other questions in uniquely salient ways.

Heterosexuality's History

Different-sex relationships stretch back through human history, but we began to call them "heterosexual" relatively recently. The German sexologist Karl Maria Kertbeny coined the words "heterosexual" and "homosexual" in the 1860s, and they did not appear in print in English until 1892, when "heterosexual" was an entry in an American medical journal. American psychiatrists and physicians took note, writing professional articles about the "heterosexual instinct" and the "homosexual invert."[29] New terminology for sexual desires proliferated. During these same years, the German sexologist Karl Heinrich Ulrichs coined the term "bisexual," one that the psychoanalyst Sigmund Freud began to use in his theories of sexuality in the 1890s. Indeed, Freud dissected "sexological notion[s] of bisexuality as the combination of male and female characteristics within a single body" as he "developed the argument that all human beings are born with a bisexual predisposition" that would, in time, morph into either a heterosexual or homosexual orientation. The British sexologist Havelock Ellis, for his part, initially explored bisexuality as "psychosexual hermaphroditism" during the late 1890s; by 1915, Ellis was coming to analyze bisexuality instead as "comparable to ambidexterity."[30]

German, French, British, and American sexologists and sex-law reformers experimented with new categories—medical and legal labels, really—to distinguish among people according to their sexual-object choices.[31] The invention of heterosexuality as a salient category was simultaneous with and coconstitutive of processes of racial differentiation that became entrenched during the late nineteenth and early twentieth centuries. Biologists, critics, and politicians propounded pseudoscientific theories to justify ideas about racial hierarchy (principally, of white supremacy deeply informed by nativism).[32] Heterosexuality emerged as a named and valued quality of "normal" sexuality amid these wideranging efforts to label and organize populations according to medical and psychological categories.

Between 1870 and 1930, a new system of describing the ostensible differences between men and women took hold in Europe and North America. As the historian Angus McLaren notes, "older notions of masculinity and femininity" no longer seemed adequate to explain "the changing nature of men's work, the rise of the white collar service sector, the reduction of the birth rate, and women's entry into higher education and the professions."[33] The solution was heterosexuality, which was never simply a descriptive term for sexual desire of men for women or of women for men. Jonathan Ned Katz has coined the phrase "different-sex erotic ideal" to refer to the new systems of meaning that surrounded relationships between people understood to be men and women by the late nineteenth century. As he explains in *The Invention of Heterosexuality* (1995), "An official, dominant, different-sex erotic ideal—a heterosexual ethic—is not ancient at all, but a modern invention."[34]

Historians of heterosexuality illuminate the risks of asserting heteronormativity as a universal constant within human history. The scholar Hanne Blank describes the "surprisingly short history of heterosexuality" since the late nineteenth century in her engaging study of the science of different-sex desires and their cultural reverberations.[35] She highlights what scholars such as Anne Fausto-Sterling have long demonstrated: that the idea of the sexual binary is itself a cultural production rooted in historical circumstances.[36] Although much of this scholarship has attended to the ways in which sexology and psychiatry produced modern categories of homosexuality and lesbianism,[37] it has also taught us a great deal about how sexology shaped emergent ideas of "the heterosexual."[38] The profusion of published advice columns that continued to include definitions of these terms into the 1940s suggests that it took many more decades for these terms to circulate widely in the vernacular. Popular print culture of the 1920s through 1940s often included minilessons about the meaning and importance of heterosexuality, a fact that demonstrates both that health professionals thought this knowledge was crucial for Americans' overall well-being and that some readers presumably learned something they did not already know.

The science of sexuality unquestionably shaped the history of heterosexuality, but we join other historians in seeking a history of heterosexuality that incorporates nonexperts, researches the grassroots, and considers multiple sources of power and authority. We, along with other historians, acknowledge that critical demographic shifts during the early twentieth century—including both urbanization and higher college attendance rates—resulted in increased mixed-sex socializing, not to mention a sexual revolution.[39] We additionally share a conviction stressed by the historian John D'Emilio: that "capitalism has led to the separation of sexuality from procreation." Indeed, if capitalism "created the material conditions for homosexual desire to express itself as a central component of some individuals' lives," we contend that material conditions and relations inform sexual desires as well as identities.[40] Sexology alone cannot explain the history of heterosexuality or its importance.

In many respects, the category of the heterosexual emerged in the early twentieth century as a necessary complement to "the homosexual," a figure of more immediate interest to queer men and, problematically, to law enforcement. As George Chauncey has argued, during the 1920s and 1930s both middle-class "queer" men and "normal" middle-class men in New York City began to reject the performative effeminacy of working-class "fairies." Queer men embraced the label of homosexuality, a name that centered "sexual desire, not gender inversion," as the name "that distinguished them from other men." "Normal" middle-class men likewise began to identify as heterosexuals and put their sexual-object choice, not simply their gender performance, at the center of their masculine identity.[41] This association between heterosexuality and the "normal" found support from the federal government and its bureaucracies. Significantly, in *The Straight State*, Margot Canaday demonstrates that the expanding federal bureaucracy "produce[d] the category of homosexuality through regulation," such that "a homosexual-heterosexual binary . . . was being inscribed in federal citizenship policy."[42] As a result of this epistemological privilege, "heterosexuality" emerged as a category of sexual identity associated with citizenship, often through programs and discourses that validated heterosexual marriage as a fundamental unit of governance, rights, and benefits.

What historians increasingly find is that heterosexuality emerged as a category and identity not simply through top-down impositions of the state but rather from multiple sources and with sometimes ambivalent results. Definitions of race and racialized class relations, not to mention notions about gendered hierarchies, shaped the meaning that people gave to their different-sex desires and the values they associated with their sexual intimacies; those intimacies might occur between two people of the same sex but be infused with opposite-sex meaning based on so-called racial difference. Certainly, a burgeoning administrative state and growing penal system in the United States played a powerful role in producing raced and classed ideas of (hetero)sexual respectability. To take one example, encounters between African American girls and women with the police, courts, and other forms of state power produced ideas about heterosexuality as a privileged status of "respectable" woman, usually but not always coded as white and often assumed to be middle class. Cheryl Hicks demonstrates the ways that juvenile courts, the policing of urban neighborhoods, and the prison system attempted to inculcate norms of middle-class heterosexuality among working-class African American girls and women in the early twentieth century. She finds that the working-class women who encountered agents of the state held distinct, if no less morally trenchant, ideas about the importance of different-sex relationships and heterosexual respectability. Rather than a top-down, middle-class imposition on a reluctantly regulated working class, heterosexuality emerged from multiple experiences of class and racial formation.[43] Hicks's work additionally reveals that, when incarcerated black and white women had sexual liaisons, administrators worried that "black women [were] function[ing] as masculine substitutes who fulfilled white women's heterosexual desire."[44] What it meant to be heterosexual, then, evolved not simply through the measured advice of medical experts like Josephine Jackson but also in the sensational reporting of crimes, in the representations of racial otherness that pervaded accounts of interracial male-female sex, and within the very prison systems intended to discipline women who violated the norms of sexual respectability.

Ideas about racial otherness and gendered power, moreover, shaped the ways in which people experienced different-sex desire and/or constructed ideas of the sexually normal. For example, as Pablo Mitchell has compellingly revealed, the perception of an individual who "pushed the boundaries of 'normal,' early twentieth-century (hetero)sexual behavior" in territorial New Mexico could be all the more complicated if that person had indigenous, Hispano, *and* Anglo heritage. Work by Victor Jew and Mary Ting Yi Lui underscores that social anxieties regarding relationships between white women and men of color during the late nineteenth and early twentieth centuries could result in Chinese and black men being demonized in ways that at once overlapped and diverged.[45] As much as cross-cultural and interracial sex could facilitate degrees of mobility or even consolidations of power, interracial and cross-cultural sexual encounters could also generate pervasive notions about sexual deviance.

The historians Amy Sueyoshi, Nayan Shah, and Peggy Pascoe have produced rather revealing work on this front. Sueyoshi considers the case of Yone Noguchi, a Japanese poet who had love affairs with a white man and with at least two white women after immigrating to the United States in the early twentieth century but who expressed himself as unabashedly heterosexual after he returned to Japan. The white women who loved him did so through the prism of their Orientalist assumptions about Japanese masculinity, Sueyoshi argues, even as Noguchi's male privilege permitted him a freedom of movement and career mobility unavailable to the educated women he courted. His life story challenges notions of presumed heterosexuality while also undermining accounts that view same-sex affairs as sites of resistance: "Heterosexuality does not simply exist everywhere unless explicitly renounced. Nor are those who resist compulsory heterosexuality necessarily exclusively 'gay.' In Noguchi's case, sexual resistance came in the 'straightest' package possible as he insistently declared his heterosexuality after his return to Japan."[46] Certainly, the US legal system cast Asians as sexual deviants. Nayan Shah argues that criminal prosecutions of South Asian men for sex with (usually younger, if still adult) white men produced narratives of "Oriental depravity" that attributed the source of sexual deviance to a foreign "other" and thus shored up the normatively masculine status of white "youth."[47] On another front, by 1940 many states had adopted anti-miscegenation laws that criminalized interracial marriage. As the historian Peggy Pascoe underscores, legislation against such intermarriage at once produced, contained, and reflected "complex and convoluted" definitions of "race." Those laws, which defined miscegenation in ways that set "Whites" against other racially defined groups, motivated some opponents of these laws to argue that interracial, different-sex attraction was especially natural. Indeed, in making such assertions, black writers such as George Schuyler and J. A. Rogers "played a role in producing a modern culture that increasingly assigned its fears of unnaturality to homosexuality rather than to race mixture."[48] Overall, the sexually normal emerged in the twentieth century as a state of being steadily defined in opposition to a racialized and classed understanding of difference. Notions about the "unnatural" nevertheless shifted away from interracial, different-sex sexuality as the century wore on.

Class, ability, and immigration status are central if often overlooked variables in the operation of ideas about the sexually "normal" and the meaning of heterosexuality. The history of the modern United States is replete with examples of individuals who engage in "heterosexual" relationships yet do not benefit from the cultural esteem afforded to "heteronormative" individuals and their families. Poverty, gender non-conformity, nonmarital pregnancy, undocumented immigration status, medical condition, and other variables produce multiple categories of heterosexuality (or, alternatively, proliferate the varieties of heterosexual perversity) that crisscross the borders of heteronormativity. Scholars of disability studies have offered historians valuable ways of interpreting the meaning of "normal" and tracing its origins. Like the contrasting spectacles of the freak show and the beauty pageant, homosexuality and heterosexuality created hypervisible (and hyperdiscursive) ways of defining the normal through the disparagement and abjection of the "other."[49]

The insights and pitfalls of whiteness studies, another field investigating the historical construction of norms that are asserted if not demonstrated to be privileged, may offer a useful comparison for the history of heterosexuality. In an assessment of whiteness studies, the historian Peter Kolchin summarizes scholars' finding that throughout North American history, "whiteness, even while omnipresent, appears unrecognized except as that which is normal." Both whiteness and heterosexuality concern social identities that define norms, and both describe positions of social, economic, legal, and political privilege. Yet those norms function in idiosyncratic and unpredictable ways. We should differentiate between different-sex desires and heteronormativity, just as scholars of whiteness differentiate between "color" and "race" in the history of "whiteness." As Kolchin cautions, "in making whiteness omnipresent, whiteness studies authors risk losing sight of contextual variations and thereby undermining the very understanding of race and whiteness as socially constructed."[50] Attending to the distinction between different-sex desires and heteronorms allows historians to discuss different-sex desires before the advent of "heterosexuality" without resorting to anachronism, and it calls attention to the gendered, racial, and class-based contingencies and exclusions that constitute heterosexuality itself.

We must be much clearer about what heterosexuality *is* and more willing to employ other terms (among them, different-sex desire, marriage, reproduction, patriarchy) that heterosexuality is too often tasked with presumptively indicating. As Rogers Brubaker and Frederick Cooper have written about the problematically expansive meanings of the term "identity," we likewise highlight the "definitional incoherence" of heterosexuality. Brubaker and Cooper challenge scholars to recognize that if a term becomes meaningful only when prefaced by a list of its permutations, variability, flexibility, contingencies, or inconsistencies, then the individuals whose analysis includes that term need to consider seriously the possibility that another word or phrase might be more useful. Along those lines, we have asked, When are historians describing heterosexuality, and when are they investigating other forms of power or other operations of gender, marriage, family, or state authority?[51] As Berlant and Warner have admonished, "Heterosexuality is not a thing. We speak of heterosexual culture rather than heterosexuality because that culture never has more than a provisional unity. It is neither a single Symbolic nor a single ideology nor a unified set of shared beliefs." Instead, they argue, "heterosexuality" becomes a facile word to consolidate "widely differing practices, norms, and institutions."[52] In many ways, it is this paradox of heterosexuality, its tendency to produce a superstructural source of power relations that affect gender, race, class, and nation and its fundamental incoherency, that has motivated our project and inspired us to bring it to fruition.

Theory and Heteronormativity

In an article playfully titled "Queer Theory for Everyone," the literary scholar Sharon Marcus argued for a more expansive interpretation of the insights of queer theory, particularly its emphasis on the instability of gender norms and sexual identities. Marcus urged other scholars not to limit queer theory's relevance to those individuals who have identified as, or who have been identified as, LGBTQ and instead to deploy queer theory as a tool to understand sexuality more broadly. Such an approach, she suggested, would help the field move beyond an analytically flat contrast between all things "straight" and all things "queer," and it would enrich our understanding of how the very idea of "straight" and "normal" shifted through historical time and cultural context.[53] Laura Doan, a historian of sexuality in Britain, similarly urges scholars to employ "queerness as method" in unpacking the creation and implications of the sexual binary, rather than conflating heterosexuality with "normal" and thus the opposite of "queer." "Queerness-as-method," Doan explains, "invites scrutiny about what is queer in all sexual practices but also invites history's intervention as a corrective to the queer faith in heteronormativity as a universal or transhistorical value."[54] Doan, Marcus, and other scholars prompt us to examine the tacit assumptions that often presuppose heterosexuality's historical ubiquity. Our effort to curate a collection of essays in the history of heterosexuality reflects our indebtedness to the insights of queer theory, yet we find such an approach compelling but incomplete without a commensurate appreciation for the feminist critique of heterosexuality.

Prior to the creation of queer theory as a field or the coinage of the term "heteronormativity," the feminist, gay liberation, and women of color movements of the 1960s and 1970s had a great deal to say about heterosexuality as a system of patriarchy (the systemic oppression of women) and about heterosexual sex. For many feminists, heterosexuality might be normal, but that very norm was the target of their activism. A fair amount of radical and lesbian feminist political writing in the late 1960s and 1970s focused on critiques of heterosexual relationships, describing them as inherently oppressive (even as necessarily violent) given the power of heteronormative patriarchy. One radical group, The Feminists, argued in their manifesto that women could not have noncoercive sex under a system of patriarchy: "Heterosexual love is a delusion in yet another sense: it is a means of escape from the role system by way of approval from and identification with the man, who has defined himself as humanity (beyond role)—she desires to be him. . . . We must destroy the institution of heterosexual sex which is a manifestation of the male-female role."[55] These feminists argued that it was the presumption of normality that made heterosexuality so deeply toxic to the cause of women's liberation.

Gay liberationists also critiqued the institution of heterosexuality. Radical gay men, such as those in The Red Butterfly, a Marxist-leaning cell of the Gay Liberation Front, theorized gay liberation as a critique of heteronormativity, militarism, racism, and capitalism in a series of pamphlets printed in 1970. Their first pamphlet, *Gay Liberation*, challenged the idea of normal sexuality and insisted that gay sex was "natural."[56] In a subsequent pamphlet by Carl Wittman, *A Gay Manifesto*, he wrote more urgently, "Exclusive heterosexuality is fucked up. It reflects a fear of people of the same sex, it's anti-homosexual, and it is frought [sic] with frustration. Heterosexual sex is fucked up, too; ask women's liberation about what straight guys are like in bed."[57] A third pamphlet, *Gay Oppression: A Radical Analysis*, argued that gay liberation affected heterosexuals both by illuminating that homosexuals were far more numerous than straight society had previously acknowledged and by challenging the idea of heterosexuality as natural or inevitable.[58]

Radical feminists produced a rich body of academic and vernacular discussions of the hetero/homo binary as a source of women's oppression. A major contribution to these conversations came in 1975 with the publication of Gayle Rubin's "The Traffic in Women." Rubin was then a graduate student in anthropology at the University of Michigan and a member of feminist groups in Ann Arbor. The essay, which has been reprinted in multiple anthologies, explored the assumptions about women's subordination within theories of Marx and Engels, Freud, Jacques Lacan, and Claude Lévi-Strauss, but it also suggested that these theories offered a powerful resource for a feminist critique. Rubin interpreted these canonical works to reveal a "sex/gender system" that each generation learned and relearned. Rubin argued that cultures "produced" gender inequality and that the sex/gender system was not embedded within, or prior to, the development of human societies.[59] Her essay described "obligatory heterosexuality" as a historically created effect of the sex/gender system that subordinated women. Her reading of this process was daringly optimistic: "Sex/gender systems are not ahistorical emanations of the human mind; they are products of historical human activity."[60] The poet and activist Adrienne Rich's widely circulated and anthologized argument about "compulsory heterosexuality," first published in 1980, extended this lesbian feminist critique of heterosexuality as a species of patriarchy. In an article in the feminist journal *Signs*, Rich described heterosexuality as a political institution that bound women into sexual servitude and economic dependency.[61] The critique of heterosexuality that Rich and other feminists advanced was of the sex/gender system of patriarchy that oppressed women and queer people, something more akin to what we today name as heteronormativity.[62]

Black women who broke off from a second-wave feminist group, the National Black Feminist Organization (NBFO), to establish the Combahee River Collective challenged what subsequent scholars would call heteronormativity, and they did so while attuned to the intersectional operations of power.⁶³ The black feminist authors of the "Combahee River Collective Statement" of 1977, including Demita Frazer, Beverly Smith, and Barbara Smith, provided a sustained analysis of the intersectional operation of heterosexism within systems of racial and class discrimination: "The most general statement of our politics at the present time would be that we are actively committed to struggling against racial, sexual, heterosexual, and class oppression, and see as our particular task the development of integrated analysis and practice based upon the fact that the major systems of oppression are interlocking. The synthesis of these oppressions creates the conditions of our lives."⁶⁴ Members of the collective did not stop there. These black feminists additionally maintained that "the liberation of all oppressed peoples necessitates the destruction of the political-economic systems of capitalism and imperialism as well as patriarchy."⁶⁵ At once socialist and anti-imperialist, the collective's pathbreaking analysis shaped generations of feminist scholarship that centered the intersections of sex, race, and class systems of privilege and oppression. What was clear to them, and what historians would be foolish to ignore, is that we should be as skeptical of the idea that heterosexism ever operates in isolation as we are to claims that heterosexuality itself is transhistorical.

Moreover, the poet Audre Lorde's 1985 pamphlet *I Am Your Sister* set forth a theory of heterosexual privilege as an operation of power and a means of oppression. Lorde offered a blunt definition: "HETEROSEXISM: A belief in the inherent superiority of one form of loving over all others and thereby the right to dominance."⁶⁶ Lorde distinguished that privileging belief from homophobia, a reflection of "terror" at the knowledge of same-sex love. Lorde additionally explained that her identity as a black lesbian was omnipresent in her activism and creative output, a source of power and an inspiration to act. If lesbianism was considered "abnormal," so too was blackness: both claims ultimately meant that Lorde was systematically oppressed by heterosexist presumptions about women's and lesbians' "place" within movements for civil rights, just as racism sought to limit her and other people of color. It was, for Lorde, nothing less than incumbent on progressive activists and thinkers to ask, "what is normal in this deranged society by which we are all trapped?"⁶⁷

Indeed, pointed interrogation of sexuality and the "normal" vitally animated work by theorists who followed Lorde. In other words, the queer theory that emerged in the late 1980s and early 1990s, which took as its starting point the existence of heteronormativity and the necessity of its undoing, built on the critique of heterosexuality's toxicity that feminist, gay liberationist, and black lesbian activists and scholars had created. Michael Warner published the first academic article to use the term "heteronormativity" in a now-canonical 1991 article in *Social Text*. In that article, Warner called on other scholars "to challenge the pervasive and often invisible heteronormativity of modern societies."[68] Warner did not explain whether heteronormativity is transhistorical or whether its contemporary power derives from the presumption that it has always existed among those who receive its benefits. His study nevertheless provides a marvelously illuminating framework for understanding how heterosexual privilege operates: "Heterosexual culture thinks of itself as the elemental form of human association, as the very model of inter-gender relations, as the indivisible basis of all community, and as the means of reproduction without which society wouldn't exist."[69] Theorists of heteronormativity point to its simultaneous ubiquity and invisibility; in this volume, we argue that the emergence of that powerful norm has a history.

We have challenged each author to define "heterosexuality" as they employ the term in their work. In this way, each author provides a history of heterosexuality as well as a historiographical case for "how to do the history of heterosexuality." Richard Godbeer even finds heterosexuality inapplicable to the people he studies. In every case, however, this approach moves the history of heterosexuality beyond the presumption that it constitutes a transhistorical yet inchoate norm against which queerness reacts or that queerness attempts to subvert. Our goals for this book are therefore to illuminate heterosexuality's antecedents, the circumstances of its creation, and its consequent effects—not to vaunt "heterosexual" as concept, practice, or identity.

* * *

Rather than organize the essays in chronological fashion, we have instead grouped them according to four rubrics: difference and desire; bodies and difference in popular culture; conceptions of marriage, family, and the domestic; and discourses about desire. Arranging essays in loose chronological order would indeed emphasize critical changes over time. Still, we have juxtaposed essays in ways that should create both productive tension and dialogue *within* each section and that should generate revealing analytical connections *across* sections regarding the historicity of heterosexuality. In each section, we have collated essays in ways that amplify "difference" across various registers. If the literary scholar Marlon Ross was explicitly interrogating "the closet as a raceless paradigm" when he observed that "racialized minorities may operate under divergent social protocols concerning what it means to be visible and invisible within normative sites like the family, . . . the workplace, . . . the street, and the community more generally," we hope that these essays will, in concert, profitably highlight a similar dynamic when it comes to a range of intimate, different-sex interactions and practices across four centuries of North American history.[70]

"Race" is not a primary concern for every author in *Heterosexual Histories*. Analyses of race constitute a through line in this anthology all the same. Several of the authors locate histories of heterosexuality within racial, gendered, and class-marked systems of power relations in ways that echo pathbreaking work on colonial sexualities by scholars such as Ann Laura Stoler.[71] Moreover, scholars in this volume benefit from and build on a raft of significant Americanist gender scholarship about race and sexuality—and on sexuality and religion, for that matter—that has been produced over the past four decades. We do not seek to delve into such scholarship here.[72] We do, however, wish to highlight a few salient points as a means of introducing the essays.

We first draw readers' attention to an observation that the cinema scholar Richard Dyer made in 1997: "All concepts of race are always concepts of the body and also of heterosexuality. Race is a means of categorising different types of human body which reproduce themselves. It seeks to systematise differences and to relate them to differences of character and worth. Heterosexuality is the means of ensuring, but also the site of endangering, the reproduction of these differences."[73] To be sure, Dyer's project was not to historicize heterosexuality. Authors featured within this collection, though, do rigorously consider how race has suffused what we now think of as "heterosexuality," not to mention how different-sex sexuality has undergirded notions about "race." Taken together, their essays reveal the persistence of these interlocking dynamics over time, how arguments regarding "race" and different-sex sexuality have changed, and how "race" can result in certain different-sex intimacies being deemed as deviant. We nonetheless join a long line of scholars who roundly reject arguments that race is a biological reality.

It seems especially pertinent and productive to turn to Karen Fields and Barbara Fields at this juncture. They rightly assert that the term "race" is actually a "shorthand," one that "stands for the conception or the doctrine that nature produced humankind in distinct groups, each defined by inborn traits that its members share and that differentiate them from the members of other distinct groups . . . of unequal rank."[74] Emphasizing that race is a conception, a doctrine, or a construction hardly means that race had—and has—no actual impact on the quotidian realities and lived experience of people. Quite critically, concepts of racial difference have profoundly informed notions about human worth *and* labor value, as have conceptions about sexed or gendered difference.[75] If the essays herein are not necessarily in conversation with scholarship on labor, the authors are attentive to matters of class. And many of the authors also speak to work that theorizes racialized gender, including studies of unfree as well as paid labor.[76]

As much as the essays in *Heterosexual Histories* are disciplinarily bound, they have interdisciplinary reach. That said, it is our aim and hope that these essays clearly establish what Jennifer Spear and Kevin Murphy have argued in another anthology of historical work on sexuality, that "careful and contextualised analysis of the shifting relationship of gender and sexuality across space and time illuminates broader historical processes."[77]

The essays in part 1, "Difference and Desire since the Seventeenth Century," offer sweeping discussions of the creation and effects of different-sex desires. They show how gender, race, religion, and nation coconstituted ideas about "normal" or "moral" sexuality at various moments in the American past. Richard Godbeer finds that "heterosexuality" is a form of sexuality unknown to his seventeenth- and eighteenth-century subjects, whose sex/gender system operated according to a distinct "poetics of desire." This poetics could, as Godbeer compellingly demonstrates, include desire for connection with the divine and be more expansive than modern understandings of erotic, different-sex interaction. In an essay that covers several centuries, Renee Romano asserts that when we consider histories of heterosexuality, we must reckon with the fact that it is bound up with interraciality, that racial difference is intrinsic to the construction of different-sex desires and to associations with sexual deviance. Nicholas L. Syrett's essay places age difference at the center of heterosexuality's history. As Syrett contends that age asymmetry has been a critical means of instantiating heterosexuality, he demonstrates how gendered ideals of age shaped desires for different-sex partners. His chapter additionally shows how the historical shift in Americans' awareness of their numerical ages led to a diminishment in age disparity in marriage, even as most American women—across ethnicity, race, religion, and region—continue to marry somewhat-older men. Judy Tzu-Chun Wu examines the history of Asian Americans through the lens of heterosexuality, finding that it served both as a negative stereotype used to justify Asian exclusion and discrimination and as a positive model for Asian Americans' self-understanding. In addition, Wu persuasively demonstrates that, by embodying heteronormativity, Asian Americans have not only claimed cultural citizenship in the United States but have shaped both racial and sexual liberalism as well. All four of these essays suggest ways of rereading American history by centering sexual differences and gendered desires.

Part 2, "Differences, Bodies, and Popular Culture," includes essays that examine specific case studies of the American history of heterosexuality within print culture, theater, and discursive production. Their topics range among racialized British colonial discourses of beauty, in Sharon Block's essay; health-reform literature that targeted interracial prostitution in antebellum New Orleans, in Rashauna Johnson's essay; and Marc Stein's study of gay satires of heterosexuality during the Cold War. Moreover, if Block analyzes the construction of sex-related beliefs that do not map onto notions about heterosexuality that gained currency after the advent of sexology, Johnson is concerned (in part) with emergent scientific norms. And while Johnson's examination of print culture underscores that certain forms of different-sex sex could unsettle prevailing notions of heterosexuality, Stein's examination of print culture produced a century later offers allied analysis of how heterosexuality could be troubled by queer commentary that offered trenchant assessments of ascendant heterosexuality. Each essay considers the words used—in eighteenth-century Atlantic-world print culture, in antebellum newspapers and health-reform literature, and in mid-twentieth-century gay camp and parody—to locate the emergence of different-sex desire as a site of gendered, raced, and embodied concern for a reading (and, in Stein's essay, theatergoing) public.

Each essay in part 3, "Embracing and Contesting Legitimacy," considers the project of defining and shoring up heteronormativity as a moral, legal, and cultural basis for American family life. Zurisaday Gutiérrez Avila and Pablo Mitchell show how, during a period of profound upheaval and dislocation, heterosexual family life factored in the experiences of Mexicans in the US Southwest between 1848 and 1900. Settler colonialism not only had profoundly negative impacts on both distinct and intermingled communities of indigenous and Mexican people but also imposed expectations of heterosexual morality on Mexicans who became Americans. Gutiérrez Avila and Mitchell find that heterosexual family life enabled Mexican women and men to counter negative Anglo assessments of their sexuality and thus became a resource for Mexican people during a traumatic period in their history. A far different picture of heterosexuality emerges from Carolyn Herbst Lewis's chapter about white, middle-class suburban "swingers" during the 1960s and 1970s. Lewis locates these enthusiastic spouse swappers at the leading edge of the sexual revolution and considers what the movement's gender conservatism might say about women's desires within (hetero)sexual liberation.[78] Indeed, Lewis reveals that swinging did not necessarily reflect egalitarian partnerships but could buttress male dominance among married couples. The third and final essay in this section turns to the legal history and rights claims of black mothers following the highly charged claims about female-headed households and "matriarchy" advanced in the 1965 publication *The Negro Family: The Case for National Action*, which was authored by then–Assistant Secretary of Labor Daniel Patrick Moynihan and is perhaps better known as "The Moynihan Report." The legal historian Serena Mayeri looks at lawsuits brought by African-descended women between 1967 and 1978 that challenged "illegitimacy penalties" in US employment law and public welfare policy. Together, these essays provide illuminating assessments of how gender, race, class, and sexual norms infused understandings of heterosexuality during a critical period of US state consolidation.

Part 4, "Discourses of Desire," includes three essays that reflect on how ways of naming and discussing heterosexuality—in medical literature, in religious language about "Judeo-Christian morality," and in a political scandal—emerged and evolved over time. Sarah Rodriguez, a historian of medicine, explains how the episiotomy, a foundational practice in obstetrics, was developed in the 1920s by the physician Joseph DeLee, in part as a way to "restore virginal conditions" (tighten the opening of the vagina) following childbirth. This physical association between women's anatomy and heterosexuality defined "normal" sexual function in terms of a male penetrative partner's satisfaction while making the episiotomy a "normal" clinical practice in obstetrical care. Heather R. White, a scholar of religion, asks how the terms "Judeo-Christian" and "heterosexuality" came to be associated in American religious discourse. She finds that religious conservatives linked their definitions of "Judeo-Christian morality" to their vision of a sexually moral, religiously guided, and heteronormative past. Andrea Friedman's essay on the politics of sexual humiliation and feminism in the Lewinsky-Clinton scandal concludes this section and rounds out our book. The scandal all at once revealed the reach, limitations, and contradictions of late second-wave feminist critiques of the sexual economy of heterosexuality. Friedman's essay illuminates how much controversy remained about the contours and content of heterosexual desire even into the early twenty-first century. Lewinsky refuted the associations with sexual humiliation that many feminists assigned to her trysts with President Bill Clinton in 1998, yet more recently she has reconsidered the relationship between power and desire in light of the #MeToo movement, which originated in 2006 with the civil rights activist and women's advocate Tarana Burke.

Together, these original essays offer myriad ways to reconsider what different-sex desire and erotic activity have meant in specific contexts and across time—not to mention what it means to write a history of heterosexuality itself. They call attention to the relationship between desire and differences of gender, race, and class. As histories of ideas and of experiences, these essays consider the relationship between differences, desires, politics, and cultures. Rather than unseen, fixed, or predetermined, heterosexuality has a complicated history. We hope this volume of essays will inspire others to continue to investigate its complex and even vexed past *and* present.

NOTES

1. "Shaws Visits Dr. Josephine Jackson, a Noted Authority on Psychology," *Blooming-ton (IL) Pantagraph*, March 26, 1924, 16.

2. Jonathan Ned Katz, *The Invention of Heterosexuality* (1995; repr., Chicago: University of Chicago Press, 2007), 92. See also Mason Stokes, "There Is Heterosexuality: Jessie Fauset, W. E. B. Du Bois, and the Problem of Desire," *African American Review* 44, nos. 1–2 (2011): 69–70.

3. Josephine Jackson, "Outwitting Your Nerves: The New Psychology in Action," *Corsicana (TX) Daily Sun*, April 21, 1930, 14.

4. Wide-ranging scholars have considered imperatives surrounding sexual respectability on various populations. One of the most influential explorations of the "politics of respectability" and race remains Evelyn Brooks Higginbotham's *Righteous Discontent: The Women's Movement in the Black Baptist Church, 1880–1920* (Cambridge, MA: Harvard University Press, 1993), 185–229. For work that analyzes the significance of class and respectability, see Michael Mason, *The Making of Victorian Sexuality* (Oxford: Oxford University Press, 1994), esp. 105–74. In *Remaking Respectability: African American Women in Interwar Detroit* (Chapel Hill: University of North Carolina Press, 2001), Victoria W. Wolcott considers both race and class in tandem. For analysis of how respectability politics could both cause and reflect tensions among African-descended Americans, see Michele Mitchell, *Righteous Propagation: African Americans and the Politics of Racial Destiny after Reconstruction* (Chapel Hill: University of North Carolina Press, 2004). For analysis of respectability and homosexuality, see Martin Meeker, "Behind the Mask of Respectability: Reconsidering the Mattachine Society and Male Homophile Practice, 1950s and 1960s," *Journal of the History of Sexuality* 10, no. 1 (2001): 78–116.

5. "A. Wilberforce Williams," *Journal of Negro History* 25, no. 2 (April 1940): 262–63; Lucius C. Harper, "Dustin' Off the News," *Defender*, May 29, 1943, 1, 4. For examples of Williams's columns about venereal disease, see Dr. A. Wilberforce Williams, "Keep Healthy," *Chicago Defender*, October 25, 1913, 4; "Dr. A. Wilberforce Williams Talks on Preventative Measures . . . ," *Chicago Defender*, January 22, 1916, 6; "Dr. A. Wilberforce Williams Talks on Preventative Measures . . . ," *Chicago Defender*, September 21, 1918, 16; "Dr. A. Wilberforce Williams Talks on Preventative Measures . . . ," *Chicago Defender*, April 7, 1923, 12. Significantly, Williams published occasional articles on health—including ones about venereal disease—into the 1930s. See, for example, Dr. A. Wilberforce Williams, "The Way to Health," *Chicago Defender*, February 16, 1935, 12.

6. See, for example, the following columns: Dr. A. Wilberforce Williams, "Keep Healthy," *Chicago Defender*, November 8, 1913, 4; "Dr. A. Wilberforce Williams Talks on Preventative Measures . . . ," *Chicago Defender*, November 20, 1915, 8; "Dr. A. Wilberforce Williams Talks on Preventative Measures . . . ," *Chicago Defender*, September 25, 1920, 12; Dr. A. Wilberforce Williams, "Keep Healthy," *Chicago Defender*, October 4, 1913, 7.

7. A search of other select African American newspapers—namely, the *Norfolk Journal and Guide*, the *Atlanta Daily World*, and the *Philadelphia Tribune*—revealed no usage of either "heterosexual" or "heterosexuality" before 1940. In 1933, however, the *Afro-American* published an article about a religious movement led by a man of African descent who was probably born as George Baker (1879–1965) but who was better known as "Father Divine." And when reporting on an investigation of Father Divine's interracial Peace Mission, the *Afro-American* noted that a committee concluded that Divine's followers were "deluded into accepting certain social, biological, and economic fallacies"—including the notion that "the human race may be propagated without heterosexual relationship in marital life." To be sure, the committee acknowledged that Divine's Peace Mission could have a positive impact on "former criminal[s] or morally loose characters." The committee took a dim view of the Peace Mission's advocacy of celibacy all the same. Coincidentally—or not—some of Divine's black female followers might have embraced "forms of desire prohibited in Divine's theology," namely, same-sex desire. If this article ultimately made no direct claims about such women, committee members did note what they considered to be a worrisome congregation of adults and children of the same sex in one Peace Mission dormitory. What do we make of the apparent reality that it was not until investigation of a heterodox movement that a leading black newspaper would invoke the term "heterosexual"? See "Are Father Divine's Angels Deluded?," *Baltimore Afro-American*, December 30, 1933, 12; Judith Weisenfeld, "Real True Buds: Celibacy and Same-Sex Desire across the Color Line in Father Divine's Peace Mission Movement," in *Devotions and Desires: Histories of Sexuality and Religion in the Twentieth-Century United States*, ed. Gillian Frank, Bethany Moreton, and Heather R. White (Chapel Hill: University of North Carolina Press, 2018), 95.

8. "Dr. A. Wilberforce Williams Talks on Preventative Measures . . . ," *Chicago Defender*, April 18, 1925, A12. The literature scholar Mary Zaborskis maintains that one of Williams's contemporaries, the African American educator and reformer Janie Porter Barrett (1865–1948), focused on the "heterosexualization" of delinquent girls at the Industrial Home School for Colored Girls in Virginia during the late 1910s and early 1920s. It is not clear, however, whether Barrett thought more in terms of encouraging sexual purity, respectability, matrimony, and "home life" or whether she actually embraced emergent notions about "heterosexuality" in a manner akin to Josephine Jackson. See Zaborskis, "Queering Black Girlhood at the Virginia Industrial School," *Signs: Journal of Women and Culture in Society* 45, no. 2 (2020): 373–94, esp. 381–86.

9. On the history of how secular and religious marriage counselors actively taught heterosexuality (and engaged deeply with social scientific and psychological theories about heterosexuality), see Rebecca L. Davis, *More Perfect Unions: The American Search for Marital Bliss* (Cambridge, MA: Harvard University Press, 2010). Newspaper searches reveal myriad advice columns that mention and explain heterosexuality in papers throughout the United States. See, for

example, "Dr. Brady Says: Did the Doctor Do Right?," *Brooklyn Eagle*, October 26, 1939, 25; Dr. George W. Crane (Northwestern University), "Case Records of a Psychologist," *Ogden (UT) Standard-Examiner*, March 30, 1938, 4; Dr. George W. Crane, "Case Records of a Psychologist," *Appleton (WI) Post-Crescent*, December 10, 1938, 8; Dr. George W. Crane, "Encourage Child to Mix Friends: Case Records of a Psychologist," *Pittsburgh Press*, April 21, 1939, 53; Dr. George W. Crane, "The Case Records of a Psychologist," *St. Louis Post-Dispatch*, August 15, 1939, 20.

10. "Dr. A. Wilberforce Williams Talks on Preventative Measures . . . ," *Chicago Defender*, July 14, 1928, A2.

11. On the need to reevaluate the Victorian-to-modern paradigm for turn-of-the-twentieth-century sexuality in the United States, see Catherine Cocks, "Rethinking Sexuality in the Progressive Era," *Journal of the Gilded Age and Progressive Era* 5, no. 2 (2006): 93–118. For a challenge to Cocks, one that embraces the "Victorian-to-modern framework," see Leigh Ann Wheeler, "Inventing Sexuality: Ideologies, Identities, and Practices in the Gilded Age and Progressive Era," in *A Companion to the Gilded Age and Progressive Era*, ed. Christopher McKnight Nichols and Nancy C. Unger (Somerset, NJ: Wiley, 2017), 102–15.

12. David M. Halperin, *How to Do the History of Homosexuality* (Chicago: University of Chicago Press, 2002), 105.

13. Daniel Wickberg, "Heterosexual White Male: Some Recent Inversions in American Cultural History," *Journal of American History* 92, no. 1 (June 2005): 155.

14. Robert A. Nye rightly observes, "As an object of disciplinary knowledge, sexuality has never been the monopoly of any single field. It has been a principal subject for ethicists, philosophers, theologians, anthropologists, sociologists, historians, creative artists, medical professionals, psychologists, and psychoanalysts." Nye nevertheless stresses that historicizing sexuality is critical: "The idea that tastes and identities appear in particular historical circumstances means that we are unlikely to understand the promise or the limits of our contemporary sexualities unless we understand those of the past." Nye, "On Why History Is So Important to an Understanding of Human Sexuality," in *Sexuality*, ed. Nye (Oxford: Oxford University Press, 1999), 3–15 (quotes on 3, 15).

15. Jeffrey Weeks, *Sexuality and Its Discontents: Meanings, Myths, and Modern Sexualities* (London: Routledge, 1985), 6.

16. See, for example, Ifi Amadiume, *Male Daughters, Female Husbands: Gender and Sex in an African Society* (London: Zed Books, 1987). Amadiume's pathbreaking *Male Daughters, Female Husbands* is not a work of transgender history but instead challenges hegemonic, Western notions about gender itself. Significantly, Amadiume shows that European colonial powers in West Africa imposed rigid ideas about binary sex differences on indigenous people and that Africans' own conceptions of gender could be notably flexible. Transgender histories have further prodded us to approach the history of heterosexuality as the effect of histori-

cal processes rather than a universal condition. Jen Manion centers the stories of female husbands who "transed gender," to show that for nearly two hundred years of British and US history, "gender was malleable and not linked entirely to sex." Manion, *Female Husbands: A Trans History* (New York: Cambridge University Press, 2020), 13.

17. Monique Wittig, *The Straight Mind and Other Essays* (Boston: Beacon, 1992), 40, 43.

18. Randolph Trumbach, *Sex and the Gender Revolution*, vol. 1, *Heterosexuality and the Third Gender in Enlightenment London* (Chicago: University of Chicago Press, 1998), 4; see also 9–10. John D'Emilio has argued that in the seventeenth and eighteenth centuries, "'heterosexuality' remained undefined, since it was literally the only way of life." D'Emilio, *Sexual Politics, Sexual Communities: The Making of a Homosexual Minority in the United States, 1940–1970* (Chicago: University of Chicago Press, 1998), 10. The historian and literary scholar Henry Abelove, by contrast, notes that the ample demographic evidence of rising fertility rates in eighteenth-century England indicates a new popularity for cross-sex "sexual intercourse so-called" as a particular kind of newly privileged erotic behavior, which together with capitalism helped create "modern heterosexuality." Abelove, "Some Speculation on the History of 'Sexual Intercourse' during the 'Long Eighteenth Century' in England," in *Beyond the Body Proper: Reading the Anthropology of Material Life*, ed. Margaret M. Lock and Judith Farquhar (Durham, NC: Duke University Press, 2007), 221.

19. Karma Lochrie, *Heterosyncrasies: Female Sexuality When Normal Wasn't* (Minneapolis: University of Minnesota Press, 2005).

20. Ruth Mazo Karras, *Unmarriages: Women, Men, and Sexual Unions in the Middle Ages* (Philadelphia: University of Pennsylvania Press, 2012), 4–5, 2.

21. Nearly thirty years ago, the philosopher Ian Hacking explained that the idea of the "normal," much like the categories of "heterosexual" and homosexual," originated in the nineteenth century. In *The Taming of Chance*, Hacking argued that by the late nineteenth century, the psychological sciences had helped create a new concept of the normal/abnormal, which supplanted the older binary of natural/unnatural. Hacking, *The Taming of Chance* (Cambridge: Cambridge University Press, 1990). The scholar Laura Doan argues in her unpublished manuscript "Birds and Bees: An Unnatural History of Modern Sexuality," however, that the older natural/unnatural system persisted long after "normality" emerged. Disability studies has further interrogated the power of ideas of the "normal" and critiqued the binary oppositions of ability/disability and its corollary of normality/freakery. See Rosemarie Garland-Thomson, *Freakery: Cultural Spectacles of the Extraordinary Body* (New York: NYU Press, 1996); Garland-Thomson, *Extraordinary Bodies: Figuring Physical Disability in American Culture and Literature* (New York: Columbia University Press, 1997); Lennard J. Davis, *The End of Normal: Identity in a Biocultural Era* (Ann Arbor: University of Michigan Press, 2013).

22. Peter Cryle and Elizabeth Stephens, *Normality: A Critical Genealogy* (Chicago: University of Chicago Press, 2017). See also Laura Doan, "Marie Stopes's Wonderful Rhythm Charts: Normalizing the Natural," *Journal of the History of Ideas* 78, no. 4 (2017): 595–620.

23. See Calvin Thomas, ed., *Straight with a Twist: Queer Theory and the Subject of Heterosexuality* (Urbana: University of Illinois Press, 2000).

24. From that issue, see especially Annamarie Jagose, "The Trouble with Antinormativity," *differences* 26, no. 1 (2015): 26–47.

25. Lochrie, *Heterosyncrasies*, xiii.

26. Lauren Berlant and Michael Warner, "Sex in Public," *Critical Inquiry* 24, no. 2 (1998): 548n2, 549.

27. Halperin, *How to Do the History of Homosexuality*, 107.

28. Marjorie B. Garber, *Vice Versa: Bisexuality and the Eroticism of Everyday Life* (New York: Simon and Schuster, 1995), 66.

29. Judit Takacs, "The Double Life of Kertbeny," in *Past and Present of Radical Sexual Politics*, ed. Gert Hekma (Amsterdam: UvA Massa Foundation, 2004), 30; Katz, *Invention of Heterosexuality*, 19–32.

30. Ross Brooks, "Transforming Sexuality: The Medical Sources of Karl Heinrich Ulrichs (1825–95) and the Origins of the Theory of Bisexuality," *Journal of the History of Medicine and Allied Sciences* 67, no. 2 (2010): 177–216; Garber, *Vice Versa*; Sigmund Freud, *Dora: An Analysis of a Case of Hysteria*, ed. Philip Rieff (New York: Collier Books, 1993), part 2; Freud, "Extract from *Three Essays on the Theory of Sexuality: 1. The Sexual Aberrations* (1905)," in *Bisexuality: A Critical Reader*, ed. Merl Storr (London: Routledge, 1999), 20–27; Henry Havelock Ellis, "Extracts from *Studies in the Psychology of Sex, Volume I: Sexual Inversion* (1897) and from *Studies in the Psychology of Sex, Volume II: Sexual Inversion* (1915)," in Storr, *Bisexuality*, 15–19. For additional consideration of Freud's theorization of bisexuality, see Birgit Lang and Katie Sutton, "The Queer Cases of Psychoanalysis: Rethinking the Scientific Study of Homosexuality, 1890s–1920s," *German History* 34, no. 3 (2016): 419–44, esp. 423–25.

31. Lucy Bland and Laura Doan, eds., *Sexology in Culture: Labelling Bodies and Desires* (Chicago: University of Chicago Press, 1998).

32. Julian Carter, *The Heart of Whiteness: Normal Sexuality and Race in America, 1880–1940* (Durham, NC: Duke University Press, 2007); Siobhan B. Somerville, *Queering the Color Line: Race and the Invention of Homosexuality in American Culture* (Durham, NC: Duke University Press, 2000). In the United States, at least, systematic processes of racial differentiation dated back to the antebellum period and the American school of ethnology. See George Fredrickson, *The Black Image in the White Mind: The Debate on Afro-American Character and Destiny, 1817–1914* (New York: Harper and Row, 1971).

33. Angus McLaren, *The Trials of Masculinity: Policing Sexual Boundaries, 1870–1930* (Chicago: University of Chicago Press, 1997), 1–2.

34. Katz, *Invention of Heterosexuality*, 14.

35. Hanne Blank, *Straight: The Surprisingly Short History of Heterosexuality* (Boston: Beacon, 2012).

36. Anne Fausto-Sterling, *Sexing the Body: Gender Politics and the Construction of Sexuality* (New York: Basic Books, 2000).

37. Lisa Duggan, *Sapphic Slashers: Sex, Violence, and American Modernity* (Durham, NC: Duke University Press, 2000); Duggan, "The Trials of Alice Mitchell: Sensationalism, Sexology, and the Lesbian Subject in Turn-of-the-Century America," *Signs* 18, no. 4 (Summer 1993): 791–814; Jennifer Terry, *An American Obsession: Science, Medicine, and Homosexuality in Modern Society* (Chicago: University of Chicago Press, 1999); Vernon A. Rosario, ed., *Science and Homosexualities* (New York: Routledge, 1997); Heike Bauer, ed., *Sexology and Translation: Cultural and Scientific Encounters across the Modern World*, Sexuality Studies (Philadelphia: Temple University Press, 2015); Harry Oosterhuis, *Stepchildren of Nature: Krafft-Ebing, Psychiatry, and the Making of Sexual Identity* (Chicago: University of Chicago Press, 2000).

38. Geertje A. Mak, "Conflicting Heterosexualities: Hermaphroditism and the Emergence of Surgery around 1900," *Journal of the History of Sexuality* 24, no. 3 (September 2015): 402; Katz, *Invention of Heterosexuality*; Kevin White, *The First Sexual Revolution: The Emergence of Male Heterosexuality in Modern America* (New York: NYU Press, 1993); Roy Porter and Lesley A. Hall, *The Facts of Life: The Creation of Sexual Knowledge in Britain, 1650–1950* (New Haven, CT: Yale University Press, 1995); Daniel Boyarin, *Unheroic Conduct: The Rise of Heterosexuality and the Invention of the Jewish Man* (Berkeley: University of California Press, 1997).

39. Important interventions on this front include the following texts: Kathy Peiss, *Cheap Amusements: Working Women and Leisure in Turn-of-the-Century New York* (Philadelphia: Temple University Press, 1986); Joanne J. Meyerowitz, *Women Adrift: Independent Wage Earners in Chicago, 1880–1930* (Chicago: University of Chicago Press, 1988); White, *First Sexual Revolution*; Margaret A. Lowe, *Looking Good: College Women and Body Image, 1875–1930* (Baltimore: Johns Hopkins University Press, 2003); Elizabeth Alice Clement, *Love for Sale: Courting, Treating, and Prostitution in New York City, 1900–1945* (Chapel Hill: University of North Carolina Press, 2006); and Christina Simmons, *Making Marriage Modern: Women's Sexuality from the Progressive Era to World War II* (New York: Oxford University Press, 2009).

40. D'Emilio additionally contends "capitalism has created conditions that allow some men and women to organize a personal life around their erotic/emotional attraction to their own sex." John D'Emilio, "Capitalism and Gay Identity," in *Powers of Desire: The Politics of Sexuality*, ed. Ann Snitow, Christine Stansell, and Sharon Thompson (New York: Monthly Review Press, 1983), 100–113 (quotes on 110, 109, 104). For allied analysis regarding capitalism and sexuality, see Robert A. Padgug, "Sexual Matters: On Conceptualizing Sexuality in History," in *Passion and Power: Sexuality in History*, ed. Kathy Peiss and Christina Simmons with

Robert A. Padgug (Philadelphia: Temple University Press, 1989), 14–31. For critical analysis of gender, the body, and the transition to capitalism, see Silvia Federici, *Caliban and the Witch: Women, The Body, and Primitive Accumulation*, rev. ed. (Brooklyn, NY: Autonomedia, 2014).

41. George Chauncey, *Gay New York: Gender, Urban Culture, and the Making of the Gay Male World, 1890–1940* (New York: Basic Books, 1994), 126.

42. Margot Canaday, *The Straight State: Sexuality and Citizenship in Twentieth-Century America* (Princeton, NJ: Princeton University Press, 2009), 3.

43. Cheryl D. Hicks, *Talk with You like a Woman: African American Women, Justice, and Reform in New York, 1890–1935* (Chapel Hill: University of North Carolina Press, 2010), 225. See also LaKisha Michelle Simmons, *Crescent City Girls: The Lives of Young Black Women in Segregated New Orleans* (Chapel Hill: University of North Carolina Press, 2015).

44. Hicks, *Talk with You like a Woman*, 225. For another crucial study of the gendering of interracial same-sex sexuality, see Regina G. Kunzel, *Criminal Intimacy: Prison and the Uneven History of Modern American Sexuality* (Chicago: University of Chicago Press, 2008).

45. Pablo Mitchell, "Accomplished Ladies and *Coyotes*: Marriage, Power, and Straying from the Flock in Territorial New Mexico, 1880–1920," in *Sex, Love, Race: Crossing Boundaries in North American History*, ed. Martha Hodes (New York: NYU Press, 1999), 331–51; Victor Jew, "'Chinese Demons': The Violent Articulation of Chinese Otherness and Interracial Sexuality in the U.S. Midwest, 1885–1889," *Journal of Social History* 37, no. 2 (2003): 389–410; Mary Ting Yi Lui, *The Chinatown Trunk Mystery: Murder, Miscegenation, and Other Dangerous Encounters in Turn-of-the-Century New York City* (Princeton, NJ: Princeton University Press, 2005); Lui, "Saving Young Girls from Chinatown: White Slavery and Woman Suffrage, 1910–1920," *Journal of the History of Sexuality*, 18, no. 3 (2009): 393–417. For important discussion of why marriages between Native American men and white women were not necessarily deemed problematic during the nineteenth century, see C. Joseph Genetin-Pilawa, "'All Intent on Seeing the White Woman Married to the Red Man': The Parker/Sackett Affair and the Public Spectacle of Intermarriage," *Journal of Women's History* 20, no. 2 (2008): 57–85. For allied analysis that explores sexuality in indigenous law, see Fay Yarbrough, "Legislating Women's Sexuality: Cherokee Marriage Laws in the Nineteenth Century," *Journal of Social History* 38, no. 2 (2004): 385–406.

46. Amy Sueyoshi, "Intimate Inequalities: Interracial Affection and *Same, Sex, Love* in the 'Heterosexual' Life of Yone Noguchi, 1897–1909," *Journal of American Ethnic History* 29, no. 4 (2010): 38.

47. Nayan Shah, "Between 'Oriental Depravity' and 'Natural Degenerates': Spatial Borderlands and the Making of Ordinary Americans," *American Quarterly* 57, no. 3 (September 2005): 703–25. See also Shah, *Stranger Intimacy: Contesting Race, Sexuality, and the Law in the North American West*, American Crossroads 31 (Berkeley: University of California Press, 2011).

48. Peggy Pascoe, *What Comes Naturally: Miscegenation Law and the Making of Race in America* (New York: Oxford University Press, 2009), 191, 119.

49. Rosemarie Garland-Thomson, "The Beauty and the Freak," *Michigan Quarterly Review* 37, no. 3 (Summer 1998), http://quod.lib.umich.edu.

50. Peter Kolchin, "Whiteness Studies: The New History of Race in America," *Journal of American History* 89, no. 1 (2002): 160. See also Thomas A. Guglielmo, *White on Arrival: Italians, Race, Color, and Power in Chicago, 1890–1945* (New York: Oxford University Press, 2003). For a decidedly different take on whiteness studies, see Wickberg, "Heterosexual White Male," 136–57.

51. Rogers Brubaker and Frederick Cooper, "Beyond 'Identity,'" *Theory and Society* 29, no. 1 (2000): 1–47.

52. Berlant and Warner, "Sex in Public," 552.

53. Sharon Marcus, "Queer Theory for Everyone: A Review Essay," *Signs* 31, no. 1 (2005): 191–218.

54. Laura Doan, "Sex Education and the Great War Soldier: A Queer Analysis of the Practice of 'Hetero' Sex," *Journal of British Studies* 51, no. 3 (2012): 663.

55. The Feminists' manifesto originally appeared in *Notes from the Second Year: Women's Liberation; Major Writings of the Radical Feminists* (New York: Radical Feminism, 1970) and was reprinted in *Radical Feminism*, ed. Anne Koedt, Ellen Levine, and Anita Rapone (New York: Quadrangle Books, 1973), 375, 376. As Martha Shelley wrote in "Lesbianism and the Women's Liberation Movement," "Love can only exist between equals, not between the oppressed and the oppressor." Shelley, "Lesbianism and the Women's Liberation Movement," in *Radical Feminism: A Documentary Reader*, ed. Barbara A. Crow (New York: NYU Press, 2000), 308. See also a critique of "the heterosexual institution" in Anne Koedt, "The Myth of the Vaginal Orgasm," in *Notes from the Second Year*, a reprint of her 1968 article, available at http://collections.mun.ca. Yet another example: Charlotte Bunch of The Furies warned that heterosexual privilege remained a problem for the women's liberation movement: "As long as women still benefit from heterosexuality, receive its privileges and security, they will at some point have to betray their sisters, especially lesbian sisters who do not receive those benefits." Bunch, "Lesbians in Revolt," in Crow, *Radical Feminism*, 336.

56. "Is Homosexuality Natural?," in *Gay Liberation* (February 1970), 5, available at http://paganpressbooks.com.

57. Carl Wittman, *A Gay Manifesto* (1970), 3, available at http://paganpressbooks.com.

58. The Red Butterfly, *Gay Oppression: A Radical Analysis* (New York, 1970), 1, available at http://paganpressbooks.com. See also John Lauritsen, "The Red Butterfly," Pagan Press, 2011, http://paganpressbooks.com.

59. Gayle Rubin, "The Traffic in Women: Notes on the 'Political Economy' of Sex," in *Deviations: A Gayle Rubin Reader* (Durham, NC: Duke University Press, 2011), 54.

60. Rubin, 61.

61. Adrienne Rich, "Compulsory Heterosexuality and Lesbian Existence," *Signs* 5 (Summer 1980): 631–60. For a series of articles under the heading of "The

Institution of Heterosexuality," see Snitow, Stansell, and Thompson, eds., *Powers of Desire*, 177–275. Feminist historians continued to explore the "institution of heterosexuality" into the mid-1980s, although subsequent works, perhaps due to the impact of queer theory in the late 1980s and early 1990s, named it less often. Feminist scholars have, however, productively engaged Rich's classic article in relation to select racialized populations. See, for example, Judy Tzu-Chun Wu, "Asian American History and Racialized Compulsory Deviance," *Journal of Women's History* 15, no. 3 (2003): 58–62; Mattie Udora Richardson, "No More Secrets, No More Lies: African American History and Compulsory Heterosexuality," *Journal of Women's History* 15, no. 3 (2003): 63–76. Leila J. Rupp notes that Rich actually prefers another iteration of her article to the one that was published in *Signs*. See Rupp, "Women's History in the New Millennium: Adrienne Rich's 'Compulsory Heterosexuality and Lesbian Existence': A Retrospective," *Journal of Women's History* 15, no. 3 (2003): 9–10. For that different iteration, see Rich, *Blood, Bread, and Poetry: Selected Prose, 1979–1985* (New York: Norton, 1994), 23–75.

62. The historian Gerda Lerner developed these theories in her history of patriarchy, in which she argued that male domination over women was the result of historical processes rooted in resource allocation and systems of domination, the results of which allow for women to remain marginal to the ideological contours and political operations of societies in which they play socially instrumental roles. Lerner, *The Creation of Patriarchy* (New York: Oxford University Press, 1986).

63. For brief discussions of this particular history, see Deborah Gray White, *Too Heavy a Load: Black Women in Defense of Themselves, 1894–1994* (New York: Norton, 1999), 242–56; Kimberly Springer, *Living for the Revolution: Black Feminist Organizations, 1968–1980* (Durham, NC: Duke University Press, 2005), 56–61; Keeanga-Yamahtta Taylor, *How We Get Free: Black Feminism and the Combahee River Collective* (Chicago: Haymarket Books, 2017), 4–8.

64. The Combahee River Collective, *The Combahee River Collective Statement: Black Feminist Organizing in the Seventies and Eighties*, Freedom Organizing Series 1 (New York: Kitchen Table: Women of Color Press, 1986), 9.

65. Combahee River Collective, 13.

66. Audre Lorde, *I Am Your Sister: Black Women Organizing across Sexualities*, Freedom Organizing Series 3 (New York: Kitchen Table: Women of Color Press, 1985), 3.

67. Lorde, *I Am Your Sister*, 3–4.

68. Michael Warner, "Introduction: Fear of a Queer Planet," *Social Text*, no. 29 (1991): 3.

69. Michael Warner, introduction to *Fear of a Queer Planet: Queer Politics and Social Theory*, ed. Warner, Cultural Politics 6 (Minneapolis: University of Minnesota Press, 1993), xxi. Karma Lochrie builds from Warner's definitions to explain how heteronormativity differs from heterosexuality: "'Heterosexuality' expands on a specific desire for the opposite sex and sexual intercourse to include moral and social virtue. 'Heteronormativity,' in brief, is heterosexuality that has become presumptive, that is, heterosexuality that is both descriptive and prescriptive, that

defines everything from who we think we are as a nation, to what it means to be human, to 'our ideals, our principles, our hopes and aspirations'" (*Heterosyncrasies*, 4). Lochrie quotes a passage from Warner's *The Trouble with Normal*, where he, in turn, is citing a woman who held a leadership position in the Mattachine Society in the 1950s; see Warner, *The Trouble with Normal: Sex, Politics and the Ethics of Queer Life* (New York: Free Press, 1999), 46.

70. Marlon B. Ross, "Beyond the Closet as a Raceless Paradigm," in *Black Queer Studies: A Critical Anthology*, ed. E. Patrick Johnson and Mae Henderson (Durham, NC: Duke University Press, 2005), 183.

71. See, for example, Ann Laura Stoler, *Race and the Education of Desire: Foucault's History of Sexuality and the Colonial Order of Things* (Durham, NC: Duke University Press, 1995); Stoler, *Carnal Knowledge and Imperial Power: Race and the Intimate in Colonial Rule* (Berkeley: University of California Press, 2002); Stoler, *Haunted by Empire: Geographies of Intimacy in North American History* (Durham, NC: Duke University Press, 2006). Important, allied analysis may also be found in Anne McClintock, *Imperial Leather: Race, Gender, and Sexuality in the Colonial Conquest* (New York: Routledge, 1995).

72. Relevant overviews include Joanne Meyerowitz, "*AHR* Forum: Transnational Sex and U.S. History," *American Historical Review* 114, no. 5 (2009): 1273–86; Cornelia H. Dayton and Lisa Levenstein, "The Big Tent of U.S. Women's and Gender History: A State of the Field," *Journal of American History* 99, no. 3 (2012): 793–817; Michele Mitchell, "Turns of the Kaleidoscope: 'Race,' Ethnicity, and Analytical Patterns in American Women's and Gender History," *Journal of Women's History* 25, no. 4 (2013): 46–73; Monica Perales, "On *Borderlands / La Frontera*: Gloria Anzaldúa and Twenty-Five Years of Research on Gender in the Borderlands," *Journal of Women's History* 25, no. 4 (2013): 163–73. For select analyses of gender, sexuality, and religion, see Susan Juster and Lisa MacFarlane, eds., *A Mighty Baptism: Race, Gender, and the Creation of American Protestantism* (Ithaca, NY: Cornell University Press, 1996); Janet R. Jakobsen and Ann Pellegrini, *Love the Sin: Sexual Regulation and the Limits of Religious Tolerance* (New York: NYU Press, 2003); Richard Godbeer, *Sexual Revolution in Early America* (Baltimore: Johns Hopkins University Press, 2004); Rebecca L. Davis, "'Not Marriage at All, but Simple Harlotry': The Companionate Marriage Controversy," *Journal of American History* 94, no. 4 (2008): 1137–63; R. Marie Griffith, "The Religious Encounters of Alfred C. Kinsey," *Journal of American History* 95, no. 2 (2008): 349–77; Gillian Frank, Bethany Moreton, and Heather R. White, "Introduction: More than Missionary: Doing the Histories of Religion and Sexuality Together," in Frank, Moreton, and White, *Devotions and Desires*, 1–16; Rebecca L. Davis, "Purity and Population: American Jews, Marriage, and Sexuality," in Frank, Moreton, and White, *Devotions and Desires*, 54–70; Weisenfeld, "Real True Buds," 90–112.

73. Richard Dyer, *White*, 20th anniversary ed. (London: Routledge, 2017), 20.

74. Karen E. Fields and Barbara J. Fields, *Racecraft: The Soul of Inequality in American Life* (London: Verso, 2014), 16.

75. Michele Mitchell and Naoko Shibusawa with Stephan F. Miescher, introduction to *Gender, Imperialism and Global Exchanges*, ed. Miescher, Mitchell and Shibusawa (Chichester, UK: Wiley-Blackwell, 2015), 4–5.

76. For important albeit select statements on racialized gender, see Eileen Boris, "'You Wouldn't Want One of 'Em Dancing with Your Wife': Racialized Bodies on the Job in World War II," *American Quarterly* 50, no. 1 (1998): 77–108, esp. 80; Evelyn Nakano Glenn, *Unequal Freedom: How Race and Gender Shaped American Citizenship and Labor* (Cambridge, MA: Harvard University Press, 2002), 7, 136, 252–56; Marisa J. Fuentes, *Dispossessed Lives: Enslaved Women, Violence, and the Archive* (Philadelphia: University of Pennsylvania Press, 2016), 75, 86, 94, 96–97, 113, 129. For analysis of "racialized orgasm," see Carolyn Herbst Lewis, *Prescription for Heterosexuality: Sexual Citizenship in the Cold War Era* (Chapel Hill: University of North Carolina Press, 2010), 43–44.

77. Kevin P. Murphy and Jennifer M. Spear, *Historicising Sexuality and Gender* (Chichester, UK: Wiley-Blackwell, 2011), 10. See also Afsaneh Najmabadi, "Beyond the Americas: Are Gender & Sexuality Useful Categories of Analysis?," *Journal of Women's History* 18, no. 1 (2006): 11–21.

78. For work that complicates Cold War–era marital sexuality in a different manner, see Lauren Jae Gutterman, *Her Neighbor's Wife: A History of Lesbian Desire within Marriage* (Philadelphia: University of Pennsylvania Press, 2020). See also Clayton Howard, *The Closet and the Cul-de-Sac: The Politics of Sexual Privacy in Northern California* (Philadelphia: University of Pennsylvania Press, 2019).

PART I

Difference and Desire since the Seventeenth Century

1

Toward a Cultural Poetics of Desire in a World before Heterosexuality

RICHARD GODBEER

In early 1630, as John Winthrop prepared to cross the Atlantic and join the Puritan settlement in New England, he bade farewell to friends and loved ones. Some, including his third wife, Margaret Tyndal, would remain in England for a time and then join him in North America. Others he would in all likelihood never see again. The latter included his "most sweet friend" Sir William Spring. Winthrop sent his friend a parting letter in which he declared as follows: "I loved you truly before I could think that you took any notice of me: but now I embrace you and rest in your love and delight to solace my first thoughts in these sweet affections of so dear a friend. The apprehension of your love and worth together hath overcome my heart and removed the veil of modesty, that I must needs tell you, my soul is knit to you as the soul of Jonathan to David: were I now with you, I should bedew that sweet bosom with the tears of affection." In the past, Winthrop wrote, when one of them set off on a trip, their good-byes had been "pleasant" because they could look forward to a reunion in the near future, but now "this addition of forever" was "a sad close." Winthrop confessed quite openly to Spring his "envy" of their mutual friend Nathaniel Barnardiston and of Spring's wife, neither of whom would suffer the anguish of long-term separation from William. Of Barnardiston, Winthrop wrote, "he shall enjoy what I desire." And as for Spring's wife, Winthrop could not but resent "the felicity of that good lady." Winthrop consoled himself with the hope that he and Spring would be reunited in heaven. Meanwhile, their mutual "prayers and affections" would "represent [them] often with the idea of each other's countenance." Winthrop prayed that Christ would bless their "bond of brotherly affection: let not distance weaken it, nor time waste it, nor change dissolve it."[1]

Envious though Winthrop was of Barnardiston and Lady Spring, there was another loving companion to whom he could entrust his friend without any twinge of jealousy: that is, their mutual savior. "I know not how to leave you," he wrote, "yet since I must, I will put my beloved into his arms who loves him best and is a faithful keeper of all that is committed to him." Winthrop described the comfort that Christ would provide in language that was even more passionate and demonstrative than his declarations of love for William Spring. In common with other Puritans, male and female, Winthrop envisaged Christ as a prospective spouse and relished "the most sweet love" of his "heavenly husband." Winthrop imagined himself as "the loving wife" in the Song of Solomon and addressed his spiritual husband-to-be in a rhapsody of romantic infatuation: "O my Lord, my love, how wholly delectable art thou! Let him kiss me with the kisses of his mouth, for his love is sweeter than wine: how lovely is thy countenance! How pleasant are thy embracings! My heart leaps within me for joy when I hear the voice of thee, my Lord, my love, when thou sayest to my soul, thou art her salvation." Winthrop would have to wait for union with his savior until the afterlife, when he hoped to join other redeemed souls in marriage to the heavenly bridegroom; but meanwhile, in his sleep, he "dreamed that [he] was with Christ upon earth" and "ravished with his love . . . far exceeding the affection of the kindest husband." On awakening after one such dream, he found that the experience "had made so deep impression in [his] heart" that he wept for joy and "had a more lively feeling of the love of Christ than ever before." Now that he was leaving England and would no longer be able to "bedew" William Spring's "sweet bosom with the tears of affection," he would find solace in Christ's love and imagine his friend in their savior's embrace.[2]

Winthrop's dreams of ravishment by a heavenly bridegroom would have neither surprised nor disturbed his contemporaries. He saw his loving relationships in this world—with three successive wives and with close male friends—as analogous to the love raptures of the world to come. In Winthrop's mind, earthly and spiritual loves were equally real and symbiotic. Looking over some of the letters that he and his first wife had written to each other, Winthrop found himself in "such a heavenly meditation of the love between Christ and [himself] as ravished [his] heart with unspeakable joy": "methought my soul had as familiar and sensible society with him as my wife could have with the kindest husband." In later years, he hoped that the love he and his third wife shared would rouse them "to a like conformity of sincerity and fervency in the love of Christ our lord and heavenly husband; that we could delight in him as we do in each other." Winthrop never referred to William Spring as a spouse (at least not in any of his surviving letters), but he did see their loving friendship as a foretaste of the bliss awaiting the redeemed in the life to come: "if any emblem may express our condition in heaven, it is this communion in love." Spring evidently felt the same way, depicting his love for Winthrop and for Christ as parallel devotions: he wrote longingly of Winthrop's "bosom, whither I desire to convey myself and to live there, as we may to [Christ] also that owns that place." Winthrop saw marital love, loving friendship, love of Christ, and Christ's love for the faithful as mutually reinforcing devotions that conflated the earthly and spiritual as well as love for men and women. He finished his letter of farewell to Spring by praying that Christ would bless their love for each other and unite them in love for their redeemer: "make us sick with thy love: let us sleep in thine arms, and awake in thy kingdom: the souls of thy servants, thus united to thee, make as one in the bond of brotherly affection."[3]

* * *

It is difficult to make sense of this seventeenth-century romantic ménage using modern categories of sexual orientation or our own assumptions about what it means to be a heterosexual male. Puritan men like John Winthrop who considered themselves quite respectable did not hesitate to express passionate love for other men and for Christ, whom they hoped to marry on the Day of Judgment and by whom they hoped to be ravished in an everlasting ecstasy that they envisaged in literal and explicitly erotic terms. They were able to do so because they inhabited a world in which neither heterosexuality nor homosexuality existed as categories of identification. Early Americans had clear notions of what we now call sexuality and gender, along with strong opinions about what constituted appropriate and inappropriate behavior, but the ways in which they understood and evaluated love and desire were very different from and in some respects much more capacious than our own. This was not simply a question of using different vocabulary to describe universal emotions or drives: because their ideas and assumptions shaped how they processed internally their own feelings and those of others, their actual experience of sexual desire and love was different from ours.

Let me pause for a moment to unpack the last few sentences. Just over a quarter century ago, the scholar David Halperin pointed out in his now-classic essay entitled "One Hundred Years of Homosexuality" that the introduction of the words "homosexuality" and (shortly afterward) "heterosexuality" at the end of the nineteenth century marked "a major reconceptualization of the nature of human sexuality." Previously, nineteenth-century medical experts had linked desire for members of the same sex to what they called "sexual inversion" (the adoption of feminine roles and traits by an anatomical man or of masculine traits and roles by an anatomical woman). But this new taxonomy shifted attention away from gender performance and focused entirely on the anatomical sex of those who were engaging in a sexual act: those who chose to have sex with persons of the same sex were *homosexual,* and those who chose instead members of the opposite sex were *heterosexual,* regardless of whether they seemed manly or effeminate. That paradigm of sexual orientation became the dominant framework used by twentieth-century Westerners to understand sexual attraction. Many people came to assume that this paradigm had a transhistorical validity, so that they could apply it to any cultural or historical setting. Yet Halperin argued that terms such as "homosexuality," "heterosexuality," and even "sexuality," far from being "the basic building-blocks of human identity for all human beings in all times and places," constitute "peculiar and indeed exceptional ways of conceptualizing as well as *experiencing* sexual desire" that would have made little sense to people living in the past (emphasis in original). Because people living before the late nineteenth century would not have described sexual desires and behavior using modern taxonomy, they would therefore have understood and even felt such desires differently. It follows that the assumptions embedded within words like "heterosexuality" present "a significant obstacle" to understanding sexual life in the past. Instead, we need to recover what Halperin called "the cultural poetics of desire," that is, the formal ideas and informal assumptions that people drew on to classify and evaluate sexual desire and behavior, along with the ways in which contemporaries disseminated and enforced those ideas and assumptions.[4]

If we are to understand what we would characterize as gender and sexuality in the context of British America and the revolutionary period, we need to take seriously the profound implications of Halperin's essay and recognize that "the cultural poetics of desire" during those periods looked and felt very different from anything we experience today. Colonists, in common with their contemporaries in early modern England and Europe, did not think about their sexual impulses in terms of a distinct sexuality that oriented men and women toward members of the same or opposite sex. Early Americans were taught to believe that all sex outside marriage—whether masturbation, casual fornication, premarital sex, adultery, or sodomy—was driven by innate moral corruption inherited from Adam and Eve; it expressed moral, not sexual, orientation. The most fundamental distinction that colonists made between licit and illicit sex depended on the marital status of those involved, not their biological sex. We know that there were men in British America who found themselves attracted to other men, and women who desired other women, yet the modern category of "homosexual" would have made little sense to them or their neighbors; they had their own conceptual frameworks through which to make sense of their urges and behavior.[5]

Early Americans understood erotic desires and acts as an expression of moral and social standing, not of intrinsic sexual identity. Consider the seventeenth-century Puritan New Englander who condemned any form of nonmarital sex as a "pollution" of the body that should be kept pure as a temple for the soul and who worried constantly about succumbing to "unclean" impulses; or the eighteenth-century southern planter who characterized sex as a demonstration of his cherished identity as a gentleman, referring to intercourse with his wife as a "flourish," or courtly gesture, to extramarital sex as "promiscuous gallantry," and to venereal infection as a "polite disorder." The first individual categorized sexual acts as part of a larger moral and spiritual endeavor, the second in terms of social identity. Both gave meaning and value to sex using categories that were not themselves intrinsically sexual. Strictly speaking, men who practiced sodomy during this period did not engage in homosexual acts, any more than the planter who gave his wife "a flourish" was engaging in a heterosexual act.[6]

In addition, and crucially, early Americans experienced love and sexual desire in the context of gender roles that adhered less rigidly to either men or women than in a modern Western setting. As we will see, women and men assumed both feminine and masculine roles, depending on the context in which they found themselves. The expectation that men could assume a female persona in certain circumstances and women a male persona reveals a culture of intricate possibilities, including the ways in which colonists enacted gendered authority. The use of spousal imagery to describe relations between savior and saved, for example, reinforced a gender-based hierarchy within the family. But Christ was much more than a masculine role model for men, who developed a range of social capacities by relating to him as brides as well as emulating him in the role of bridegroom, just as women performed the role of husband in the absence of male spouses and adopted masculine characteristics in a spiritual context that would astonish modern Christians.

Setting aside our own assumptions about sexuality is not easy. Consider the insistence by many otherwise astute and careful scholars that we should read expressions of love between male friends living in the past (such as John Winthrop and William Spring) as at least implicitly homoerotic. These scholars assume that expressions of loving devotion must necessarily imply a desire for sexual intimacy or, to put it another way, that people who are in love with each other must want to have sex. That many modern readers would make this assumption is perhaps not surprising: the paradigm of sexual orientation teaches us that romantic feelings generally go hand in hand with sexual attraction and that sexual orientation impels most of us sexually and romantically toward members of the same or opposite sex. That paradigm has established a firm and tenacious grip on our hearts, minds, and bodies.[7] Yet early Americans did not automatically conjoin romantic love with erotic desire, as would become the case once the paradigm of sexual orientation took hold. Equally important, their conception of how gender worked enabled them to embrace combinations of love and desire that would later become problematic. This essay uses two particular categories of romantic and erotic relationship in early America to illustrate how necessary it is for us to set aside our most deeply felt assumptions if we are to understand past men's and women's experiences of sexual desire and love.

* * *

Let us now visit briefly with another seventeenth-century New Englander in the happy grip of two symbiotic love affairs that defy, among other things, our persistent stereotypes of what it meant to be a Puritan.

Edward Taylor, the young pastor at Westfield, Massachusetts, was about to be married. In September 1674, two months before his wedding to Elizabeth Fitch, Taylor sent his prospective wife a passionate love letter. "I know not how to use a fitter comparison to set out my love by," he wrote, "than to compare it unto a golden ball of pure fire rolling up and down my breast, from which there flies, now and then a spark like a glorious beam from the body of the flaming sun." Yet Elizabeth Fitch was not the only love on Edward Taylor's mind, as the young man openly confessed. Love for a human spouse, however sincere and intense, must always be "limited and subordinate" to the devotion that united believers to Christ. The love that Taylor expressed for his savior was intimate, romantic, sensual, and often explicitly erotic. In poems written between the 1680s and 1720s, Taylor envisaged Christ as "a spotless male in prime" and addressed his savior in language of utter infatuation:

> Thou art the loveli'st object over spread
> With brightest beauty object ever wore
> Of purest flushes of pure white and red
> That ever did or could the love allure.
> Lord make my love and thee its object meet
> And me in folds of such love raptures keep.

Faith would prepare Taylor's heart as a "feather-bed . . . with gospel pillows, sheets, and sweet perfumes" to welcome Christ the lover. The young pastor yearned for divine arousal of his spiritual "fancy" in vividly sexual terms. "Yea," he wrote, "with thy holy oil make thou it slick till like a flash of lightning it grow quick." Taylor's poems leave no room for doubt that he anticipated union with Christ through the ecstatic experience of orgasm and penetration. According to Taylor, the soul was "the womb," Christ "the spermadote," and "saving grace the seed cast thereinto." Once "impregnate[d]" by Christ, the soul was "with child" and in due course would produce "the babe of grace." That infant was the fruit of matchless passion, conceived "in folds of such love raptures" as only Christ could provide.[8]

There was nothing unusual or unconventional about Edward Taylor's dual passion for Elizabeth Fitch and his heavenly bridegroom. In early 1718, the Boston magistrate Samuel Sewall, a few months after the death of his first wife, was already contemplating another loving union. The prospective spouse about whom he enthused to his diary was not, however, one of the widows before whom he would later lay his suit: "I had a sweet and very affectionate meditation concerning the Lord Jesus; nothing was to be objected against his person, parentage, relations, estate, house, home! Why did I not resolutely, presently close with him! And I cried mightily to God that he would help me so to do." That April, Sewall officiated at a marriage and wrote afterward, "Oh! that they and I might be married to CHRIST; and that our marriage might be known to ourselves, and others!" During the same year in which Sewall was contemplating Christ's unimpeachable qualifications as a spouse, the influential minister Increase Mather published a sermon in which he described marriage with Christ as "the most desirable one that ever was or that possibly can be." No "greater dignity" was imaginable than marrying "the only son of the King of Heaven," no "greater felicity" than to have as a husband "the wisest and richest that can be thought of." The bride of such a groom would be "made happy for ever."[9]

Different Christian cultures have responded to biblical images of Christ as bridegroom and lover in various ways. Most modern Westerners downplay or ignore biblical passages that contain this imagery. Medieval mystics described union with Christ in terms of feelings and relationships that they shunned in an earthly setting: members of religious orders yearned for marriage with their savior and yet committed themselves to celibacy here on Earth as a prerequisite for sanctity. This reaffirmed the opposition of physical and spiritual realms as well as their belief that devotion necessarily involved transcendence of the body. New England Puritans, by contrast, welcomed the sensual possibilities embedded within such passages of the Bible. Eager to celebrate marriage and family life as an agent of grace and social order, they drew direct parallels between human marriage and the soul's espousal to Christ. They hoped that the latter would provide a model for husbands and wives as they sought to build and sustain their relationships, just as human marriage would inspire believers to strive for union with their other, greater spouse. Marriage and marital sex became a foretaste of what the redeemed would experience when they joined their divine husband in heaven.[10]

Over the course of the seventeenth century, New England pastors became increasingly effusive in their evocation of Christ as an object of romantic, sensual, and erotic infatuation. Faced with the maturation of young men and women who had not chosen to live in a godly commonwealth and who would decide as adults whether or not to embrace orthodoxy, ministers sought to seduce youngsters into the community of faith by stressing the voluptuous pleasures that awaited them in the form of union with their savior. Pastors described the soul's marriage to Christ in ever more elaborate detail, occasionally devoting entire sermons to the subject. In so doing, they acted not only as teachers whose duty it was to explicate a recurring scriptural metaphor but also as self-styled "friends of the bridegroom" who courted on Christ's behalf. The days on which they preached became Christ's "wooing days," when the savior would "deck and array himself with all his glory and beauty," hoping to bedazzle the objects of his love. Since pastors hoped to become brides in their own right, they served simultaneously as interpreters, advocates, and potential recipients of the redeemer's advances.[11]

Ministers encouraged their flocks to feel Christ's love as an intensely voluptuous experience. "Here he comes," rhapsodized Samuel Willard, "to give us the caresses of his love, and lay us in his bosom and embraces. And now, oh my soul! Hast thou ever experienced the love of a saviour?" Edward Taylor was by no means alone in using sexual and reproductive metaphors to convey Christ's bestowal of grace, which would "quicken" the believer's spiritual womb, the same word used to describe the first stirrings of life in a physical womb. Christ's gift, explained Willard, was as much "physical" as "moral": "he withal puts in his finger, and makes a powerful impression."[12] Prayer also afforded an opportunity to enjoy "soul-ravishing communion" with Christ. Believers would emerge from such experiences "refreshed with those close embraces which he receives from him whom his soul loves." Cotton Mather, admittedly idiosyncratic in many regards, confided to his diary the extravagantly sensual experiences he underwent during spiritual exercise, describing "the rapturous praelibations of the heavenly world" in which he was "swallowed up with the ecstasies of [Christ's] love." So "inexpressibly irradiated from on high" was Mather that he was sometimes unable "to bear the ecstasies of the divine love, into which [he] was raptured": "they exhausted my spirits; they made me faint and sick; they were insupportable; I was forced even to withdraw from them, lest I should have swooned away under the raptures."[13]

Early modern assumptions about gender made possible the acknowl-edgment and celebration of raptures such as these. Anglo-American settlers, in common with their contemporaries across the Atlantic, as-sociated particular attributes and roles with masculinity and others with femininity, but they did not assume that those attributes or roles were or should remain attached only to one sex or the other: any man or woman could and indeed should embody both masculine and feminine attributes in appropriate contexts.[14] Puritan men could thus cultivate a loving and passionate devotion to Christ, envisaging him as a prospec-tive bridegroom, and meanwhile marry women on Earth, developing ardent relationships with their wives that prefigured eventual union with their male savior. In relation to their wives on Earth, they were functionally male, whereas in relation to Christ in the spiritual realm (which was to them very real), they became functionally female. In this world and the next, Puritans could find romantic and sexual fulfilment in a combination of passions that many modern Westerners would find incomprehensible.[15]

Just as men would become the brides of Christ, so godly women would adopt male attributes through spiritual redemption. Ministers assured their flocks that those who received God's grace would become "members of Christ," dedicated to his service and empowered by their regeneration. Contemporaries used the word "member" to denote a penis, and Puritans often wrote of their "spiritual ejaculations," referring to spontaneous prayer but surely aware of the word's double meaning. Thus, while the awakened souls of both men and women surrendered themselves to be penetrated and fertilized by their savior, they also be-came phallic and ejaculatory extensions of Christ. The repeated use of phallic images to denote spiritual power reminds us how dominant pa-triarchal conceptions were within Puritan culture and of the limits to gender fluidity. Yet women could assume masculine attributes and be-come correspondingly potent. A virtuous woman as much as any man had "the image of Christ and God upon her," and on the Day of Judg-ment, her soul would "be marvellously changed into the likeness of the Lord Jesus Christ himself."[16]

Meanwhile, images of the divine in clerical writings were sometimes explicitly maternal and reproductive. Willard referred to "the womb of providence" and spoke of the world as "a sucking infant depending on the breasts of divine providence." Nehemiah Walter urged his readers to "lay" their "lips unto the breasts of the gospel" so as to take from it "spiritual food." Clergymen, the congregations over which they presided, and the colleges at which they trained also assumed maternal, reproductive personas. William Adams referred to ministers as "travailling in birth with souls till Christ be formed in them." Samuel Danforth, reminiscing about the early years of settlement, recalled the "pious care" taken of "sister churches, that those that wanted breasts might be supplied." John Wise described Harvard College as "our dear mother," producing "fair, and numerous offspring." Contemporaries endowed body parts and the physical processes associated with them with clearly gendered attributes (the breast and womb representing maternal nourishment and fecundity, the penis connoting virility). Yet men, women, and even institutions could acquire male and female organs, along with their functions and the cultural significations that they carried.[17]

Men adopted a bride-like posture not only as Christians but also in other contexts. They made sense of situations in which they deferred to male-identified authority by assuming in those contexts a female persona. John Cotton, in whose Boston congregation John Winthrop was a member, declared that the relationship between rulers and subjects in a commonwealth was equivalent to that between "husband and wife in the family," so that men who became empowered as voting citizens on election days should then defer to those whom they elected, as wives should obey their husbands.[18] Meanwhile, women could assume masculine roles in particular circumstances and be treated as if male figures by men and women around them. If a husband was ill or absent, a wife could step into his shoes and expect male neighbors to engage with her as if they were dealing with her husband. As household mistresses, women routinely exercised authority over male servants and other dependents. Their doing so might seem incompatible with patriarchal assumptions, but as the historian Phyllis Mack reminds us, a subordinate male was "functionally feminine in relation to his female superior," who in turn was "functionally masculine in relation to her apprentices or dependents." By no means all women had the opportunity to embody patriarchal authority as household heads, but hierarchies of age and status routinely placed women in positions of precedence over men. Rank or status often outweighed biological sex in deciding who had authority in a given position; whoever had that authority became male-identified. Dominance and subjection found expression through gendered language, but social and political order rested just as firmly on male as on female submission to those placed above them. Gendered power operated more in terms of situation than with regard to the sex of those involved: it did not belong exclusively to any one sex.[19]

That measure of flexibility in gender roles depended in part on biological assumptions that made a much less absolute distinction between men and women than later conceptions of the body would claim to exist. Most contemporaries believed that four fundamental fluids or humors (blood, choler, melancholy, and phlegm), present in all human bodies, governed physical functions and emotions. The humors were in constant flux, which led to a never-ending struggle against disequilibrium. (Contemporaries believed that humoral imbalance caused disease, thus the use of bleeding and purging to restore a healthy balance between the four fluids.) Men and women differed from each other to some degree because they had a distinct combination of these four fluids; the physical and moral frailty of women resulted from their distinctive humoral makeup. Yet those differences between men and women were as unstable as the humors themselves. From this perspective, there could be no clear-cut distinction between the sexes. Equally significant in its implications for gender was Galen's still-influential "one-sex" model of the body. This model assumed that female reproductive organs were nothing more than male organs inverted (the uterus an internal version of the scrotum, the ovaries resembling male testicles, and the penis appearing in women as the cervix and vagina). According to Galen, a failure of heat prevented female organs from thrusting outward, so that women, according to this model, were beings who had failed to develop fully into men. This denial of any clear-cut boundaries between male and female bodies, in humoral and one-sex models, would have legitimated and facilitated the flexibility of gender roles in early modern culture.[20]

That Puritans could envisage for each believer, including men, two intensely passionate marital relationships, one with an earthly spouse and the other with a heavenly bridegroom, was due, then, to specific conceptions of gender and even of anatomical sex that the colonists brought with them across the Atlantic. There is no evidence to suggest that Native American traditions and practices influenced English settlers' understanding of gender or sexuality. Early reports from the New World had described a category of Native American men, often referred to by Indians as "half man / half woman," who lived as women, dressed in female clothing, and engaged in sexual relations with other men. There were also Indian women who assumed male clothing and roles, though this phenomenon seems to have been less widespread. From a Native American perspective, the "half man / half woman" seems to have embodied and promoted a harmony that resulted from reconciling opposites within the physical and spiritual realms. The composite identity of these individuals enabled them to mediate between the polarities of male and female as well as between those of spirit and flesh. Yet European explorers and settlers neither understood nor respected the assumptions underlying Native American conceptions of gender: that Indians revered men who lived as women and who made themselves sexually available to other men in their communities exemplified for Europeans the immorality and savagery of Indian culture. Indeed, Europeans used the word "berdache" (an Arabic word meaning "male prostitute") to describe such men. English and Indian conceptions of gender did share an assumption that men and women could combine male and female attributes, but whereas the "half man / half woman" tradition conferred on particular individuals a gender identity that combined male and female components, English and specifically Puritan conceptions of gender involved everyone adopting a range of gender roles and attributes in particular contexts.[21]

The performance of these gendered roles within Anglo-American society proceeded according to a complex and strictly regulated protocol. Whether colonists considered an individual's adoption of male or female roles appropriate depended entirely on the context. Yet a clear commitment to order and regulation within early modern society should not blind us to the degree of flexibility in gender roles and categories that contemporaries used to make sense of their lives. Moreover, that "fluidity of self-perception" (to quote Phyllis Mack) framed all interactions because contemporaries used gendered and familial metaphors to describe social, political, and religious relationships. Puritans inhabited a world in which earthly bridegrooms could anticipate eagerly becoming heavenly brides, in which both men and women embraced a polymorphous sexuality through which they would bear "the babe of grace" even as they rejoiced in their phallic credentials as "members of Christ." Thus, John Winthrop could refer to Christ as "my love, my dove, my undefiled," praying that he might be "possesse[d]" by his savior in "the love of marriage," and recommend that romantic union to his third wife, Margaret Tyndal, as a "pattern" for their own loving relationship. In ways that may seem bizarre and alien to us, Winthrop became both husband and wife, alongside his effusively loving friendship with William Spring.[22]

* * *

A few months after Winthrop penned his letter of loving farewell to Spring, as the Puritan flotilla journeyed across the Atlantic, he revealed in a lay sermon that he delivered aboard the *Arbella* how central the ideal of "brotherly affection" was to his vision for a godly life and godly society. Just as a body would fall apart without the ligaments that held its bones together, he declared, so the members of a godly commonwealth would fall prey to contention and disorder unless "knit together" by "the sweet sympathy of affections." It was that "fervent love" for one another and for Christ that had united the faithful throughout Christian history. Winthrop proposed that his audience take from scripture two models for that love between brothers and sisters in Christ, which he called "the bond of perfection." The first of these was the relationship between Adam and Eve in the Garden of Eden, each eager for "nearness and familiarity," sharing in each other's sadness or distress, and happiest when the other was "merry and thriving." Many generations later, the spirit of that first human relationship had been "acted to life" anew in another consummate expression of Christian love: the friendship between David and Jonathan. Winthrop described that friendship in a deeply affecting passage of his sermon: Jonathan loved David "as his own soul," Winthrop assured his audience. Even when facing a brief separation, "they thought their hearts would have broke for sorrow, had not their affections found vent by abundance of tears." Inspired by the example of these two men, New Englanders should "entertain each other in brotherly affection" and "love one another with a pure heart fervently." Love between brethren would inspire love for Christ, who would then be "formed in them and they in him, all in each other knit together by this bond of love." Relationships such as these were not limited to men: "other instances," Winthrop noted, "might be brought to show the nature of this affection, as of Ruth and Naomi and many others." Mutual love and devotion among faithful men and women, modeled on the first human marriage and loving same-sex friendships, would enable a truly redemptive society, preparing believers for union with Christ.[23]

Expressions of loving friendship suffused official statements and private correspondence in early New England. When Connecticut's colonial assembly called in 1638 for a treaty of friendship between the northern colonies, urging that New Englanders should "walk and live peaceably and lovingly together," it invoked the example of Jonathan and David, whose "love was great each to other" and who "made a covenant to perpetuate the same."[24] Winthrop's son and namesake inspired effusive declarations of love from his brothers in Christ. "I do long for your company as much as the teeming earth for the rising sun," wrote Hugh Peter. "Oh how my heart is with you." Peter assured the governor's son that he loved him "as mine own soul" and declared in one letter, "Oh that I were to die in your bosom." Edward Howes, writing from England, addressed Winthrop Jr. as "charissime" (dearest one), "gaudium meae vitae" (joy of my life), and "optatissime amice optime" (best and most desired friend). Howes declared that Winthrop's virtue had "kindled" in him "such a true fire of love" that "the great Western Ocean cannot quench": "it shall be with you," he assured his friend, "wheresoever you are."[25]

For seventeenth-century New England Puritans, as for early Americans in general, context was everything. Male intimacy could nurture and reinforce or corrupt and undermine their commonwealth, depending on how it expressed itself. The year prior to John Winthrop's celebration of "brotherly affection" in his sermon aboard the *Arbella*, "five beastly sodomitical boys" were exposed on the *Talbot* and subsequently sent back to England for punishment, so "foul" was their offense. As the scholar Michael Warner has pointed out, Winthrop's glorification of male love "was thus delivered in the very space of the repudiation of sodomy, en route to the New Canaan." Warner suggests that Winthrop and others may have feared sodomy as a warped version of the "brotherly affection" that, in Winthrop's words, should unite New England's citizens as "members of the same body." The "bonds of brotherly affection" would provide the sinews of a godly commonwealth, but the distortion of that affinity could pollute and destroy it. To put this another way, though sex between men was illegal and denounced by religious leaders as an abominable sin, Puritans saw intense love between godly men—and, we might add, godly women—as decent, honorable, praiseworthy, and indeed indispensable to the success of a godly commonwealth.[26]

Puritans were by no means unique in stressing the importance of impassioned and loving friendship. Revivalists who took the colonies by storm in the mid-eighteenth century and Methodist preachers who traveled through the South in the early decades of independence adopted a similarly fervent tone in describing their feelings for one another.[27] By no means all eighteenth-century Americans saw evangelical preachers as worthy role models. Yet throughout the century, men across the colonies and the new republic formed and often maintained over many decades loving friendships that were emotionally intense and physically affectionate. To give just two examples: In September 1763, Joseph Hooper, a recent graduate from Harvard College, sat down in Marblehead, Massachusetts, to compose a letter addressed to his former classmate Benjamin Dolbeare. He wrote as follows: "The sun never rose and set upon me since I parted from you, but he brought to my longing imagination the idea of my bosom friend; my faithful memory daily represents him in all the endearing forms that in his presence ever rose in my mind. My fancy paints him in the most beautiful colours, and my soul is absorbed in contemplating the past, wishing for a reiteration and longing to pour forth the expressions of friendship." In December 1798, as Daniel Webster prepared to leave Dartmouth College on vacation, he dreaded the prospect of having to spend several weeks apart from his friend George Herbert. "The thought distracts my soul and fills me with dismay," Webster wrote. "I go, but George, my heart is knit with thine." Webster was convinced that he would "sink in dark despair" were it not for knowing that he and his friend would soon be reunited on his return to Dartmouth. "Roll on the hour," the young man exclaimed in fervent anticipation.[28]

Many of these friendships lasted far beyond young adulthood and flourished alongside relationships with women, providing emotional support through various trials and reminding friends of an earlier phase in their lives that seemed, at least in retrospect, happy and carefree. In 1813, when the Philadelphia Quaker Henry S. Drinker came across a letter written by his dear friend Richard Thomas twenty years before, it still touched him deeply: "it spoke to my heart's best feelings, as I well remember, and I now again read it with emotion." At Drinker's request, Thomas then unearthed the response that Drinker had sent to that letter. "How sweet to the heart is the interchange of such kindness," Thomas now wrote, "such 'flow of soul' as melts in these letters." Since his departure from Philadelphia, separation from his "favorite friend and brother" had resulted in "gloom" and "depression." His chief pleasure in life now was correspondence with Drinker and other friends "whose hearts are susceptible of the sorrow and distress of others, and who are kind enough to allow me that intercourse." In Drinker's original response, he had celebrated "a social sympathy which heaven has implanted in the feeling heart, in mitigation of its own sufferings."[29]

Loyalties associated with friendship seem for the most part to have complemented rather than clashed with those of blood and marriage. Early Americans took it for granted that loving relationships between men and between women could coexist with heartfelt love for a person of the opposite sex. Eighteenth-century male friends often referred to each other as brothers and so characterized their relationships as a form of kinship. Family incorporated biological kin, conjugal relatives, and friends with whom one felt a sense of affinity into one loving and supportive community. Describing friends as kinfolk was neither perfunctory nor merely honorary: it indicated a very real and meaningful connection between individuals. That conflation of kinship and friendship enabled a much more expansive network of personal association than that encompassed by blood or marital connection.[30]

Yet circles of friendship were generally exclusive and indeed explicitly exclusionary. Those who belonged to communities of faith might refer to one another as loving brothers and sisters in Christ, but they rarely characterized those who belonged to other denominations or faiths as part of their family. Literate, privileged young men celebrated their friendships with one another as cultivating social sophistication, sensibility, and learning, as well as religious faith; they generally assumed that similarity in temperament, background, and social status would draw potential friends together. In effect, this ethos operated as a form of class and gender solidarity. Though we know that less privileged white Americans were exposed to celebrations of friendship through sermons and newspaper articles (which they might hear read aloud even if they could not read themselves), we have no way of telling how they responded to such encomia. Some less privileged listeners may have thought of friendship as a kind of bond that people of all social classes could experience, but the culture of friendship most certainly did not encourage people to form friendships that traversed social classes, let alone racial boundaries. Though some antislavery activists in the late eighteenth century urged white Americans to recognize and embrace their fundamental commonality with African slaves as brothers and sisters in one great human family, few privileged white Americans were willing to contemplate welcoming even less privileged whites, let alone people of color, into a fictive brotherhood. Though representatives sent by royal governors, colonial assemblies, and later state and federal governments to negotiate treaties with Native Americans sometimes adopted Indian rhetoric that invoked loving brotherhood and friendship in order to grease the wheels of diplomacy, Americans of European descent had little interest in understanding Indian conceptions of friendship other than through a European lens. Nor did they intend to treat Indians as brothers and sisters in practice unless the exigencies of the particular situation demanded that they do so. In the aftermath of the American Revolution, as political thinkers stressed the importance of fraternal collaboration between citizens in making a republic feasible, that nationalized conception of brotherhood was intrinsically exclusive, defining carefully who had the right to citizenship and to which nations the United States would extend the hand of fraternal amity.[31]

Early Americans routinely asserted that ties between friends had a broad public significance, creating affective bonds between individuals that would then serve as the emotional sinews of a larger identity. They understood society not as an abstract entity but as the sum of individual and intensely personalized relationships. That legitimization and celebration of loving friendship as a public good acquired a particular and explicitly political significance for North Americans during the revolutionary period. Personal friendship became a way of encouraging empathy between citizens in a society that no longer cohered through shared loyalty to a monarch. Friends would encourage in each other a generosity of spirit that would then inform and enrich social and public interactions, creating a sympathetic and magnanimous citizenry. According to the scores of essays and poems celebrating friendship that appeared in newspapers and magazines in the late eighteenth century, male friends found personal happiness through these relationships and inspired one another in their pursuit of knowledge and virtue. Those qualities and accomplishments would then radiate outward and transform postrevolutionary society, encouraging citizens to look beyond their own selfish interests to comprehend and empathize with the interests and feelings of others.[32]

The postrevolutionary press actively encouraged and celebrated loving and sympathetic friendships between men as the quintessence of republican masculinity. One particularly vivid essay exemplified this idealization of male friendship and its tone of unabashed sentimentality:

> Tell me ye of refined feelings—have you ever found pleasures equal to those derived from friendship? What can be more delightful to the eye of benevolence than the prospect of a connection where the sentiments and affections are sweetly united? Picture to yourself, reader, two young men mutually bound by a sacred friendship—a friendship established upon the experience of years. See them with interlocked arms walking the pleasant grove, reciprocally breathing forth, without reserve, the sentiments of their bosoms! Observe the essence of benevolence glowing on their cheeks, and the gleams of participated ecstasy sparkling in their eyes. View them sweetly seated at the enchanted shrine of their goddess— friendship—unbosoming every sensation, and even mingling heart with heart! Notice them saluting each other after being separated for a season by the calls of interest—with what cordiality—with what emotions of joy—with what exquisite delight they embrace.

Author after author emphasized the yearning for intimacy and support that brought men together, as well as the broad social benefits that such friendships produced. The sentimental friend figured, then, both as a personal good in his own right and as a means to a larger social good. Friendship also played an important role in reenvisaging the family as a model for society as a whole, shifting attention away from the hierarchical authority of paternal figures to the more democratic bonds that bound brothers together in service to the new republic.[33]

Much of that postrevolutionary conversation focused on male friendship as a foundation for enlightened male citizenship. Yet printed discussions of same-sex friendship often depicted the nurturing of love between friends as a duty and pleasure that men and women shared in common. Literate women wrote of their feelings for one another in letters that bore a remarkable resemblance to those passing back and forth between male friends. Indeed, some men were eager to learn about the experience and expression of sympathetic friendship from female relatives and neighbors. Because women living in the seventeenth-century and early eighteenth-century colonies left behind them far fewer letters and diaries than did men and because male diarists and letter writers were for the most part from the upper ranks of colonial society, we know much more about elite male friendships in the colonial period than about those of women and less privileged men. But we can be confident that all Americans who had access to newspaper and magazine articles or sermons praising friendship (regardless of whether they could read them or heard them read aloud) would have been familiar with the notion that same-sex friendships played a central role in nurturing civic and religious society.[34]

Context and moral tone remained all-important. Eighteenth-century Americans worried that male rakes and profligates might corrupt other young men who kept company with them. Yet they also believed that men could influence each other for good, quelling their corrupt tendencies and appealing to each other's potential for virtue—despite a new thread of anxiety about male desire that wove its way across the Atlantic. By the early eighteenth century, there had emerged in London a distinct subculture that catered to men seeking sexual intimacy with members of the same sex; such men could meet in specific parks or taverns, the latter known as "molly" houses because of the self-consciously effeminate and often cross-dressing men who frequented such establishments. Lurid descriptions of these gathering places appeared in printed accounts of police raids on such establishments and transformed sodomy from an indistinct threat, often associated with foreigners, to a much more immediate and concrete phenomenon. At the same time, the notion of sodomy as an immoral act that anyone might be tempted to engage in was giving way to the image of the sodomite, a distinct social category referring to a specific cadre of men consistently attracted to other men. Some scholars have argued that these developments made men much more reluctant to express affection that might be confused with sexual interest, so that by the middle of the eighteenth century, Englishmen were shaking each other's hands rather than embracing and kissing each other.[35]

Yet no such discernible subculture had emerged in British America. A wide spectrum of city dwellers on the eastern seaboard were exposed to imported images of the homoerotic through accounts of police raids and prosecutions in London as well as through literary representations such as Lord Strutwell and Captain Whiffle, characters in Tobias Smollett's popular novel *Roderick Random*. Yet American newspapers still depicted sodomy as an alien vice and more specifically as a prime example of British decadence; they generally kept silent about its possible occurrence in their own midst. Though descriptions of physical affection between men did occasionally suggest that untoward intimacies might be taking place, especially in attacks on groups that were otherwise suspicious, such as the Freemasons, contemporaries seem to have viewed these instances as aberrations. Male friendship enjoyed an almost entirely positive and respected place within colonial and post-revolutionary society.[36]

Modern readers often assume that loving friendships such as these must have included an element of sexual attraction, even if the men or women involved did not act on such desires. Physical affection assuredly did play an important role in many of these relationships. Male friends often referred to the pleasure that they took in touching and holding each other, delighting in the proximity of each other's bodies. Daniel Webster recalled "press[ing]" Thomas Merrill's hand and wrote that he wanted to pour the effusions of his "heart," which was "now so full," into his friend's ear "till it ran over." William Wirt, a Virginian lawyer who had established a close friendship with Dabney Carr in the 1790s as the two men traveled together in search of clients, later wrote, "O! That you were here. Am I ne'er to see you more?—I long for your hand—I hunger after your face and voice—can you not come down this winter, if not sooner?"[37] Some male friends commented in their letters how much they enjoyed sleeping together. When Israel Cheever wrote to Robert Treat Paine complaining that he had "no sweet chum to confabulate with upon a bed of ease," his turn of phrase was by no means metaphorical: he went on to declare how much he missed his "dear chum, with whom I have lain warm so many nights." Wirt and Carr almost certainly slept together as they traveled looking for work, perhaps from choice as well as for practical reasons. Wirt recalled that period with "a swelling of the heart": "gone forever," he lamented, "are those pleasures!"[38]

But what exactly were those pleasures? Early Americans often shared their beds with visitors, including complete strangers. Few private homes or even taverns offering accommodation had enough space to allow for the kind of privacy that most modern Westerners take for granted. Because adult Westerners now generally invite people into their beds only if they are in a sexual relationship or having a more casual sexual encounter, they tend to read more into nocturnal companionship than people living in the past would have done. In some instances, sleeping together may have included erotic stimulation or even sexual activity; and there were doubtless cases in which society's validation of same-sex affection provided a cover for erotic intimacies and instances of coercion. Yet early Americans would not have assumed that love, even an intense romantic love, included or implied erotic attraction, because their conception of sexuality was different from ours, so that they did not leap to the same conclusions as we would. Families and neighbors would hardly have encouraged the formation of close same-sex friendships if they thought they would lead to sexual intimacy, given that sex between men or between women was a criminal offense as well as denounced by ministers as a heinous sin. Yet they did encourage such relationships and often allowed their sons to spend the night together, because for them neither expressions of love nor physical affection automatically signified sexual attraction.[39]

Very occasionally, journals and letters that survive from the colonial and revolutionary periods do hint at the possibility of erotic attraction. The Virginian John Randolph wrote in a 1795 letter that he "burned with desire to see" his college friend Henry Rutledge, though he also celebrated their friendship as "pure affection between man and man." Perhaps he wanted to distinguish his feelings from those of other men whom he suspected of being less "pure" in the expression of their love, or perhaps he sought to disown feelings within himself that he feared and condemned. One surviving letter that expresses nostalgia for nights spent in the past with a close friend is much more suggestive. Virgil Maxcy, who lived in Smithfield, Rhode Island, assured his "chum" William Blanding in Rehoboth, Massachusetts, that he missed sleeping with him: "I get to hugging the pillow," he declared, "instead of you." One night when a visiting stranger slept in the same bed with Maxcy, the stranger commented in the morning that Maxcy had "hugged him all night," and indeed Maxcy remembered waking up several times to find his arms "tight around him." Maxcy clearly enjoyed sleeping curled up with someone. We cannot know for certain if the physical intimacy that Maxcy missed had any sexual component to it, but he did make a very striking remark in that same letter. "Sometimes," he wrote, "I think I have got hold of your doodle when in reality I have hold of the bedpost." A "doodle" that could be confused with a bedpost was hardly in a state of repose, and Maxcy signed this particular letter, "your cunt humble." This may have been a humorous reference to Blanding having had erections in his sleep that may or may not have had anything to do with attraction to his bedmate, even though Maxcy ended up as the butt (so to speak) of his friend's nocturnal arousal. Young male adults often experience spontaneous sexual arousal and have wet dreams in the night. But perhaps Blanding really did lust after Maxcy, who perhaps welcomed his friend's "doodle," though this would have been a risky thing to acknowledge, even in private correspondence.[40]

Historians have often downplayed or suppressed evidence of sexual intimacy between men and between women in the past that they do not wish to acknowledge. Thankfully, a growing number of scholars are now giving that surviving material the careful attention that it deserves, as part of a much larger project to recover the lives and experiences of people previously erased from historical accounts.[41] Yet in avoiding undue reticence or actual suppression of historical evidence, we should take care not to fall into the trap of seeing what we expect or want to see. Whether or not particular friendships did have a sexual component, declarations of love between men or between women would not automatically have suggested to relatives or neighbors that sexual relations were taking place. Indeed, most Anglo-Americans living in the colonial and revolutionary periods had no difficulty envisaging a passionate yet nonsexual love between two men or two women. Cassandra Good's recent book on cross-sex friendships shows that eighteenth-century Americans distrusted male-female relationships, fearing that those involved would give way to physical attraction and become lovers. It is surely significant that contemporaries were much less anxious about loving same-sex friendships and happily made room for them as a personal, social, and political good.[42]

Only once we set aside our own assumptions and even our categories of analysis—no easy task—can we appreciate that sexualized love was just one possibility in a rich repertoire of possibilities open to premodern men and women as they expressed their feelings for one another. There must surely have been cases in which that spectrum of possibilities provided a cover for erotic intimacy that would otherwise have endangered the individuals concerned (not only because of the legal penalties for sodomy but also through social and self-inflicted stigma). Some friends may have explored the boundary between physical affection and erotic expression, perhaps occasionally venturing across that boundary and discovering something new about themselves. Yet as the historian Alan Bray has pointed out, "the inability to conceive of relationships in other than sexual terms says something of contemporary poverty; or, to put the point more precisely, the effect of a shaping concern with sexuality is precisely to obscure that wider frame." The literary scholar Ivy Schweitzer makes a similar point: "Without denying the erotic and sexual potential of friendship," we should recognize that "a very different logic guided its understandings in this period." That logic "enabled an array of social and political relations that critics have frequently overlooked."[43]

* * *

Alan Bray's characterization of modern sexual paradigms as *obscuring* instead of illuminating the past and Ivy Schweitzer's argument that scholars' own preconceptions have led them to *overlook* the logic that framed relationships in the past echo David Halperin's insistence that words like "heterosexuality," "homosexuality," and even "sexuality" constitute "*a significant obstacle* to understanding the distinctive features of sexual life in non-Western and pre-modern cultures" (emphasis added).[44] A short essay such as this cannot hope to provide a comprehensive discussion of the challenges involved in recovering premodern conceptions of gender and sex, let alone a complete reconstruction of what that conceptual world may have looked like. But I do hope to have illustrated through a brief examination of two particular types of relationship, both endorsed enthusiastically by early Americans, just how unhelpful are our most fundamental assumptions and beliefs about what we now refer to as gender and sexuality in making sense of the past. The loving and passionate relationships that early American men were encouraged to develop with Jesus Christ and with one another, even as legal and religious codes condemned sex between men, can seem very bizarre to a modern Western sensibility, because our cultural wiring is so different from theirs. That wiring extends deep inside us. Because most modern Westerners have internalized the paradigm of sexual orientation, it is extremely difficult for us to wrap our minds around a world in which gendered expression and the relationship between love and sex operated according to a different logic. Even finding words that are not freighted with the baggage of modernity poses a huge challenge (as many of us who have tried to write about sexual cultures in the past will attest). Yet try we must. Otherwise, we will achieve little more than to project our sense of ourselves onto the past.[45]

That daunting yet exciting project of reconstructing the "cultural poetics of desire" by which people lived in the past has important implications for historians of modern sexuality. Scholars working on the experience, articulation, and policing of heterosexuality in the modern United States and Europe should consider that the rest of the world, including large numbers of migrants making their way into Western countries, do not necessarily think about sex in the same way (even as Western values seek to establish cultural hegemony across the globe). In an era of massive migration, the paradigm of sexuality that took hold in the twentieth-century West now coexists alongside very different models for making sense of love and desire. Meanwhile, alternative ways of understanding and evaluating sexuality articulated by theorists, evangelicals, and many young people who embrace a much more fluid sense of their sexual identities are creating an even more variegated and volatile cultural landscape. Heterosexuality is not only a recent and idiosyncratic phenomenon but may also turn out to be much more fragile and transient than we often assume.

NOTES

1. John Winthrop to William Spring, February 8, 1630, in *Winthrop Papers*, ed. Samuel Eliot Morison et al., 5 vols. (Boston, 1929–47), 2:203, 205–6.

2. Winthrop to Spring, 2:206; John Winthrop, "Experiencia," in *Winthrop Papers*, 1:166, 202–4.

3. Winthrop, "Experiencia," 1:202–3; Winthrop to Spring, February 8, 1630, 2:205–6; William Spring to John Winthrop, n.d. [March 1637], in *Winthrop Papers*, 3:365; John Winthrop to Margaret Winthrop, October 3, 1623, in *The Life and Letters of John Winthrop*, ed. Robert C. Winthrop, 2 vols. (Boston, 1864–67), 1:193.

4. David M. Halperin, *One Hundred Years of Homosexuality, and Other Essays on Greek Love* (New York: Routledge, 1990), 9, 15, 16, 18, 29. Halperin was building

on Michel Foucault's argument that we should seek to understand sexuality not as
a biological fact but instead as a cultural production, for which see Foucault, *The
History of Sexuality, Volume 1: An Introduction*, trans. Robert Hurley (New York:
Pantheon Books, 1978), esp. 127. For other helpful formulations of this approach,
see Bruce R. Smith, *Homosexual Desire in Shakespeare's England: A Cultural Poetics* (Chicago: University of Chicago Press, 1991), 10–11; and Jonathan Ned Katz,
The Invention of Heterosexuality, 2nd ed. (Chicago: University of Chicago Press,
2007), viii–ix.

5. See Richard Godbeer, *Sexual Revolution in Early America* (Baltimore: Johns Hopkins University Press, 2002), esp. 62–71.

6. For southern planters and their incorporation of sex into their sense of themselves as gentlemen, see Godbeer, 190–93.

7. Theorists have challenged the model of sexual orientation from a range of perspectives, and many young people reject as artificial the clear-cut distinctions on
which the homo/heterosexual paradigm depends, invoking instead a more fluid
understanding of sexual desire and identity. Meanwhile, some Christian denominations insist that our selection of sexual partners results from moral choice
and not an innate sexuality. Yet the basic assumptions underlying this paradigm
remain powerful and indeed predominant within Western culture.

8. Edward Taylor to Elizabeth Fitch, September 1674, in *The Unpublished Writings
of Edward Taylor*, ed. Thomas M. Davis and Virginia L. Davis, 3 vols. (Boston:
Twayne, 1981), 3:37–41; Edward Taylor, *The Poems of Edward Taylor*, ed. Donald
E. Stanford (New Haven, CT: Yale University Press, 1960), 142, 164, 212, 230, 248,
259, 295, 362–63, 448. Taylor drew extensively on the language of Canticles. See,
for example, his adaptation of "Let him kiss me with the kiss of his mouth" (Cant.
1:2) in *Poems of Edward Taylor* (254–55) and of "I am my beloved and my beloved
is mine" (Cant. 6:2; 323–25).

9. Samuel Sewall, *The Diary of Samuel Sewall*, ed. M. Halsey Thomas, 2 vols. (New
York: Farrar, Straus and Giroux, 1973), 2:864 (October 19, 1717), 882 (February
6, 1718), 891 (April 4, 1718); Increase Mather, *Practical Truths Plainly Delivered*
(Boston, 1718), 59–60.

10. See Peter Brown, *The Body and Society: Men, Women, and Sexual Renunciation in
Early Christianity* (New York: Columbia University Press, 1988); E. Ann Matter,
The Voice of My Beloved: The Song of Songs in Western Medieval Christianity (Phil-
adelphia: University of Pennsylvania Press, 1990); and Dyan Elliott, *Spiritual Mar-
riage: Sexual Abstinence in Medieval Wedlock* (Princeton, NJ: Princeton University
Press, 1993). For discussions of marital imagery in early-modern English litera-
ture, see Barbara Kiefer Lewalski, *Protestant Poetics and the Seventeenth-Century
Religious Lyric* (Princeton, NJ: Princeton University Press, 1977); Stanley Stew-
art, *The Enclosed Garden: The Tradition and the Image in Seventeenth-Century
Poetry* (Madison: University of Wisconsin Press, 1966); Jonathan Jong-Chu Won,
"Communion and Christ: An Exposition and Comparison of the Doctrine of
Union and Communion with Christ in Calvin and the English Puritans" (PhD

diss., Westminster Theological Seminary, 1989); and Amanda Porterfield, *Female Piety in Puritan New England: The Emergence of Religious Humanism* (New York: Oxford University Press, 1992), chap. 1.

11. Cotton Mather, *Ornaments for the Daughters of Zion* (Boston, 1692), 64; Mather, *A Glorious Espousal* (Boston, 1719), 12; Mather, *A Union with the Son of God by Faith* (Boston, 1692), 13–15; Mather, *The Mystical Marriage* (Boston, 1728), 6; Joshua Moodey, *A Practical Discourse Concerning the Choice Benefit of Communion with God in His House* (Boston, 1685), 24–25.

12. Samuel Willard, *A Complete Body of Divinity* (Boston, 1726), 459, 533, 556; Willard, *The High Esteem Which God Hath of the Death of His Saints* (Boston, 1683), 15; Willard, *Some Brief Sacramental Meditations* (Boston, 1711), 4; Cotton Mather, *Bethiah* (Boston, 1722), 30.

13. I. Mather, *Practical Truths*, 175; Willard, *Complete Body of Divinity*, 892; C. Mather, *Diary of Cotton Mather*, ed. Worthington C. Ford, 2 vols. (1911; repr., New York: Ungar, 1957), 1:98 (May 13, 1685), 426 (April 16, 1702), 471 (March 12, 1703), 483 (May 15, 1703).

14. See Richard Godbeer, "Performing Patriarchy: Gendered Roles and Hierarchies in Early Modern England and Seventeenth-Century New England," in *The Worlds of John Winthrop: England and New England, 1588–1649*, ed. Francis J. Bremer and Lynn Botelho (Boston: Massachusetts Historical Society, 2005), 290–333.

15. Male New Englanders' conception of themselves as brides of Christ would have been facilitated by their pastors' depiction of the soul as not adopting the sex of the body it inhabited: they characterized the soul sometimes as female and sometimes as sexually indeterminate. This mattered because Christ would marry not men and women but their souls. Elizabeth Reis has argued that a gendered distinction between body and soul allowed Puritan men to think of their souls as feminine while retaining a masculine "sense of themselves." I would suggest that such a distinction functioned as one component of a broad gender fluidity. See Godbeer, *Sexual Revolution in Early America*, 79–82; and Reis, *Damned Women: Sinners and Witches in Puritan New England* (Ithaca, NY: Cornell University Press, 1997), 93–120 (quote on 101). Margaret Masson argues that ministers could use "the female role as a typology for the regenerate Christian" without creating "role conflict" for men because New Englanders "had not yet arrived at definitions of sex roles or personality structure that were as fixed or mutually exclusive as those found in the nineteenth century." Masson, "The Typology of the Female as a Model for the Regenerate: Puritan Preaching, 1690–1730," *Signs: Journal of Women in Culture and Society* 2 (1976): 305, 315; see also Porterfield, *Female Piety*, 6–7, 156.

16. C. Mather, *Ornaments for the Daughters of Zion*, 39, 42.

17. Willard, *Complete Body of Divinity*, 131, 145; Nehemiah Walter, *Unfruitful Hearers Detected and Warned* (Boston, 1696), 52; William Adams, *The Necessity of the Pouring Out of the Spirit* (Boston, 1679), A4; Samuel Danforth, *A Brief Recognition of New England's Errand into the Wilderness* (Cambridge, MA, 1671), 12; John Wise, *A Word of Comfort to a Melancholy Country* (Boston, 1721), 11. John

Oxenbridge likened magistrates to "a nursing father" who "bears the sucking child." Oxenbridge, *New England Freemen* (Cambridge, MA, 1673), 36–37. For an extended discussion of maternal imagery in Puritan literature, see David Leverenz, *The Language of Puritan Feeling: An Exploration in Literature, Psychology, and Social History* (New Brunswick, NJ: Rutgers University Press, 1980).

18. John Cotton, *The Way of the Churches of Christ in New England* (London, 1645), 4; see also John Winthrop, *The History of New England from 1630 to 1649*, ed. James Savage, 2 vols. (Boston, 1825–26), 2:281.

19. Phyllis Mack, *Visionary Women: Ecstatic Prophecy in Seventeenth-Century England* (Berkeley: University of California Press, 1992), 49. See also Lisa Wilson, *Ye Heart of a Man: The Domestic Life of Men in Colonial New England* (New Haven, CT: Yale University Press, 1999); Laurel Thatcher Ulrich, *Good Wives: Image and Reality in the Lives of Women in Northern New England, 1650–1750* (New York: Knopf, 1982), 3, 38; Anthony Fletcher, *Gender, Sex, and Subordination in England, 1500–1800* (New Haven, CT: Yale University Press, 1995), 403; and Susan Dwyer Amussen, *An Ordered Society: Gender and Class in Early Modern England* (New York: Columbia University Press, 1988), 3. Gender flexibility applied only within particular contexts: women who tried to exercise male-identified prerogatives in circumstances that others saw as inappropriate or who challenged the need to conceptualize power in male terms, appropriating authority in their own right as women, became extremely vulnerable. See, for example, "Proceedings of Excommunication against Mistress Ann Hibbens of Boston," in *Remarkable Providences: Readings in Early American History*, ed. John Demos (Boston: Northeastern University Press, 1991), 262–82.

20. A growing number of early-modern writers challenged this anatomical paradigm, depicting the female organs as distinct and arguing that women's bodies were perfect in their own right. But during this transitional period, elements of the Galenic model were often combined with newer ideas, so that distinctions between maleness and femaleness remained much less absolute than in later periods. Fletcher, *Gender, Sex, and Subordination*, 33, 41, 44, 79, 82, 108; Thomas Laqueur, *Making Sex: Body and Gender from the Greeks to Freud* (Cambridge, MA: Harvard University Press, 1990). See also Janet Adelman, "Making Defect Perfection: Shakespeare and the One-Sex Model," in *Enacting Gender on the English Renaissance Stage*, ed. Viviana Comensoli and Anne Russell (Urbana: University of Illinois Press, 1999), 23–52; and Stephen Orgel, *Impersonations: The Performance of Gender in Shakespeare's England* (Cambridge: Cambridge University Press, 1996), 21–23.

21. See Evelyn Blackwood, "Sexuality and Gender in Certain Native American Tribes: The Case of Cross-Gender Females," *Signs* 10 (1984): 27–24; Walter L. Williams, *The Spirit and the Flesh: Sexual Diversity in American Indian Culture* (Boston: Beacon, 1986); Raymond E. Houser, "The 'Berdache' and the Illinois Indian Tribe during the Last Half of the Seventeenth Century," *Ethnohistory* 37 (1990): 45–65; Sue-Ellen Jacobs, Wesley Thomas, and Sabine Lang, eds., *Two-Spirit People:*

Native American Gender Identity, Sexuality, and Spirituality (Urbana: University of Illinois Press, 1997); Will Roscoe, *Changing Ones: Third and Fourth Genders in Native North America* (New York: St. Martin's, 1998); Qwo-Li Driskell, *Asegi Stories: Cherokee Queer and Two-Spirit Memory* (Tucson: University of Arizona Press, 2016); and Gregory D. Smithers, "Cherokee 'Two Spirits': Gender, Ritual, and Spirituality in the Native South," *Early American Studies* 12 (2014): 626–51.

22. Mack, *Visionary Women*, 50; Winthrop, *Life and Letters of John Winthrop*, 1:136 (John Winthrop to Margaret Tyndal, April 4, 1618), 397 (John Winthrop to William Spring, February 28, 1629).

23. John Winthrop, "A Model of Christian Charity," in *Winthrop Papers*, 2:284, 288–94; for another invocation of Ruth and Naomi as a model for friendship, see Thomas Brooks, *Heaven on Earth* (1654; repr., London: Banner of Truth Trust, 1961), 251.

24. Roger Ludlow, in behalf of General Assembly of Connecticut to Governor and Assistants of Massachusetts, May 29, 1638, in *Winthrop Papers*, 4:36.

25. Hugh Peter to John Winthrop Jr., September 30, 1638, June 23, 1645, ca. April 1647, March 15, 1649, in *Winthrop Papers*, 4:63, 5:30, 146, 319–20; Edward Howes to John Winthrop Jr., November 9, 1631, March 7, 1632, March 26, 1632, February 25, 1640, in *Winthrop Papers*, 3:54, 66, 72, 4:203.

26. Michael Warner, "New English Sodom," in *Queering the Renaissance*, ed. Jonathan Goldberg (Durham, NC: Duke University Press, 1994), 339, 345. Scholars of early-modern England have noted that the specter of sodomy did occasionally cast a shadow over loving male friendships. Alan Bray, for example, discusses "dark suggestions of sodomy" in Elizabethan literary representations of male friendship, in "Homosexuality and the Signs of Male Friendship in Elizabethan England," in Goldberg, *Queering the Renaissance*, 40–61 (quote on 49).

27. For examples of these evangelical friendships and the rhetoric that endorsed them, see Richard Godbeer, *The Overflowing of Friendship: Love between Men and the Creation of the American Republic* (Baltimore: Johns Hopkins University Press, 2009), 94–113.

28. Joseph Hooper to Benjamin Dolbeare, September 4, 1763, Dolbeare Family Papers, Massachusetts Historical Society, Boston; Daniel Webster to George Herbert, December 20, 1798, in *The Writings and Speeches of Daniel Webster*, ed. J. W. McIntyre, 18 vols. (Boston: Little, Brown, 1903), 17:71.

29. Richard Thomas to Henry S. Drinker, October 1, 1793; Drinker to Thomas, October 8, 1793; Drinker to Thomas, March 18, 1813; Thomas to Drinker, April 19, 1813; all in Drinker and Sandwith Papers, vol. 4, file 67, Historical Society of Pennsylvania, Philadelphia.

30. See Anya Jabour, *Marriage in the Early Republic: Elizabeth and William Wirt and the Companionate Ideal* (Baltimore: Johns Hopkins University Press, 1998), 5; and Jabour, "Male Friendship and Masculinity in the Early National South: William Wirt and His Friends," *Journal of the Early Republic* 20 (2000): 83–111. See Naomi Tadmor, *Family and Friends in Eighteenth-Century England* (New York: Cam-

bridge University Press, 2001); Godbeer, *Overflowing of Friendship*; and Anne S. Lombard, *Making Manhood: Growing Up Male in Colonial New England* (Cambridge, MA: Harvard University, 2003), 54.

31. For examples of abolitionists invoking brotherhood as a justification for emancipation, see Godbeer, *Overflowing of Friendship*, 170. For Cherokee conceptions of friendship in the eighteenth century and the role that friendship played in relations between the Cherokee and British officials along with Anglo-Americans, see Gregory D. Smithers, "'Our Hands and Hearts Are Joined Together': Friendship, Colonialism, and the Cherokee People in Early America," *Journal of Social History* 50 (2017): 609–29.

32. For a fuller version of this argument, see Godbeer, *Overflowing of Friendship*, chap. 5. Republican thinkers also accorded women crucial roles as wives and mothers in fostering a virtuous male citizenry. See Ruth Bloch, "American Feminine Ideals in Transition: The Rise of the Moral Mother, 1785–1815," *Feminist Studies* 4 (1978): 101–26; Linda Kerber, *Women of the Republic: Intellect and Ideology in Revolutionary America* (Chapel Hill: University of North Carolina Press, 1980); Mary Beth Norton, *Liberty's Daughters: The Revolutionary Experience of American Women, 1750–1800* (Boston: Little, Brown, 1980); Ruth Bloch, "The Gendered Meanings of Virtue in Revolutionary America," *Signs* 13 (1987): 37–58; Jan Lewis, "The Republican Wife: Virtue and Seduction in the Early Republic," *William and Mary Quarterly* 44 (1987): 689–721; Laurel Thatcher Ulrich, "Daughters of Liberty: Religious Women in Revolutionary New England," in *Women in the Age of the American Revolution*, ed. Ronald Hoffman and Peter J. Albert (Charlottesville: University of Virginia Press, 1989); Rosemary Zagarri, "Morals, Manners, and the Republican Mother," *American Quarterly* 44 (1992): 192–215; and Godbeer, *Sexual Revolution in Early America*, chap. 8.

33. *Cumberland Gazette*, November 9, 1789. For loving male friendships in colonial North America and the early republic, see Caleb Crain, "Leander, Lorenzo, and Castalio: An Early American Romance," *Early American Literature* 33 (1998): 6–38; Crain, *American Sympathy: Men, Friendship, and Literature in the New Nation* (New Haven, CT: Yale University Press, 2001); Jabour, "Male Friendship and Masculinity"; Ivy Schweitzer, *Perfecting Friendship: Politics and Affiliation in Early American Literature* (Chapel Hill: University of North Carolina Press, 2006); Godbeer, *Overflowing of Friendship*; Smithers, "Our Hands and Hearts Are Joined Together"; and Janet Moore Lindman, "'This Union of the Soul': Spiritual Friendship among Early American Protestants," *Journal of Social History* 50 (2017): 680–700. See also Allan Silver, "Friendship in Commercial Society: Eighteenth-Century Social Theory and Modern Sociology," *American Journal of Sociology* 95, no. 6 (1990): 1474–1504.

34. See Lillian Faderman, *Surpassing the Love of Men: Romantic Friendship and Love between Women from the Renaissance to the Present* (New York: William Morrow, 1981); Carroll Smith-Rosenberg, "The Female World of Love and Ritual: Relations between Women in Nineteenth-Century America," in *Disorderly Conduct: Visions*

of Gender in Victorian America (New York: Knopf, 1985), 53–76; Carol Lasser, "'Let Us Be Sisters Forever': The Sororal Model of Nineteenth-Century Female Friendship," *Signs* 14 (1988): 158–81; and Joan R. Gundersen, "Kith and Kin: Women's Networks in Colonial Virginia," in *The Devil's Lane: Sex and Race in the Early South*, ed. Catherine Clinton and Michele Gillespie (New York: Oxford University Press, 1997), 90–108.

35. See Alan Bray and Michel Rey, "The Body of the Friend: Continuity and Change in Masculine Friendship in the Seventeenth Century," in *English Masculinities, 1660–1800*, ed. Tim Hitchcock and Michele Cohen (New York: Longman, 1999), esp. 80. Bray discusses the emergence of this subculture in *Homosexuality in Renaissance England* (London: Gay Men's Press, 1982), chap. 4; see also Rictor Norton, *Mother Clap's Molly House: The Gay Subculture in England, 1700–1830* (London: Gay Men's Press, 1992). Randolph Trumbach argues that the emergence of the adult effeminate sodomite as a "third gender" had profound implications for the ways in which other men perceived and enacted their own versions of manhood as they sought to distinguish themselves from this new effeminate persona; see his *Sex and the Gender Revolution: Heterosexuality and the Third Gender in Enlightenment London* (Chicago: University of Chicago Press, 1998).

36. See Thomas A. Foster, "Antimasonic Satire, Sodomy, and Eighteenth-Century Masculinity in the *Boston Evening Post*," *William and Mary Quarterly* 60 (2003): 171–84; and Clare A. Lyons, "Mapping an Atlantic Sexual Culture: Homoeroticism in Eighteenth-Century Philadelphia," *William and Mary Quarterly* 60 (2003): 152.

37. Daniel Webster to Thomas Merrill, May 1, 1804, in *Writings and Speeches*, 17:166; William Wirt to William Pope, August 5, 1803, Wirt Papers, Maryland Historical Society, Baltimore; Wirt to Dabney Carr, April 1, 1810, Wirt Papers; Wirt to Carr, June 10, 1814, Library of Virginia, Richmond. Anya Jabour discusses Wirt's friendships in "Male Friendship and Masculinity."

38. Israel Cheever to Robert Treat Paine, July 27, 1749, in *Papers of Robert Treat Paine*, ed. Stephen T. Riley and Edward Hanson, 3 vols. (Boston: Massachusetts Historical Society, 1992), 1:58; William Wirt to Dabney Carr, March 19, 1802, Wirt Papers.

39. William Benemann castigates Anya Jabour for holding back from the conclusion that the language used in letters written by the southern lawyer William Wirt and his male friends "imply actual sexual relations." Jabour does acknowledge that a few of these letters "contained erotic overtones," but as she points out, the letters between these men "give no indication that their prized reunions included sexual intimacy" ("Male Friendship and Masculinity," 93). Benemann goes on to declare that Jabour's "reticence stems from a reluctance to make definitive statements about the past which are unsupported by surviving evidence" and that "proper interpretation of ambiguous language" is the only alternative to leaving the subject of male-male intimacy "unexplored." Others may be disturbed by the claim that one can make "definitive statements about the past which are unsupported by surviving evidence." It is surely disingenuous to claim that we face a stark choice between doing so and leaving topics such as this "unexplored." There is a middle

way that involves circumspect presentation of evidence. Acknowledging that the language used by Wirt might indicate sexual attraction on his part is one thing, but to conclude that this "impl[ies] sexual relations" is quite another. Benemann, *Male-Male Intimacy in Early America: Beyond Romantic Friendships* (New York: Haworth, 2006), 16.

40. John Randolph to Henry Rutledge, quoted in William Cabell Bruce, *John Randolph of Roanoke, 1773–1833*, 2 vols. (New York: G. P. Putnam's Sons, 1922), 1:127, 135; Cheever to Paine, July 27, 1749, 1:58; Wirt to Carr, March 19, 1802; Virgil Maxcy to William Blanding, January 1, 1800, Blanding Family Papers, Massachusetts Historical Society, Boston. Recent scholars of early modern England and Europe have also uncovered examples of male friendship in which love and sexual attraction intermingled. See, for example, George Haggerty, *Men in Love: Masculinity and Sexuality in the Eighteenth Century* (New York: Columbia University Press, 1999); and Guido Ruggiero, *Machiavelli in Love: Sex, Self, and Society in the Italian Renaissance* (Baltimore: Johns Hopkins University Press, 2007).

41. Most biographers of Alexander Hamilton, for example, either ignore suggestive passages in Hamilton's correspondence with John Laurens, some playfully flirtatious and others deeply loving, or simply insist that their friendship must have been entirely nonsexual. As William Benemann points out, while there is "no irrefutable proof that Laurens and Hamilton were lovers," there is "sufficient circumstantial evidence to render indefensible any unqualified pronouncement that they were not" (*Male-Male Intimacy*, xii–xiii). Unfortunately, Benemann goes on to claim that other male friendships probably did have an erotic component even when there is no evidence at all to suggest sexual attraction, let alone that sexual relations were taking place.

42. Cassandra Good, *Founding Friendships: Friendships between Men and Women in the Early Republic* (New York: Oxford University Press, 2015). Historians such as Lillian Faderman (*Surpassing the Love of Men*) and Caroll Smith-Rosenberg ("Female World of Love and Ritual") have uncovered a world of female friendship that incorporated a broad range of possibilities for emotional and physical intimacy.

43. Alan Bray, *The Friend* (Chicago: University of Chicago Press, 2003), 6; Ivy Schweitzer, *Perfecting Friendship: Politics and Affiliation in Early American Literature* (Chapel Hill: University of North Carolina Press, 2006), 6. David Halperin makes a similar point in his introduction to *Love, Sex, Intimacy, and Friendship between Men, 1550–1800*, ed. Katherine O'Donnell and Michael O'Rourke (Basingstoke, UK: Palgrave Macmillan, 2003), 8–11.

44. Halperin, *One Hundred Years of Homosexuality*, 18.

45. See also Kathryn Wichelns, "From *The Scarlet Letter* to Stonewall: Reading the 1629 Thomas(ine) Hall Case, 1978–2009," *Early American Studies* 12 (2014): 523: "In seeking to bring in from the margins those whose experiences were suppressed or ignored for so long, we must avoid the temptation to make them seem too familiar."

2

The Strange Career of Interracial Heterosexuality

RENEE ROMANO

In 1603, long before there was any category we now know as heterosexuality, William Shakespeare penned *Othello*, which famously features a love affair and marriage between the beautiful white Desdemona and the "Moorish" Venetian general Othello. That love affair ends badly, as interracial relationships often do in cultural representations, when a jealous Othello kills his wife after being misled by the duplicitous Iago into believing that she is having an affair. In Shakespeare's tale, Othello's passionate love and desire for his wife does not make him manly. It does not make him "normal." Instead, as the literary critic Rebecca Ann Bach has shown, at the time when the play was written, a man's unbridled desire for a woman made him weak, even effeminate. Othello's excessive desire for his wife marked him as racially other in the seventeenth century, a degraded Moor who did not exhibit the kind of self-control suitable for a proper man.[1]

Heterosexuality, Hanne Blank writes in *Straight: The Surprisingly Short History of Heterosexuality*, is "like air, all around us and yet invisible."[2] It is the task of this volume to make visible what has been elusively invisible, to make historically specific a category, identity, and norm that have remained stubbornly ahistorical. The changing reception to the character of Othello offers one small clue to the early emergence of what Bach calls the "heterosexual imaginary" over the course of the eighteenth century. If in Shakespeare's day, Othello's excessive desire for his wife marked him as a racially inferior man, by the eighteenth century, commentators on the play had begun to laud Othello for his passion as an emerging heterosexual order recoded male sexual desire for women as a key marker of masculinity. Over the course of the eighteenth century, Bach argues, "what was originally part of Othello's racial stigma became part of the dominant male identity."[3]

That transition of course did not reach completion in the eighteenth century. Even in the early twentieth century, a medical dictionary still defined heterosexuality as "abnormal or perverted appetite toward the opposite sex."[4] And while this new category might have helped Othello's reputation with theater critics, did it really, as Bach's analysis seems to imply, somehow help legitimize the idea of interracial love? Shakespeare's problematic characterization of his overly jealous Moor reflected what scholars have recognized as an extraordinarily powerful aspect of the emergence of race: the ways in which ideologies about racial difference and especially the supposed inferiority of nonwhites drew on portrayals of sexual difference and deviance. As race cohered as an ideology for categorizing the people of the world in a hierarchy (especially in slave societies like that which developed in the United States), hypersexuality—or supposedly illicit and excessive, uncontrollable sexual desire—became a key marker of racial inferiority. The changing reception of a character like Othello makes one wonder, might the acceptance of sexual desire signaled by the emergence of heterosexuality somehow diminish the stigma of sexual racism and undercut the opposition to cross-race relationships that served as a foundation of the United States' racial/sexual system?

Or would history show that as the sexual system evolved in the United States, middle-class whites could legitimate their own more passionate sexual desires as respectable and properly heterosexual by defining them against a stigmatized other, an other that would include not only the new category of "homosexuals," who engaged in same-sex acts, but also interracial couples, who too engaged in sexual acts with what most saw as an improper object choice? As heterosexuality became decisively normative, shifting from its turn-of-the century definition of a "perverse" desire for the opposite sex to its 1934 dictionary definition of "normal sexuality,"[5] was it in part because same-race couples could go to a "black and tan" club, watch interracial mixing, and craft their own more respectable heterosexual identity in opposition to a deviant margin? Othello's story did not end in the eighteenth century; instead, black men like him who desired and married white women would again end up as outsiders, heterosexuals perhaps but certainly not heteronormative, at least not in the nineteenth or twentieth centuries and, arguably, still not today.

This chapter asks what interraciality, or the experience of interracial couples, can tell us about the history of heterosexuality. And it explores what a focus on heterosexuality might reveal about the history of interracial sexuality, too. My analysis takes seriously the historian Kevin Mumford's call that we consider interraciality as a category of analysis. In his book *Interzones: Black/White Sex Districts in Chicago and New York in the Early Twentieth Century*, Mumford contends that "interracial relations on the margins" are "central to understanding the character of modern American culture."[6] What does heterosexuality look like when we move interraciality from the margins to the center? What do we learn about the power and limits of heterosexuality, as well as how it became and has served as a normative category that structures politics, society, and culture, when we focus on the history and experience of interracial couples?

Drawing on both my own work on black-white interracial marriage and a wide scholarship on interracial sexual and marital relationships throughout US history, I argue that interraciality and heterosexuality have a complicated and ambivalent relationship, one that ensures that the experiences of heterosexual interracial couples differ not only from white heterosexual couples but also from same-race nonwhite ones. Interraciality magnifies and overdetermines heterosexual interpretations of male-female interactions. As a result of the intense sexualization of the color line, all kinds of cross-racial male-female interactions are presumed to be sexual. Heterosexual interracial couples are thus hypervisible, while same-sex desire across racial lines is frequently invisible and culturally illegible. Yet even as cross-race male-female relationships are incessantly read as heterosexual, they are not heteronormative and have not been accorded the full privileges of heterosexuality.

While we know, thanks to the work of Siobhan Somerville, that race played an important role in shaping cultural conceptions of the emerging category of homosexuality, scholars have paid less attention to how race has worked to construct the boundaries of what constituted "proper" heterosexuality.[7] Yet for much of US history, cross-race different-sex relationships have been as "queer" in their challenge to heterosexuality as homosexuality has. Heterosexual interracial relationships have historically threatened notions of white racial purity. They have challenged a social and national order constructed to maintain white supremacy and white male patriarchal privilege. Stigmatized as illicit and deviant, they served as an "other" against which the heterosexual norm could define itself. In many ways, different-sex interracial couples, especially those involving a white woman, have proved as much of, or even more of, a threat to the heteronormative social order as same-sex couples have.

Reproduction

Without the regulation of different-sex interracial relationships, it would have been nearly impossible to build a race-based society where privileges and opportunities were granted based on a racial hierarchy. Colonial and later state prohibitions against different-sex interracial relationships helped construct and define racial boundaries and categories and in particular allowed for the imagining of whiteness as a space of racial "purity," uncontaminated by the taint of "blood" of racial groups that were rapidly being defined in opposition to whiteness. If European settlers to the Americas had freely mixed with both the indigenous people and the Africans imported as laborers, race as we know it today may not have ever developed. But the colonies and later states chose a different course, passing laws that had two major functions: to create a sharp division, especially between those considered white and those of African descent; and to ensure that race would correspond first with slave status and later with privilege.[8]

The web of antimiscegenation laws that marked the American landscape in some form or another for over three hundred years (from the passage of the first law targeting interracial sex in Maryland in 1661 to the 1967 Supreme Court ruling in *Loving v. Virginia* that declared all remaining state antimiscegenation laws unconstitutional) sought to create and protect a mythic "pure" whiteness from the contamination of interracial mixing.[9] Virginia's 1662 law decreed that "any Christian" who fornicated with a black man or woman would have to pay double the fines typically incurred for such an act. That law also announced a profound break with English common law because it ruled that a child's legal status would follow from that of its mother rather than its father. The law laid out the reasons for the change quite clearly. "Whereas some doubts have arrisen whether children got by any Englishman upon a negro woman should be slave or free, Be it therefore enacted and declared by this present grand assembly, that all children borne in this country shall be held bond or free only according to the condition of the mother."[10] White men, in other words, could have sex with enslaved women, and any resulting children would inherit their mother's slave status. But mixed-race children of white women would be born free. Thus, all interracial relationships between white women and black men potentially threatened the system of racial slavery, as well as the authority of white men.

These regulations and social customs helped create the astounding racial fiction that mixed-race children born to white women would "pollute" the white race, while those born to women of color would not affect whiteness, as long as the white father did not try to legitimate them through marriage or some other legal means. The greater policing of white women's reproductive capacities reflected a patriarchal perspective on heterosexual sex: men were the active partners, who through the sex act transferred their semen—and metaphorically their blood—to women. But the passive female partners did not have the same potential to pollute men. Thus, a white man "injected" his white blood into nonwhite races when he had sex with a woman of color. But a white woman was polluted and tainted by nonwhite blood if she had sex with a man of color. The segregationist Mississippi senator Theodore Bilbo starkly acknowledged this gendered construction of interracial sex in a 1947 screed against integration. "We deplore the conditions which have poured a broad stream of white blood into black veins," Bilbo wrote, "but we deny that any appreciable amount of black blood has entered white veins. As disgraceful as the sins of some white men may have been, they have not in any way impaired the purity of the Southern Caucasian blood."[11]

Bilbo reassured his readers that southern white women had "preserved the integrity of their race" so that no one could "point the finger of suspicion in any manner whatsoever at the blood which flows in the veins of white sons and daughters of the South."[12] Yet his seeming need to defend white female purity reflects the fundamental insecurity that heterosexuality causes for whiteness: even as whiteness must be reproduced to ensure a secure future for the white race, the very process of reproduction carries within it the seeds of the destruction of whiteness itself. Concepts of race are inherently linked to the body; race offers a

mechanism to categorize bodies in a way that reproduces itself. Heterosexual reproduction thus operates as both the mechanism to ensure the
maintenance of racial difference and the site that endangers the production of race.[13]

Cross-racial sex, especially that between white women and nonwhite
men, had to be policed in order to construct racial categories and then
later to maintain them. The late nineteenth-century emergence of heterosexuality as a sexual system only intensified fears about the dangers
that different-sex interracial relationships could pose to white racial purity. Heterosexuality both placed erotic satisfaction at the core of modern sexual identity and revalued women's sexuality in a positive way.[14]
As the literary scholar Mason Stokes explores, this shift to a pleasure-
driven sexuality increased anxiety about racial mixing. Heterosexuality "located desire outside family, race, and nation," Stokes argues, thus
bringing with it a heightened possibility for perversion and corruption.[15]

Regulating interracial sex was especially crucial since the same racialized sexual stereotypes that developed as a way to differentiate nonwhites from whites could also serve to generate cross-racial desire. Even
as white men insisted that black men posed a threat to white women
because of their ostensibly heightened sexual appetite, their alleged lack
of self-control, and their supposedly enormous penises, they worried
that white women freed to explore their own sexual satisfaction might
find such men appealing. Sexual racism—or ideas of racial difference
articulated through constructions of sexual difference—had perhaps
the unintended consequence of turning many racial "others" into attractive sexual partners; stereotypes about black men particularly threatened whiteness since they portrayed them in ways that emphasized their
sexual prowess and that could, theoretically, make them attractive to
white women, the guardians of white racial purity.[16] The emergence of
heterosexuality, Stokes thus argues, led white men to focus obsessively
on the dangers of racial mixing, to engage in a "compulsive imagining of
interracial sex" between black men and white women.[17]

Given the threat that heterosexuality posed to whiteness, it seems perhaps inevitable that Stokes finds that American literature from the nineteenth and early twentieth centuries demonstrates the importance of white
male homosociality to the project of white supremacy. It was relationships *between* white men—who took on the project of controlling white

womanhood—that served to protect whiteness, Stokes suggests. Homosocial kinship between white men was far safer for whiteness than was
the heterosexual desire of men for women—or, even worse, of women for
men of their choice. Even relationships between white men that blurred
the line between the social and the sexual were thus less of a threat to the
existing racial and social order than differently sexed interracial relationships were. As Stokes writes, in turn-of-the century American literature,
"homoeroticism becomes, paradoxically, the only structure of desire that
can keep whiteness white."[18] Robert Young, in his 1995 work *Colonial
Desire*, makes the same point more explicitly. Same-sex sex, he writes,
"posed no threat because it produced no children; its advantage was that
it remained silent, covert, unmarked. . . . In fact, in historical terms, concern about racial amalgamation tended if anything to encourage same-
sex play."[19] Heterosexual interraciality, given its ability to blur racial lines
through the birth of mixed-race children, proved more threatening than
homosexuality to a racial system predicated on notions of white purity.

Reproducing the Nation

It was not just white racial purity that heterosexuality threatened; its new
"pleasure-centered dispersal of sexual energy" had within it the seeds "of
the fall of the white state," Stokes concludes, a possibility brought to the
screen in the famous 1915 silent film *Birth of a Nation*, directed by D. W.
Griffith.[20] *Birth of Nation* dramatized Griffith's version of the history of
Reconstruction, as the South sought to rebuild after the Civil War. In
Griffith's version, based loosely on Thomas Dixon's novels *The Klans-
man* and *The Leopard's Spots*, the threat to white southerners was both
the mentally and socially inferior freed blacks who no longer accepted
their rightful place as subordinate to whites and the northern whites
who falsely believed that blacks could ever be equal to whites. The political drama focuses on the birth of the Ku Klux Klan and its efforts to
restore white supremacy in the South, but its romantic drama focuses
on two heterosexual couples, each involving one child of the pro-Union
white northern Stoneman family and one child of the pro-Confederacy
white southern Cameron family. For the Stoneman-Cameron couples
to achieve their happy ending, the white northern partners must both
come to recognize the threat that blacks present to the social order and

to realize the danger posed by interracial relationships. Here the most conniving blacks are those who are racially mixed themselves, and what black men really want as the symbol of their newfound freedom is a white wife. In *Birth of a Nation*, interracial sex threatens not only white racial purity—indeed, the character presented as the paragon of white female purity, a teenager known only as "Little Sister," jumps to her death rather than face defilement at the hands of a black man—but also the fledging post–Civil War national order. The white northerners can only be happily united in matrimony with their white southern lovers when they realize how threatening black political, social, and sexual equality really is. As one of the intertitle cards in a climactic scene near the end of the silent film reads, "The former enemies of North and South are united again in defense of their Aryan birthright."[21] Birthing a nation, the film makes quite clear, required promoting certain kinds of relationships while prohibiting others.

Heterosexuality is not simply the sexual desires and practices that are socially defined as "normal." Rather, as Stevi Jackson writes, "the coercive power of compulsory heterosexuality derives from its institutionalization as more than merely a sexual relation."[22] Heterosexuality is institutionalized through laws and public policy that privilege certain kinds of relationships and familial arrangements over others. Government policies that promote marriage, that encourage male-headed households, that link government benefits to one's marital status, and that view marriage and family creation as a solution to poverty or juvenile delinquency have all worked to portray the ideal citizen as heterosexual. As Joane Nagel explains in her work on the intersections of race, sexuality, and ethnicity, "Implicit in the idea of the nation . . . are certain prescriptions and proscriptions for sexual crossings—what good citizens should and should not do sexually, and whom they should and should not have sex with."[23] Gender plays a vital role in this nation building, with women given responsibility for reproducing the nation and men for running and defending it. As a result, nationalist politics goes "hand-in-hand" with forms of "hegemonic masculinity" that promote and affirm a patriarchal, heteronormative social order that justifies monitoring and controlling women's sexuality. Nationalist discourse across the globe, Nagel concludes, defines "proper places for men and women," "valorize[s] the heterosexual family as the bedrock of the nation," and condemns "those considered outside the sexual boundaries of the nation."[24]

Peggy Pascoe's sweeping history of the United States' antimiscegenation regime highlights just how much energy has been expended to place heterosexual cross-race relationships outside the "sexual boundaries of the nation." Legislation regulating interracial relationships were among the first racial laws passed in the colonies, and they were the last segregation laws to fall in the civil rights era. Antimiscegenation laws, which existed in some form from 1661 to 1967, proved the most pervasive and enduring forms of legal racial discrimination. The antimiscegenation regime, Pascoe reminds us, was a national one, not just a southern one. Laws prohibiting interracial marriage existed in all but nine of the fifty states at one time or another. They targeted relationships not only between blacks and whites but also between whites and Asians, Malays, and, in some cases, Native Americans. Antimiscegenation laws thus grouped together all nonwhites as a threat to white purity and made clear that preventing interracial marriage was a vital part of constructing a system of white supremacy and building a stable nation.[25]

The sexuality scholar Steven Seidman insists that critical sexuality studies must focus more attention on "analyzing the way in which regimes of normative heterosexuality create hegemonic and subordinate forms of heterosexuality."[26] If so, then exploring the antimiscegenation regime needs to be at the top of the priority list. The widespread and intense regulation of interracial relationships suggests that different-sex cross-race relationships were among the most deviant forms of heterosexuality, viewed by authorities as highly threatening to the state. Institutionalized heterosexuality typically promotes monogamous, marital relationships, with marriage being so important to the state that long-term cohabiting different-sex couples are presumed to be part of a "common-law marriage" even when they have made no legal contract with each other. But in the case of interracial pairings, marriage actually made a relationship more threatening to the state, not less. Interracial marriages had to be regulated in order to prevent the transfer of wealth and assets from whites to nonwhites. They needed to be prohibited to ensure that any children born of interracial sex would be considered illegitimate. And they needed to be stigmatized as a way to promote a construction of a stable national order where whites held a privileged place.

Indeed, the regulation of interracial marriage was so important to states that even white men would find their rights limited. While the regulation of interracial sex sought to control the actions of white women while allowing white men to freely engage in sex with nonwhite women, the prohibition of interracial marriage affected both men and women alike. While Pascoe notes that this impingement on the rights of white men was among the "hardest won—and most unstable—achievement" of the antimiscegenation regime, the fact that patriarchal privilege did not extend to white men's rights to legitimize their mixed-race children or to leave their assets to their nonwhite partners demonstrates that interraciality could, to put it crudely, trump heterosexuality.[27] Courts regularly denied nonwhite long-term partners of white men the status of common-law wives, which would have granted them the right to their partner's estates and legitimacy for their children. Many of the miscegenation cases that reached the courts concerned the disposition of property or estates after the death of a white spouse. Some states designed laws specifically to prevent this kind of wealth transmission. Mississippi law awarded inheritances to any white descendant, regardless of legitimacy and no matter how remote, over any mixed-race descendant.[28]

Yet while the antimiscegenation regime placed some limits on white men's freedom for the sake of the nation, it was white women who had the power to truly disrupt the national order through engaging in interracial relationships. Women, perceived as the guardians of the purity of their communities, have been charged with reproducing and upholding the identity of racial nations. As the legal scholar Leti Volpp argues, "Nationalism entwines with race so that women are subjected to control in order to achieve the aim of a national racial purity."[29] White women who explicitly chose nonwhite men challenged not only the white men in their own lives but also the entire edifice of a racial system justified by the need to defend white women's racial purity. White men defended segregation, the denial of political equality, and the practice of lynching on the grounds that they needed to protect precious white womanhood from nonwhites, and especially black men, who might come to see themselves as equal to whites if not confined to a subordinate racial status.[30] It is no wonder that white women who became involved in interracial relationships were frequently portrayed as mentally ill and even institutionalized by their parents.[31] "But would you want your daughter to marry one?" the famous "final" question, invoked as late as the 1960s as a way to silence critiques of segregation, made clear the ways in which interracial relationship between white and nonwhite men directly threatened white male patriarchal authority. "A Negro having relations with a white man's daughter, his own precious virgin, is in effect a storming of the castle, the penultimate act of castration," a 1966 magazine article colorfully explained.[32]

And what is castration but the ultimate denial of patriarchal power? While feminist scholarship tells us that heterosexuality has served as an institution of male control over women, interracial heterosexuality instead threatened white male patriarchal control over white women. In a seminal 1980 essay, Adrienne Rich argued that women's emotional, economic, and physical bonds with each other represented the most powerful threat to compulsory heterosexuality and male control over women. But white men's response to the possibility of relationships between white women and nonwhite men suggests that heterosexual interraciality could be as threatening to patriarchal power as lesbianism was.[33] Interraciality, like same-sex relationships, challenged the stability of a heterosexual national order.

While nonwhites have not had an equal place to whites in the nation, they have at least had the possibility of inclusion if they adhered to heteronormative conventions through same-race marriages and nuclear family formation. Indeed, understanding how "regimes of normative heterosexuality create hegemonic and subordinate forms of heterosexuality" requires that we also explore how blacks, Asians, and other racialized communities viewed cross-racial relationships. Communities of color participated in the construction of a heteronormative order that stigmatized interracial relationships even if their full inclusion in that order remained elusive. That has been the case whether they have sought to further themselves on the basis of their similarity to white Americans or whether they have sought power and purchase in the nation on the basis of their differences from whites.

For racialized groups stigmatized as sexually deviant and licentious, embracing the respectability politics associated with heteronormativity— monogamy, marriage, and middle-class cultural practices—has long served as one path toward racial equality. Both blacks and Asian Americans, for example, promoted images of their own family life as "normal"

in order to further their claims for cultural and political inclusion. As
Judy Wu has argued, the experience of being defined as sexually deviant
as a result of racial discrimination "reinforces the value of heteronormativity" for nonwhite groups.[34] Of course, since the entire antimiscegenation regime marked nonwhites as inferior to whites, people of color did
not necessarily support or advocate bars on intermarriage themselves.
Indeed, they feared that such bans would only serve to make it easier for
white men to sexually exploit women of color. But, like whites, many
associated interracial relationships with exploitative and illicit sex, characterized those who would engage in such relationships as degraded,
and feared that open involvement in or support for such relationships
would tarnish the entire community as lacking in respectability. In 1868,
all eight of the black delegates to the Arkansas Constitutional Convention joined white delegates in voting to condemn "all amalgamation . . .
legitimate or illegitimate."[35] Black club women in the late nineteenth and
early twentieth centuries promoted "ladylike" behavior and sexual self-
control as a way for black women to challenge the "myth of black promiscuity," a myth fueled by even consensual interracial relationships.[36]
The impulse to associate interracial relationships with immorality and to
condemn them as detrimental to the race continued well into the twentieth century. "All decent colored people disapprove of mixed marriages,"
a self-described "Loyal American Negro Mother" wrote in 1949, while
the black sociologists St. Clair Drake and Horace R. Cayton Jr. found in
their 1945 study of black Chicago that having a white spouse could hurt
blacks' social position with other blacks.[37] Blacks or other racial groups
who sought to normalize their racial difference by publicly performing
heteronormativity tended to be wary of cross-racial relationships.[38]

This common ground between whites and nonwhites again highlights the deviant nature of heterosexual interracial relationships. These
relationships have been sexualized to the extent that respectability politics has proven a limited avenue for advancement for interracial couples. The antimiscegenation legal regime had the effect of stigmatizing
all kinds of interracial relationships as immoral and licentious even if
the relationship was stable, long term, monogamous, or resulted in a
marriage.[39] Marriage, in other words, did not normalize heterosexual
interraciality; it did not confer respectability on an interracial couple
as long as there were laws barring intermarriage. Even in states where

intermarriage was legal, white women with black men and black women with white men were presumed to be prostitutes, not wives. Elaine Neil, a white woman, had to threaten to sue the state of New York in the early 1950s to stop a police campaign against her and her black husband. Police arrested Elaine on prostitution charges, called her a "whore," and questioned the legitimacy of her marriage to her black husband. Nor did marriage protect couples from speculation that their relationships were motivated by sexual curiosity, mental instability, or economic gain.[40]

That is not to say that heterosexual interracial couples have not engaged in a politics of respectability. Indeed, cross-race couples have sought to distance themselves from negative stereotypes of illicit interracial sex by stressing exactly the kinds of behaviors that heteronormativity requires: that they married for love, that they are no different from same-race heterosexual couples, that they are stable and monogamous, and that they have children and form nuclear families. But this project has been, at best, incomplete. The 1951 intermarried couple who insisted to *Ebony* magazine that they were ordinary people, "nothing spectacular nor side show freaks," differed little in perspective from couples in the 1980s who railed against the negative portrayal of interracial relationships on television talk shows from current couples who feel they must constantly work to deflect negative stereotypes and to position themselves as normal, legitimate, and "in love."[41] Normalizing heterosexual interracial love through a politics of respectability remains an elusive strategy for full acceptance because it is not the status of an interracial relationship—commercial or not, married or not, stable or not—that makes it deviant. It is the fact of the relationship at all. As with queer couples, heterosexual interracial couples have had to fight to be considered respectable because their object choice automatically renders their relationship nonnormative.

It is not only respectability that has eluded interracial couples but also the possibility of participating in a politics of nation building. Interracial relationships not only have threatened the construction of a white heteronormative state but also have been viewed with disgust by other racial groups who envisioned constructing a sense of nationhood based on their ethnic or racial heritage. The preeminent black nationalist leader Marcus Garvey, the head of the Universal Negro Improvement Association, went so far as to praise the white-supremacist Ku Klux Klan in

1922 because that organization, like his, believed in racial purity. Garvey and the Klan shared similar antimiscegenation views. "Whilst the Ku Klux Klan desires to make America absolutely a white man's country, the Universal Negro Improvement Association wants to make Africa absolutely a black man's country," Garvey explained. Interraciality threatened both of these nation-building projects.[42] In the 1960s and 1970s, black nationalists attacked blacks who intermarried for betraying the race and "sleeping with the enemy." Malcolm X echoed Garvey in his opposition to intermarriage. "Let the white man keep his women and let us keep ours," he instructed blacks. Black nationalists described interracial relationships, in the words of Eldridge Cleaver, as a "revolutionary sickness," a sign of one's desire to be white. Building a strong black nation required, as one black woman explained, that blacks eschew interracial relationships and "want to see the blood of our heritage running in and through the veins of our children."[43] There is no space for interraciality in racial nationalism, whether espoused by whites or by other racialized groups.

Although there have always been a handful of Americans who have praised racial mixing as a way to fulfill the United States' destiny, it has proven difficult for interracial couples to imagine themselves as engaged in their own political project. The historian Greg Carter, who writes about the understudied intellectual American tradition of viewing racial mixing as a positive good rather than a threat or sign of degradation, shows how advocating racial mixing could be part of a vision of full equality for all races in a transformed country.[44] Thus, the radical abolitionist Wendell Phillips urged people of all races to mix freely in the United States, while more recently, groups created by and for mixed-race couples and families have sometimes described interracial love as one avenue toward reducing racial tensions. As one magazine for interracial couples insisted in 1977, "Love is the answer, not legislation."[45] But whatever nation-building project interracial couples and their families might be involved in has always been viewed as utopian, as even the title of Carter's book—*The United States of the United Races: A Utopian History of Race Mixing*—suggests.

Interracial couples, moreover, have found that their relationships are stigmatized and discredited if there is even the slightest hint that their actions are politically motivated. While same-race heterosexual couples can be part of a nation-building project—even an explicit one—and not have the status and legitimacy of their relationship called into question, interracial couples have been much more easily charged with being together for reasons that heterosexuality deems illegitimate, such as marrying to promote a political agenda. Not surprisingly, different-sex interracial couples have historically taken great pains to insist that their marriages are respectable, traditional, and loving.[46] The earliest clubs for interracial couples, the Manasseh Society, which was founded in Milwaukee and Chicago in the late nineteenth century, and the Penguin Club, founded in New York in 1936, explicitly required that all members be legally married and even demanded proof of character. The Manasseh Society required that members attend church regularly; the Penguin Society forbid childless couples on the ground that the presence of children indicated a more stable marriage.[47] Being seen as "crusaders" for interracial love served to reinforce negative stereotypes about these relationships in ways that placed them even further outside heteronormativity. For same-race couples, building stable nuclear families has been considered a key aspect of nation building, but cross-race couples have found little place for themselves in that project.

Deviant or Other? The Visibility of Hetero Interraciality

Scholars of normative heterosexuality tell us that there are many ways to be a "bad" heterosexual. While the invention and institutionalization of heterosexuality served most powerfully to regulate and stigmatize same-sex acts, it also created hierarchies that privileged heterosexuals who were involved in monogamous, gender-conventional, long-term (preferably married) relationships based on love over those who engaged in casual sex or commercial sex, who had multiple partners, or who in some ways challenged gender norms. As Steven Seidman argues, "normative heterosexuality not only establishes hierarchy with homosexuals, but creates hierarchy among heterosexualities" as well.[48] Interracial couples might be considered the poster children for deviant heterosexuality; adhering to heteronormative conventions has done little to normalize them historically.

The exclusions of different-sex interracial couples from the most basic aspects of heterosexual privilege raise the question of whether they are really lesser heterosexuals, ranked lower on a hierarchy than normative heterosexuals, or are perhaps instead defined as outside the norm entirely. One of the most powerful aspects of heterosexual privilege, Hanne Blank writes, is the right to go through the world without your relationship attracting much notice. "Having your sexuality and your relationships be perceived as 'normal' provides unearned privilege," Blank argues. "It accrues automatically and invisibly to everyone *who is perceived as being heterosexual* for as long as they continue to be perceived that way."[49]

Are different-sex interracial couples "perceived as being heterosexual" under this definition? If being heterosexual means one has the right to go through the world without your relationship attracting much attention, they certainly have not had that right. Different-sex interracial couples in the United States have historically encountered disapproval and even violent opposition. Historically and currently, different-sex couples complain about the stares, comments, and scrutiny they experience when they are in public. Whether those comments are hostile or affirming, they make clear that interracial relationships are not normative.[50]

As a sexual regime, heterosexuality stigmatizes same-sex relationships as the ultimate boundary against which normative practices are judged, making homosexuality suspect and highly visible while making heterosexuality the invisible norm. But the color line has been sexualized in a way that makes different-sex interracial pairings far more visible than same-sex interracial relationships. It is heterosexual interracial pairings that raise the specter of the loss of white racial purity and the threat to the project of constructing a racial nation. Cross-racial interactions between a man and woman—particularly the most taboo of those crossings between blacks and whites but also sometimes those between white men and Asian women—serve as visible triggers of a history of sexual racism and illicit desire, and that history is so powerful that even men and women of different races who are only acquaintances are often construed as sexually involved. The sociologist Amy Steinbugler argues that "racial difference may actually heighten presumptions of heterosexual intimacy." Some pairings are so associated with racial and sexual deviance that "others may read this historic symbol onto two individuals who are simply occupying the same physical space."[51]

While heterosexual interracial couples experience a heightened sense of public visibility, queer interracial couples often feel profoundly invisible. In interviews with contemporary queer interracial couples, Steinbugler found that most felt that their interraciality lacked any public identity and indeed made them culturally illegible. All of the cultural scripts about interraciality relate to different-sex pairings, a category that carries with it long-standing "historical, social, and political meanings."[52] In fact, crossing the color line has been so deeply linked to deviant heterosexual desire that at times even same-sex interracial pairings have been understood as fundamentally heterosexual. In 1913, the psychologist Margaret Otis explained the relationships between young black and white women at a reform school as an example of white women's heterosexual attraction to men, with race difference standing in for gender difference. "The difference in color, in this case," Otis argued, "takes the place of difference in sex."[53] Other twentieth-century reformers also attributed interracial lesbian relationships in prison to black women taking on masculine roles and temporarily substituting for male partners for their supposedly straight white female lovers.[54] This understanding of interracial lesbian relationships demonstrates the power of the "heterosexualization" of the color line.

This relative invisibility of same-sex interracial relationships is particularly noteworthy because demographic evidence suggests that today—and perhaps historically—queer couples are in fact more likely to be interracial than straight ones are. In 2010, the US Census found that same-sex couples were more likely to be interracial or interethnic than any other kind of couples; 20.6 percent of all same-sex couples were interracial or interethnic, as compared to 18.3 percent of different-sex unmarried couples and 9.5 percent of different-sex married couples.[55] Nevertheless, queer interraciality often remains invisible in public. The black law professor I. Bennett Capers explains the different treatment that he encounters when he is out with his white husband than when his black brother visits with his white wife. His brother and sister-in-law "are still suspect, subject to the look, an 'interracial tax,'" while he feels he is actually made safer and less threatening by having a white male partner.[56]

Rather than different-sex interraciality being a form of "bad" heterosexuality, it might perhaps be more aptly considered as akin to same-sex relationships: one of the "others" that heterosexuality as a new sexual regime defined itself against. The reorganization of the systems of gender and sexuality that took place in the late nineteenth century and resulted in the "invention" of the categories of heterosexuality and homosexuality drew on and developed from ideas already in circulation about race and racialized bodies. In *Queering the Color Line*, Siobhan Somerville argues that scientific discourses about race shaped the ways in which sexologists articulated emerging models of homosexuality. Sexologists scrutinized bodies of so-called inverts for biological markers of difference just as scientists had scrutinized black bodies for markers of racial inferiority. They described gender ambiguity—or what seemed to be a mixed-gendered body—as akin to a mixed-race body. And they developed a new focus on sexual-object choice that linked homosexual and interracial desire as both unnatural and deviant.[57] The emerging system of heterosexuality defined homosexuality as deviant, in other words, by associating it with interracial sex, which was already understood as illicit and overly sexualized.

Heterosexuality as a new sexual regime associated with different practices and behaviors became socially acceptable in part through contrasting it both to interracial heterosexuality and to homosexuality, which in fact were often geographically linked. What Kevin Mumford calls "interzones," or sites that allowed interracial mixing that developed in northern cities in the early twentieth century, also became sites associated with same-sex relationships. Interracial sex became the marker of vice; these deviant spaces, Mumford suggests, provided space for the emergence of new gay subcultures. Both different-sex cross-racial mixing and same-sex relationships became the stigmatized other that a new, more sexually permissive heterosexual center could redefine itself against. A dance hall could be respectable as long as it did not allow racial mixing, Mumford argues in his study of New York and Chicago. In California, fears of mixing between white women and Filipino men led to city bans on mixed-race dancing, not to mention bans on all dance halls in the 1920s.[58]

The historian Chad Heap similarly demonstrates that the new heterosexual system based on the acceptance of female sexual desire and of the erotic as central to one's identity legitimated itself and became respectable through the practice of middle-class whites defining themselves against an "other" that included both same-sex and different-sex interracial relations. Heap focuses on the practice known as "slumming," in which middle-class whites (and new immigrants seeking whiteness) visited neighborhoods and clubs associated with primitivism, illicit desire, and commercial sex and in so doing shifted the boundaries of what was considered respectable sexual behavior (dating and oral sex, Heap argues, were two practices that slumming helped validate). Whites could maintain their own respectability, even while embracing new sexual practices, by positioning themselves against a degraded, exotic other. "Slumming provided the mechanism through which its participants could use both race and sexual encounters to mediate their transition from one system of sexual classification to another," Heap writes.[59] Both black and tan slumming and the subsequent "pansy" craze, in which middle-class whites visited first spaces in black neighborhoods and then spaces associated with same-sex coupling, helped reshape middle-class sexual boundaries and legitimate the idea of sexual pleasure and desire linked to the emergence of heterosexuality. Interraciality, in short, helped establish the boundaries of what constituted proper and normative heterosexuality and became one of the markers that served to stigmatize same-sex relationships as deviant.

Heterosexuality Post-*Loving*?

In 1967, the US Supreme Court declared the entire antimiscegenation legal regime unconstitutional after Richard and Mildred Loving challenged the state of Virginia's ban on interracial marriage. Richard, a white man, and Mildred, a woman of African and indigenous ancestry, had been childhood sweethearts in Caroline County, Virginia.[60] But after they married in 1958, they were charged with violating Virginia law and forced to leave the state to avoid a jail sentence. Seeking to return home, they eventually began a court challenge that would result in the invalidation of all the remaining miscegenation laws nationwide. Marriage, the Supreme Court ruled in the *Loving* case, was a fundamental right that states could not abridge or deny on the basis of race.[61]

Since that ruling, the number of heterosexual interracial couples in the United States has increased dramatically, especially those involving Asians and Latinos. In 1967, only 3 percent of all newlyweds married across race lines. Today, 17 percent of different-sex new marriages are interracial or interethnic (meaning Latino/non-Latino). The number of black-white married couples has increased from 51,000 in 1960 to 422,250 in 2010. Public opposition to interracial relationships has also declined dramatically since the *Loving* decision. In 1958, 94 percent of Americans disapproved of black-white marriages; today, only 11 percent do. Americans of all racial groups are more open to intermarriages involving members of their own families. In 2000, 31 percent of Americans indicated that they would disapprove of a family member marrying someone of another race; in 2015, that number stood at only 10 percent. And 39 percent of Americans in a 2017 Pew Research Study said that more people marrying across race lines would be good for society; only 9 percent claimed that more intermarriages would harm society.[62]

But if cross-race different-sex relationships have been as challenging to heterosexuality as same-sex relationships have and both interraciality and homosexuality have served as the "other" against which heterosexuality was defined, what does the lessening of the taboo against interraciality suggest about the stability and future of the sexual regime of heterosexuality?

To be fair, not everyone agrees that there really has been any meaningful decrease in opposition to interracial relationships since *Loving*. Pointing to the still small number of interracial couples and to other indicators, many scholars and social commentators argue that interracial pairings remain rare and socially deviant. Fifty years after *Loving*, whites remain four times more likely than random to marry another white person, and a recent study attributes most of the increase in the number of interracial marriages to demographic change, especially the growth in the US population of Asians and Hispanics and the decline in the white population, rather than to more tolerant attitudes toward interracial relationships among whites.[63] Ethnographic studies of heterosexual interracial couples find that they still report feeling hypervisible in public, while studies that seek to probe people's private racial feelings find that many whites still find interracial relationships off-putting and even something that inspires disgust.[64] A recent edited collection of essays by law professors about the 1967 *Loving* decision almost uniformly takes the glass-half-empty approach, emphasizing all the ways that heterosexual privilege remains outside the reach of different-sex interracial couples. As one writer explains, "mixed race remains a threat to political stability and social respectability," while another stresses that black-white relationships remain "sexualized spectacles" that observers see as deviant and perverse. Interracial couples, a third essay points out, rarely see relationships like theirs represented in the media or affirmed as normal for their children.[65]

But given the changes in the past thirty years and the fact that today one in six newlyweds is married to a partner of a different race or ethnicity and that the rate of interracial pairings is even higher among cohabiting but unmarried couples, it seems useful to conclude with at least some questions about what a greater openness to interraciality might suggest about the future of heterosexuality.

Siobhan Somerville lays out one possible answer in her 2005 essay "Queer Loving," in which she argues that heterosexual interracial relationships became normative—at least in the legal arena—through the increased demonization and stigmatization of same-sex relationships. Normative citizenship, Somerville argues, had been articulated through both discourses of race and discourses of sexuality, as reflected in laws that prohibited interracial marriage and criminalized homosexuality. But just weeks before the Supreme Court handed down the *Loving* decision, it upheld a 1952 law that made homosexuals and adulterers ineligible to naturalize. For Somerville, this timing is evidence that "the interracial couple was imagined as having a legitimate claim on the state at the same time that the nation was defensively constituted as heterosexual, incapable of incorporating the sexually suspect body." *Loving* thus expanded marriage rights by consolidating heterosexuality as a prerequisite for recognition by the state, Somerville insists. Interracial marriage became legitimized in law "in relation to its thorough heterosexualization."[66] In this reading, different-sex interracial relationships became normative—at least in the eyes of the law—because they could be defined against same-sex relationships. Thus, one possibility is that interraciality and homosexuality no longer operate in tandem as others against which heterosexuality defines itself.

While Somerville argues that interraciality became normative by the intensified exclusion of the homosexual, developments since she made that argument in 2005 raise the very different possibility that different-race and same-sex relationships have both become less oppositional to heterosexuality in the past forty years as long as they adhere to certain heteronormative (or homonormative) conventions. It is telling that the past fifty years have witnessed not only the legalization of interracial marriage and an increased acceptance for interracial relationships but also the legalization of same-sex marriage and a lessening of the taboo against homosexuality. Indeed, the popularity of the *Loving* analogy—or the argument by proponents of gay marriage that since the court upheld individuals' freedom to marry across racial lines in 1967, it should uphold the right of individuals to marry someone of the same sex— indicates that the increased acceptance of interraciality has helped spur the acceptance of homosexuality too. It seems that both kinds of relationships that heterosexuality defined itself against have become more socially acceptable as long as they do not challenge gender conventions, they link sex to love and marriage, they uphold family values, and they limit their public displays of affection. The history of interraciality may tell us, in short, that heteronormative heterosexuality is today "constituted as much by the 'other' being incorporated in a subordinate position within the dominant category as by the 'other' being excluded."[67] Even though the division may no longer be solely between same-race/ interracial or hetero/homo, heteronormativity in this reading still creates a hierarchy between "good sexual citizens" and those "bad" sexual citizens who engage in erotic behaviors unmoored from intimacy and monogamy.[68]

Or—and this final possibility seems as likely to me as the others—the legalization of interracial marriage and at least a lessening of the taboo against interracial relationships may signal that we are near the end of the sexual regime known as heterosexuality. Jonathan Ned Katz ends his book about the invention of heterosexuality with evidence that the sexual regime was already becoming less stable beginning in the 1970s and 1980s. Katz points to increasing divorce rates, falling marriage rates, less distinction between "gay" and "straight" sex acts, and a general convergence of gay and straight lifestyles.[69] While Katz does not include anything about race on his list, the growing number of interracial couples might be yet another indicator that the era of heterosexual supremacy is coming to an end.

Whatever the future holds for heterosexuality, it is clear that its past is inextricably linked to interraciality. Yet these links remain woefully unexplored. Scholars of sexuality rarely identify monoraciality as a key prerequisite to heterosexual privilege, while scholars of interracial relationships have failed to recognize heterosexuality and heteronormativity as important influences on heterosexual interracial intimacy. In other words, heterosexuality remains an area where monoraciality is assumed, while interraciality is an area of intellectual inquiry where heterosexuality is assumed.[70] But as this chapter has attempted to demonstrate, neither interraciality nor heterosexuality can be fully understood without reference to the other.

NOTES

1. Rebecca Ann Bach, "17th and 18th Century Othello and Desdemona: Race and Emerging Heterosexuality," in *Feminisms and Early Modern Texts: Essays for Phyllis Rackin*, ed. Bach and Gwynne Kennedy (Selinsgrove, PA: Susquehanna University Press, 2010), 81–98.

2. Hanne Blank, *Straight: The Surprisingly Short History of Heterosexuality* (Boston: Beacon, 2012), xvi.

3. Bach, "17th and 18th Century Othello and Desdemona," 81.

4. Quoted in Jonathan Ned Katz, *The Invention of Heterosexuality* (Chicago: University of Chicago Press, 1995), 92.

5. Katz, *Invention of Heterosexuality*.

6. Kevin Mumford, *Interzones: Black/White Sex Districts in Chicago and New York in the Early Twentieth Century* (New York: Columbia University Press, 1997), xi, xii.

7. See Siobhan B. Somerville's seminal work, *Queering the Color Line: Race and the Invention of Homosexuality in American Culture* (Durham, NC: Duke University Press, 2000). Her argument about the ways in which race served as a key reference point for understanding homosexuality is discussed in more detail later in the essay.

8. For more on the process of constructing whiteness as a space of "purity," see Kirsten Fischer, *Suspect Relations: Sex, Race, and Resistance in Colonial North Carolina* (Ithaca, NY: Cornell University Press, 2002); Joanne Nagel, *Race, Ethnicity, and Sexuality: Intimate Interactions, Forbidden Frontiers* (New York: Oxford University Press, 2003), 37–62.

9. The 1661 Maryland law mandated that a "free-born" English woman who married a black slave serve the same master during the life of her husband and that any children of the couple would be slaves as well. There is a large literature on the history of antimiscegenation laws in the United States and the role such laws played in shaping racial and gender hierarchies. See, for example, Peggy Pascoe, *What Comes Naturally: Miscegenation Law and the Making of Race in America* (New York: Oxford University Press, 2009). A good introduction is Peter Bardaglio, "'Shamefull Matches': The Regulation of Interracial Sex and Marriage in the

South before 1900," in *Sex, Love, and Race: Crossing Racial Boundaries in North America*, ed. Martha Hodes (New York: NYU Press, 1999), 112–40.

10. Governor and Council of Virginia, "Statutes (1630–70)," in *Race in Early Modern England: A Documentary Companion*, ed. Ania Loomba and Jonathan Burton (New York: Palgrave Macmillan, 2007), 229.

11. Theodore Bilbo, *Take Your Choice: Separation or Mongrelization* (Poplarville, MS: Dream House, 1947), 57–58.

12. Bilbo, 57–58.

13. Richard Dyer, *White* (New York: Routledge, 1997), 20; Mason Stokes, *The Color of Sex: Whiteness, Heterosexuality, and the Fictions of White Supremacy* (Durham, NC: Duke University Press, 2001), 16.

14. For more on this, see Katz, *Invention of Heterosexuality*, 88.

15. Mason Stokes, "White Heterosexuality: A Romance of the Straight Man's Burden," in *Thinking Straight: The Power, Promise, and Paradox of Heterosexuality*, ed. Chrys Ingraham (New York: Routledge, 2005), 133.

16. For a good overview of racial sexual stereotypes and their social implications, see Nagel, *Race, Ethnicity, and Sexuality*.

17. Stokes, *Color of Sex*, 17.

18. Stokes, 18.

19. Robert C. Young, *Colonial Desire* (1995), quoted in Stokes, "White Heterosexuality," 146.

20. Stokes, "White Heterosexuality," 146.

21. *Birth of a Nation*, directed by D. W. Griffith, based on the novel by Thomas Dixon Jr. (Triangle Film Corp., 1915).

22. Stevi Jackson, "Sexuality, Heterosexuality, and Gender Hierarchy: Getting Our Priorities Straight," in Ingraham, *Thinking Straight*, 18.

23. Nagel, *Race, Ethnicity, and Sexuality*, 141. See also Diane Richardson, *Rethinking Sexuality* (London: Sage, 2000), 80.

24. Nagel, *Race, Ethnicity, and Sexuality*, 159, 166.

25. See Pascoe, *What Comes Naturally*.

26. Steven Seidman, "From the Polluted Homosexual to the Normal Gay: Changing Patterns of Sexual Regulation in America," in Ingraham, *Thinking Straight*, 40.

27. Pascoe, *What Comes Naturally*, 11.

28. Stetson Kennedy, *Jim Crow Guide: The Way It Was* (Boca Raton: Florida Atlantic University Press, 1990), 67; originally published as *Jim Crow Guide to the U.S.A.* (London: Lawrence and Wishart, 1959). Pascoe's *What Comes Naturally* explores this issue of wills, estates, and miscegenation law in great depth.

29. Leti Volpp, "American Mestizo: Filipinos and Antimiscegenation Laws in California," in Loving v. Virginia *in a Post-racial World: Rethinking Race, Sex, and Marriage*, ed. Kevin Noble Maillard and Rose Cuison Villazor (New York: Cambridge University Press, 2012), 71.

30. While relationships between white women and black men were deemed particularly threatening, other kinds of interracial relationships also challenged the social

and patriarchal order. As Mary Ting Yi Lui has shown, the murder of a white woman, allegedly by her Chinese lover, in early twentieth-century New York City generated efforts by authorities to "restore moral and spatial order" with intensified surveillance of Chinatown, intensified spatial segregation, and efforts to police the behavior of white women. See Lui, *The Chinatown Trunk Mystery: Murder, Miscegenation, and Other Dangerous Encounters in Turn-of-the-Century New York City* (Princeton, NJ: Princeton University Press, 2005).

31. Renee Romano, *Race Mixing: Black-White Marriage in Postwar America* (Cambridge, MA: Harvard University Press, 2003), 66–69.
32. Romano, 197–98.
33. Adrienne Rich, "Compulsory Heterosexuality and Lesbian Existence," *Signs: Journal of Women in Culture and Society* 5, no. 4 (Summer 1980): 631–60.
34. Judy Tzu-Chun Wu, "Asian American History and Racialized Compulsory Deviance," *Journal of Women's History* 15, no. 3 (Autumn 2003): 60.
35. Hannah Rosen, *Terror in the Heart of Freedom: Citizenship, Sexual Violence and the Meaning of Race in the Postemancipation South* (Chapel Hill: University of North Carolina Press, 2009), 164.
36. For more on black club women's adherence to and promotion of "respectable" middle-class sexual norms, see Stephanie J. Shaw, *What a Woman Ought to Be and to Do: Black Professional Women Workers during the Jim Crow Era* (Chicago: University of Chicago Press, 1996), 13–25.
37. Both quoted in Romano, *Race Mixing*, 85.
38. Mason Stokes, "Father of the Bride: Du Bois and the Making of Black Heterosexuality," in *Next to the Color Line: Gender, Sexuality, and W. E. B. Du Bois*, ed. Susan Gillman and Alys Eve Weinbaum (Minneapolis: University of Minnesota Press, 2007), 289–316.
39. Pascoe, *What Comes Naturally*, 59–62.
40. For more, see Romano, *Race Mixing*, 48–49, 127–32.
41. Romano, x, 277–79; Amy C. Steinbugler, *Beyond Loving: Intimate Racework in Lesbian, Gay, and Straight Interracial Relationships* (New York: Oxford University Press, 2014), chap. 5.
42. "Hon. Marcus Garvey Tells of Interview with Ku Klux Klan," *Negro World*, July 15, 1922, 7; quoted in Bob Blaisdell, introduction to *Selected Writings and Speeches of Marcus Garvey* (Mineola, NY: Dover, 2004), viii.
43. Romano, *Race Mixing*, 216–47 (quotes on 221, 222, 243).
44. Greg Carter, *The United States of the United Races: A Utopian History of Race Mixing* (New York: NYU Press, 2013).
45. *Interracial*, March 1977, title page.
46. Romano, *Race Mixing*, 139–40.
47. Will Kuby, *Conjugal Misconduct: Defying Marriage Law in the Twentieth-Century United States* (New York: Cambridge University Press, 2018), 226–27.
48. Seidman, "Polluted Homosexual," 40.
49. Blank, *Straight*, 164 (emphasis added).

50. For more on the visibility of heterosexual interracial couples, see Romano, *Race Mixing*; Steinbugler, *Beyond Loving*, 55.
51. Amy Steinbugler, "Hiding in Plain Sight: Why Queer Interraciality Is Unrecognizable to Strangers and Sociologists," in *Interracial Relationships in the 21st Century*, 2nd ed., ed. Earl Smith and Angela Hatterly (Durham, NC: Carolina Academic Press, 2013), 97.
52. Steinbugler, 99.
53. For more on this, see Somerville, *Queering the Color Line* (quote on 34).
54. See Cheryl D. Hicks, *Talk with You like a Woman: African American Women, Justice, and Reform in New York, 1890–1935* (Chapel Hill: University of North Carolina Press, 2010), 204–36.
55. Daphne Lofquist, Terry Lugaila, Martin O'Connell, and Sarah Feliz, "Households and Families: 2010" (US Census Bureau, Washington, DC, April 2012), 18, www.census.gov. Note these numbers refer to both interracial relationships and same-race Hispanic/non-Hispanic relationships, or what the US Census Bureau considers as interethnic marriages. If only *interracial relationships* are considered, the corresponding numbers for interracial couples are 6.9 percent of all heterosexual married couples, 14.2 percent of unmarried different-sex couples, and 14.5 percent of same-sex couples.
56. I. Bennett Capers, "The Crime of Loving: *Loving, Lawrence*, and Beyond," in Maillard and Cuison Villazor, Loving v. Virginia *in a Post-racial World*, 106.
57. Somerville, *Queering the Color Line*, 39.
58. Mumford, *Interzones*, 56; Rick Baldoz, *The Third Asiatic Invasion: Migration and Empire in Filipino America, 1898–1946* (New York: NYU Press, 2011), 130–34.
59. Chad Heap, *Slumming: Sexual and Racial Encounters in American Nightlife, 1885–1940* (Chicago: University of Chicago Press, 2009), 10.
60. Mildred Loving, who was from the triracial community of Hunter's Point, Virginia, was of mixed Native American and African ancestry, and recent scholarship has revealed that she defined herself as Indian rather than black. Indeed, Arica Coleman argues that from Lovings' own perspective, their marriage adhered to Virginia law, which allowed marriages between whites and some Native Americans. Outsiders, however, including the media and the courts, defined Mildred Loving as black, and the 1967 case of *Loving v. Virginia* was viewed at the time as affirming the rights of blacks and whites to marry. For more on this issue, see Arica Coleman, *That the Blood Stay Pure: African Americans, Native Americans, and the Predicament of Race and Identity in Virginia* (Bloomington: Indiana University Press, 2013).
61. Romano, *Race Mixing*, 188–91.
62. Frank Newport, "In U.S. 87% Approve of Black-White Marriage, vs. 4% in 1958," Politics, Gallup, July 25, 2013, www.gallup.com; Gretchen Livingston and Anna Brown, "Intermarriage in the U.S. 50 Years after *Loving v. Virginia*," Pew Research Center, May 18, 2017, www.pewsocialtrends.org.
63. Dan Kopf, "Why Is Interracial Marriage on the Rise?," *Priceonomics*, September 1, 2016, https://priceonomics.com.

64. Allison L. Skinner and Caitlin M. Hudac, "'Yuck, You Disgust Me!': Affective Bias against Interracial Couples," *Journal of Experimental Psychology* 68 (January 2017): 68–77.

65. Kevin Noble Maillard, "The Multiracial Epiphany, or How to Erase an Interracial Past," in Maillard and Cuison Villazor, Loving v. Virginia *in a Post-racial World*, 95; Camille A. Nelson, "Love at the Margins: The Racialization of Sex and the Sexualization of Race," in Maillard and Cuison Villazor, Loving v. Virginia *in a Post-racial World*, 103, 104; Angela Onwuachi-Willig and Jacob Onwuachi-Willig, "Finding a *Loving* Home," in Maillard and Cuison Villazor, Loving v. Virginia *in a Post-racial World*, 184.

66. Siobhan B. Somerville, "Queer Loving," *Gay and Lesbian Quarterly* 11, no. 3 (2005): 357, 358.

67. Carol Johnson, "Heteronormative Citizenship and the Politics of Passing," *Sexualities* 5, no. 3 (2002): 330.

68. Seidman, "Polluted Homosexual," 58.

69. Katz, *Invention of Heterosexuality*.

70. Steinbugler, *Beyond Loving*, xix, xx.

3

Age Disparity, Marriage, and the Gendering
of Heterosexuality

NICHOLAS L. SYRETT

In a series of columns in the *New York Tribune* in 1850 and 1851, the
women's rights advocate and poet Elizabeth Oakes Smith addressed
what she called "woman and her needs." The greatest need in Smith's
eyes was for women to have the chance to develop as individuals, just
as men were able to do. She thought this personal development would
be possible if girls could delay marriage and if, in the interim, they were
educated and afforded access to fulfilling work. Too often, Smith wrote,
girls stepped directly "from the baby-house to the marriage altar." She
believed that there was "something painfully sad, to say nothing of
humiliating, in the sight of these baby wives to men old enough to be
guides and fathers to them, and girl mothers, hardly escaped from pan-
talets." She believed that the marriage of legal minors (those below the
age of twenty-one) was wrong because they did not know their minds
enough to make such an important commitment, especially so when
coverture made marriage oppressive for all women. Sizable numbers of
women married as minors throughout the nineteenth-century United
States, and nearly all marriages across the country were characterized by
a gendered age disparity: the girl or woman was younger than the man.[1]

Smith's voice joined a chorus of others who argued over the benefits
and dangers of youthful marriage and gendered marital age differences.
Together, these stories reveal how age has shaped the history of heterosexuality, mostly in the marital relation but often in the courtship
that led to marriage. Despite this long history of discussions about age
and marriage, historians of North America have overlooked the importance of age to heterosexual behaviors and ideals almost entirely.
My argument about its significance is twofold. First, gendered understandings of age—in the realm of both physical characteristics and life

accomplishments—have informed what made a man or woman an at-tractive prospect for marriage. Since the birth of the United States (and indeed during the colonial era as well), popular culture, advice givers, and social commentators have framed ideals of heterosexually alluring femininity around youthfulness and masculinity in terms of maturity. For many couples, understandings of age have been intrinsic to marital suitability. Attractiveness and eligibility for marriage have historically been built on age difference: men's greater age has meant that they had accomplished enough to support a family, whereas women's or girls' suitability has been predicated on their beauty and their supposed fer-tility. Men have traditionally had an age threshold for marriage linked to accomplishment; women have not.

Second, the consequences of age difference within marriages have di-minished over the course of American history just as the numerical age gaps have also shrunk. In the nineteenth century, the vast majority of American marriages united an older husband and a younger wife; their relationship with each other was shaped by the fact that the husband was more mature than his wife, at least initially. Spouses chose each other in part by evaluating life stage, rather than chronological age. A man's pre-cise age was not especially important, but he had to be independent and self-sustaining enough to support a family. This meant that he was likely to be older than his prospective bride, who herself brought youthful fer-tility to the marriage. A man's greater age was one part of what defined his masculinity and his dominance in the marital relationship. In the second half of the nineteenth century, the rise of age consciousness—of individuals knowing their dates of birth and thus their numerical years of age—shifted perceptions about whether it was beneficial to have a marital age disparity. As more and more people came to know their ages, lending credence to the notion that age was a fundamental part of one's identity, the gap in the ages of marital partners shrank. What had previously been understood in terms of a necessary difference in life stages was now recast in terms of chronological age, a more precise demarcation of identity. Because Americans were coming to believe that age—not just for courting couples but for everyone—structured one's temperament and sensibilities, prospective spouses began to choose more similarly aged marriage partners. This trend began in the later nineteenth century and accelerated over time.

Significantly, growing age consciousness occurred at the same time that more Americans came to understand marriage as the complementary or companionate union of two souls joined as one. Significant age disparities did not support this vision of marriage, and as a result, age gaps diminished over the course of the twentieth century. Broader shifts in American gender politics brought the issue of marital age disparities to the fore yet again in the 1960s and 1970s. As some activists in the women's movement encouraged Americans to see women and men as fundamentally more similar than different, marital age gaps that had shrunk but still persisted lessened even further. More couples chose similarly aged partners as spouses, partially a consequence of thinking of a spouse as a "partner" in the first place, rather than the much more gendered "wife" and "husband," words that I argue had long been coded in terms of asymmetrical age. As of 2017, large age gaps are in the minority in the United States, and more people marry similarly aged spouses than at any other time in the nation's history.[2]

Gendered marital age disparities nevertheless persist in the contemporary United States; the age gaps are just much smaller, usually only about two years. It is a testament to that persistence that the percentage of women who marry younger men is still small in comparison to those men who marry younger (sometimes much younger) women. When women marry younger men, their ages typically differ only by a year or two. Far fewer "cougars" prowl for young men than older men "rob the cradle." Age disparities in marriage partners may once have been rooted in demography and gendered expectations surrounding financial support and fertility—that is, in patriarchy—but they persist even when heterosexual marriage in the twenty-first century is no longer as tightly linked to these structural conditions. Most women now support themselves both before and after marriage, no longer solely relying on their husbands for income, and most women wait later to reproduce, meaning that youthful fertility does not drive most of them to the altar. While the phenomenon has its roots in structural forces in the American past, the tradition lives on as a symbolic form of gender differentiation within the heterosexual couple.[3]

The Changing Meanings of Age

Chronological age has a history that is overlaid with gender and race. In the United States, age was one means by which white men perpetuated what Gayle Rubin famously called "the traffic in women," moving women from dependents in one household to dependents in another, never allowing them the autonomy that came with full adulthood. In the nineteenth century, manhood was defined in large part through the adulthood gained via independence—a status explicitly impossible for enslaved men and often withheld from free black men. Although some Americans, particularly the white working classes and African Americans, were unaware of their precise ages, stage of life was correlated with status. White men who had reached independent adulthood were perceived as more manly than boys or African American adults, while white youth and adult men of color were trapped in a state of semi-dependence, in the historian Joseph Kett's memorable phrasing. For many white men, adulthood arrived at age twenty-one, both the age of majority and the age at which they could vote. The connections between manhood, adulthood, whiteness, and citizenship were thus solidified through the linkages between gender and age.[4]

For women and almost all people of color, however, chronological age was far less meaningful. No women and very few African Americans were able to vote upon reaching age twenty-one. Most black Americans were enslaved during the antebellum period, which meant that their ages were far less significant than for whites. Even following emancipation, African Americans were denied most of the perquisites of citizenship well into the twentieth century. They and poor whites also remained far less likely to be aware of their chronological ages. Impoverished people moved into some semblance of premature adulthood via work when they were big enough, not old enough. White women who reached legal adulthood often had their rights and privileges curtailed when they married because of coverture, leading many women's rights activists to refer to women as "perpetual minors," a phrase they used to denote the similarities that women (and African and Native Americans) shared with children.[5]

Age disparities within nineteenth-century marriages thus heightened white men's power both in marriage and in the outside world; women and people of color were denied the powers that came with increased age. An older white man might enter a marriage having already demonstrated several years of independent living, the ability to sustain himself economically, and perhaps the sexual experience gained through visits

Figure 3.1. James Baillie, *The Life and Age of Woman: Stages of Woman's Life from the Cradle to the Grave*, 1848 (Courtesy of the Library of Congress)

to prostitutes. The younger woman he married, especially if she had not yet reached her majority, moved seamlessly from being a dependent in her father's household to becoming her husband's dependent. She had little way of supporting herself in a world where women's wages lagged far behind those of men. She probably had little education, and she was probably a virgin. From the perspective of the wife, the spouses were often an unfortunately matched pair.[6]

Age was thus far more than simply a numeral one called oneself or the number of years one's body had been on Earth. It had a cultural meaning associated with power, status, and adulthood, though largely only for white men. White women's attractions were usually perceived, then as now, to rest in their youthful beauty. But this beauty garnered them power largely in the realm of courtship, and even then they had the ability only to refuse, never to initiate, at least if they were in the middle classes. White women's beauty was perceived to fade over time, whereas a white man's physical appearance, at least until senescence, was usually depicted as gaining in stature as he aged. As Corinne T. Field has

Figure 3.2. James Baillie, *The Life and Age of Man: Stages of Man's Life from the Cradle to the Grave*, 1848 (Courtesy of the Library of Congress)

shown, images that depicted the life course as a series of steps gained widespread popularity after the 1830s as a way for Americans to understand the gendered dynamics of aging. A white man or woman moved upward to the apex of middle age and then descended thereafter. In these images, white women tended to advance to decrepitude and unattractiveness much more quickly than white men. In the popular 1848 images by James Baillie, the woman is a bride by the fourth stage and a mother by the fifth, and at the apex of her life, she is wrinkled and haggard, already having outlived her usefulness. Although she is stooped by the seventh stage, she still has three stages left before she dies. There is no valorization here of the wisdom or capabilities of the older woman. The man, by contrast, is depicted upright and moving forward through the eighth stage; at the height of his powers, he is joined by the US flag, "proudly associating his individual journey of life with the fate of the nation," as Field has argued.[7]

The patriarchal legal regime undergirding these cultural representations of older men and women persisted through the nineteenth century.

Perhaps the most significant manifestation of these laws regulated marriage. However, over the course of the twentieth century, legislatures and courts gradually removed many of the age-related legal disabilities that women suffered in the nineteenth century. A constitutional amendment granted to most women in 1920, and eventually all women, the ability to vote upon reaching the age of majority. The percentage of women who worked for wages dramatically increased over the course of the twentieth century, giving some women a measure of autonomy over their lives unavailable when women's wages lagged much more significantly behind those of men. The gradual, piecemeal dismantling of coverture through litigation and legislation, which was not complete until states had outlawed marital rape by the 1990s, now means that women do not forfeit their legal identities or full rights when they marry. And far more women live periods of their lives as single people before marrying, if they ever choose to do so.[8]

Simultaneously, however, chronological age has become more significant than stage of life as nearly all Americans possess a birth certificate and know their birthday. Advertisers, medical practitioners, organizations for senior citizens, and various state bureaucracies bombard Americans with the meanings associated with their precise ages. However, the legal incapacities that once bound age and gender together have attenuated over the past half century. As a result, the age disparities that inhered in nineteenth- and early twentieth-century marriages had more consequence for wives and husbands than most age gaps do for contemporary American couples. Earlier marital age gaps were rooted in a patriarchal sociolegal system where men supported and controlled women via the institution of marriage. Age gaps among courting couples owed their existence to that system but also perpetuated inequality after unions were solemnized. While heterosexual marriage in the American context is no longer predicated on stark gender inequality, age disparities continue because most people continue to choose asymmetrically aged partners. Our current heterosexual marital age gaps persist as vestigial symbols of gender differentiation rather than as one of its causes.

Age asymmetry also demonstrates the socially constructed nature of heteronormativity: as some gender differences have lessened—especially related to education, work, and income—choosing an asymmetrically aged spouse allows both halves of a couple to enact the fantasy of gender differentiation on which heterosexuality depends. In this chapter, I thus make no claims to whether men and women intrinsically desire younger or older spouses. Rather, my contention is that the inclination to prefer an asymmetrically aged spouse is a product of various societal forces. The key factors shaping this choice were more often economic and structural in the nineteenth century; by the early twenty-first century, the gendered marital age disparity instead reflects the persistence of cultural expectations for heterosexual marriage in the United States. Age asymmetry remains one way of acting out heterosexuality in a world where gender differences have lessened, of performing courtship and marriage in a way that affirms one's own masculinity or femininity.[9]

The Nineteenth Century

To understand where age gaps originated, it helps to start with prescriptive expectations before looking at practice. Among these are the laws that regulated men's and women's abilities to marry. English common law, which had its antecedents in medieval canon law and Roman civil law, mandated twelve as the age of consent for marriage for girls and fourteen for boys. In Spanish and French colonies, the Catholic Church set the marriageable minimums at eleven for girls and thirteen for boys. In European settlements in North America, many colonies, and later states, legislated higher ages, but almost all maintained some age gap in their statutes until well into the twentieth century. These age disparities were premised on expectations about when boys and girls reached puberty. Of course, most people did not take advantage of the marriage minimums, but women married before men—sometimes much earlier—in all the American colonies, and legislators across the country presumed that girls and women both could and should marry before men did.[10]

A few states serve as useful examples. When Massachusetts entered the union in 1788, it imported its colonial statute on marriage with it. It set no marriageable minimums, which means it relied on the differential common-law minimums of twelve and fourteen, and then set the ages of eighteen and twenty-one as those below which a girl or boy, respectively, needed parental permission to wed. Massachusetts tinkered with its laws over the course of the nineteenth and twentieth centuries, but it maintained a differential marital consent age until the late twentieth century. When the midwestern state of Iowa entered the union in 1846, legislators set fourteen and eighteen as the minimum marriageable ages for girls and boys, respectively, mandating parental consent below eighteen and twenty-one. They lowered boys' age to sixteen in 1851 and maintained those different ages through the mid-twentieth century. Almost all states followed similar patterns, maintaining some difference in when boys and girls could marry.[11]

Beyond what legislatures permitted by statute, many nineteenth- and twentieth-century Americans believed in the salutary effects of a gendered marital age disparity. From the nineteenth through the mid-twentieth century, authors of prescriptive guides to love, romance, and marriage consistently advocated for a male-dominant age gap between husband and wife. Those writing such guides recommended ideal ages based on what they believed were physiologically the best times for women and men to marry. These were framed as recommendations about bodies, but the authors were clearly concerned about the effects of age gaps on the gendered social dynamics of marriage as well. The age gap these guides recommended was often greater than those written into state laws. William Alcott, author of more than fifty books on sex and hygiene and among the most widely read authors on the subject, published his *Philosophy of Marriage* in 1857. In it, he recommended that "first marriages should not take place, in the case of males, sooner than about the twenty-fifth or twenty-sixth year; nor in that of females sooner than the twenty-first or twenty-second year." Alcott justified these ages by explaining that this was when the "physical frames" of the sexes would be ready for marriage. Alcott never advocated for very wide gaps in marriage ages, but he nevertheless believed that men should be older than their wives. In 1847's *The Young Ladies and Gentlemen's Hymeneal Instructor*, Edward Caswall explained that "from twenty-three to twenty-six is the best age for males; and for females, from twenty to twenty-three." L. N. Fowler, in *Marriage: Its History and Ceremonies*, explained that "woman is as well qualified at twenty as man is at twenty-five."[12]

Those who dispensed advice directly to courting couples rarely advocated for gaps more than five years. Still, they also did not condemn older men marrying younger women, taking it almost for granted that young men would be unlikely to marry older women (though they might become infatuated with them in youth) but explaining that "many old men who marry young wives are aware of the nourishing effects of such unequal unions, are not such 'old fools' as many pronounce them." In 1858, *Courtship Made Easy* by Harry Hazen Jr. explained that "there should be at least four or five years difference in the ages of man and wife, the man being the oldest. It is more natural and suitable that the husband should be of superior age, and a girl that marries a man twenty years her senior will do better than she who marries one five years younger than herself." An 1870 edition of *How to Woo and How to Win* simply concluded that "as to age, it is generally conceded that the wife should be younger than the husband," noting what was by that point the consensus view. While none of these guides advocated for an older-wife/younger-husband combination, there was some variation in the justification for age gaps. For instance, in 1843, Harvey Newcomb's *The Young Lady's Guide to the Harmonious Development of Christian Character* advised that "*The person of your choice must be* NEARLY YOUR OWN AGE. Should he be younger than yourself, you will be tempted to look upon him as an inferior; and old age will overtake you first." Here Newcomb seems to acknowledge two things simultaneously, one based in biology, the other in perceptions about biology. He advises a woman not to marry a younger man because she might die first, which he presumes would be a greater inconvenience for a husband than a wife, but more interestingly he argues that women should never marry a younger man because she would perceive his youthfulness as a mark of inferiority. This particular age discrepancy would upset what he believes should be the proper arrangement within a marriage: the man is superior to his wife. Age was but one more means of assuring this marital arrangement.[13]

Beginning in the colonial era and continuing through the nineteenth century, in a wide variety of locations in the United States (and its prior colonies), and even for Americans who might have been unaware of laws or courtship-advice manuals, there were real demographic explanations for why men were older than their wives. Mostly these had to do with a shortage of women, especially in areas that were settled for commercial reasons and in areas where families did not make up the preponderance of settlers. In colonial Maryland, in the far northern reaches of nineteenth-century Alta California and New Mexico, and on the Overland Trail that stretched from Missouri to California and Oregon, girls and very young women married men who were older than they were in large part because there were so few women.[14]

Age gaps were greater in these areas because of demographic constraints, but even in areas of settlement with relatively even sex ratios— colonial New England, for instance—men were older than their brides because of the expectation that men needed to have reached an age where they were capable of supporting a wife and family. The ages at first marriage among eighteenth-century residents of Hingham, Massachusetts, for instance, varied between 24.6 and 28.4 for men, whereas women married between the ages of 22 and 24.7. Average gaps were three or four years depending on the decade, but at no time did the average age of marriage for women exceed that for men. By the nineteenth century, men needed to have inherited or been given land or trained for a profession or found some sort of job before they were ready to marry. Women, by contrast, needed only to have reached physical maturity. Among antebellum enslaved people, as well, historians estimate that the age of first marriage was higher for men than it was for women, even though male slaves were unable to support their wives financially because both men and women were enslaved by whites who controlled their labor. Assumptions about gendered maturity, in other words, exceeded their economic justifications. While most American communities encouraged girls to wait until well past menarche to wed, there nevertheless was not a structural age constraint on marriage for girls in a way that operated similarly for boys. This is where our tradition of age-asymmetrical marriage originates: men discouraged from marrying by their parents and others around them until they could support a family, girls able to marry once they reached puberty. And it continued through the nineteenth and twentieth centuries, largely because of the continued expectation that a man was responsible for supporting his wife.[15]

We have state-produced numbers for age at first marriage only beginning in the middle of the nineteenth century, when states began to collect vital statistics, at first only sporadically and semireliably. In New York State, for instance, we know that in the years 1847 and 1848, about 28 percent of girls married below the age of twenty, whereas only about 2 percent of boys did so. An average of 38 percent of both men and women married between the ages of twenty and twenty-five, but after that, numbers begin to skew, with higher numbers of men—as much as two to three times higher—in all other age brackets through the eighties. While large numbers of men and women probably married similarly aged spouses in the twenty to twenty-five bracket, there is no other way to account for the large percentage of under-twenty brides and the much higher numbers of twenty-five-plus grooms than that men were marrying women and girls younger than they were.[16]

In the mid-1850s, we have numbers for a variety of locations that confirm the pattern. In Massachusetts, Rhode Island, South Carolina, and Kentucky, between 6.5 percent (Kentucky) and 1.72 percent (Massachusetts) of grooms were below the age of twenty, whereas 22.5 percent (Massachusetts) and 42.03 percent (Kentucky) of brides were. Again the most popular age bracket for grooms or brides was between twenty and twenty-five, Massachusetts having the highest percentages in that category for women and men, and thereafter the numbers rise for men but not for women. Over 2 percent of all grooms in all four states were between fifty and sixty, and yet less than 1 percent of brides were similarly aged. Combined with the larger numbers of girls marrying under the age of twenty, it is clear that men were marrying younger women.[17]

Massachusetts, the first state to systematically collect vital statistics, actually spells out these age gaps explicitly in its reports. Between 1853 and 1856, for instance, the state's statisticians calculated that the vast majority of brides under twenty married men who were older than they were: 95 percent did so. Even at the next age bracket, twenty to twenty-five, the most popular time to marry in Massachusetts for men or women, nearly half of all brides were still marrying men who were older than they were, including a handful of men in their fifties and sixties. As the report's authors note, "fifty-one gentlemen between 50 and 60 were married, 3 to maidens under 20, 4 to females between 25 and 30, 10 between 30 and 35, 9 between 35 and 40." These annual reports' authors had been noting what they perceived as unusual age gaps since they began publishing their reports in the 1840s. The spread of age consciousness, to which the state of Massachusetts was contributing by compiling such age-based statistics in the first place, was making marriage with large age gaps seem more and more unusual as calendar age came to be further incorporated into Americans' sense of self. These gaps clearly still occurred, but they were becoming rarer and more noteworthy when they did happen.[18]

The Turn of the Century

Concerns about marital age intensified by the later nineteenth and early twentieth centuries, as age itself became much more deeply entrenched in people's understandings of their own selves. Not only did more Americans know how old they were, but they also learned to assign new and significant importance to different age-based stages of their lives. These shifts had multiple causes, among them federal age-based pension programs, Progressive-era innovations around mandatory age-graded schooling, anti-child-labor legislation, statutory rape laws, and the further spread of medical and state bureaucracies, one facet of which made birth certificates and the ability to document one's age much more widespread. In keeping with these changes, over the course of the later nineteenth and early twentieth centuries, a majority of states raised their minimum marriageable ages, and many shrank the gap between when a boy and girl might marry. This demonstrated both that lawmakers did not believe that young children should marry and also a growing recognition—at least in some states—that young women should not be permitted to enter into marriages with older men. Because legislators did not want to restrict a grown man's ability to marry, they simply restricted his prospective bride's.[19]

Commentators continued to advise readers against large age gaps but still retained the fundamental prescription that men be older than their brides. Thus, when Paul Popenoe published his best-selling *Modern Marriage* in 1925, he asserted that "a man must marry a woman who is at least slightly younger than he is." Only a slight difference in age was, of course, unlikely to have resulted in vastly different life experiences, but in the 1920s, reversing the age asymmetry of marriage would still have been seen as upending the gendered order of marriage. The point, then, was that men were meant to be older than their wives; this gendered age disparity supported the male dominance that was, for Popenoe and many others, part of what made an ideal heterosexual couple. Men took the lead in marriages, and women followed.[20] If Popenoe had softened his attitude in a 1943 revised edition, noting that about 10 percent of men married women older than they were, he still took it for granted that "the man's age also determines his wife's age, to some extent, because he tends to marry a girl a few years younger than himself, as the census figures show." In this case, Popenoe was being descriptive, but he certainly did not question the notion that men both could and would choose girls who were younger than they were.[21]

Wide marital age gaps began to appear disadvantageous only as the American middle classes adopted new ideals of marriage as the union of two complementary souls. As a result of a peer-oriented social world that developed in the later nineteenth century and that flourished by the early twentieth—a development augmented by the increasing prevalence of mandatory high school for all Americans—age gaps shrank. Young men and women were much more likely to meet future spouses in settings surrounded by people of similar ages. One study found that the percentage of couples with only a two-year age gap went from 34.7 percent in Providence, Rhode Island, in 1864 and 23.6 percent in Omaha, Nebraska, in 1875, to 43.3 percent in Providence in 1921 and 44.4 percent in Omaha in 1925. Couples separated by only three years saw similar increases. More and more Americans were marrying those who were similar to themselves in age, even though outliers continued to exist. Despite this real shift, the vast majority of men continued to marry women who were younger than they were; the size of the gap just lessened.[22]

The Postwar Years

The trends that had begun at the turn of the century continued unabated through the twentieth century: first, the importance of chronological age grew, and second, more and more Americans began to insist that marriage should be a complementary, rather than a hierarchical, relationship. This latter development was aided by the second wave of the women's movement. American lawmakers followed suit, and by the 1970s, a majority of states had equalized the minimum marriageable ages for girls and boys as well as the ages below which they required parental consent. Iowa, for instance, maintained the ages of fourteen and sixteen for boys and girls, respectively, until 1961, when it raised both ages by two years (to sixteen and eighteen), which it maintained until 1975, when it equalized the age of marriage without consent at eighteen and set as the absolute minimum sixteen with consent for both sexes.[23]

States like Iowa made these changes for two main reasons. The first was that they lowered the age of majority itself to eighteen; it had previously been twenty-one in most states (though only eighteen for girls in some). Equalizing the age of official adulthood with that for the ability to decide to marry made logical sense. Legislators were also reacting to a world transformed by the second wave of the women's movement, after which it became difficult to justify allowing girls and boys to be treated differently in the realm of age, not just in marriage law but in a whole host of other realms that lawmakers set about equalizing during this decade. That said, a number of states (Arkansas, Mississippi, New Hampshire, Ohio, and Rhode Island) continue to set differential marriageable ages, and many states allow exceptions to their minimums in one very particular set of sex-based circumstances; in cases where the prospective bride is pregnant, she may marry at an earlier age than may boys in that state.[24]

More recent courting-advice literature has increasingly emphasized characteristics other than age when evaluating a prospective marital partner. Many advice givers do not discuss age at all, beginning their tutorials either after a couple has married or once they have already met. The authors of these guides seem to believe that men and women will choose their dates and spouses on their own; their role is then to guide their readers either toward engagement or through a successful marriage. Since the mid-twentieth century, marriage advisers have presumed that Americans prioritize romance over pragmatic concerns; young people will decide for themselves whether they have met "the one." Popenoe, for instance, begins *Sex, Love, and Marriage* (1963), his follow-up to *Modern Marriage*, after the wedding; the first chapter concerns the honeymoon. Carl Rogers's *Becoming Partners* (1972) dedicates a chapter to "Shall We Get Married?" but does not weigh in on proper ages. The best-selling *The Rules: Time-Tested Secrets for Capturing the Heart of Mr. Right* (1995) also assumes that its female reader can decide on her own how old Mr. Right should be. As eHarmony, the dating website whose model is built on evaluating suitability based on "29 dimensions of compatibility," explains in wishy-washy language, "Age is relative—someone may be 60 yet have the health, looks and vitality of a 40 year old while conversely some people in their forties seem ready to collect their pensions." These givers of advice seem to presume that readers can make up their own minds who is, or is not, a suitably aged partner. They do so in a country in which most are already choosing spouses of similar ages anyway.[25]

In the meantime, the average age of first marriage has crept steadily upward over the course of the twentieth century and into the twenty-first—from 20.3 for women and 22.8 for men in 1960 to 26.1 for women and 28.2 for men in 2010. No longer are most men and women marrying in their early twenties. The idea that a man needed to be older than his wife and have the requisite professional or educational experience in order to support her at home remained popular from the time of Alcott to that of Popenoe (at least in 1943), but most couples no longer plan on such an economic and marital quid pro quo. Heterosexual couples today wait to marry until later in life, and the majority of women continue to work after marriage. As marriage has at least theoretically been transformed into more of an egalitarian love relationship between spouses, the imperative for men to be older than their wives has diminished.[26]

All that said, in 64 percent of contemporary heterosexual couples (married or otherwise), the man is still older than the woman, although the average age gap is now just 2.3 years. In 23 percent of heterosexual couples, the woman is older than the man, and in 13 percent, the difference is less than twelve months. These numbers include people of all races and ethnicities. Recent studies investigating racial difference in what demographers call "age heterogamy" indicate that there are not significant differences between racial groups. One exception is among African American women in their thirties and forties: due to a relative shortage of black men in this age cohort (eighty-nine for every one hundred women), black women are more likely than white women to date and have sexual relationships with men who are at least five years older than they are.[27]

The percentage of older-male couples has clearly diminished over time, though numbers show that the older that people marry, the greater the age gap. Indeed, older men who remarry are far more likely to have larger age gaps with their second wives than with their first. Twenty percent of remarrying men in 2013 married a woman ten or more years younger than they were; 18 percent married women six to nine years their junior. By contrast, just 5 and 10 percent of men marrying for the first time, respectively, married women with the same age gaps. Of course, this is partially because the men marrying for the first time are themselves younger and the floor below which they cannot marry is closer to their own ages, but the numbers do point to the continued salience of age gaps—and the youthfulness of women—in determining marital suitability.[28]

Studies by online dating companies, OkCupid among them, demonstrate that men are much more likely to set their age parameters for women younger than they are, whereas women are more open to experiment with men slightly younger than they are but are much more likely to date older men. Actual messaging activity is even more imbalanced. As one study explained, "men tend to focus on the youngest women in their already skewed preference pool, and, what's more, they spend a significant amount of energy pursuing women *even younger than their stated minimum*. No matter what he's telling himself on his setting page, a 30 year-old man spends as much time messaging 18 and 19 year-olds as he does women his own age." This trend persists at older ages as well, even among men who are not interested in having children, one ostensible reason they might have for being interested in younger women. One academic study found that 47 percent of men aged thirty-five to forty-four in its sample preferred a partner younger than thirty-five, whereas only 8 percent of similarly aged women did so. Another found that, among personal ads for men and women aged forty to sixty-nine, 64 percent of men but only 17 percent of women preferred a partner at least five years younger. In the twenty-first century, we continue to live in a society in which heterosexual men and women are still likely to date and marry in age-asymmetrical pairs, in part because women's attractiveness remains dependent on youth, whereas men's is linked to maturity. Age asymmetry remains embedded within what many people consider to be the DNA of heterosexuality. There are few structural reasons for this to be the case. Maintaining age differentials in marriage allows heterosexual couples to nod toward "traditional" marriage, even as their own partnerships may actually be very different from the marriages of their grandparents or great-grandparents.[29]

Coda: Consequences

Just as age gaps have declined over the course of American history, so too have their repercussions. It was simply more consequential for a young woman in the antebellum era to marry a man ten to twenty years her senior than it would be for a woman today to marry a man similarly aged or, the much more likely scenario, only two years her senior. In order to investigate some of the consequences of age gaps that do persist, however, it is helpful to return to Elizabeth Oakes Smith, with whom we began. Smith believed that the greatest problem with youthful marriage, aside from the fact that it robbed girls of girlhood, was that it made for incompatible couples and led to divorce. Young wives were not adequately prepared for either the domestic or sexual duties of their marriages, and young motherhood followed soon thereafter. Men gained a helpmeet, and women were thrust into an intimate relationship with men they might not know all that well, especially given the traditions of courtship prevalent in nineteenth-century America, in which couples often did not spend much time together alone prior to marriage. As Smith described her wedding at sixteen to her thirty-one-year-old husband in the unpublished autobiography she would write many years later, "I was so foreign to all this: so unfit for the occasion. I, a dreamy, undeveloped child—living my own life, in which worldliness did not form a single ingredient. My poor little head was not furnished with a fibre of the actual." Elizabeth Oakes Smith and her husband, Seba Smith, remained married until he died in 1868, forty-five years after their wedding. She did not consider the marriage to be a happy one, but she was opposed to divorce for religious reasons. The couple had five children together. Smith attributed a good part of her unhappiness to the "lack of sympathy" between her husband and herself, which itself was partially caused by the fifteen-year difference in their ages.[30]

In sum, age-asymmetrical marriages, especially in an era before divorce was either acceptable or available, could lead to unhappy unions between ultimately incompatible spouses. Studies show that in contemporary marriages, the larger the age gap, the more likely the couple is to divorce. One 2014 study found that a one-year age gap led to only a 3 percent chance of divorce. The rate rose to 18 percent for a five-year gap, 39 percent for a ten-year gap, and 95 percent for a gap of twenty years or more. One need not be crassly predictive with results like these, but they suggest that incompatibilities are more likely to exist between spouses separated by large numbers of years.[31]

Elizabeth Oakes Smith lived an additional twenty-five years as a widow following the death of Seba Smith. Widowhood is the statistical likelihood for women who marry older men and always has been, especially because women tend to live longer than men in the first place. According to the US Census Bureau's American Community Survey, in 2009, 3.6 percent of men aged fifteen or over had ever been widowed, whereas 10 percent of women had. Only 2.6 percent of the same sample of men remained widowers; 8.9 percent of the women did. In 2003, 29.4 percent of American women aged sixty-five to seventy-four were widowed, compared with only 8.8 percent of men of the same age; the difference between the two rates only increases as both men and women age. A number of factors account for the preponderance of widowhood, but two of them are linked to trends we have already seen. Women live longer than men do, and while the longevity of both has increased over the twentieth century and into the twenty-first, the effect has simply been to extend the period during which women remain widowed. Combined with the fact that women tend to marry men who are their seniors, they are more likely to experience widowhood than men are. Men are also more likely to remarry after becoming widowers, and men's second marriages tend to be to women who are even younger than their first wives were when they married them. The effect of this is to reduce the number of same-aged male peers that elderly widows themselves might remarry *and* to create more widows when these remarried men predecease their younger wives and leave a new set of widows behind. The overall result of age asymmetry in marriage—first, second, and subsequent—is to create a disproportionate number of widows. Almost all contemporary studies have shown that widowhood negatively affects the "health, survival, and well-being of the surviving spouse."[32]

The preference of men and women for asymmetrically aged mates also reduces the overall number of prospective husbands for women looking to marry. While the odds of a woman marrying after age forty are not, as the now famously debunked 1985 *Newsweek* cover story warned, less than the odds of being killed by terrorists, more and more women are eschewing marriage altogether. Many are doing so by choice, but large numbers of heterosexual women are also reevaluating the lives they thought they might lead as they find themselves at forty, fifty, and sixty years old without husbands. This is neither positive nor negative, in and of itself, and it is clearly a consequence of changed expectations for marital partnership on behalf of women, as well as the availability of eligible men in some populations (the high mortality and incarceration rate of black men, to name the most obvious factor). Yet, statistically, it is also clear that men's preference for younger wives has contributed to the growing rate of lifelong singlehood for women.[33]

A two-year gap in marriage ages between husband and wife, which is the average in the contemporary United States, probably has little consequence for the happiness or compatibility of the couple. If the marriage is marred by inequality—the wife performing more housework and child care than her husband, as is the case for most American marriages—it is unlikely that this labor differential is due to age disparity but instead is more likely due to the unwillingness of most American men to shoulder an equal share of domestic responsibilities. And as we have also seen, ever-growing numbers of women actually are dating and marrying younger men.

As more and more white women have joined their husbands and brothers in the workforce over the course of the twentieth century and in much more recent years as more couples join the ranks of those in which the wife actually outearns the husband, perhaps age disparities remain one way for men and women to feel they are acting out the gender differences inherent to heterosexual marriage, to have the differential age reinforce their ideas of proper wife- and husband-hood. It is not dissimilar from how some heterosexual couples also enact wedding scripts in ways that hark back to earlier traditions rooted in the patriarchal exchange of women: men asking fathers' permission to marry their daughters; men proposing to women; only women wearing engagement rings; fathers giving away their daughters in marriage ceremonies. For many contemporary brides and grooms, the gendered history behind these rituals might be noxious, but clinging to these traditions speaks to an imagined marital past that symbolically marks their union as a real marriage.[34]

The age contrast may also account for part of what brought the couple together in the first place. As sociologists of gender have long demonstrated, masculinity and femininity are mutually defining. In the history of American heterosexuality, age disparity helps constitute the very notions of masculinity and femininity. A man is a suitable partner if he is older, a woman if she is younger. While the structural forces that created the age contrast may have been dying out for the past century, age asymmetry lives on as a symbol of a bygone "traditional" heterosexuality.

NOTES

1. E. Oakes Smith, "Woman and Her Needs," no. 6, *New-York Daily Tribune*, March 21, 1851; Smith, "Woman and her Needs," no. 4, *New-York Daily Tribune*, January 23, 1851, 7; Smith, "Woman and Her Needs," no. 5, *New-York Daily Tribune*, March 4, 1851, 3.

2. On the development of age consciousness, see Howard Chudacoff, *How Old Are You? Age Consciousness in American Culture* (Princeton, NJ: Princeton University Press, 1989), chap. 2. On the transformations in marriage, see Stephanie Coontz, *Marriage, a History: From Obedience to Intimacy* (New York: Viking, 2005), chaps. 9 and 10. On the convergence of the two, see Nicholas L. Syrett, *American Child Bride: A History of Minors and Marriage in the United States* (Chapel Hill: University of North Carolina Press, 2016), chap. 5; Jonathan Vespa, Jamie M. Lewis, and Rose M. Kreider, "America's Families and Living Arrangements, 2012" (US Census Bureau, Washington, DC, 2013), 21.

3. Milaine Alarie and Jason T. Carmichael, "The 'Cougar' Phenomenon: An Examination of the Factors That Influence Age-Hypogamous Sexual Relationships among Middle-Aged Women," *Journal of Marriage and Family* 77 (2015): 1250–65.

4. Gayle Rubin, "The Traffic in Women: Notes on the 'Political Economy' of Sex," in *Toward an Anthropology of Women*, ed. Rayna Reiter (New York: Monthly Review Press, 1975), 157–210; E. Anthony Rotundo, *American Manhood: Transformations in Masculinity from the Revolution to the Modern Era* (New York: Basic Books, 1994); Joseph Kett, *Rites of Passage: Adolescence in America, 1790 to the Present* (New York: Basic Books, 1977), 29; Jon Grinspan, *The Virgin Vote: How Young Americans Made Democracy Social, Politics Personal, and Voting Popular in the Nineteenth Century* (Chapel Hill: University of North Carolina Press, 2016).

5. Corinne T. Field, *The Struggle for Equal Adulthood: Gender, Race, Age, and the Fight for Citizenship in Antebellum America* (Chapel Hill: University of North Carolina Press, 2014); Corinne T. Field and Nicholas L. Syrett, introduction to *Age in America: The Colonial Era to the Present*, ed. Field and Syrett (New York: NYU Press, 2015), 7–8.

6. Syrett, *American Child Bride*, chap. 4; Rotundo, *American Manhood*, chap. 7.

7. Field, *Struggle for Equal Adulthood*, 99, 102.

8. Nancy Cott, *Public Vows: A History of Marriage and the Nation* (Cambridge, MA: Harvard University Press, 2001); Hendrik Hartog, *Man and Wife in America: A History* (Cambridge, MA: Harvard University Press, 2000).

9. On heteronormativity, see Michael Warner, introduction to *Fear of a Queer Planet: Queer Politics and Social Theory*, ed. Warner (Minneapolis: University of Minnesota Press, 1993), 3–17. On the connections between age and sexual identities, see Nicholas L. Syrett, "Age," in *The Routledge History of American Sexuality*, ed. Kevin P. Murphy, Jason Ruiz, and David Serlin (New York: Routledge, 2020), 21–31.

10. Nicholas L. Syrett, "Statutory Marriage Ages and the Gendered Construction of Adulthood in the Nineteenth Century," in Field and Syrett, *Age in America*, 120–23.

11. Syrett, *American Child Bride*, 23–24; *Acts and Resolves Passed by the General Court of Massachusetts in the Year 1971* (Boston: Wright and Potter, 1971), 129–30; *Massachusetts Statutes*, Chapter 207, § 7, 24, 25; *Revised Statutes of the Territory of Iowa* (Iowa City: Hughes and Williams, 1843), 434; *Code of Iowa, Passed at the General Assembly of 1850–51* (Iowa City: Palmer and Paul, 1851), 221.

12. William Alcott, *The Moral Philosophy of Courtship and Marriage* (Boston: John P. Jewett, 1857), 49, 66 (on his influence, see Charles Rosenberg's introduction to *The Physiology of Marriage*, by William Alcott [Boston: Dinsmoor, 1866; repr., New York: Arno, 1972]); Edward Caswall, *The Young Ladies and Gentlemen's Hymeneal Instructor; or, The Philosophy of Love, Courtship, and Marriage* (New York: John Nicholson, 1847), 9; L. N. Fowler, *Marriage: Its History and Ceremonies, with a Phrenological and Physiological Exposition of the Functions and Qualifications for Happy Marriages*, 19th ed. (New York: Fowler and Wells, 1848), 127.

13. Edward B. Foote, *Medical Common Sense: Applied to the Causes, Prevention and Cure of Chronic Diseases and Unhappiness in Marriage* (New York: published by the author, 1863), 47; Harry Hazen Jr., *Courtship Made Easy; or, The Mysteries of Making Love Fully Explained* (New York: Dick and Fitzgerald, 1858), 6; *How to Woo and How to Win: Containing Rules for the Etiquette of Courtship, with Directions Showing How to Win the Favor of the Ladies; How to Begin and End a Courtship; and How Love Letters Should Be Written* (New York: Dick and Fitzgerald, 1870), 9; Harvey Newcomb, *The Young Lady's Guide to the Harmonious Development of Christian Character*, 5th ed. (Boston: James B. Dow, 1843), 289 (emphasis in original).

14. Lois Green Carr and Lorena S. Walsh, "The Planter's Wife: The Experience of White Women in Seventeenth-Century Maryland," *William and Mary Quarterly* 34, no. 4 (October 1977): 542–71; Syrett, *American Child Bride*, chap. 2.

15. Daniel Scott Smith, "The Demographic History of Colonial New England," *Journal of Economic History* 32, no. 1 (1972): 165–83, esp. 177; Richard Archer, "New England Mosaic: A Demographic Analysis for the Seventeenth Century," *William and Mary Quarterly* 47, no. 4 (1990): 477–502; Syrett, *American Child Bride*, 46, 59.

16. *Report of the Secretary of State, of the Number of Births, Marriages and Deaths, for the Year 1847*, Senate Report No. 73, April 12, 1848, chart following p. 7, New York State Archives, Albany; *Report of the Secretary of State, of the Number of Births, Marriages and Deaths, for the Year 1848*, Senate Report No. 86, April 10, 1849, chart following p. 7, New York State Archives, Albany.

17. *Sixteenth Report to the Legislature of Massachusetts Relating to the Registry and Return of Births, Marriages, and Deaths, in the Commonwealth of Massachusetts for the Year Ending December 31, 1857* (Boston: William White, 1858), 187.

18. *Fifteenth Report to the Legislature of Massachusetts Relating to the Registry and Return of Births, Marriages, and Deaths in the Commonwealth, for the Year Ending December 31, 1856* (Boston: William White, 1857), 149.

19. Chudacoff, *How Old Are You?*, chap. 2; Syrett, *American Child Bride*, 130–33.

20. Field and Syrett, introduction to *Age in America*, 4; Chudacoff, *How Old Are You?*, chap. 4; Paul Popenoe, *Modern Marriage* (New York: Grosset and Dunlap, 1925), 48–49.

21. Paul Popenoe, *Modern Marriage: A Handbook for Men*, 2nd ed. (New York: Macmillan, 1943), 10.

22. Chudacoff, *How Old Are You?*, 96–97.

23. Syrett, *American Child Bride*, 30–32, 134–35; *The Code of Iowa Passed at the Session of the General Assembly of 1850–1* (Iowa City: Palmer and Paul, 1851), 222; *Iowa Code*, Chapter 595, § 2.

24. Syrett, "Statutory Marriage Ages," 117–18; Syrett, *American Child Bride*, 259–60.

25. Paul Popenoe, *Sex, Love, and Marriage* (New York: Belmont Books, 1963); Carl Rogers, *Becoming Partners: Marriage and Its Alternatives* (New York: Delacorte, 1972); Ellen Fein and Sherrie Schneider, *The Rules: Time-Tested Secrets for Capturing the Heart of Mr. Right* (New York: Grand Central, 1995); eHarmony, "Does Age Matter?," accessed October 15, 2016, www.eharmony.co.uk.

26. "Table MS-2: Estimated Median Age at First Marriage, by Sex: 1890 to Present" (US Census Bureau, Washington, DC), www.census.gov.

27. Mona Chalabi, "What's the Age Difference in a Couple?," FiveThirtyEight, January 22, 2015, http://fivethirtyeight.com; Alarie and Carmichael, "'Cougar' Phenomenon," 1250, 1263.

28. Gretchen Livingston, "Tying the Knot Again? Chances Are, There's a Bigger Age Gap than the First Time Around," *FacTank: News in the Numbers*, Pew Research Center, December 4, 2014, www.pewresearch.org; Paula England and Elizabeth Aura McClintock, "The Gendered Double Standard of Aging in US Marriage Markets," *Population and Development Review* 35, no. 4 (December 2009): 797–816.

29. Christian Rudder, "The Case for an Older Woman," *Oktrends: Dating Research from OkCupid* (blog), February 16, 2010, http://blog.okcupid.com (emphasis in original); Alarie and Carmichael, "'Cougar' Effect," 1251.

30. Elizabeth Oakes Smith, "A Human Life. Being the Autobiography of Elizabeth Oakes Smith," 252, manuscript copy, Microfilm Reel 1, New York Public Library; Joy Wiltenburg, "Excerpts from the Diary of Elizabeth Oakes Smith," *Signs: Journal of Woman in Culture and Society* 9, no. 31 (1984): 540.

31. Andrew M. Francis and Hugo M. Mialon, "'A Diamond Is Forever' and Other Fairy Tales: The Relationship between Wedding Expenses and Marriage Duration," September 15, 2014, https://papers.ssrn.com; "The Bigger the Age Gap, the Shorter the Marriage," *New York Post*, November 11, 2014, http://nypost.com.

32. "Widowhood: Demography of the Widowed," *Marriage and Family Encyclopedia*, accessed October 15, 2016, http://family.jrank.org; Rose Kreider and Renee Ellis,

"Number, Timing, and Duration of Marriages and Divorces: 2009" (US Census Bureau, Washington, DC, May 2011), table 6, p. 15, www.census.gov; Wan He, Manisha Sengupta, Victoria A. Velkoff, and Kimberley A. DeBarros, "65+ in the United States: 2005" (US Census Bureau, Washington, DC, 2005), 147, www.census.gov.

33. Alarie and Carmichael, "'Cougar' Effect," 1252; Rebecca L. Traister, *All the Single Ladies: Unmarried Women and the Rise of an Independent Nation* (New York: Simon and Schuster, 2016), 29; Ralph Richard Banks, *Is Marriage for White People? How the African American Marriage Decline Affects Everyone* (New York: Dutton, 2011), 30–33.

34. On the persistence of outdated and sexist traditions in modern weddings, see, for instance, Chrys Ingraham, *White Weddings: Romancing Heterosexuality in Popular Culture* (New York: Routledge, 1999); Jaclyn Geller, *Here Comes the Bride: Women, Weddings, and the Marriage Mystique* (New York: Seal, 2001).

4

"Deviant Heterosexuality" and Model-Minority Families

Asian American History and Racialized Heteronormativity

JUDY TZU-CHUN WU

In our golden state . . . land monopoly has seized upon all
the best soil in this fair land. . . . Here, in San Francisco, the
palace of the millionaire looms up above the hovel of the
starving poor with as wide a contrast as anywhere on earth.
To add to our misery and despair, a bloated aristocracy has
sent to China—the greatest and oldest despotism in the
world—for a cheap working slave. . . . Their dress is scant
and cheap. Their food is rice from China. They hedge twenty
in a room, ten by ten. They are wipped [*sic*] curs, abject in
docility, mean, contemptible and obedient in all things. They
have no wives, children or dependents.

They are imported by companies, controlled as serfs,
worked like slaves, and at last go back to China with all their
earnings. They are in every place, they seem to have no sex.
Boys work, girls work; it is all alike to them.
—Dennis Kearney, president, and H. L. Knight, secretary,
"Appeal from California: The Chinese Invasion: Workingmen's Address," *Indianapolis Times*, February 28, 1878

At a time when Americans are awash in worry over the
plight of racial minorities—One such minority, the nation's
300,000 Chinese-Americans, is winning wealth and respect
by stint of its own hard work.

In any Chinatown from San Francisco to New York, you
discover youngsters at grips with their studies. Crime and
delinquency are found to be rather minor in scope.

Still being taught in Chinatown is the old idea that people
should depend on their own efforts—not a welfare check—in
order to reach America's "promised land." . . .

"We're a big family. If someone has trouble, usually it can be solved within the family. There is no need to bother someone else."
—"Success Story of One Minority Group in U.S.," *U.S. News and World Report*, December 26, 1966

Asian Americans are the highest-income, best-educated and fastest-growing racial group in the U.S., with Asians now making up the largest share of recent immigrants. A Pew Research survey finds Asian Americans are more satisfied than the general public with their lives, finances and the direction of the country, and they place a greater value on marriage, parenthood, hard work and career success.
—Pew Research Center, "The Rise of Asian Americans," June 19, 2012

Since the arrival of large numbers of Asian people on US soil, Asian Americans have been racialized in the United States through popular media, political rhetoric, legislation, and even academic studies in two primary ways. Beginning in the mid- to late nineteenth century, people of Asian ancestry have been feared as the "yellow peril," fundamentally and perpetually alien and threatening to US society. Beginning in the mid-twentieth century, Asian Americans also have been depicted as "model minorities," individuals who excel through hard work and who demonstrate the superfluousness of mass protest or legal intervention to redress racial discrimination.

Both the yellow peril and the model minority reveal the interconnectedness between race, class, nation, and politics in the externally imposed as well as internally constructed representations of Asian Americans. Opponents of immigration from Asia portrayed the yellow peril as a cheap, racialized, and foreign labor force that undermined the jobs, wage scales, and livelihoods of American white male laborers. The depiction of Asian people as the yellow peril helped to justify their exclusion from United States territory and polity, beginning in the late nineteenth century. At first glance, the stereotype of the model minority could not seem more different from the yellow peril. Rather than a racial threat, the model minority is a salve to a racially divided nation. In the 1950s and 1960s, the model-minority representation served as a political solution to the civil rights and racial liberation movements. During the same decades that the United States engaged in Cold War proxy battles with the Soviet Union and People's Republic of China around the globe and witnessed clashes between civil rights demonstrators and police in its streets at home, the idea of a "model minority" struck a powerful chord. The model minority affirmed an American ideal of meritocracy and rejected the need for radical systemic change to achieve social justice. Stable and nonthreatening, the model minority is a highly trained and educated professional, needed for the globalized, high-tech service economy of the mid- to late twentieth century and beyond. The representation of Asian Americans as model minorities, however, masked social-economic and ethnic disparities within these communities and overlooked Asian Americans' engagement with social activism and protest as well.

Normative understandings of gender and sexuality— heteronormativity—served as a foundation to portray both the threatening alienness of Asian people and their exemplary minority status. Chinese male immigrants, according to the Workingmen's Party of California in 1878, lacked hetero-nuclear families: "they have no wives, children or dependents." As a result, Chinese immigrants had no loyalty to the United States, choosing instead to return to China and take "all their earnings" with them. These anti-Chinese advocates also decried the lack of gender differentiation among immigrant communities: "They seem to have no sex. Boys work, girls work; it is all alike to them." These perceived qualities situated Chinese immigrants as outsiders to US society, not only due to their race and economic status but also due to their heterosexual deviancy.[1] Asian American model minorities, on the other hand, are hypernormative with regard to their family values. The Pew Research Center, a self-described nonpartisan "fact" tank on social trends affecting the United States, reported in 2012 that "Asian Americans . . . place a greater value on marriage, parenthood, hard work and career success."[2] This litany suggests that Asian Americans' commitment to heteronormativity is synonymous with their work ethic, economic achievements, and exemplary model-minority status.

Heteronormativity has shaped externally imposed racialization as well as self-identification and practices. This chapter offers a synthetic rereading of Asian American history through an intersectional analysis. This lens foregrounds the centrality of sexuality and gender for the construction of race, class, and citizenship.[3] The first two sections of the chapter focus on the interconnectedness of racial and sexual representations of Asian Americans, as exemplified by the yellow peril and the model-minority discourses, respectively. The last part of the chapter examines Asian American practices and self-depictions. In response to charges of what Jennifer Ting has described as "deviant heterosexuality," both Asian American individuals and scholars of Asian American history have emphasized the importance of nuclear family formation.[4] The ability to embody heteronormativity helped to racially and sexually integrate Asian Americans, allowing them to claim cultural citizenship in the United States.

However, Asian American individuals and communities also expanded and at times challenged racialized heteronormativity. I use the term *racialized heteronormativity* to foreground the interconnectedness between racial, gender, and sexual hierarchies that work together to privilege whiteness and heterosexuality. Some Asian Americans gained inclusion and recognition through political activism and kinship practices that advanced racial and sexual liberalism. John D'Emilio and Estelle Freedman describe *sexual liberalism* as the decoupling of sexuality from procreative and marital contexts, a trend that developed throughout the twentieth century.[5] For example, the increased accessibility of birth control helped to decrease the likelihood that heterosexual activity would result in pregnancy. *Racial liberalism*, which challenged legal, cultural, and social practices of racial hierarchy, also emerged in the twentieth century, particularly in the post–World War II era. For instance, the civil rights movement demanded equal access to voting, public accommodations, education, and jobs, regardless of race. Asian American sexual and kinship practices helped to promote both racial and sexual liberalism but in uneven ways. The formation of interracial families through marriage violated laws and social practices that protected whiteness. Transnational and transracial adoption also decoupled procreation from reproduction by making racial difference visible within American nuclear family units. The valuing of extended families and the existence of gay, lesbian, and transgender communities among Asian Americans have expanded understandings of normative kinship networks. Yet each of these practices both deviated from and also reinforced dominant understandings of sexuality, family, and race. Racialized heteronormativity, deeply embedded in US society, has structured the terms of both exclusion and inclusion for Asian Americans.

Foreign and Queer

From the mid-nineteenth century through the early decades of the twentieth, Asian American communities in the United States were predominantly male. Just over one million Asian immigrants arrived in the United States during this time period. Among the approximately 430,000 Chinese, 180,000 Filipino, and 8,000 Korean migrants, women constituted between 10 and 13 percent of the population. Out of approximately 7,000 South Asians, fewer than a dozen were women. Japanese in the United States were the only exception to this drastic gender disparity; women constituted just over one-third to slightly less than one-half of the 380,000 Japanese immigrants in this community. Higher numbers of Japanese women lived in Hawai'i, where they were recruited for labor and family-formation purposes.[6] Nevertheless, the overall skewed gender ratios fueled racialized and sexualized representations of Asian Americans, particularly on the mainland, as heterosexually deviant and hence irredeemably foreign. Both the demographic gender imbalance among Asian Americans and the cultural representations of their deviancy emerged in response to a confluence of historical factors. The expansion of the US empire with its attendant labor needs across the continent and overseas, nativist anxieties about US borders, and the increasing importance of heteronormativity in defining social order in the late nineteenth and early twentieth centuries all contributed to gendered migration patterns for Asian American communities and their racialized and sexualized representations.

Asian immigrants began arriving in large numbers in the United States as the nation itself expanded westward across the continent and overseas. Chinese, Japanese, Korean, South Asian, and Filipino laborers, most of them male, responded to the gendered labor market that drew manual laborers to the US West and to other parts of North and South

America.[7] They helped build railroads, develop agricultural and fishing industries, and manufacture consumer goods. Just as the US labor market, particularly in the West, prioritized male laborers, sending communities tended to adopt gendered migration strategies. Like other communities around the world, Asian villages and extended kinship networks primarily sent men abroad first in order to obtain work and resources for their families. Overall, most migrant communities tended to become more gender balanced over time.[8] In the case of Asian immigrants, however, exclusion laws, with one notable exception, tended to exacerbate and perpetuate gender imbalance.

As migrants around the world arrived in the United States and transformed the economic and social fabric of the nation, xenophobic movements emerged to restrict migration and limit the political rights of immigrants. The anti-Asian movements, initially based in the West, achieved national success through a series of immigration exclusion laws and court decisions that both restricted migration and designated almost all Asians as "aliens ineligible for citizenship."[9] Filipinos, whose country was subject to US colonial control, were "nationals," not aliens, but they were still not US citizens either.

While Asian male laborers were the primary targets of these exclusion laws, Asian women also felt the impact of these policies based on three heteronormative logics. First, the United States excluded Asian women on the basis of their perceived sexual deviancy and threat to white heteronormative families. The Page Act of 1875 sought to prevent the entry of contract Asian laborers as well as female prostitutes. At the time, immigration officials and the American public tended to regard all Chinese women as sex workers. This perception made it extremely difficult for any Chinese woman to enter the country.[10] They were regarded as threatening the health of white men and boys by offering "cheap" sexual services and spreading "loathsome" diseases. One white male medical doctor, who testified in the California State Senate investigation of Chinese immigration in 1876, a year after the passage of the Page Act, stated, "I am satisfied from my experience, that nearly all [white] boys in town, who have venereal disease, contracted it in Chinatown. They have no difficulty there, for the prices are so low that they go whenever they please. The women do not care how old the boys are, whether five years old or more, as long as they have money."[11] The sexually infected white men, in turn, according to another white male medical expert, then "go among white girls and distribute these diseases very generously."[12] Chinese women, in the eyes of anti-Chinese critics, represented a particularly vile threat to US society. Their inexpensive labor was blamed as the primary source of sexual contagion among white males, who in turn infected white females.

Second, the legal principle of *coverture*, a heteronormative idea that defined women's relationship to legal rights, effectively excluded many Asian women. Under coverture, a woman's legal status was determined by that of her husband or the male head of household. If a husband or father was excludable under immigration policies, then Asian women, presumed to be economically and legally dependent, were excludable as well.

Finally, Asian women were excluded due to historical timing. The exclusion policies were instituted before Asian families and communities began developing more gender-balanced migration streams. The only exception resulted from the 1907 Gentlemen's Agreement, a diplomatic bargain between the United States and Japan. At the time, Japan was a more highly respected country compared to other Asian nations.[13] Japan acceded to US requests to stop the migration of Japanese male laborers. In exchange, however, Japanese immigrant men were allowed to send for their wives. Given the expense of trans-Pacific travel, these marriages tended to be arranged ones and finalized through an exchange of photographs. This picture-bride migration allowed many Japanese and some Korean immigrants, whose country became a colony of Japan in the early 1900s, to create heteronormative intraethnic families on US soil. Other Asian immigrant communities were denied the legal opportunities to do so during the late nineteenth and early twentieth centuries.

Legal restrictions not only exacerbated gender imbalances among Asian immigrants but also deterred interracial heterosexual marriage formation. Antimiscegenation laws originated in the South to demarcate whiteness from blackness and indigeneity. These state-based policies proliferated geographically and expanded their coverage to other racialized groups. In fact, the number of states that banned Asian-white marriages increased from five in 1869 to fourteen in 1939.[14] Fears of interracial sexuality especially targeted Filipino men, who arrived in large numbers in the 1920s and early 1930s. During the "flapper" era, described as the first sexual revolution in US history, some white women crossed the racial line to dance with, date, and even marry nonwhite men. Anger at these sexualized border crossings led to riots against and even killings of Filipinos.[15] The combination of legal and social policing of interracial sexuality, in conjunction with immigration exclusion laws, sought to contain the presence of Asian people in the United States in order to protect white female racial purity. Asian Americans were unwanted outsiders to the nation, the political citizenry, and the white American family.

Cultural depictions of Asian people in the United States as the yellow peril emphasized how their racial difference, economic status, and lack of heteronormative families combined to symbolize their fundamental and threatening alienness to US society. A 1908 pamphlet, *Meat vs. Rice: American Manhood against Asiatic Coolieism*, included a section entitled "Have Asiatics Any Morals?"[16] The authors, Samuel Gompers and Herman Gutstadt of the American Federation of Labor, recounted the lack of normative families in Chinese enclaves. Citing investigations into urban slums, the authors indicated "that whatever may be the domestic family relations of the Chinese empire, here the relations of the sexes are chiefly so ordered as to provide for the gratification of the animal proclivities alone, with whatever result may chance to follow in the outcome of procreation. There are apparently few families living as such, with legitimate children."[17] While labor activists condemned these seemingly disorderly and uncivilized living arrangements, the scholar Nayan Shah has characterized these practices as a form of "queer domesticity."[18] Fascination with and moral condemnation of "queer domesticity" helped to generate a national movement for Chinese exclusion. Economic arguments resonated most strongly in the US West and among the working class. Recruited as "cheap labor" to create the economic infrastructure of the West, Asian immigrants became targets of the racial and economic resentments of the white laboring classes. As Karen Leong points out, moral critiques about their gender abnormality resonated beyond this regional political context, shaping a national conversation about Asian sexual otherness among the white middle classes that valued the sanctity of the home.[19]

Mainstream Americans' prejudices added up to an impossible set of expectations for Asian American sexuality. Subject to discriminatory immigration and marriage policies that produced "bachelor societies," Asian Americans became despised for their inability to create and perceived lack of interest in forming normative families. Anti-Asian movements even charged Japanese American families with heterosexual deviancy. They portrayed picture-bride marriages as fraudulent unions and Japanese American women as overly fecund. In the words of Senator James Phelan of California, "So long as women are admitted from Japan, so prolific are they, that even with an exclusion law, we shall have the economic evil of their presence for a great many generations."[20] Biological reproduction by Asian immigrants on US soil circumvented the intent of exclusion laws as well as other discriminatory laws, like the state-based Alien Land Laws that prevented "aliens eligible for citizenship" from owning property. As a result, Asian American women's reproductive capabilities were targeted for political critique. As the historian Kevin Starr has observed, "The Anti-Japanese lobby . . . bristled at the possibility that Japanese men might turn to white women for wives rather than remain in the enforced celibacy that characterized the Chinese experience," but the lobby also "did not want Japanese immigrants to have Japanese wives, lest they produce too many Japanese children."[21] In the midst of the emerging eugenics movement of the late nineteenth and early twentieth centuries, Japanese immigrant women were feared and condemned for their "prolific" reproductive capabilities that could result in "too many Japanese children." The representation of Asians as a "yellow peril" simultaneously produced, exaggerated, and demonized nonnormative sexuality among Asians and their descendants living in the United States. In fact, these racialized depictions of deviancy even made those who conformed to intraracial heteronormativity vulnerable to accusations of disorderly sexuality.

Profound shifts in American sexual norms at the turn of the twentieth century intensified these criticisms of Asian American gender and sexuality. Heteronormativity increasingly defined the boundaries of social acceptability and deviancy. Homosociality, or organizing one's primary social relationships with people of the same gender, had been the norm for much of the nineteenth century. By the early twentieth century, the belief that men and women had distinctly different but complementary social and sexual roles became a fundamental principle of US society. Heteronormativity became even more central for the organization of social life and the basis for defining civilized and modern society with the intense industrialization of the turn of the century and US imperial expansion. The economic pressures and social pleasures offered by modern, urban cities promoted heterosociality.[22] Also, as white Americans encountered racialized others in imperial contexts, white heteronormativity served as the basis for demarcating civilization from savagery.[23] Asian immigrants on US soil represented a foreign threat with regard to race, class, and sexuality. As one anti-Chinese movement advocate decried as early as 1878, "The [white] father of a family is met by them at every turn. Would he get work for himself? Ah! A stout Chinaman does it cheaper. Will he get a place for his oldest boy? He can not. His girl? Why, the Chinaman is in her place too! Every door is closed. He can only go to crime or suicide, his wife and daughter to prostitution, and his boys to hoodlumism and the penitentiary."[24] The white male breadwinner in this diatribe experienced economic decline simultaneously as a racialized invasion by foreigners and as the loss of gendered responsibilities and privilege. Heteronormativity constructed what was acceptable with regard to gender roles and sexuality as well as racial, class, and national citizenship.

Model-Minority Families

The recuperation of Asian Americans from aliens ineligible for citizenship and heterosexual deviants to model minorities with strong family values occurred in the middle decades of the twentieth century. As the United States formed alliances with Asian nations during World War II and the Cold War, racially discriminatory immigration policies, like the 1924 Johnson-Reed Act, which banned aliens eligible for citizenship from entering the country, became political liabilities. From 1943 to 1952, the United States Congress repealed or reformulated exclusion laws to admit token numbers of Asian immigrants and to allow them access to naturalized citizenship.[25] These rather-grudging reforms, which allowed 100 to 105 immigrants a year from Asian countries, reflected the context of decolonization and the Cold War. From 1945 to 1960, forty countries in Asia, Africa, and Latin America achieved independence from their colonial rulers. In 1955, at the Bandung Conference, Third World countries sought to assert their neutrality and independence from the Cold War battles between the United States and the Soviet Union. To win the "hearts and minds" of the Third World, the United States had to address its history and the daily reality of racial discrimination. The Jim Crow South and white resistance to the emerging civil rights movement, in particular, generated embarrassing publicity and skepticism about the United States.[26] The model-minority representation of Asian Americans that emerged in this historical moment addressed both domestic and global concerns regarding race. The model-minority emphasis on heteronormativity also reveals the centrality of gender and sexuality for demarcating racial acceptance and national security.

Scholars debate when the model-minority representation emerged in US society. More recent scholarship emphasizes that the ideal of the model minority appeared as early as World War II, as some Asian American groups were praised for their loyalty and exemplary service at the expense of other racial groups, including other Asian Americans. The concept of the "model minority" is most commonly associated with the sociologist William Peterson's January 1966 article published in the *New York Times Magazine* about the success of Japanese Americans; a similar story appeared in a December issue of *U.S. News and World Report*, celebrating the achievements of Chinese Americans.[27] Both articles lauded Japanese and Chinese Americans for their ability to overcome discrimination through hard work. As the *U.S. News* article stated, "Still being taught in Chinatown is the old idea that people should depend on their own efforts—not a welfare check—in order to reach America's 'promised land.'"[28] Similarly, Peterson's article portrayed Japanese Americans as having experienced the worst of US discrimination, including incarceration during World War II; yet the community was still thriving "by their own almost totally unaided effort."[29] These celebrations of Asian American resiliency and initiative contrasted with perceptions of African Americans as being mired in a culture of poverty, freeloaders who depended on government assistance and engaged in protest to demand redress. The articles explicitly denigrated blackness. One commented that, "at a time when it is being proposed that hundreds of billions be spent to uplift Negroes and other minorities, the nation's 300,000 Chinese-Americans are moving ahead on their own—with no help from anyone else."[30] In the aftermath of civil rights legislative victories and the growing urban riots in northern cities during the mid-1960s, the model-minority image of Asian Americans affirmed that meritocracy existed in the United States. Even if racial discrimination persisted, minorities should be able to rise above these conditions. And if they did not, then they were misguided and prone to "self-defeating apathy or a hatred so all-consuming as to be self-destructive."[31]

Heteronormativity demarcated the presumed racial exceptionalism of Asian Americans. In popular commentary about Asian Americans, the low crime rates and hard work ethic were attributed to strong family structures and values. Even ethnic spokespersons affirmed this portrayal by explaining, "The parents always watch out for the children, train them, send them to school and make them stay home after school to study."[32] The champions of the model-minority narrative even blamed social dysfunction on deviations from a patriarchal family structure. A Chinese American judge observed, "As the Chinese become more Westernized, women leave the home to work . . . , we see greater problems within the family unit—and a corresponding increase in crime and divorce."[33] The model-minority myth not only disciplined other racial groups but also Asian American women who sought alternative gender roles to that of housewife and mother.

The correlation between increased social problems and the "breakdown" of patriarchal nuclear families was central to the racial and gendered discourses of the middle decades of the twentieth century. The white, middle-class home served as a haven in the midst of fears of nuclear annihilation.[34] The hetero-nuclear family also served as a yardstick to measure social and national acceptability. Indeed, the two-parent household became the benchmark for normality during the postwar decades. The Cold War initiated both a "Red Scare," or communist witch hunt, and a "Lavender Scare," which targeted gay, lesbian, and queer individuals as supposed security risks.[35] The proliferation of white heteronormative suburbs in the post–World War II era also became the basis to critique the so-called social dysfunction of racialized inner cities. *The Negro Family: The Case for National Action* (1965), informally known as the Moynihan Report and commissioned by Assistant Secretary of Labor Daniel Patrick Moynihan, posited that the lack of traditional nuclear families among African Americans, and particularly the dominance of black women as matriarchs, fostered a culture of poverty.[36] Asian Americans as model minorities served as a racial and gender contrast to these representations of African Americans. As Ellen Wu has argued, Asian Americans during the middle decades of the twentieth century transitioned from "definitely not white" to "definitely not black."[37]

Changing demographics among Asian Americans, aided by immigration laws that privileged heterosexual families, helped Asian Americans shed associations with the "yellow peril" and instead come to be perceived as having strong nuclear families. The second- and third-generation children of Asian immigrants were certainly more gender balanced compared to the first generation. Also, the immigration policies and laws of the post–World War II era privileged heteronormative family formation. The War Brides Act of 1945, amended in 1947 to include Asian women, facilitated marriage migration for alien women who married US servicemen. The 1952 Immigration Act eliminated racial restrictions but also maintained exclusions based on mental disorders or psychopathic personalities, clauses that allowed the exclusion of individuals who were nonnormatively gendered or sexed.[38] The 1965 Immigration Act, which overhauled the 1924 immigration law by allotting equal immigration quotas for each country, facilitated large-scale migration from Asia. However, the law gave priority to skilled migration as well as heteronormative family reunification. Past immigration legislation also protected heteronormativity, as evinced by the Page Act, which sought to bar prostitution. The policies of the late nineteenth and early twentieth centuries socially engineered Asian Americans to be heterosexually deviant. By the middle to late twentieth century, Asian Americans achieved racial inclusion, both literally and figuratively, through their ability to embody heteronormativity. Their ability to enter as highly skilled and educated professionals or as members of family units gave demographic credence to the ideal of the model minority. The cultural representation of the model minority in turn upheld neoliberal approaches to governance. This political philosophy minimized government involvement in the economy and in social welfare. Strong, stable families, according to social commentators who celebrated the model-minority representation, meant that government intervention, including efforts to address historical and continuing racial inequalities, was unnecessary.

Embracing and Resisting Racialized Heteronormativity

Asian American individuals, communities, and spokespersons recognized the cultural power of heteronormativity and tended to embrace or promote gender and familial normality as a form of cultural citizenship.[39] However, Asian American kinship formations and sexual practices also deviated in practice from hegemonic understandings of family and sexuality. Interracial marriage, transnational and transracial adoption, extended kinship systems, and gay, lesbian, bisexual, transgender, and queer sexuality all challenged white heteronormativity in different ways and advanced sexual and racial liberalism. However, each of these practices also had the potential to reinscribe dominant understandings of sexuality, family, and race.

Asian American marital patterns simultaneously undermined and reinforced heterosexual norms. Once feared for their sexual transgression of the color line, Asian Americans in 2015 had the second highest rate of interracial marriage, at 28 percent.[40] This means that more than one in four Asian American have married a partner of a different racial background. Even before the 1967 Supreme Court case *Loving v. Virginia* finally ruled antimiscegenation laws unconstitutional, Asian Americans tested these racial marital boundaries. Some crossed state lines or married aboard ships to circumvent state-based marriage laws. Others hoped to find lenient or confused county clerks who would issue marriage licenses.[41] A significant community of Punjabi men and Mexican women formed families and farming communities in California, beginning in the early twentieth century. Their marriage licenses reveal a lack of consensus as to how to racially categorize these two groups and whether the marriages were permissible in light of antimiscegenation laws that prevented interracial marriage between whites and non-whites.[42] During World War II and the Cold War, Asian women married American men, of varying racial backgrounds, whom they met on or near US military bases abroad. These individual crossings of the racial line led to court cases as well as community advocacy. As Peggy Pascoe argues, organizations like the Japanese American Citizens League played a key role in helping to overturn racially discriminatory marriage laws.[43]

These recent patterns of high rates of interracial marriage, however, do not mean that Asian Americans have triumphed over racial discrimination or heteronormativity. Asian American women are more than twice as likely as Asian American men to marry interracially.[44] Asian American women also tend to marry white men more often than they marry men of other racial backgrounds. These interracial marriages do not symbolize the triumph of a color-blind society. Rather, the particular couplings reflect ingrained beliefs regarding racialized sexuality. As Ji-Yeon Yuh has argued, Korean women who marry white American military men are searching for "Prince Charming," coded white and economically well-off; correspondingly, the US soldiers are looking to fulfill their fantasy of a "Lotus Blossom," an exotic Asian woman who will cater to their every need.[45] Also, the heterosexual unions of racially and often economically privileged men with foreign women from colonial or neocolonial contexts illuminate the symbolic power of marriage. Marrying across racial, national, and class lines transforms transgressive relationships into socially legitimate kinship units. The narratives of romantic love that accompany these marriages help to mask the power inequalities between partners as well.

Asian Americans have transformed the racial composition of American families not only through marriage but also through adoption. Like international marriages, international adoptions from Asia were a by-product of militarism. The first adoptees from Korea, in the midst and aftermath of the Korean conflict, were multiracial children of American GIs and "native" women. Over time, as Kimberly McKee describes, a transnational industrial adoption complex was created by social service agencies, Christian churches, and government agencies in the United States and Asia.[46] This network also eventually facilitated the adoption of monoracial Asian children overseas, with the United States as the most popular receiving country and white, middle-class nuclear families as the most likely to successfully adopt.

Transnational as well as transracial adoptions have the potential to disrupt white heteronormativity. The racial difference between parents and adoptees draws public attention to nonnormative forms of reproduction. "Race-matching" adoption practices that were more common for the first half of the twentieth century attempted to hide adoption, thereby rendering invisible heterosexual infertility. In contrast, mixed-race families formed through adoption broadcast the disassociation of reproduction of children from biological procreation. Also, the presence of nonwhite adopted children in predominantly white families disrupts the valuing of families that maintain racial borders.

Nevertheless, international, transracial adoptions can also reaffirm white heteronormativity. White, middle-class, American families have broadcast their national, racial, and class superiority by seeking to rescue Third World children from poverty, gender discrimination, and/or communism. In addition, some white American parents also express a preference for Asian adoptees, particularly Chinese girls, because of the perception of their docility, attractiveness, and potential to become model minorities.[47] Although some gay, lesbian, and queer individuals utilize adoption for kinship formation, adoption social service agencies, religiously based organizations, and government agencies still tend to give preference to heteronormatively married and economically well-off families. A 2010 US government report indicates that adopted children, compared to stepchildren and children living with biological parents, are more likely to be living in households with married parents and with higher median family incomes.[48]

In addition to interracial marriages and transnational adoptions, other forms of Asian American kinship also can challenge dominant models of family. Nuclear families tend to be regarded as the basic social unit by most Americans. In contrast, Asian American kinship structures are often much more expansive. The so-called bachelor societies of the late nineteenth and early twentieth centuries masked a variety of kinship arrangements. Immigrant men had transnational families in Asia, and sometimes they had more than one wife. Many Asian American men lived and worked with brothers and uncles. Some of these relationships were biological and represented an extension of Asian kinship ties. Others were "fictive," created by those struggling to survive in a hostile land and seeking allies. Still others were formalized into family associations that provided social services, information about jobs and lodging, avenues for communication back to the homeland, and advocacy.

Asian American attachment to extended family commitments confounded US immigration and refugee officials. The architects of the 1965 Immigration Act had not anticipated the large-scale migration from Asia that resulted from the family reunification clause of the policy. Since most Americans had ancestral connection to Europe, the designers of the policy expected white Americans to utilize this clause. To their surprise, Asian Americans became the fastest growing racial group in the United States, increasing from one million in 1965 to nearly twenty million in 2013.[49] They entered not just as medical personnel, engineers, and entrepreneurs but also as immediate and extended members of family already in the United States. Southeast Asian refugees who arrived in the aftermath of the US war in Vietnam also challenged resettlement policies that tried to scatter nuclear families around the country to lessen the financial and cultural burden of refugee relocation on the US public. After this initial resettlement, Vietnamese, Cambodian, Laotian, and Hmong refugees frequently engaged in secondary resettlement to reconstitute extended families and clans. These kinship ties were not fully recognized by humanitarian, resettlement, or welfare agencies, but they were crucial for refugee communities.[50]

These extended kinship networks, which countered heteronormative nuclear forms of family, nevertheless tended to reassert patriarchal forms of family. Even so, the impact of war and refugee relocation also provided opportunities to reshape gender roles. Women became heads of households, at times due to war-related deaths or due to the mental and economic distresses of refugee migration and dislocation. Women also could "bargain" with patriarchy.[51] Due to the changed circumstances of living as racialized refugees in the United States, some Vietnamese women gained greater leverage within their families given their relative earning power compared to Vietnamese refugee men. Southeast Asian Americans have been lauded as model minorities, and there are economically successful as well as highly educated members within this community. However, overall, Southeast Asian Americans (namely, Vietnamese, Cambodian, Laotian, Thai, and Hmong) have the lowest educational attainment rates and the highest rates of poverty among all Asian Americans. As a result of the abrupt circumstances of refugee relocation and the trauma of fleeing war-torn societies, substantial portions of the Southeast Asian American community have higher indices of socioeconomic poverty, even in comparison with the national average.[52] Facing structural forms of discrimination based on race, language, culture, and refugee status, Southeast Asian Americans frequently turn to their extended kinship network for social and economic support.

Finally, Asian American gay, lesbian, trans, bisexual, and queer individuals also challenge white heteronormativity.[53] Nayan Shah illuminates a range of "stranger intimacies" practiced by Asian American men during the late nineteenth and early twentieth centuries with partners of varying racial, class, and gender backgrounds in the US West.[54] My past work also explored the interracial, homoerotic intimacies of Margaret Chung, the first US-born woman of Chinese descent to become a physician.[55] She never married but instead engaged in romantic and intense relationships with the lesbian poet Elsa Gidlow and the singer Sophie Tucker. Chung even formed her own alternative family by adopting over one thousand American soldiers, politicians, and entertainers as an expression of her dual patriotism toward the United States and China during World War II.

In contemporary society, Asian American queer individuals and organizations navigate both racialized heteronormativity and "homonationalism."[56] Asian American LGBTQ individuals and scholars challenge the presumption that homosexuality is a "Western disease"; this position is commonly articulated by Asian as well as Asian American critics, seeking to mark nonnormative sexuality as foreign to their cultures and communities.[57] Asian American queers also critique the white LGBTQ community for either marginalizing nonwhites or else eroticizing their racial differences. In the post-9/11 era, Jasbir Puar has identified a political movement to incorporate white, middle-class, gay men as well as lesbians and feminists, recuperating them as legitimate and respectable members of the US nation.[58] This form of "homonationalism," however, comes at the expense of racialized and Orientalized bodies, who are marked as terrorist and queer, subject to detention, deportation, and torture. Just as other sexual and kinship practices partially challenge white heteronormativity, Asian American LGBTQ individuals face continued predicaments. The privileging of heterosexuality has not disappeared, either in US society or within ethnic communities or in Asian countries. Homonationalism promises inclusion for some but also reinforces religious, racial, class, and sexual boundaries.

Conclusion

Heteronormativity is foundational to the racialization of Asian Americans. As both yellow peril and model minority, Asian people in the United States have been alternately despised and respected. The presumed gender and sexual deviancy of Asian Americans during the late nineteenth and early twentieth centuries reinforced their perceived alienness from US society. In contrast, the depiction of Asian Americans as members of model families from the mid-twentieth century onward was crucial to their rebranding as model minorities.

Neither of these externally imposed representations fully captured the range of Asian American kinship formations and sexual practices. In many ways, interracial marriage, transnational and transracial adoption, extended and fictive kinship networks, and the lives of LGBTQ-identified individuals reveal how Asian Americans have contested white heteronormativity and advanced both racial and sexual liberalism. At the same time, each formation also reveals the persistent power of racialized heterosexuality to shape not only normative society but also those who challenge those values.

The dominant image of Asian Americans as a "yellow peril" shifted to the idea of the "model minority" nearly seventy years ago, yet both representations continue to have enormous cultural power. The recent uproar over Amy Chua, the author of the 2011 *Battle Hymn of the Tiger Mother*, demonstrates how easily Americans conflate the model-minority and the yellow-peril images. Chua, a law professor at Yale, gained notoriety for revealing her draconian methods of raising high-achieving children. Her approach of long hours of musical practice, high expectations of children's grades, and no play dates drew some praise but also much criticism for her excessive parenting style. In the words of *Time*'s writer Vivia Chen, "Amy Chua is an easy whipping post. . . . Overnight, she became the archetype of the nightmare Asian mom, hell bent on raising uber-achievers at all cost."[59] Chua's methods produced model-minority children, ready to compete in a globalized and neoliberal economy. However, the criticism of Chua also evoked yellow-peril rhetoric. Chua was both model minority and yellow peril, a tiger mom and a dragon lady. Representing her methods as traditionally Chinese, Chua symbolized both supercompetitive Asian Americans (outperforming even whites) and the specter of China (a global economic power that threatens the US economy). The tiger-mom controversy reminds us of the persistence of racialized and sexualized representations of Asian Americans and how these cultural scripts can be exploited by individuals seeking recognition and acceptance in US society.

NOTES

My thanks to Rebecca Davis and Michele Mitchell for their insightful comments and encouragement. I also want to express my deep appreciation to members of our Asian American Women's History Writing Group for their support and suggestions. They are Kelly Fong, Dorothy Fujita-Rony, Jane Hong, Valerie Matsumoto, Isabela Quintana, and Susie Woo.

1. Dennis Kearney, president, and H. L. Knight, secretary, "Appeal from California: The Chinese Invasion: Workingmen's Address," *Indianapolis Times*, February 28, 1878, http://historymatters.gmu.edu. Karen J. Leong, "'A Distinct and Antagonistic Race': Constructions of Chinese Manhood in the Exclusionist Debates, 1869–1878," in *Across the Great Divide: Cultures of Manhood in the American West*, ed. Matthew Basso, Laura McCall, and Dee Garceau (New York: Routledge, 2001), 131–48; Nayan Shah, *Contagious Divides: Epidemics and Race in San Francisco's Chinatown* (Berkeley: University of California Press, 2001).

2. Pew Research Center, "The Rise of Asian Americans," June 19, 2012, updated April 4, 2013, www.pewsocialtrends.org.

3. Yu-Fang Cho, *Uncoupling American Empire: Cultural Politics of Deviance and Unequal Difference, 1890–1910* (Albany: SUNY Press, 2014); Amy Sueyoshi, *Discriminating Sex: White Leisure and the Making of the American "Oriental"* (Urbana: University of Illinois Press, 2018).

4. Jennifer Ting, "Bachelor Society: Deviant Heterosexuality and Asian American Historiography," in *Privileging Positions: The Sites of Asian American Studies*, ed. Gary Y. Okihiro, Marilyn Alquizola, Dorothy Fujita Rony, and K. Scott Wong (Pullman: Washington State University Press, 1995), 271–79.

5. John D'Emilio and Estelle B. Freedman, *Intimate Matters: A History of Sexuality in America*, 3rd ed. (Chicago: University of Chicago Press, 2012).

6. Ronald Takaki, *Strangers from a Different Shore: A History of Asian Americans* (Boston: Little, Brown, 1998).

7. Erika Lee, *The Making of Asian America: A History* (New York: Simon and Schuster, 2015).

8. Donna Gabaccia, *From the Other Side: Women, Gender, and Immigrant Life in the U.S., 1820–1990* (Bloomington: Indiana University Press, 1995). Some exceptions to this gendered pattern include Irish and Jewish migrations to the United States.

9. The legislation and treaties included the 1882 Chinese Exclusion Law, the 1907 Gentlemen's Agreement, the 1917 Asiatic Barred Zone, the 1924 Immigration Act, and the 1934 Tydings-McDuffie Act. Along with the 1790 Naturalization Act, which restricted naturalization to free, white individuals, the Supreme Court cases of *Ozawa* (1922) and *Thind* (1923) affirmed Asian immigrant ineligibility for US citizenship.

10. Sucheng Chan, *Entry Denied: Exclusion and the Chinese Community in America, 1882–1943* (Philadelphia: Temple University Press, 1991); Martha Gardner, *The Qualities of a Citizen: Women, Immigration, and Citizenship, 1870–1965* (Princ-

eton, NJ: Princeton University Press, 2005); Erika Lee, "Exclusion Acts: Chinese Women during the Chinese Exclusion Era, 1882–1943," and Jennifer Gee, "Housewives, Men's Villages, and Sexual Respectability: Gender and the Interrogation of Asian Women at the Angel Island Immigration Station," in *Asian/Pacific Islander American Women*, ed. Shirley Hune and Gail M. Nomura (New York: NYU Press, 2003) 77–105; George Pfeffer, *If They Don't Bring Their Women Here: Chinese Female Immigration Before Exclusion* (Urbana: University of Illinois Press, 1999).

11. Quoted in Shah, *Contagious Divides*, 86.

12. Quoted in Shah, 87.

13. Japan's victory in the 1904–5 Russo-Japanese War signaled that it was a rising world power.

14. Peggy Pascoe, *What Comes Naturally: Miscegenation Law and the Making of Race in America* (New York: Oxford University Press, 2009).

15. Rick Baldoz, *The Third Asiatic Invasion: Empire and Migration in Filipino America, 1898–1946* (New York: NYU Press, 2011).

16. Samuel Gompers and Herman Gutstadt, *American Manhood against Asiatic Coolieism: Which Shall Survive?* (San Francisco: Asiatic Exclusion League, 1908).

17. Gompers and Gutstadt, 17–18.

18. Shah, *Contagious Divides*, 77–104.

19. Leong, "Distinct and Antagonistic Race," 145.

20. Quoted in Catherine Lee, *Fictive Kinship: Family Reunification and the Meaning of Race and Nation in American Migration* (New York: Russell Sage Foundation, 2013), 63.

21. Kevin Starr, *Embattled Dreams: California in War and Peace, 1940–1950* (New York: Oxford University Press, 2002), 61.

22. Kathy Peiss, *Cheap Amusements: Working Women and Leisure in Turn-of-Century New York* (Philadelphia: Temple University Press, 1986); Carroll Smith-Rosenberg, *Disorderly Conduct: Visions of Gender in Victorian America* (New York: Oxford University Press, 1986).

23. Gail Bederman, *Manliness and Civilization: A Cultural History of Gender and Race in the United States, 1880–1917* (Chicago: University of Chicago Press, 1996); Jonathan Ned Katz, *The Invention of Heterosexuality* (Chicago: University of Chicago Press, 2007); Victor Roman Mendoza, *Metroimperial Intimacies: Fantasy, Racial-Sexual Governance, and the Philippines in U.S. Imperialism, 1899–1913* (Durham, NC: Duke University Press, 2015); Setsu Shigematsu and Keith L. Camacho, eds., *Militarized Currents: Toward a Decolonized Future in Asia and the Pacific* (Minneapolis: University of Minnesota Press, 2010).

24. Kearney and Knight, "Appeal from California."

25. Cindy I-Fen Cheng, *Citizens of Asian America: Democracy and Race during the Cold War* (New York: NYU Press, 2013); Madeline Y. Hsu, *The Good Immigrants: How the Yellow Peril Became the Model Minority* (Princeton, NJ: Princeton University Press, 2015); Ellen D. Wu, *The Color of Success: Asian Americans and the Origins of the Model Minority* (Princeton, NJ: Princeton University Press,

2014). Also see Iyko Day, *Alien Capital: Asian Racialization and the Logic of Settler Colonial Capitalism* (Durham, NC: Duke University Press, 2016); Moon-Ho Jung, *Coolies and Cane: Race, Labor, and Sugar in the Age of Emancipation* (Baltimore: John Hopkins University Press, 2008); and Lisa Lowe, *The Intimacies of Four Continents* (Durham, NC: Duke University Press, 2015), for model-minority-like representations of Asian Americans prior to the twentieth century.

26. Mary L. Dudziak, *Cold War Civil Rights: Race and the Image of American Democracy* (Princeton, NJ: Princeton University Press, 2011).

27. William Petersen, "Success Story, Japanese-American Style," *New York Times Magazine* January 9, 1966; "Success Story of One Minority Group in U.S.," *U.S. News and World Report*, December 26, 1966.

28. "Success Story of One Minority Group in U.S."

29. Peterson, "Success Story, Japanese-American Style."

30. "Success Story of One Minority Group in U.S."

31. Peterson, "Success Story, Japanese-American Style."

32. "Success Story of One Minority Group in U.S."

33. "Success Story of One Minority Group in U.S."

34. Elaine Tyler May, *Homeward Bound: American Families in the Cold War* (New York: Basic Books, 2008).

35. David K. Johnson, *The Lavender Scare: The Cold War Persecution of Gays and Lesbians in the Federal Government* (Chicago: University of Chicago Press, 2006).

36. *The Negro Family: The Case for National Action* (Washington, DC: Office of Policy Planning and Research, US Department of Labor, March 1965).

37. Wu, *Color of Success*, 2.

38. Margot Canaday, *The Straight State: Sexuality and Citizenship in Twentieth-Century America* (Princeton, NJ: Princeton University Press, 2011).

39. Shah, *Contagious Divides*.

40. Wendy Wang, "Interracial Marriage: Who Is 'Marrying Out'?," Pew Research Center, June 12, 2015, www.pewresearch.org.

41. Karen Leonard, *Making Ethnic Choices: California's Punjabi Mexican Americans* (Philadelphia: Temple University Press, 1994); Pascoe, *What Comes Naturally*.

42. Antimiscegenation laws did not prevent nonwhite individuals of different racial backgrounds from marrying each other. However, Mexican Americans were at times categorized as "white," and South Asians, accordingly to anthropological studies, were "Caucasians." However, both Mexican and South Asian Americans were also treated and legally categorized as nonwhite as well. The variability in racial status for Mexican and South Asian Americans caused confusion and provided leeway for local marriage-license clerks who could prevent or allow interracial marriages. Also see Ian F. Haney López, *White by Law: The Legal Construction of Race* (New York: NYU Press, 2006).

43. Pascoe, *What Comes Naturally*.

44. While 17 percent of Asian American men marry interracially, 37 percent of Asian American women marry interracially. Wang, "Interracial Marriage."

45. Ji-Yeon Yuh, *Beyond the Shadow of Camptown: Korean Military Brides in America* (New York: NYU Press, 2004).

46. Kimberly McKee, *Disrupting Kinship: Transnational Politics of Korean Adoption in the United States* (Urbana: University of Illinois Press, 2019); Catherine Ceniza Choy, *Global Families: A History of Asian International Adoption in America* (New York: NYU Press, 2014); Arissa H. Oh, *To Save the Children of Korea: The Cold War Origins of International Adoption* (Stanford, CA: Stanford University Press, 2015).

47. Andrea Louie, *How Chinese Are You? Adopted Chinese Youth and Their Families Negotiate Identity and Culture* (New York: NYU Press, 2015).

48. Rose M. Kreider and Daphne A. Lofquist, "Adopted Children and Stepchildren: 2010" (US Census Bureau, Washington, DC, April 2014), www.census.gov.

49. "Asian/Pacific American Heritage Month: May 2015" (US Census Bureau, Washington, DC, 2015), www.census.gov.

50. Nazli Kibria, *Family Tightrope* (Princeton, NJ: Princeton University Press, 1995); Eric Tang, *Unsettled: Cambodian Refugees in the New York City Hyperghetto* (Philadelphia: Temple University Press, 2015); Khatharya Um, *From the Land of Shadows: War, Revolution, and the Making of the Cambodian Diaspora* (New York: NYU Press, 2015); Chia Youyee Vang and Faith Nibbs, *Claiming Place: On the Agency of Hmong Women* (Minneapolis: University of Minnesota Press, 2016).

51. Kibria, *Family Tightrope*.

52. White House, "Critical Issues Facing Asian Americans and Pacific Islanders," Initiative on Asian Americans and Pacific Islanders, accessed July 15, 2016, www.whitehouse.gov.

53. David L. Eng and Alice Y. Hom, *Q&A: Queer in Asian America* (Philadelphia: Temple University Press, 1998); Gayatri Gopinath, *Impossible Desires: Queer Diasporas and the South Asian Public Cultures* (Durham, NC: Duke University Press, 1995); Russell Leong, *Asian American Sexualities: Dimensions of the Gay and Lesbian Experience* (London: Routledge, 1996); Marin F. Manalansan IV, *Global Divas: Filipino Gay Men in the Diaspora* (Durham, NC: Duke University Press, 2003).

54. Nayan Shah, *Stranger Intimacy: Contesting Race, Sexuality and Law in the North American West* (Berkeley: University of California Press, 2012). Also see Amy H. Sueyoshi, *Queer Compulsions: Race, Nation, and Sexuality in the Affairs of Yone Noguchi* (Honolulu: University of Hawai'i Press, 2012).

55. Judy Tzu-Chun Wu, *Doctor "Mom" Chung of the Fair-Haired Bastards: The Life of a Wartime Celebrity* (Berkeley: University of California Press, 2005).

56. Jasbir Puar, *Terrorist Assemblages: Homonationalism in Queer Times* (Durham, NC: Duke University Press, 2007).

57. Monisha Das Gupta, *Unruly Immigrants: Rights, Activism, and Transnational South Asian Politics* (Durham, NC: Duke University Press, 2006).

58. Puar, *Terrorist Assemblages*.

59. Vivia Chen, "Why the Tiger Mom's New Book Makes You Nervous," *Time*, January 31, 2014, www.time.com.

PART II

Difference, Bodies, and Popular Culture

5

Defining Sexes, Desire, and Heterosexuality in Colonial British America

SHARON BLOCK

Colonists in North America wrote about sex and sexed bodies regularly. They gossiped about sex acts, joked about eroticized bodies, and peppered their writings with sexual innuendos. Beliefs about how bodies were meant to interact erotically and between whom sexual acts were expected to occur underlay these conversations and commentaries. When writers discussed "the sexes" or referred to women as "the sex," they relied on a shared understanding of how male and female bodies were naturally differentiated. When Anglo-American colonists told stories about sexual escapades or commented on an individual's erotic appeal, they were both relying on and instantiating the ways that people labeled "men" or "women" were supposed to relate to one another. These definitions of sexed bodies were inseparable from assumptions of innate sexual attraction between women and men. Rather than taking such ideologies for granted, this chapter explores the constructed nature of sex-related beliefs. It reveals the many ways that expectations and practices of heterosexuality undergirded not only sexuality and gender but an array of broad social constructs. Analyzing the subtle operations of heterosexual discourse in colonial America recasts seemingly unremarkable commentaries into important evidence about a fundamental organizing structure of colonial society.

The history of sexuality has come a long way from one scholar's assertion in 1986 that the topic was worth studying because "the sex-drive . . . has repercussions on how men relate to other people and how they go about their work."[1] Modern historians of sexuality do not generally focus on an innate sex drive unencumbered by cultural meaning, let alone one that is primarily applicable to men. Scholarship on early American sexuality in particular has exploded in recent decades, building a more sophisticated understanding of its intersections with gender, masculinity, patriarchy, and racial hierarchies.[2] Yet as this anthology shows, studies of sexuality have had their own limitations: historians have too often relied on unquestioned assumptions of the naturalness of male-female sexual interactions in their studies. This oversight has persisted, despite decades-old calls for "a heterosexual history which needs to be recognized and explored, rather than simply taken for granted."[3]

Such overlooked definitional questions are essential to the history of early America, an era of settler colonialism that lay the groundwork for definitions of bodies, belonging, race, and sexuality. Thus it makes particular sense to interrogate eighteenth-century heterosexuality as a system of practices and ideals, rather than limiting the term to a contemporaneously explicit category of sexualized identity. Heterosexuality, as a broadly understood and intrinsically racialized norm of sexual relationships between men and women, structured colonial American men's patriarchal power over their own and other men's sexual access to women.[4] And yet most scholars of early American sexuality have not seen heterosexuality as an explicit conceptual theme: the indexes of a dozen books important to the development of early American sexuality reveal almost no entries for the term.[5] Nevertheless, the central place of heterosexuality to colonial definitions of women's and men's gender roles necessitates that scholars better analyze and mark its often unstated power. Part of better integrating the histories of same-sex sexual relations into histories of sexuality requires decentering what Jen Manion productively terms "heteroessentialism," which Manion defines as "the widespread failure by historians to consider the role that heterosexuality plays in giving meaning and stability to individual subjects as well as to social, political, legal, and economic institutions."[6] Naming heterosexuality as an analytic category does not negate possibilities of sexual fluidity or varieties of practiced sexual ideologies; instead, it helps to better explain the structure of gendered and sexed power in the eighteenth century.

Manion's important work is not the first feminist scholarship to critique the ways that scholars' implicit assumptions of heterosexuality have erased the relationship between heterosexual norms and the history of same-sex desires. From Carroll Smith-Rosenberg's foundational work on the female world of love and ritual to Adrienne Rich's essay about compulsory heterosexuality to Judith Bennett's examination of the "lesbian problem," scholars have interrogated women's desire, love, and affection for each other and have chided historians for viewing the past "in heteronormative terms" that presume most historical actors desired members of the "opposite" sex.[7] Their critiques ring true about early American historical scholarship. For example, in a 2003 introduction to a special issue on the history of sexuality in the *William and Mary Quarterly*, Kathleen M. Brown and I asked how best to study "relationships between masters and enslaved women [that] present one of the most challenging examples of how difficult it can be to analyze the relationship of sex to power in the past."[8] Undoubtedly, historians still have much work to do in documenting and analyzing the sexual abuse of enslaved women.[9] But that sentence also wrongly presumed the sexual abuse of enslaved women by masters while eliding that reality for enslaved men.[10]

While feminist theorists may have offered early critiques of assumed heteronormativity, social history scholarship on same-sex sexual relations in colonial America has largely focused on men. This is partly a result of colonists' tendency to more explicitly define male-male sexual interactions as legally transgressive, thus producing documentary evidence for historical interrogation.[11] More recently, scholars have productively employed theories of queerness and creatively analyzed expressions of desire to show that we can write histories of same-sex homoeroticism, sexuality, and desire and to question the very nature of an early American category of "sexuality" that is divisible from other social structures.[12] Such work has been important in correcting mainstream assumptions of unexamined heteroessentialism.

Moving beyond heteronormative assumptions requires marking that which is regularly unmarkable, in other words, working to define a history of heterosexuality. Some scholars would argue that "heterosexuality" is irrelevant before the late nineteenth-century rise of sexology and sexual identities. Jonathan Ned Katz, following Michel Foucault's groundbreaking *History of Sexuality*, importantly argued that heterosexuality was modern invention and that its fabrication required the language of the dialectic of homosexuality/heterosexuality. For this chapter, I am less interested in the timing of the development of that historically significant language than in thinking through how we can move beyond "our usual assumption of an eternal heterosexuality" to interrogate how heterosexual norms operated in early American society.[13] As a scholar of the eighteenth century, I find myself unwilling to cede the meaning of heterosexuality to the modern period's rise of psycho-medical definitions.[14]

I use "heterosexuality" in the broadest sense of practices and systems, rather than the post-Freudian development of an individual's sexual identity. To be sure, this means a different concept of heterosexuality than that which would come to dominate in the twentieth century. The development of the homo/heterosexual binary, to my mind, does not have to negate the value of deconstructing the implicitly heterosexual ideologies and practices of earlier times. I view heterosexuality in earlier periods as a set of organizing features that linked intimacy and social structure to transform desire into cultural capital. Heterosexual norms might include the naturalized expectations of oppositional features in men's and women's bodies, the assumptions that sexualized desire should find outlets in male-female marriages, or that settler-colonial men's racialized erotic power was a key to productive civilization.

The field of critical race studies informs my approach to the history of heterosexuality. In 1990, the literary scholar Ann duCille wrote a critique of the first comprehensive survey of the history of sexuality, *Intimate Matters* by John D'Emilio and Estelle Freedman. "'Othered' Matters" recognized the massive accomplishments of *Intimate Matters* while questioning the dangers of replicating the "sexuality of the othered."[15] Since duCille's piece, numerous scholars in African American, postcolonial, and Indigenous studies have interrogated the means by which we build archives and claim evidence. Only by paying attention to the silences in our sources and our histories—that which is not named, not spoken, and often literally unremarkable—do we see the underpinnings of a society's most central features.[16] Deconstructing the objectivity of the archive pushes us to think about how presumably normative forms of sexuality were encoded in historical records. To what degree have early American historians missed opportunities to critically analyze the period's heterosexual institutions by treating them as natural reality, in a way that they would not, for instance, treat racial divisions?

Colonial understandings of heterosexuality shaped how British American colonists discussed and understood the concept of the sexes.

In the decades before the American Revolution, colonial publications mentioned the sexes not just as demographic identifiers but in reference to romantic and sexual relations that were presumed to be heterosexual. Discussion of women as a group surfaced largely in relation to sexual matters, linking their sexed bodies to expected erotic behavior. Recentering corporeality suggests that evaluations of desirability, beauty, and erotic appeal were a means to implement eighteenth-century heterosexuality. Both private and public writings show how descriptions of individuals' appearance worked to naturalize different-sex attraction and to create what we can describe as a heterosexual norm.[17] Public ideals of beauty foregrounded male evaluations of women, again setting desire into a male-defined heterosexual framework. Men regularly described women as objects of their attraction, tying desirability to heterosexual and marital relations. Women's extant personal writings suggest that they, too, might evaluate men through a framework of heterosexual desire, thus strengthening a system beyond the overtly male gaze of early American print culture. In a society increasingly defined by a race-based slave-labor system, British colonists limited expressions of erotic desirability to those identified as being of European heritage. Whether referring to sexed bodies, employing generic classifiers based around heterosexual norms, or not noting the beauty of non-European women, colonists simultaneously instantiated colonial racial and heterosexual divisions. They relied on a system of intimate relations that positioned men as sexual pursuers of women, giving naturalized meaning to heterosexual beliefs and practices.

Defining the Sexes

While colonists did not use terms of binary opposition between men and women—the term "opposite sex" did not enter widespread usage until the twentieth century—their assumptions about the naturalness of male-female sexual relations conveyed their presumptions about sex-identified bodies.[18] Colonists had a range of sexed-body related phrases to choose from: "sexes," "both sexes," "two sexes," "the sexes," and "the sex" (referring to women) all appeared in colonial print. Scholars have scrutinized the degree to which a one-sex (female bodies as an inferior version of male bodies) or two-sex (male and female bodies as oppositional) model held sway in early modern Europe.[19] Aspects of both models coexisted in eighteenth-century popular thought. Moreover, bodies did not have to be understood in oppositional male-female terms (two-sex model) for colonists to see them as belonging together sexually. This expression of what we might call complementary heterosexuality appears repeatedly in late-colonial newspapers' terminology related to the sexes.

Colonists were comfortable using "sexes" to reference basic demographics of colonial social structure. The *America's Historical Newspapers* database identifies over nine hundred mentions of the "sexes" in the colonial eighteenth century. "Sexes" appeared in print with no definite or indefinite article (i.e., "a" or "the") to mark demographic divisions: a census might track "all colours, sexes, and ages," a funeral sermon could be addressed to people of "all Nations, Sexes, and Ages," or "Dr. Ryan's Incomparable Worm Destroying Sugar Plums" could claim to cure disorders in persons of "All Ages, Sexes and Constitutions."[20] By aligning sex alongside age, constitution, and nationality, colonists revealed their humoral understandings of bodies in contrast to modern notions of inherent biology of sex and race. Colonists understood the sexes as male and female, but they also saw that bodily division intersecting with other determinative life experiences.

The inclusive term, "both sexes," appeared in advertisements as a way to signal the social appropriateness of the product or service for women and men, implicitly marking male and female gender expectations. Late-colonial newspapers regularly advertised schooling for "Children of both Sexes" or entertainment for "both Sexes."[21] Occasionally, such advertisements did have some relation to sexual behavior: one doctor claimed that he could cure "gonorrhea . . . in both sexes," while an advertisement for "Keyser's Pills" offered a cure of the "*secret disease*" in "both sexes."[22] "Both sexes" in these advertisements seemed to be used to emphasize women's inclusion in an arena that might not necessarily be understood to apply to them.

Colonists added an article or adjective before "sexes" (such as "the" or "both") in order to invoke male and female difference. Print mention of "the sexes" emphasized the hetero-nature of men and women by constructing them as opposites or as two halves of a whole. A column on matrimony focused on the "Battle of the Sexes."[23] As one Revolutionary-era newspaper proclaimed, "the two Sexes ought to be perfected by one another."[24] Colonial print culture regularly used "the sexes" to divide bodies into male and female within the context of heterosexual relationships and behavior. Newspaper essays on men's and women's intimate relationships used the terms "both Sexes" or "two Sexes"; authors offered matrimonial advice to "both Sexes of all Ages."[25] A risqué memoir from 1750 discussed the "commerce that is carried on between the two Sexes" and rhetorically asked, "what is Love, but the Union of the two Sexes?"[26] Despite the generic classificatory usage of "sexes," the term's use was based in a heterosexual understanding of human sexuality.[27]

It was not just that men and women were conceptualized as markedly different from one another but that those divisions were understood primarily in the context of male-female intimate relationships. In many cases, colonial British writers and editors employed the term "the sexes" to warn against nonmarital heterosexual interactions. There was "the illicit intercourse of the sexes" and the "illicit commerce between the sexes."[28] Another writer criticized women's focus on "continual parties of jolity between the sexes" rather than marriage.[29]

Colonists also invoked sex-based language by referring to women as representatives of "the sex" when the topic addressed women's marital or sexual relations with men. These references to women as "the sex" naturalized men's desire toward women into bodily categorization. A musing on happiness in 1751 asked whether Adam would again give up Eden for the possibility of "Perfection in the Sex."[30] A Virginia newspaper's lengthy discourse on love and marriage the following year espoused the popular belief that "the sex appear admirably formed by Nature . . . to engage the hearts of Men."[31] Likewise, "the sex" was repeatedly mentioned in discussions of marriage. A "Maid's Soliloquy" about the necessity of marriage noted that nature requires "an alliance" of "an husband to the sex."[32] A commentary on the foundations of marriage again discussed "the sex," and a letter commenting on another essay on marriage focused on its portrayal of the "female sex."[33] Heterosexual norms were central to gender-based bodily categorization and differentiation.

On other occasions, British colonists spoke of "the sex" when focusing on women's illicit sexual behavior. This usage defined women as a group in terms of the degree to which they adhered to heterosexual marital limitations on sexual activity. A political commentary mentioned "the sex" in reference to "the reputation of their chastity."[34] A man who spent time with dissolute women was said to have "contempt for, the sex in general."[35] Another writer observed that toasts "in regard to the sex" tended to focus on "those who have trespassed against chastity."[36] Perhaps most explicitly, a "Letter to Parents" began by decrying the "Sluttery" of women who have premarital sex and then warned parents that without proper education and rearing, "the *Sex*" would behave badly.[37] In all of these examples, a belief in women's natural tendency toward sexual misbehavior informed a bodily division of the sexes.

Colonial print thus referenced femaleness via a categorization of "the sex" to emphasize heterosexual desire and marital relationships. Mentions of "the sex" could have referred to a wide range of issues associated with women: perhaps gardening and farming, washing and sewing, childbirth and child rearing, or any of the myriad gender-based responsibilities in which many colonial women engaged. But "the sex" seemed to be the term that colonists most reached for when discussing erotic appeal and male-female intimate marital relationships. Colonial Americans rarely used the term "male sex"—in several decades of publications, it only appeared a scant handful of times.[38] Still, when it did appear, it too was used in the context of heterosexual relations. A history of Britain published in 1748 noted "the Judgment of the Male Sex" in choosing a woman to marry.[39] An account of Moravians proclaimed that "the Male Sex consists of married Men, unmarried ones, and Widowers," again referencing heterosexual ties with its focus on marital status.[40]

A story from a popular British novel illustrates the degree to which British colonial print culture tied the definition of sexed bodies to expectations of heterosexual sexual behavior. Reprinted in the colonies in the mid-eighteenth century, *The Memoirs of the Remarkable Life and Surprising Adventures of Miss Jenny Cameron* was a sexualized adventure novel. The sensationalized tale took aim at Scotswoman Jean Cameron after her involvement with the 1745 Jacobite uprisings. In one of the novel's episodes, a young Jenny, the "Mistress of the Revels," is looking for (mis)adventure. Jenny sets out to replicate "a Masquerade in the Town, where Men and Women chang'd Habits, or put on such as best agreed with their own Fancy, without any Regard to the Distinction of Sexes." Fascinated by the idea of crossing sartorial gender boundaries, Jenny decides to clothe herself and the female servants in suits that belonged to her male cousins, while insisting that the footman be dressed "in the female Habiliments of Miss *Jenny*." Once Jenny is wearing men's clothes, she "was resolv'd to act the virile Part as high as she could possibly carry it." Jenny and her group of men's-clothed women come across another group of women. This new group was "Girls that had dress'd themselves up for a Market, and were looking out for Customers," a description that sexualizes those young women as promiscuous if not actual sex workers. Being "eager to carry on the Joke as far as she could," Jenny and her male-dressed compatriots "kiss'd, and toy'd, and prattled with them with as much Assurance as if they really had been those pretty Fellows they appear'd to be."[41] In other words, the proof of the women's successful impersonation of maleness was that they made sexual overtures toward women. Indeed, Jenny's group was so successful that the "Harlots" became angry when the supposed-men would not take their sexual overtures further. Maleness was proved by the ability to express sexual desire toward women, reaffirming the ways that heterosexual relations defined sexed bodies.

Despite seeming to be generically applied, terms related to sexed bodies supported developing racial hierarchies. Enslaved people, who were generally forbidden to legally marry, were marginalized from references to "the sex" made in the context of marriage and related courting behavior. Public discussions of marital or romantic heterosexual relations did not include "Negroes." Instead, eighteenth-century colonial print sources employed "the sexes" to refer to people defined as "Negroes" only when discussing demographics. In fact, colonists only referenced African-descended people with the demographic use of "sexes" when they were being bought and sold. Joseph Blewer offered "Seventy Gold Coast SLAVES" of "both Sexes" for sale.[42] An expert in "All Maritime Business" offered to procure "Negroes of both Sexes," and the sale of a Rhode Island farm included "several Negroes of both Sexes" as part of the transaction.[43] In such examples, sex was a sign of potential economic value, not used to comment on sexual interactions or marital guidelines. Even when not explicitly referencing enslaved people as property, mention of the sexes of African American people did not stray into heterosexual commentary. For instance, a Boston newspaper article worried about the plans of a "half a Score of Negro Servants of both Sexes assembled at a free Negroe's House."[44]

In print, at least, colonists excluded people of African descent from the heterosexual implications of "sexes" that they so commonly employed to describe people whose heritage was unspecified. This omission reflected the close association in colonial consciousness between "Negroes" and unmarriable chattel. There is no question that Euro-American colonists knew about and participated in sexual relations with enslaved people. But any discussion of such relationships tended to emphasize its irregularity rather than its bodily based naturalness. For example, an eighteenth-century health care guide claimed that "the pious *Spaniards* catch'd" the Pox "from their *Negro* Mistresses in the *West-Indies*, and had the Honour of propagating it from thence to all the rest of the World," referring to sexual relations with enslaved women as a public health hazard.[45] A satirical epitaph for a deceased Anglo-American teacher published in the 1760s described him as a "wicked old Lecher / And most abandoned of all Scoundrels That God ever gave Life to." The proof of the headmaster's misdeeds included not only his generically committing "every Vice" but "Black fornication in particular," by obtaining "The Charcoal Charms" of a "Negroe Wench."[46] Rather than emphasizing such interactions in terms of illicit but normative heterosexuality, Euro-American colonists publicly emphasized the racial degradation that accrued to Euro-American men who had sexual relations with women of African descent.

These nuanced public uses of sexed bodies matter because they contributed to the daily acceptance of unstated meanings of heterosexuality.[47] Likewise, Indigenous studies scholars have written about the ways that the "settler common sense" of Euro-Americans' possessions of Indigenous territories became "lived as given, as simply the unmarked, generic conditions."[48] So too were heterosexual relations discursively produced as an unmarked norm. References to "the sexes" or "the sex" in colonial America defined gender through heterosexual relations. These understandings of sexed bodies would offer a starting point for more overt expressions of heteroerotic desire among British colonists.

Making Heterosexual Beauty and Desire

In published and personal writings, colonial discussions of beauty reinforced notions of necessarily heterosexual desire. When male colonists used their personal writings to describe what people looked like, they most often focused on women's appearance as a sign of their desirability. This male-on-female gaze was a function of a heterosexually structured society. Although not as common, the few women who commented on men's appeal suggest that they, too, adjudged appearance through heterosexual appeal. While descriptions of women's heteroerotic appeal might seem universal, it actually marked whiteness by publicly excluding African Americans from large categories of expressed erotic desirability.

Colonists did not compose personal records about desire, attraction, and erotic appeal on a regular basis: they were far more likely to note a person's physical condition than describe their physical features. Private letters and diaries noted when family members were "all in perfect health" or when someone was looking "very poorly."[49] This emphasis on health and sickness crossed gender lines: the southern tutor Philip Vickers Fithian wrote down when inflamed tick bites left a woman covered with poxes, mentioned a man whose middle finger was cut off to the bone, and commented repeatedly on his own illnesses and injuries.[50] Elizabeth Drinker, a Philadelphia Quaker, filled many pages of her diaries with descriptions of illness and injuries, including commentaries on who was unwell, her own headaches, and family members' various sore throats, agues, fevers, or colds.[51]

When colonists did comment on individuals' appearance or attractiveness, they were making purposeful statements beyond the rote recitations of the health of family and friends. Men most commonly evaluated women's appearance, suggesting their heterosexual nature of desire. A few months of Philip Vickers Fithian's diary show that most of his commentary on appearance detailed his evaluation of women's appeal. While employed as a tutor in Virginia, Fithian wrote descriptions of a "small" woman with a "winning Presence"; "an elegant, beautiful woman"; a woman who was "something below what Ladies call elegant, neat but not *flashy* in her dress"; "two young ladies pretty well gone in what we call the Bloom of Life"; a "young, Handsome, polite lady"; and a young woman who was "about sixteen, neat, handsome, genteel, & sociable." Fithian judged women's appeal via their appearance (elegant, beautiful, handsome) and character (winning, polite, elegant, sociable). Fithian's evaluations of men in the same time period focused instead largely on actions—what they had done or what had happened to them.

He referred to a man's finger getting chopped off, a "fatigued" looking student who had stayed out late, and a "slovenly" student and gave a detailed description of a visitor's unique attire.[52] Fithian's assessment of women's attractiveness focused on the degree to which women appealed to him, rather than the factual recitation of events (accident, lack of sleep, details of attire) that affected men's appearances. His descriptions of men were unladen with the erotic evaluations that permeated his descriptions of women's appearance. This discursive practice set women as objects of men's desire.

A comparison of two exceptionally detailed descriptions further shows the implicit differentiations of Fithian's evaluations of men's and women's appearances. The unique visitor mentioned earlier was described largely in terms of what he was wearing: "black superfine Broadcloth; Gold-Laced hat; laced Ruffles; black Silk Stockings; & to his Broach on his Bosom we wore a Masons Badge inscribed 'Virtue and Silentio' cut in a Golden Metal! Certainly he was fine!" Fithian described this male visitor for his exceptional clothing and offered detailed evidence of that uniqueness. In contrast, Fithian's most detailed description of Elizabeth (Betsy) Lee included fewer objective details and far more personal evaluation in the almost four hundred words he used to describe her. He included some factual descriptors: Betsy was twenty-six years old, was "well set" with "a full face, sanguine Complection"; "her Nose is rather protuberant," and her hair was "a dark Brown." Yet Fithian's more evaluative commentary dwarfed the number of specific details he offered. She was "of a proper Height" with a "masculine & dauntless" aspect when she sat. Fithian resorted to mythical figures to convey his admiration of her features: her eyes "are exactly such as *Homer* atributes to the Goddess *Minerva*; & her Arms resemble those which the same Poet allows to *Juno*." Indeed, Betsy Lee was "truely elegant; her carriage neat & graceful; & her presence soft & beautiful." Overall, she was, despite her "embelishments of Dress & good Breeding, not much handsomer than the generality of Women."[53] Fithian's assessment of Betsy's desirability was far more elaborate than his focus on her exact features. He repeatedly set Betsy's appeal in terms of masculinity and femininity: he described that she sat in a "masculine" manner; he compared her to Roman goddesses, and ended by evaluating her in comparison to women as a whole. In contrast, his lengthy descriptions of the man's appearance only offered a two-word evaluation of his fineness in attire, not a wholesale evaluation of his allure.

Fithian was not the only male colonial writer who repeatedly described women in terms of their appeal to men. Women's value to men had long been a feature of patriarchal systems, where men's sexual power was inextricable from their social and economic power. The Virginian William Byrd's diaries and travel narratives are well-plumbed sources for his commentaries on people, places, and sexual pursuits.[54] Byrd's *Histories of the Dividing Line* was a combined secret and official record of his travels while border-surveying. Byrd, too, focused on his own evaluation of women's desirability. Byrd labeled numerous "handsome" or "handsome enough" women, as well as noting "pretty Girls," "Beauty's [sic] enough," "fair Beauty's [sic]," or "not much Beauty" among groups of women.[55] In contrast, Byrd's descriptions of men tended to focus far more on injuries, infirmities, and unusual features. In one notable incident, Byrd described how a man who had been hit by lightning alongside a pine tree was left with "an exact Figure of the Tree upon his Breast, with all its Branches, to the wonder of all that beheld it." In the same day, Byrd described a landlord who walked on crutches, "having the Gout in both his Knees," followed by a description of "2 truss Damsels . . . that were handsome enough."[56] These women rated commentary on their well-formed body shapes (truss) and their overall appeal to Byrd (handsome enough). In contrast, Byrd had explained the specific cause of the male landlord's infirmity: details about his illness and use of crutches rather than the heterosexual-infused judgment with which he described the pair of women. The landlord might merit sympathy for his condition, but the unnamed women rated only a ranking of their desirability. On another occasion, a Mr. Kinchin was described as "a Man of Figure in these parts, & his Wife a much better Figure than he."[57] The wordplay on the dual meanings of "figure"—a masculine notion of a person of important stature compared to the importance of a woman's bodily shape—epitomizes the differential standards of gendered judgment that emphasized women's appeal to men. European-descended women were notable for the figure of their bodies, European-descended men for the way they figured in society.

Other travel writers likewise described women via their presumed potential desirability to men. William Black described many people he met on his midcentury travels, including "Mr. Levy's a Jew." Mr. Levy merited no other depiction. Yet his sister, Hettie Levy, was a "Young Lady" who "was of the middle Stature, and very well made her Complection Black but very Comely, she had two Charming Eyes, full of Fire and Rolling, Eyebrows Black and well turn'd, with a Beautiful head of Hair, Coal Black. . . . She was a Lady of a great Deal of Wit, Join'd to a Good Understanding, full of Spirits, and of a Humour exceeding Jocose and Agreeable."[58] Black was an unusual writer in the amount of detail he offered but was typical in conveying his opinions of Hettie's physical appearance and temperament. Words like "comely," "charming," "beautiful," "well turn'd," and "agreeable": these were evaluations of her appeal to him, not simple reports of physical features. These descriptive tactics rooted men's descriptions of women in assumptions of heterosexual desire.

Various young men offered evaluations of women's desirability against a backdrop of heteroerotic or heteroromantic desire focused on potential romantic partners: women of European descent. Robert Bladen Carter apparently wrote the names of more than a dozen local "young ladies" in the margins of an old book, recording what was described as his "taste, & the Medications of his heart." Polly Taylor was simply "the Lovely of Mount-Airy"; Lydia Pettit "has d-m'd ugly Freckles in her Face, otherways She is handsome & tolerable"; Jenny Washington "is very Pretty"; "Miss Steerman is a beautiful young Lady."[59] All of these descriptions— "handsome," "pretty," "beautiful"—circulated around Carter's opinion of the young women's desirability, making that evaluation a way for men to assess women's heterosexual appeal. Likewise, every one of Philip Vickers Fithian's mentions of beauty were evaluations of European-descended women's appearance. There were "beautiful Quaker Girls," "a beautiful young Lady," and a friend's fiancée who had "a good share of personal beauty." Jenny Washington "has not a handsome Face, but is neat in her Dress, of an agreeable Size, & well proportioned, & has an easy winning Behaviour."[60] Literate men discussed their view of the allure of the women with whom they socialized. Men's heterosexually directed commentary reinscribed social and courting status onto appropriate women's bodies.

On the rare occasions that male colonists discussed the appearance of women of non-European descent, they connected desirability to heterosexual acts rather than to personal beauty. Philip Vickers Fithian described the appeal of a woman named Sukey only when he was describing other men's sexual pursuit of her. Fithian first described Sukey when a man was thought to have broken into the house at one o'clock in the morning to "commit fornication with *Sukey*, (a plump, sleek, likely Negro girl about sixteen)."[61] On another occasion, he described being hesitant to believe that Robert Bladen Carter had locked himself in a stable with this "likely Negro Girl" "for a considerable time." He preferred to believe that these incidents involved "one of the warm-blooded, well fed young Negroes, trying for the company of buxom *Sukey*."[62] In these comments, Fithian described Sukey's overtly sexualized appearance (plump, sleek, buxom) in reference not just to men's heterosexual desire but to men's sexual claiming of her.

Similarly, William Byrd recounted a story that coupled a non–European American woman's appealing appearance with a man's sexual assault. He and his compatriots met "a Dark Angel" whose "Complexion was a deep Copper, so that her fine Shape & regular Features made her appear like a Statue en Bronze done by a masterly hand. Shoebrush was smitten at the first Glance, and examined all her neat proportions with a critical Exactness. She struggled just enough to make her Admirer more eager."[63] In this passage, Byrd describes the physical appeal of a woman of Indigenous and/or African heritage as a precursor to his compatriot's sexual force toward her. In both this and the Vickers example, the male writers presented men's sexual desire toward nonwhite women in the context of aggressive and forced heterosexual overtures, suggesting that men's sexual rights to socially vulnerable women was an outgrowth of the naturalness of such women's erotic appeal to men.

The imagined prospect of heterosexual relations structured how colonial women evaluated men's desirability. While women's perspectives are largely absent from print commentaries, there are occasional records that offer a woman's perspective on heterosexual appeal. The diary of Sally Wister, a sixteen-year-old Quaker living outside of Philadelphia, is noteworthy for its focus on the many soldiers and officers with whom Wister interacted. Wister evaluated the appearance and character of about two dozen men. It may have been a particular set of circumstances that led to Sally Wister's detailed recordings: in addition to her literacy, the British occupation produced a seemingly near-constant parade of young men in her vicinity. Wister's diary thus offers a clear picture of the ways that young women might share their opinions on men's appeal, behavior, and desirability. The attractiveness of the men Wister met was central to many of her commentaries. Captain Alexander Furnival had, "excepting one or two, the handsomest face I ever saw." Colonel Gist was "very pretty; a charming person"; Robert Tilly was "rather genteel, [with] an extreme pretty, ruddy face," to which a horseback ride added "the most beautiful glow." Heabard Smallwood was a "very genteel, pretty little fellow," while Captain Jones was "tall elegant and handsome." A man named Finley was "wretched ugly," and a dragoon from Maryland "has very few external charms."[64] This young woman recorded descriptions of men that made clear her evaluative stance on their appeal.

At various points, Sally Wister also noted the shared conversations about men within her social circle of young women. She described her rising appreciation of a Major Jameson but noted, "We girls differ about him. Prissa and I admire him, whilst Liddy and Betsy will not allow him a spark of beauty." On another occasion, Betsy (probably Eliza Wister) and Liddy (Foulke) shared Wister's opinion on Alexander Spotswood Dandridge's appeal, apparently "coincid[ing] in [Sally's] opinion" that he was "the handsomest man in existence."[65] Among themselves, these women shared in the project of evaluating men's appeal.

Alongside Wister's evaluations of men's heterosexual desirability, she repeatedly peppered descriptions with assessments of their success at masculine performance. A colonel was "one of the most amiable of men," another had "a truly martial air, the behaviour and manner of a gentleman." William Stoddert was "manly," and a man named Jameson was "tall and manly."[66] In all of these descriptions, Wister set her commentary on the men's appearance into her understanding of what made a successful and attractive man, effectively tying heteroerotic appeal to a culturally produced categorization of bodies.

Similar to most male writers, Wister focused her evaluations of erotic appeal on Euro-American men. The one African American person she mentioned was "Seaton's negro." Unlike her loquaciousness about the many Euro-American men she mentioned, that phrase was the sum total of information Wister offered about this person. We do not know his name, and we are left to assume his sex (male?) and his status (enslaved?). To be sure, others went unnamed in the diary—but they often had a description attached to them. There was a "genteel officer," the "sensible young" lawyer, and the unnamed parson who was exceptionally tall, "thin and meagre" with "not a single personal charm."[67] But this "negro" remains heterosexually invisible to Wister. If not considered an appropriate object of (however fantasized) intimacies, description of his bodily individuality was irrelevant.

Sally Wister's writing gives a sense of the range of commentaries on heterosexual evaluation in daily life. In print, however, the appellation of "beauty" was a trait largely restricted to women as a generic group or to Euro-American women as individuals. For example, in the middle decades of the eighteenth century, "beauty" appeared in up to one-quarter of published almanacs, almost exclusively in reference to women. Colonial print culture cast women's beauty in explicitly heterosexual terms, as a tool women deployed to attract men. A 1772 newspaper allegory described Beauty as Love's daughter, sent down to mankind, thus seeing women's beauty as a promoter of intimate relationships. These sources did not always (or even often) represent women's desirability as a positive attribute: a popular conduct book published in the 1760s warned about women "who by their beauty enslaved" men, and an editor claimed that "the Pains of Love" toward "a beautiful" woman had led the previous editor to forget to publish the almanac on time.[68] In these and many similar examples, Anglo-American publications found women's beauty worth mentioning because of its power over men in heterosexual relationships. They did not consider female beauty of much concern to friends or children. Heterosexuality undergirded these commentaries on beauty with beliefs in the naturalness and necessity of male-female sexual and marital relationships.

As the product of a settler-colonial society, this idealized version of beauty's heteroeroticism reinforced society's racial and sexual hierarchies. Mentions of "beauty" were remarkably absent from public discussions of African American bodies. A search of digitized newspapers from 1750 to 1780 yielded only one use of the root word "beaut-" within ten words of "negro" or "negroe": a report of a Revolutionary War battle mentioned, among the many dead and wounded, the author's personal losses. He reported the death of his "poor" assistant and then reported, "my fine valuable Negro carpenter was [killed on] the 7th, and a beautiful mare, that cost me 20 guineas was shot through the head the same day."[69] Unlike the sympathy expressed for the "poor" assistant, both the mare and the "Negro carpenter" were commodified by their value, and while the mare could be "beautiful," the enslaved carpenter was "fine"—a generic term referring to the quality of a range of objects in the eighteenth century. Chattel slavery placed people of African descent in a position that made public recognition of their hetero-appeal exceedingly rare.

Stephanie M. H. Camp posited, in one of her last pieces of scholarship, that "there is no better lens through which to chronicle the mutability of race than another moody and somatic social category: beauty."[70] Colonial discussions of bodily appeal and imputed desirability indeed reflected the many means through which bodies made up the raced and gendered categories that led to the appellation of beauty. African-descended women, not publicly seen to inhabit that category of potential spouse for the European-descended print audience, would thus be erased from the womanly beauty that signified attraction to a potential heterosexual mate. In a society where only some members had the right to formal recognition of heterosexual coupling in marriage, expressions of desire and appellations of beauty suggest the importance of teasing out heterosexuality from patriarchy. Doing so helps us see the institution of marriage as a patriarchal construction built around a belief in the naturalness of heterosexual sexual relations.

Conclusion

Heteronormativity underlay discussions of men's and women's sexed bodies and shaped the ways that men formulated women's beauty and desirability. What we might label colonial heteropatriarchy was created through innumerable quotidian interactions, some of which appear to us in the skeletal remains of written language. Colonists' mentions of sexed bodies tied physicality to expectations of heterosexual behaviors. Men's descriptions of women emphasized their relative suitability for heterosexual relationships. Certain women's beauty was notable in terms of its ability to appeal to men's desire—in other words, against a backdrop of the naturalness and necessity of heterosexual relations. Such hetero-erotic desire was situated within racialized economic structures that marked some women by their erotic appeal to men and others through the eroticization of sexual assault. And although sources are limited, it appears that those evaluations were reciprocal, with women also evaluating some men's appeal as sexual, romantic, or marital partners.

To be sure, this construction of heterosexuality bears only limited resemblance to the homosexual/heterosexual identity binaries that increasingly took hold of US society at the turn of the twentieth century. But that does not negate the importance of the structural precursors that made heterosexual behaviors and ideologies the norm for centuries. Colonial evaluations of bodily appearance or the sexualization of bodily divisions were part of a system that relied on a naturalized, unstated heteronormativity. It also has thrived under historians' own heteroessentialism that resisted questioning both our subjects' and our own assumptions about what is sexually natural, making colonial women and men's erotic relationships seem unremarkable rather than historically constructed.

NOTES

1. Ronald Hyam, "Empire and Sexual Opportunity," *Journal of Imperial and Commonwealth History* 14, no. 2 (January 1986): 40.

2. For just some early examples, see Kathleen Brown, "'Changed . . . into the Fashion of Man': The Politics of Sexual Difference in a Seventeenth-Century Anglo-American Settlement," *Journal of the History of Sexuality* 6, no. 2 (October 1995): 171–93; Kirsten Fischer, *Suspect Relations: Sex, Race, and Resistance in Colonial North Carolina* (Ithaca, NY: Cornell University Press, 2002); Thomas Foster, *Sex and the Eighteenth-Century Man: Massachusetts and the History of Sexuality in America* (Boston: Beacon, 2007); Richard Godbeer, *Sexual Revolution in Early America* (Baltimore: Johns Hopkins University Press, 2002); Jennifer L. Morgan, *Laboring Women: Reproduction and Gender in New World Slavery* (Philadelphia: University of Pennsylvania Press, 2004); Merril D. Smith, *Sex without Consent: Rape and Sexual Coercion in America* (New York: NYU Press, 2002).

3. Jonathan Ned Katz, *The Invention of Heterosexuality* (New York: Dutton, 1995), 9.

4. See Kathleen M. Brown, *Good Wives, Nasty Wenches, and Anxious Patriarchs: Gender, Race, and Power in Colonial Virginia* (Chapel Hill: OIEAHC at University of North Carolina Press, 1996), 4–5.

5. I include my own book *Rape and Sexual Power in Early America* (Chapel Hill: OIEAHC at University of North Carolina Press, 1995) in this list. Because my point is about the field, not individual authors, I do not cite other scholars here.

6. Jen Manion, "Historic Heteroessentialism and Other Orderings in Early America," *Signs* 34, no. 4 (Summer 2009), 998.

7. Carroll Smith-Rosenberg, "The Female World of Love and Ritual: Relations between Women in Nineteenth-Century America," *Signs: Journal of Women in*

Culture and Society 1, no. 1 (1975): 1–29; Adrienne Rich, "Compulsory Heterosexuality and Lesbian Existence," *Signs* 5, no. 4 (1980): 631–60; Judith M. Bennett, *History Matters: Patriarchy and the Challenge of Feminism* (Philadelphia: University of Pennsylvania Press, 2006), 108.

8. Sharon Block and Kathleen M. Brown, "Clio in Search of Eros: Redefining Sexualities in Early America," *William and Mary Quarterly* 60, no. 1 (January 2003): 11.

9. For recent important work in this area, see Sowande M. Mustakeem, *Slavery at Sea: Terror, Sex, and Sickness in the Middle Passage* (Urbana: University of Illinois Press, 2016), esp. 85–90; Marisa J. Fuentes, *Dispossessed Lives: Enslaved Women, Violence, and the Archive* (Philadelphia: University of Pennsylvania Press, 2016), 83–85.

10. Thomas A. Foster, "The Sexual Abuse of Black Men under American Slavery," *Journal of the History of Sexuality* 20, no. 3 (2011): 445–64.

11. Richard Godbeer "'The Cry of Sodom': Discourse, Intercourse, and Desire in Colonial New England," *William and Mary Quarterly* 52, no. 2 (April 1995): 259–86; "Colonial America: The Age of Sodomitical Sin," OutHistory, accessed September 19, 2017, http://outhistory.org. Women's same-sex relationships figure more prominently in early nineteenth-century scholarship, such as Karen V. Hansen, "'No Kisses Is Like Youres': An Erotic Friendship between Two African-American Women during the Mid-Nineteenth Century" *Gender & History* 7 no. 2 (1995): 153–82; and Rachel Hope Cleves, *Charity and Sylvia: A Same-Sex Marriage in Early America* (New York: Oxford University Press, 2014).

12. For example, see Ann Myles, "Queering the Study of Early American Sexuality," *William and Mary Quarterly* 60, no. 1 (January 2003): 199–202; Clare Lyons, "Mapping an Atlantic Sexual Culture: Homoeroticism in Eighteenth-Century Philadelphia," *William and Mary Quarterly* 60, no. 1 (January 2003): 119–154; John Saillant, "The Black Body Erotic and the Republican Body Politic, 1790–1820," *Journal of the History of Sexuality* 5, no. 3 (1995): 403–28; Bruce Burgett, "The History of *x* in Early America," *Early American Literature* 44, no. 1 (2009): 215–25.

13. Katz, *Invention of Heterosexuality*, 14–15, 13 (quotation).

14. On turn of-the-century medicalization of homosexuality, see Jennifer Terry, *An American Obsession: Science, Medicine, and Homosexuality in Modern Society* (Chicago: University of Chicago Press, 1999); Michel Foucault, *The History of Sexuality: An Introduction, Volume I* (New York: Vintage Books, 1978); Vernon A. Rosario, ed., *Science and Homosexualities* (New York: Routledge, 1997).

15. Ann duCille, "'Othered' Matters: Reconceptualizing Dominance and Difference in the History of Sexuality in America," *Journal of the History of Sexuality* 1, no. 1 (1990): 103.

16. Brian Connolly and Marisa Fuentes, eds., "From Archives of Slavery to Liberated Futures?," special issue, *History of the Present* 6, no. 2 (Fall 2016): 105–116; Fuentes, *Dispossessed Lives*; Ashley Glassburn Falzetti, "Archival Absence: The Burden of History," *Settler Colonial Studies* 5, no. 2 (October 2014): 1–17; Avery F. Gordon, *Ghostly Matters: Haunting and the Sociological Imagination* (Minneapolis: University of Minnesota Press, 2008); Ann Laura Stoler, *Along the Archival*

Grain: Epistemic Anxieties and Colonial Common Sense (Princeton, NJ: Princeton University Press, 2010).

17. Sources for this project include eighteenth-century personal letters and diaries by Anglo-American colonists, as well as serial and stand-alone publications. Digital databases (including Archive of Americana and Accessible Archives) were particularly useful in comparing the frequency and use of particular terms related to sexual behavior and sexed bodies.

18. For the twentieth-century rise in "opposite sex," see Google ngram, reachable at https://tinyurl.com/oppositesexngram (click search). For an exceptional mention of the "opposite sex," in reference to the practices of ancient Scandinavians, see "From the Pennsylvania Magazine," *Connecticut Gazette*, May 24, 1776, 1.

19. See Thomas Laqueur, *Making Sex: Body and Gender from the Greeks to Freud* (Cambridge, MA: Harvard University Press, 1990); Katherine Park and Robert A. Nye, "'Destiny Is Anatomy,' Essay Review of Thomas Laqueur, *Making Sex: Body and Gender from the Greeks to Freud* (1990)," *New Republic*, February 18, 1991, 53–57; Karen Harvey, "The Substance of Sexual Difference: Change and Persistence in Representations of the Body in Eighteenth-Century England," *Gender & History* 14, no. 2 (August 2002): 202–23. For early theorizing of meanings of "women" as an increasingly sexualized category by the eighteenth century, see Denise Riley, "Does a Sex Have a History?," in *Am I That Name? Feminism and the Category of "Women" in History* (London: Macmillan, 1998), 1–17. On the intersection of one-sex and two-sex models in seventeenth-century Puritan constructs of gender and sexuality, see Elizabeth Maddock Dillon, "Nursing Fathers and Brides of Christ: The Feminized Body of the Puritan Convert," in *A Centre of Wonders: The Body in Early America*, ed. Janet Moore Lindman and Michele Lise Tarter (Ithaca, NY: Cornell University Press, 2001), 129–43.

20. "Quebec," *Boston Post-Boy*, August 13, 1759, 4; *England's Timely Remembrancer, or The Minister Preaching His Own Funeral Sermon . . .* [Boston?]: [publisher not identified], [1752?], 5; *New York Gazette*, July 13, 1772, 3.

21. For example, *Essex Gazette*, April 13, 1773, 148; *New-Hampshire Gazette*, September 12, 1775, 2; *Pennsylvania Chronicle*, May 1, 1769, 124.

22. *Pennsylvania Chronicle*, May 31, 1773, 289; *Newport Mercury*, June 28, 1773, 3.

23. "Rules and Maxims for Promoting Matrimonial Happiness," *New-Hampshire Gazette*, December 19, 1760, 2.

24. *Virginia Gazette*, March 4, 1773.

25. "REFLECTIONS on GALLANTRY; and on the EDUCATION of WOMEN," *Pennsylvania Gazette*, November 11, 1772; "The CONTRAST or a Parallel between Courtship and Matrimony," *Virginia Gazette*, November 26, 1772; *Boston News-Letter*, June 7, 1708, 2; *Pennsylvania Evening Post*, June 17, 1775, 251.

26. Arnold Arbuthnot, *Memoirs of the Remarkable Life and Surprizing Adventures of Miss Jenny Cameron, a Lady* (Boston: D. Fowle, 1750), 109, 74.

27. On the overlaps between sexed, gendered, and sexualized bodies in early American and early modern history, see Elizabeth Reis, *Bodies in Doubt: An American*

History of Intersex (Baltimore: Johns Hopkins University Press, 2009), 1–54; Barbara Chubak, "Imagining Sex Change in Early Modern Europe," Nursing Clio, September 19, 2017, https://nursingclio.org; Jen Manion, *Female Husbands: A Trans History* (Cambridge: Cambridge University Press, 2020). For an important early theoretical intervention to these relationships, see Judith Butler, *Bodies That Matter: On the Discursive Limits of "Sex"* (New York: Routledge, 1993).

28. "To the Printer of the Public Ledger," *Providence Gazette*, January 26, 1765, 2; "Lisbon, Feb 28," *Pennsylvania Packet*, June 7, 1773, 1.

29. "A Defence of Cuckoldom," *Rivington's New York Gazettteer*, February 24, 1774, 1; "Extract of a Letter from Bath," *Essex Journal*, April 6, 1774, 3; "Thoughts on the Influence of Card Playing," *Boston Post-Boy*, September 5, 1768, 1.

30. "From a Late Philadelphia Paper," *Boston Gazette*, April 2, 1751, 1.

31. *Virginia Gazette*, August 7, 1752.

32. "To the Printer of the Newport Mercury," *Newport Mercury*, May 2, 1763, 1.

33. *Georgia Gazette*, September 14, 1768, 1; *Pennsylvania Chronicle*, September 14, 1767.

34. "London," *Providence Gazette*, August 20, 1763, 1.

35. "From the Lady's Magazine, for Sept 1771," *Boston Post-Boy*, February 15, 1773.

36. *South Carolina Gazette*, July 6, 1767. See also *New-York Gazette*, July 27, 1767, 1.

37. "A Letter to Parents," *Boston Post-Boy*, February 8, 1773, 2.

38. Based on a March 2017 America's Historical Imprints search, between 1740 and 1775 "male sex" appeared in approximately half a dozen individual colonial publications, while "female sex" appeared at least six times more frequently.

39. James Burgh, *Britain's Remembrancer; or, The Danger Not Over* (Philadelphia: Godhard Armbrister, 1748), 45.

40. Heinrich Rimius, *A Candid Narrative of the Rise and Progress of the Herrnhuters, Commonly Call'd Moravians, or Unitas Fratrum . . .* (Philadelphia: William Bradford, 1753), 62.

41. Archibald Arbuthnot, *Memoirs of the Remarkable Life and Surprising Adventures of Miss Jenny Cameron . . .* (Boston: Fowle, 1750), 32–35.

42. *Pennsylvania Gazette*, July 25, 1765. See also *Boston Evening-Post*, May 3, 1742, 2; *Boston News-Letter*, August 3, 1727, 2.

43. *New-York Mercury*, June 16, 1766; *Providence Gazette*, Supplement, February 17, 1770, 30. See also *New-Hampshire Gazette*, September 12, 1775, 2; *Virginia Gazette*, April 22, 1773; *Pennsylvania Gazette*, September 8, 1757; *Pennsylvania Gazette*, February 7, 1765; *South Carolina Gazette*, December 28, 1769.

44. "To Old Master Janus," *New-England Courant*, November 16, 1724, 1.

45. John Tennent, *Every Man His Own Doctor; or, The Poor Planter's Physician* (Williamsburg, VA: W. Parks, 1736), 58. This was widely reprinted. For example, George Fisher, *The American Instructor; or, Young Man's Best Companion* (Philadelphia: Franklin and Hall, 1753), 369. For pre-eighteenth-century European discussions of African women's beauty, see Jennifer L. Morgan, "'Some Could Suckle over Their Shoulder': Male Travelers, Female Bodies, and the Gendering

of Racial Ideology, 1500–1770," *William and Mary Quarterly* 54, no. 1 (January 1997): 170; Stephanie M. H. Camp, "Making Racial Beauty in the United States: Toward a History of Black Beauty," in *Connexions: Histories of Race and Sex in North America*, ed. Jennifer Brier, Jim Downs, and Jennifer L. Morgan (Urbana: University of Illinois, 2016), 113–26.

46. *A Conference between the D[evi]l and Doctor D[ov]e: Together with the Doctor's Epitaph on Himself* (Philadelphia, 1764).

47. As the historian Carol F. Karlsen analogously noted about colonial New England, "the association [between women and witches] was never made explicit in New England culture" because the belief was so naturalized as to be literally unremarkable. Karlsen, *The Devil in the Shape of a Woman: Witchcraft in Colonial New England* (New York: Norton, 1998), 3.

48. Mark Rifkin, "Settler Common Sense," *Settler Colonial Studies* 3, nos. 3–4 (November 2013): 322–23.

49. John B. Reeves, "Extracts from the Letter-Books of Lieutenant Enos Reeves, of the Pennsylvania Line (Continued)," *Pennsylvania Magazine of History and Biography* 21, no. 2 (1897): 236; Henry Laurens to John Bartram, August 9, 1766, in *The Papers of Henry Laurens*, ed. David R. Chesnutt, vol. 5 (Columbia: University of South Carolina Press, 1974), 153.

50. Philip Vickers Fithian, *Journal and Letters of Philip Vickers Fithian, 1773–1774: A Plantation Tutor of the Old Dominion* (Charlottesville: University of Virginia Press, 1978), 158, 51, 194.

51. Elizabeth Drinker, *The Diary of Elizabeth Drinker*, ed. Elaine Forman Crane (Boston: Northeastern University Press, 1991). See also Rebecca Tannenbaum, *Health and Wellness in Colonial America* (Santa Barbara, CA: Greenwood, 2012), 219–21.

52. Fithian, *Journal and Letters*, 49–76 (period of January 1–March 12, 1774).

53. Fithian, 130.

54. For just some of the voluminous scholarship on Byrd, see Kenneth A. Lockridge, *On the Sources of Patriarchal Rage: The Commonplace Books of William Byrd II and Thomas Jefferson and the Gendering of Power in the Eighteenth Century* (New York: NYU Press, 1994); Brown, *Good Wives, Nasty Wenches, and Anxious Patriarchs*.

55. William Byrd and William Kenneth Boyd, *William Byrd's Histories of the Dividing Line Betwixt Virginia and North Carolina* (Raleigh: North Carolina Historical Commission, 1929), 51, 75, 53, 69, 113, 113. See also 149, 311, 89.

56. Byrd and Boyd, 75.

57. Byrd and Boyd, 111.

58. "Journal of William Black, 1744," ed. R. Alonzo Brock, *Pennsylvania Magazine of History and Biography* 1, no. 4 (1877): 415–16.

59. Fithian, *Journal and Letters*, 136.

60. Fithian, 135, 136, 104, 123.

61. Fithian, 184. The only other person described as "likely" (in this case surprisingly so) was a deaf and dumb man on p. 188. On the use of "likely" as part of the "special lexicon" applied to enslaved people, see Stephanie Smallwood, *Saltwater Slavery: A Middle Passage from Africa to American Diaspora* (Cambridge, MA: Harvard University Press, 2009), 52, 63; Sharon Block, *Colonial Complexions: Race and Bodies in Eighteenth-Century America* (Philadelphia: University of Pennsylvania Press, 2018), 49–51.

62. Fithian, *Journal and Letters*, 86, 185, 187.

63. Byrd and Boyd, *Histories of the Dividing Line*, 57.

64. Sarah Wister, *Sally Wister's Journal: A True Narrative; Being a Quaker Maiden's Account of Her Experiences with Officers of the Continental Army, 1777–1778* (Philadelphia: Ferris and Leach, 1902), 84, 122, 123, 150, 86, 143.

65. Wister, 156–58.

66. Wister, 81–82, 85, 144.

67. Wister, 128, 134, 93, 95.

68. "On Beauty," *South Carolina Gazette*, October 8, 1772; James Fordyce, *Sermons to Young Women* (London: A. Millar and T. Cadell, 1767), 202, 203, 214; Matthew Boucher, *The Pennsylvania Almanack, for the Year of Christ, 1745* . . . (Philadelphia, [1744]). See an extended discussion in Sharon Block, "Early American Bodies: Creating Race, Sex, and Beauty," in *Connexions*, 85–112.

69. *Connecticut Journal*, December 29, 1779.

70. Camp, "Making Racial Beauty in the United States," 113–26.

6

Spectacles of Restraint

Race, Excess, and Heterosexuality in Early American Print Culture

RASHAUNA JOHNSON

When, therefore, a young marriageable maiden exhibits
the symptoms of the approach of any of these diseases, she
should, if possible, be united to the object of her affections.
—Alphonse Broussais, 1843

Amalgamation—Francis Pitt, a "white man," was arrested on
Marigny street, at 12 o'clock on Monday night, for walking
with a colored *ladi*, with his arm around her neck and for
harboring other designs.
—*Daily Orleanian*, May 19, 1852

With an elegantly dressed white man kissing an ebony-hued enslaved
woman to the left and a casually dressed white man preparing to lash
a black man to the right, the famed *Virginian Luxuries* painting (artist
unknown, ca. 1815) shows that production and profit, punishment and
pleasure lay entangled at the heart of the Atlantic plantation complex.[1]
The kiss and the lash, the different-sex and same-sex contact, were part
of the same spectrum of sexuality and domination during chattel slavery.[2] "Scandal and excess inundate the archive," Saidiya Hartman writes.
The documents housed in these aseptic repositories "take for granted
the traffic between fact, fantasy, desire, and violence."[3] Far from being
secreted away in some dusty cove, the paper trail of slavery in New
Orleans lays bare the hunger to consume black bodies that animated
antebellum society.[4] Notarial archives record the frenzy with which
humans were bought and sold. Thanks to *partus sequitur ventrum*,
which meant enslaved women could only give birth to enslaved chil-

dren, planters' papers record in detail the so-called natural increase of their human capital. Mythic quadroon balls promised (if not delivered) an endless supply of free women of color to satisfy the sexual fantasies of even the most unabashed white male libertine. Antebellum New Orleans, it seemed, was a headquarters of what, by century's end, would be called heterosexuality.[5]

Yet not all modes of sexual expression, including different-sex sex, were met with uniform approval. Over the nineteenth century, reformers increasingly emphasized the benefits of what we now call heterosexuality. "An official, dominant, different-sex erotic ideal—a heterosexual ethic—is not ancient at all, but a modern invention," Jonathan Ned Katz writes.[6] At first blush, these attempts to esteem the pleasure derived from different-sex sex as a value unto itself, one divorced from procreative imperatives, might be told as story of modern progress from sexual repression to sexual liberation.[7] Such a perspective, however, would leave unacknowledged the many ways that the discursive production of boundaries around acceptable different-sex pleasure would marginalize most queer and many different-sex intimacies due to intersecting hierarchies of gender, race, class, status, and sexuality. People talked about sex, producing parables and treatises designed to instruct—and, barring that, to shame—members of society in the ways of proper sexual expression. In New Orleans, a city known for its "spectacular wickedness," reformist literature created spectacles of restraint that, the authors hoped, would rein in perceived sexual excesses through appeals to scientific, moral, and legal authority.[8] In so doing, they helped to create norms that rendered deviant anything other than different-sex intimacies between "proper" partners.

This chapter uses two texts to chart the emergence of a racialized heterosexuality in the antebellum United States. The first text, Alphonse Broussais's *Self-Preservation; or, Sexual Physiology Revealed*, was published in New York City in 1843.[9] Though now obscure, at the time *Self-Preservation* reached readers in New Orleans through the Literary Depot, a bookshop located at the heart of the city. Although now it would be considered a work of "pseudoscience," the text relies on attributed and unattributed sources to advocate the pleasurable and procreative benefits of different-sex sex.[10] An examination of Broussais's boundaries around healthy heterosexuality from the standpoint of antebellum New Orleans shows that the denial of enslaved people's autonomous sexual subjecthood

and pleasure divorced from procreation—essentially, the denial of enslaved heterosexuality—was essential to free people's economic profit and
sexual pleasure. The second text is the *Daily Orleanian*, a newspaper published in New Orleans in the 1840s and 1850s, which ran a regular column
that publicly identified and ridiculed white women and black men who
had sex with each other. Though the paper did not incite vicious mobs to
prevent these intimacies (which became one pretext for lynchings after
emancipation), it did not necessarily "tolerate" them either, as one scholar
suggests.[11] Instead, the newspaper tacitly endorsed the state's racialized
punishments for those who were accused of engaging in prostitution, especially when it involved white women and black men. The newspaper's
accounts of these arrests offered vicarious access to titillating acts even
as it surveilled and shamed some of society's most vulnerable members.
Taken together, these texts show different ways that authors used print
culture to encourage proper heterosexual expression and to discourage
liaisons that threatened to destabilize the social order.

The significance of this effort is twofold. First, it contributes to ongoing efforts to explore the "prehistory of heterosexuality" in early
America.[12] The heterosexual subject remains the default in much of the
historical scholarship, particularly in the early American period. As a
result, queer lives and experiences go unremarked, and different-sex intimacies are considered unremarkable. Second, this study contributes to
ongoing efforts to examine the ways that norms that governed different-
sex desire cleaved along hierarchies of race, class, gender, and status.
Scholars such as George Chauncey and Siobhan Somerville have called
our attention to the role of racism in the "invention of homosexuality"
in the late nineteenth and early twentieth centuries, and now scholars
of early America are giving similar attention to racism in the invention
of heterosexuality as well.[13] In charting this contested history of heterosexuality, we see how elites attempted to impose sexual norms and the
ways that marginalized peoples reclaimed their own bodies by insisting
on the sexual pleasure that others would deny them.[14]

"Alphonse Broussais" and Medically Necessary Restraint

The March 15, 1840, edition of the *Daily Picayune* carried items typical
of any antebellum New Orleans newspaper. It listed steamboat arrival

and mail-ship departure notices and the lottery pot. Under the heading "Amusements," it listed upcoming shows at the Theatre D'Orleans and an apartment for rent near the St. Charles Theater. The Orleans Ballroom advertised "Dress and Masquerade Balls," and a Mr. Fuertes, "member of the Musical Conservatory of Madrid, Spain," advertised piano, guitar, and vocal lessons to "the ladies and gentlemen of New Orleans." In runaway-slave ads, the laborers whose sweat financed the trappings of refinement imprinted brief records of their resistance onto these pages. David, "a slender black man, about 18 years old, 5 feet 10 or 11 inches high, long arms, large hands and feet, rather a downcast look when spoken to," and "a black or griffe colored boy, named SCOT; about 28 or 30 years old . . . a pretty good barber, and was acting in the capacity of dining room servant at the City Hotel when he left," rejected the bondage that operated just below the veneer of luxury. Yet runaway ads, however arresting, were only the most obvious of the textual sites of racial formation visible on that single page. "New Orleans Literary Depot," one advertisement pronounced: "Current literature of the day, No. 13 Exchange Place," in the heart of the city. "Always for sale at the above place, either by the single copy or year, all the principal MAGAZINES AND NEWSPAPERS in the United States, of the *latest dates*; together with miscellaneous collection of *Juvenile Books, Novels, Engravings, Prints, Blank Books, Stationery, &c.*"[15] And in stocking one particular text, Alphonse Broussais's *Self-Preservation*, the Literary Depot would introduce a text to the local audience designed to entertain and instruct white men on how to regulate different-sex sexual pleasure toward optimizing their own pleasure, reproduction, and efficacy. In a slaveholding center like New Orleans, this different-sex pleasure for free people came at the expense of the enslaved, for whom procreation, not pleasure, remained more essential than ever to the planter and merchant way of life.[16]

By the 1840s, such books as Broussais's competed with other racialized amusements for the public's eye—and dollar. "Cheap Books, Recently Published by Burgess, Stringer & Co, 222 Broadway, cor. of Ann-Street," proclaimed an 1846 advertisement for Broussais's publishing house.[17] Located in New York City, "under Barnum's American Museum," the publishers and booksellers shared space with a man remembered as "a genius in promotion."[18] Unlike most American theaters, which were known meeting spots for prostitutes and their clients, P. T. Barnum's museum ostensibly excluded sex workers in favor of "family audiences."[19] But his "museum" was nonetheless steeped in erotic racist performance. Only decades before its opening, Barnum's predecessors displayed Saartjie Baartman, the so-called "Hottentot Venus," before massive crowds in Europe as a living specimen, before her body suffered a postmortem dissection at the hands of the French paleontologist George Cuvier.[20] Barnum exhibited Joice Heth, an enslaved woman, as George Washington's 161-year-old former nurse.[21] These ethnographic displays of different "types" of people furthered emerging ideas about the biological basis of racial difference.[22] The shows proved extraordinarily popular, as one historian of Barnum notes: "Some 38 million customers paid the 25 cents admission to attend the museum between 1841 and 1865. The total population of the United States in 1860 was under 32 million."[23] Undoubtedly inspired by Barnum's marketing techniques, Burgess, Stringer & Co. ran ads for Broussais's text at least five times in the nationally circulated *National Police Gazette Journal* between June and July 1846, and the printers tailored the advertisement to the *Police Gazette*'s largely working- and middle-class readership: "The great author of the present work has, in the present practical treatise, thrown out to the world matter, the value of which will present itself instantly to the mind of the simplest reader. It treats on subjects, the want of knowledge which, has made thousands unhappy in family and social relations."[24] These ads were certainly effective, and Broussais's text circulated from New York to the Lower Mississippi River Valley.

In New Orleans, a centrally located bookstore called the Literary Depot stocked Broussais's book and other curiosities. During the 1840s, that establishment underwent a series of name changes, location changes, ownership changes, and expansions as it became a node of local and Atlantic print communication.[25] An August 1840 post in the *Daily Picayune* noted that "Curn's Literary Depot," located at 13 Exchange Place, carried "a neat little journal called 'The Crisis,' devoted to politics and in favor of the election of Gen. [William Henry] Harrison to the Presidency, [that] has just been started in this city."[26] Throughout the fall, Curns continued to advertise his shop, such that by Christmas Eve a local columnist declared, "Curns's establishment is getting to be a sort of fashionable lounge. His little oddities, varieties and delicacies in the reading way, form an attraction exceedingly novel and pleasant."²⁷ Curns ordered and supplied everything from the *New York Truth Teller* to Goshen butter.²⁸ By early 1842, J. C. Morgan became the listed proprietor in ads: "Graham's Magazine for May, and all the other recent journals most popular with the public, are lying upon Morgan's tables, at the Literary Depot. The supplies come in continually, and all the attractive light reading of the day may be found there as usual."²⁹ Shortly thereafter, the Depot moved to 18 Exchange Place, and in January 1843, Morgan opened a second branch of the Literary Depot in Natchitoches, Louisiana.³⁰ The business continued to expand. A few months later, "Morgan & Bravo" ran ads for the Literary Depot in New Orleans and New York newspapers. In an October 1843 ad in New York's *New World*, Bravo & Morgan noted that it was located "At the 'Merchants' Exchange,' Adjoining the Post-Office," in New Orleans. It described itself as "Publishers, Booksellers, Stationers, &C, . . . Venders of all the cheap books and publications of the day—Periodical Literature, Reviews, Magazines, Journals of Science, Newspapers from all parts of the United States and Great Britain." It boasted selections from across disciplines and across the world, and it sought an equally wide audience: "In a word, they repeat their great object is to make the Literary Depot in every way useful to their supporters, and the public generally; from whom they solicit support and patronage, if they are found to deserve it."³¹

In February 1844, Bravo & Murray advertised its copies of Broussais's *Self-Preservation* alongside nearly forty other works, "by the most popular authors of the day," "at unprecedented low prices." The list began with biographies of big men: President Andrew Jackson and Congressman John Randolph. Then it listed *A Christmas Carol* by Charles Dickens, *Sketches of Everyday Life* by Fredrika Bremer, *The American in Paris* by Jules Janin, and two works by James Fennimore Cooper: *Ned Myers; or, A Life Before the Mast* and *Wyandotté*, a work of historical fiction that presents a sympathetic treatment of Native Americans during the American Revolution. Another title was *Judith Bensaddi, the Jewess*, by the southern abolitionist Henry Ruffner, a Presbyterian minister who was relatively sympathetic to Jews: "Judith Bensaddi is the standard fictional Jewess, beautiful, dark, romantic, refined, noble, and Christian proselyte."³² An educational text promised "French, German, Italian and

Spanish, without a Master, in six easy lessons." In other words, Broussais's text was part of an eclectic mix of holdings.[33]

Bravo & Morgan listed Broussais's book next to two other self-help books for men and women, which shows that the sellers assumed a sufficient supply of gendered anxieties to boost sales. The following texts appear one after the other: *The Book of Beauty, with Modes of Improving and Preserving It, in Man and Woman*; *Self-Preservation*, by A. Broussais; and *Manhood, Causes of Its Premature Decline*. Broussais's text claims its author's authority on its title page: "Alphonse Broussais, M.D. member of the First Medical Institutions of London and Paris; Revised and amended by a physician of Philadelphia." Yet the text bears the hallmarks of subterfuge. The "Philadelphia physician" goes unnamed, and the author perhaps attempts to surrogate the authority of the prominent French physician François Jean Victor (F. J. V.) Broussais (1772–1838).[34] Whatever its dubious origins, fake narratives have real consequences, and whatever his credentials, Alphonse Broussais proceeded to explain human sexuality. "'Know thyself.' The injunction is handed down to us by the moralists of all ages," he wrote. "How can we . . . unless we acquaint ourselves with those momentous facts which have reference to our sexual organisation?"[35]

The advice Broussais gave was emblematic of a trend among antebellum sexual reformers to castigate masturbation as a health risk that ultimately threatened heterosexual relationships. In the 1830s and 1840s, reformist white women campaigned against masturbation because they wanted to preserve their sexual vitality and establish their own purity. White reformist women's conceptions of purity, one scholar argues, "did not merely exclude women of color; it depended on their sexual debasement and effected their continued exploitation."[36] Despite this implicit exclusion, however, medical practitioners nonetheless outlined universalist ideas about human sexuality while also perpetuating the idea that there are biological differences between races. Broussais, like these reformers, argued that "self-pollution or onanism is, then, that detestable practice, by which persons of either sex may defile their own bodies, alone, in secresy [*sic*], and whilst yielding to lascivious imaginations, and endeavor to imitate and procure to themselves, those sensations, which nature has appended to the commerce of the sexes."[37] Masturbation, then, was universally harmful because it diminished the pleasure that was supposed to be derived only through different-sex sex. The consequences of masturbation, Broussais warned, include loss of vitality, insomnia, blindness, insanity, and the "diminution of the size of the penis."[38] Broussais and the other reformists believed that masturbation was an uneconomical use of limited sexual capacity.

If masturbation was a waste of sperm and vitality, Broussais argued, then different-sex sex under the proper conditions could be salubrious. "The male dreams of the female: the latter of the male. One of the opposite sex is continually present to the mind, and eyes, and imagination."[39] "It is evident that the cure of nymphomania," Broussais continued, "must consist in marriage."[40] As such, Broussais suggested eligible women marry male partners of their choice rather than be subject to nymphomania. Marriage also prevented the other, equally unhealthy extreme, celibacy, which caused convulsions, hysteria, prostitution, and other such excesses.[41] In Broussais's eighth chapter, "Necessity of Intermarriage—Expediency of Early Marriages—Female Diseases Subject to be Relieved Thereby—Greater Chances of Longevity Possessed by Married People—Cases Wherein Matrimony Should be Discouraged," he warned that celibacy among women "of an erotic temperament" led to "hysterism [sic]," an "epileptic uterus," "uterine cholics [sic], and nervous diseases."[42] Reading was similarly troubling: "Women who . . . exercise the mental organs severely and continually are in most cases barren," Broussais elaborated, "while in others they become subject to serious accidents in pregnancy, because they carry all their powers toward the brain, and deprive the sexual organs of their natural energy."[43] The cure for these ills was the pleasure of sex within marriage: "When, therefore, a young marriageable maiden exhibits the symptoms of the approach of any of these diseases, she should, if possible, be united to the object of her affections."[44]

Yet New Orleans readers in the Literary Depot would have understood that marriage was a privilege available only to free citizens who could enter into legal contracts and that marriage did not guarantee personal satisfaction, sexual or otherwise. For example, white women could attempt to enter into mutually beneficial marriages with white men, but things did not always go as planned. Indeed, on the same sheet as the Literary Depot's advertisement for Broussais's text, a short article appears about a Mrs. Mary Murphy of Kentucky, described as "young and beautiful—about 25 years of age," whose husband was "confined in the Lunatic Asylum since 1840, and it was represented that his case was incurable." Kentucky's state senators did not grant her petition for a legislative divorce, with senators denying her petition eighty votes to one. "Too bad for Mrs. Mary Murphy," the paper quipped.[45] The marital possibilities for people of color were even more constrained. Interracial marriages became illegal in 1808, so free women of color whose partners were white men could not enjoy the rights and moral imprimatur of marriage. Free women of color could marry free men of color, which many did.[46] Enslaved men and women did not have the right to marry. Though some entered into what they hoped would be long-term relationships, the law did not protect their bonds, and they had little control over their bodies.[47]

Broussais elaborated on the protoeugenic implications of this racialized heterosexuality by plagiarizing Alexander Walker's chapter "Crossing," which focused on procreation as one of several beneficial outcomes of appropriate, pleasure-centered, different-sex intimacy.[48] For Broussais, although the law did not uniformly recognize free women's right to give and withhold sexual consent, nature did. According to him, a woman's volition was essential for conception. Rape could not result in pregnancy, and if a pregnant woman claimed to have been raped, she was lying: "on this subject, the assertions of women are of no weight."[49] Therefore, pleasure-centered procreation was essential to the improvement of the various human races. Walker-as-Broussais takes for granted the discredited (but seemingly indefatigable) idea that human "breeds" exist and that they can be ranked on a continuum from Europeans at the summit to Africans at the bottom.[50] Through strategic reproduction with whiter people, the authors write, a group could elevate their status: elite Persians, "by introducing handsome individuals to breed," including Georgians and Circassians, "have, by this means, completely succeeded in washing out the stain of their Mongolian origins."[51] "In Paraguay," Walker asserts and Broussais parrots, "the mixed breed . . . constitutes . . . a great majority of the people termed Spaniards or white men; and they are said to be a people superior in physical qualities to either of the races from which they have sprung, and much more prolific than the aborigines."[52] However "destitute of principles as is crossing among the varieties of mankind," Broussais writes, "its advantages have been generally observed and acknowledged."[53]

The "crossing" of European and African races, however, does not enter Broussais's imaginary, though it was ubiquitous in New Orleans and across the slaveholding Americas, and it would have destabilized his theory about the necessity of pleasure for reproduction. When the chapter turns its attention to crossings among people of African descent, it limits its focus to so-called mixtures within that group. "It is not only, however, in the mingling of distinct races that we observe an amelioration or improvement in the progeny. Results nearly equal, perhaps, arise from intermarriages amongst different tribes of the same caste."[54] Walker and Broussais allege a "striking superiority" of American-born "Creole negroes" "in corporeal and mental powers, compared with their African parents who came from different tribes."[55] This is one of the closest references to the Middle Passage and chattel slavery in the text, though it was written during the "second slavery," when Brazil, Cuba, and the US South deepened their investment in that institution to produce cotton, sugar, coffee, and other staples for global consumption.[56] Rape and the sexual exploitation of enslaved men and women were endemic to that process. Yet, as mentioned earlier, in Broussais's estimation, reproduction could only happen in the context of a heterosexual—that is to say, mutually desired and pleasurable—union.[57] In other words, the very fact of black reproduction in the context of slavery was evidence not of rape but of enslaved people's sexual agency and pleasure.[58]

Perhaps the greatest irony of this "Crossing" chapter, then, is that it cited the antebellum United States as the exemplar of the political and economic power of interbreeding without reference to slavery: "The Americans—a melange of all the different nations of Europe, though mostly of English, Scottish and Irish descent, are noted for activity and enterprise: and their march of improvement, in practical science, the mechanical arts, and commerce, has surpassed what could have been anticipated in a people cast into a wilderness so distant from the civilized world. Their rapid increase and improvement has attracted the admiration of Europe, and they have offered to the world a splendid example of justice and national freedom."[59] This passage defined "Americans" as people of English, Scottish, and Irish extraction and excluded other Euro-Americans, to say nothing of Indigenous and African peoples. The chapter attributed US success to interbreeding among Europeans, yet it made no mention of slavery or the foundational role that the production and reproduction of black bodies played in US commerce.

"Snowy and Sooty": Disciplining Desire through Display

While Broussais's text certainly reached the New Orleans market, works of reform physiology were generally unpopular in slaveholding regions. Slaveholders associated such texts with abolitionist and women's movements.[60] So perhaps after perusing a copy of Broussais's text, a reader at the Literary Depot then turned his attention to one of the local newspapers, such as the *Daily Orleanian*, "Official Journal of Third Municipality."[61] Like Barnum and Broussais, its "egotistical" editor, J. C. Prendergast, used his platform to impart a version of reformist norms onto southern print culture.[62] In the nineteenth century, in light of slave emancipation across much of the northern United States, Saint-Domingue, and the British Caribbean, US slaveholders sought to bolster their power abroad through efforts to annex or support the other proslavery states, such as Cuba and Brazil.[63] At home, southern elites reinforced their concentrated political and economic power by hoarding for themselves the right to sexual pleasure.[64] Local judges and journalists manned the boundary between acceptable expressions of heterosexuality and their "unacceptable" counterparts, such as prostitution. Like Barnum and Broussais, the *Daily Orleanian* put people and their sexualities on display. When it editorialized about court proceedings against alleged Irish American prostitutes, the paper sought to shame the immigrant women away from "vices"—alcohol, sex work, and recreational sex with black men—and toward the bourgeois marriages that would bring them into patriarchal, white households and, by extension, the nation. Together, the courts of law and public opinion ensured that elite white men's sexual excesses were sated, while marginalized women and men faced punishment for seeking to enjoy the same prerogatives.

If explicit discussions of chattel slavery were hard to come by in *Self-Preservation*, its imperatives were stamped into every page of the *Daily Orleanian*. Antebellum New Orleans rested on a foundation of sugar and cotton plantations—and the hierarchies that sustained them.[65] "Sale of a plantation," the *Daily Orleanian* announced in February 1849. Its contents included a lot in the city's Third Municipality on Casa Calvo Street between Clouet and Louisa Streets, a sugar refinery, and three enslaved persons: "Tony, a negro man aged about 37 years, drayman"; "Ben, a negro man, aged about 35 years, sugar boiler"; and "Fanny, a negro girl, aged about 33 years, a plain cook."[66] This sugar plantation was not adjacent to the city; it was in the city. The plantation and city shared space, and they shared values. "Like ideas about honor and manhood, independence, and whiteness," one historian writes, "the collective sexual aggressiveness enabled and valorized by the slave trade helped form a group identity for slave-owning white men." Slave traders and owners alike "spoke of themselves as if they were animated, erect penises, one-eyed men watching for mulatto women to rape."[67] While this attention concentered on the bodies of so-called fancy women of a lighter phenotype, all enslaved women and men were subject to sexual violence. Perhaps that pervasive threat in part explains why the enslaved woman Betsey, "aged about 40 years—height about 5 feet 4 inches; black hair, black eyes and bad teeth," ran away from her owner, who then posted a runaway slave advertisement in the *Daily Orleanian* in hopes of her return to bondage.[68]

The systematic rape of enslaved persons is harder to detect on the pages of the *Daily Orleanian*, but the paper virtually exhibited the supposed sexual availability of free women of color when it published advertisements for quadroon balls, through which white men and free women of color entered financial and sexual arrangements. Although so-called interracial sex occurred across the nation, the fancy trade and quadroon balls made New Orleans one headquarters of interracial heterosexuality.[69] "The proprietors of this splendid Ball Room," one *Daily Orleanian* advertisement reads, "respectfully inform the public that this establishment will be open during the season; for White Balls on THURSDAY, FRIDAY and SUNDAY evenings." "For Quarteroon Balls on WEDNESDAY and SATURDAY evenings," the advertisement continues, "Nothing has been neglected to make it one of the most brilliant and agreeable of the city. A superior Orchestra is engaged . . . and the liquors are choice description. A Restaurant at fixed price is attached to the establishment." The manager who published this advertisement guaranteed civility: "The strictest order will be observed."[70] Notwithstanding the inherent asymmetry of these arrangements, white men's pursuit of heterosexual pleasure with free women of color could be classed as acceptable and even "orderly" activities.

By contrast, white "women" whose gender and sexual expression contravened bourgeois norms became spectacles and, at times, objects of scorn. "A female in male attire was arrested in Birmingham, Conn.," the *Daily Orleanian* reported via a lengthy quotation from the *New Haven Palladium*. "Her assumed name is Charles Crandall, and she gave Lydia Ransom, as her real name." Crandall was born in Providence, Rhode Island, before being "enticed from her home when only 11 years of age, by a young man of 18, and entered on board of a ship with him for a whaling voyage, she acting as cabin boy."[71] This narration evokes the popular seduction plots in which rakish men took advantage of naïve girls and young women. As such, Crandall's presentation and labor as a "cabin boy" who might have engaged in a sexual relationship with the older man queers the seduction narrative even as it preserves such tales' age-based asymmetries.[72] After the unnamed man died aboard the ship, Crandall went to the US consul and returned to an unnamed port in the US South (possibly New Orleans). "According to her story, it is five years since she left home, most of the time having been spent on shipboard as a seaman. When arrested, she says she was on her way to New York in search of occupation as a seaman."[73] When Prendergast reprinted this story in the New Orleans newspaper, he made Crandall into a spectacle, which at once enforced and troubled binary notions of gender.[74]

The paper also displayed white women, many of them Irish immigrants, who operated outside norms of bourgeois marriage, whether by choice, circumstance, or some combination of the two. Poor "famine" immigrants from Ireland became a highly visible, if vulnerable, population in the Third Municipality, and the *Daily Orleanian* could be sympathetic. In January 1850, the paper criticized the local government's tax of 12.5 cents per immigrant: "Were it apportioned to each of the municipalities, for the purpose of relieving the distressed located therein, then, there would be no questionings nor complainings; nor would paupers be so frequently encountered. Now, that there are hundreds of poor, half famishing immigrants in our midst, if a quota of the monies, mentioned, were placed in the hands of the Irish Union Immigrant Society, what immense good could be achieved?"[75] To be sure, Prendergast had an investment in securing such funding: he was a founder of the short-lived

Irish Union Immigrant Society.[76] Still, he was a Whig when most southern Irishmen supported the Democrats; as one historian explains, Prendergast "saw himself as a friend of the working man. He believed Whig policies in support of national improvements were a boon to immigrants and other poor whites looking for work."[77] Women were among the most vulnerable of the poor immigrants. The *Daily Orleanian* ran an advertisement for a "young widow lady whose baby has recently died" who sought "a situation as a wet nurse."[78] The ad does not mention her nationality, but she might have been an immigrant woman who used Prendergast's platform as one route to relief.

Concern shaded into scorn when working-class women engaged in behavior that reformists deemed immoral, such as alcohol consumption, especially when it occurred in public. "Spatial inequalities," the historians Elsa Barkley Brown and Gregg D. Kimball argue, "made many activities engaged in by the working-class more visible because, lacking private facilities, their work and leisure were more public."[79] Prendergast, who supported the temperance movement, used the pages of his newspaper to shame working-class women who struggled with alcohol addiction. For example, he describes a scene in Recorder Pierre Seuzeneau's office, wherein the latter man presided over hearings: "we were pained by the exhibitions of feminine *loveliness* which met our gaze," Prendergast condescended. He mocked the "bloated features, vacant-stare [*sic*], and unwashed garb" of one woman.[80] In a similar column, he criticized a woman named Mary Waters, "who belies her nomenclature, as she is fonder of any other liquid than water; rarely mixes her name up with Holland gin, or brings it in contact with brandy." Prendergast deemed her a member "of the frail sisterhood, remarkable for any other attribute than virtue."[81]

As with alcohol addiction, sex work also carried physical risks. The 1830s marked a turning point in public concern over prostitution across the United States and Atlantic world. Elites were concerned that working-class women were moving beyond the reach of patriarchal power.[82] Reformist women's organizations, such as the New York Female Moral Reform Society, sought to rescue downtrodden women in urban slums.[83] Concerns about sexually transmitted infections and public health were also part of this shift.[84] Such infections were individual ailments that threatened the general public's health and therefore became cause for collective mobilization. This panic about prostitution did not manifest itself the same way across the country. In Savannah, for example, poor white women faced arrest for drunkenness, vagrancy, and prostitution but not necessarily to the same extent as in New Orleans.[85] In New York, leaders hired Dr. William Sanger, resident physician at Blackwell's Island Hospital, to investigate prostitution. With assistance from police, Sanger produced the monumental *History of Prostitution*.[86] That work includes a cautionary tale about a "girl, eighteen years of age, born in Louisiana, of highly respectable parents," who "was induced to elope from a boarding-school in the vicinity of New Orleans with a man who accorded with her romantic ideal of a lover." Sanger continues with the morality tale: "No marriage vows ever passed between them; she trusted him as the heroine of a modern novel would have done, and he deceived her, as all modern rakes deceive their victims." They lived together until the man left her dishonored and "destitute." After his departure, "she had no other means of support than open and avowed prostitution." Sanger blamed boarding schools and education in general, which coaxed white women out of the safety of traditional roles.[87] Locally, however, this prostitution panic was driven in part by electoral politics. In a bitter election in 1850 New Orleans, Recorder Seuzeneau's challenger accused him of being soft on prostitution and "white slavery," a charge that included details about immigrant women being forced to work in brothels.[88] In part to compensate for that earlier vulnerability and to placate local reformers such as Prendergast, Seuzeneau increased enforcement of antiprostitution laws, which effectively increased surveillance and incarceration of a vulnerable—yet, in some ways, increasingly independent—group of women.

Local law enforcement and Prendergast's paper together aimed particular vitriol at white women who, by necessity or choice, entered into "liaisons" with men of African descent, slave or free.[89] In a column titled "Snowy White and Sooty," a play on the tale by the Brothers Grimm, Prendergast specifically shamed white women and enslaved men who had been arrested for cohabitation. On January 15, 1852, the paper mentioned "Eliza Saucier, or *Liz*, for short, and Mary Darcy, a pair of fallen angels—dwellers in *Sanctity Row*, on *Elysian* Fields street [who] were arrested for cohabiting with two snow balls one of them Spencer, owned by the Cotton Press Co.; the other Ambrose, the property of Mr. Cu-

cullu. The frail fair ones were sent to the parish prison—the darkies received a half hundred lashes between them."[90] The following month, the paper ran a similar article, this time a case from the Second Municipality: "Margaret Campbell, a white woman, and Scott, a negro, were arrested for cohabitation, and brought before his Honor of the Second Municipality, who sent 'Snowy White' to the workhouse for a quarter of a year, and ordered 'Sooty' to be flogged. The frail female woman ought to be flogged also."[91] Rather than tolerate these intimacies, Prendergast called for corporal punishment for white women and black men who chose to engage in interracial cohabitation.

A few months after those columns appeared, the *Daily Orleanian* called attention to white women accused not of cohabitation with a specific man but of sex work more broadly, with no mention of the race and status of their alleged clients. "Recorder Seuzeneau seems determined on ridding the Third district of the lewd and abandoned women who prowl about and infest it; more particularly those of that famed locality on Elysian Fields street, denominated Sanctity Row." Prendergast named all fourteen suspected "ladies of easy virtue" in the column.[92] In a column of the same name the following month, Prendergast noted the upswing in enforcement: "The recorders and police seem to be extremely vigilant just now, in arresting and punishing the frail and fair, who have strayed from virtue's paths."[93] These so-called lewd women included "Mary White, Julia Ann Clarke and Mrs Mitchel, alias 'Irish Suze,' [who] were arrested as 'nymphs of the pave,' yesterday, and caged. Mary Bruel, a 'green horn,' who was washing for Suze at the time the officers appeared, was also arrested. Mrs. McGee, the female wife of Ned McGee, who paid a visit to the guardhouse yesterday to see her liege lord, who is in quod for keeping a house of ill fame, was herself caged as ones of 'em.[94] Here, at least two women—"Irish Suze" Mitchel and Mrs. McGee—who were presumably married to white men, nonetheless came in for public scrutiny due to their alleged roles as brothel keepers.

Finally, the paper makes at least one cryptic reference to an enslaved woman who reportedly serviced a white male client at her owner's command. In a column entitled "Amalgamation," the headline proclaimed the following: "Francis Pitt, a 'white man,' was arrested on Marigny street, at 12 o'clock on Monday night, for walking with a colored *ladi*, with his arm around her neck and for harboring other designs."[95] Unlike wealthy men, who could own women of color as slaves or enter into *plaçage* arrangements with free women of color, all in private, this man's attempt to enjoy a similar pleasure had taken place in public. This left him vulnerable to arrest, as authorities could not fathom a legitimate reason for him to socialize with an enslaved woman at midnight. Pitt's being caught with a bondswoman at midnight—and then strategically deployed quotation marks in Prendergast's account—rendered Pitt's whiteness probationary. Second, the woman of color is referred to as a "ladi" to ensure that readers understood that she was anything but. Prendergast and the local authorities assumed that she was a sex worker, and they punished both participants accordingly. Pitt "was fined a V, or ten days in the parish prison, and the wench was sentenced to twenty five lashes."[96] Their racialized punishments reflected and reinforced social hierarchies: the white man was fined and incarcerated; the enslaved woman endured corporal punishment. The latter punishment, the paper alleged, would perhaps rehabilitate the woman's owner: "This will interfere with the legal business of the boquet sellers, and curtail the profits of their owners, whi [sic] send them out, ostensibly, to sell flowers."[97] This oblique reference situates this woman at the intersection of peddling and prostitution, suggesting owners sent their bondswomen into the streets under the pretext of lawful peddling but in reality to sell their own bodies, for the master's profit. For Prendergast, however, this was yet another form of unacceptable heterosexuality, one that raised the specter of cross-racial reproduction.

Conclusion

In the early American period, reformers as different as Broussais and Prendergast used texts to circulate ideas about the benefits of proper heterosexuality as well as the harms of its improper manifestations. Whether from an appropriated perch in the Ivory Tower or in the middle of a slavery-centered metropolis, these authors used print culture to call attention to spectacles of approved and proscribed heterosexuality.

Taken together, these texts show that heterosexuality gained ascendance in early America by cleaving along intersecting hierarchies of race, gender, status, and class. For Broussais, a man's ability to control urges toward masturbation showed the ability to master himself and to preserve his limited sexual abilities for proper enjoyment within a mutually agreeable, heterosexual union. For men in the slaveholding South, by contrast, one of the perquisites of wealth and status was the ability not to have limits placed on one's sexual appetites but instead to claim access to the bodies of every subordinate. Those most subordinate were enslaved women, whose supposed hypersexuality rendered them ever available in the minds of many men. What this meant in practice, however, is that enslaved women lived under the constant threat of rape. Free women of color could exercise some measure of choice in the matter, but they remained vulnerable to exploitation in the patriarchal society. Finally, white women who engaged in sexual relationships outside of marriage became vulnerable to charges of immorality and prostitution. Those who had sex with black men were particularly stigmatized and criminalized.

The history of sexuality is inseparable from the history of racism. Even as heterosexuality became hegemonic, rendering same-sex desire criminal and hidden, all members of society could not expect to enjoy different-sex pleasures equally. In the antebellum United States, pleasure was an entitlement for heterosexual, white male citizens. For many others, whether those who enjoyed same-sex intimacies or so-called straight people who lacked the social standing to exercise choice, acceptable heterosexuality—elite people's enjoyment of different-sex intimacies—could become the vector of marginalization and oppression. In this way, heterosexuality could become pathological, a means of producing and reproducing the hierarchies and inequalities that perpetuate elite people's pleasure at great cost to all others.

NOTES

1. Alex Bontemps, "Seeing Slavery: How Paintings Make Words Look Different," *Common-Place* 1, no. 4 (July 2001), www.common-place-archives.org.
2. Fred Moten, *In the Break: The Aesthetics of the Black Radical Tradition* (Minneapolis: University of Minnesota Press, 2003), 4.
3. Saidiya Hartman, "Venus in Two Acts," *small axe* 26 (June 2008): 5. See also Marisa J. Fuentes, *Dispossessed Lives: Enslaved Women, Violence, and the Archive* (Philadelphia: University of Pennsylvania Press, 2016).
4. Vincent Woodard, *The Delectable Negro: Human Consumption and Homoeroticism within U.S. Slave Culture* (New York: NYU Press, 2014); Carlyle Van Thompson, *Eating the Black Body: Miscegenation as Sexual Consumption in African American Literature and Culture* (Durham, NC: Duke University Press, 2006).

5. Emily Clark, *The Strange History of the American Quadroon: Free Women of Color in the Revolutionary Atlantic World* (Chapel Hill: University of North Carolina Press, 2013); Doris Garraway, *The Libertine Colony: Creolization in the Early French Caribbean* (Durham, NC: Duke University Press, 2005); Jennifer L. Morgan, *Laboring Women: Reproduction and Gender in New World Slavery* (Philadelphia: University of Pennsylvania Press, 2004); Adrienne Davis, "'Don't Let Nobody Bother Yo' Principle': The Sexual Economy of American Slavery," in *Sister Circle: Black Women and Work*, ed. Sharon Harley and the Black Women and Work Collective (New Brunswick, NJ: Rutgers University Press, 2002), 103–27. On the fancy trade, see Alexandra Finley, "'Cash to Corinna': Domestic Labor and Sexual Economy in the 'Fancy Trade,'" *Journal of American History* 104, no. 2 (September 2017): 410–30; Edward E. Baptist, "'Cuffy,' 'Fancy Maids,' and 'One-Eyed Men': Rape, Commodification, and the Domestic Slave Trade in the United States," *American Historical Review* 106, no. 5 (December 2001): 1619–50; Walter Johnson, *Soul by Soul: Life inside the Antebellum Slave Market* (Cambridge, MA: Harvard University Press, 1999). For critiques of the heteroessentialism of this literature, see Jim Downs, "With Only a Trace: Same-Sex Sexual Desire and Violence on Slave Plantations, 1607–1865," in *Connexions: Histories of Race and Sex in North America*, ed. Jennifer Brier, Jim Downs, and Jennifer L. Morgan (Urbana: University of Illinois Press, 2016), 15–37; Thomas A. Foster, "The Sexual Abuse of Black Men under American Slavery," *Journal of the History of Sexuality* 20, no. 3 (September 2011): 445–64; Jennifer Manion, "Historic Heteroessentialism and Other Orderings in Early America," *Signs: Journal of Women in Culture and Society* 34, no. 4 (Summer 2009): 981–1003.
6. Jonathan Ned Katz, *The Invention of Heterosexuality* (1995; repr., Chicago: University of Chicago Press, 2014), 14.
7. As Michel Foucault contends, rather than assume a transhistorical silencing around sexuality, we would do well to consider the excess of such discourse and its attendant purposes. "One had to speak of sex," he writes: "A policing of sex: that is, not the rigor of a taboo, but the necessity of regulating sex through useful and public discourses." Foucault, *History of Sexuality, Volume I: An Introduction*, trans. Robert Hurley (New York: Pantheon Books, 1978), 24–25.
8. Emily Epstein Landau, *Spectacular Wickedness: Sex, Race, and Memory in Storyville, New Orleans* (Baton Rouge: Louisiana State University Press, 2013); Alecia P. Long, *The Great Southern Babylon: Sex, Race, and Respectability in New Orleans, 1865–1920* (Baton Rouge: Louisiana State University Press, 2004). While these studies focus on the late nineteenth and early twentieth centuries, they both situate the later period within a longer context that dated to the earlier antebellum period.
9. The full title is *Self-Preservation; or, Sexual Physiology Revealed; being facts of vital importance to the married and unmarried: with practical remarks on love, courtship, marriage, its proper seasons, how to choose a partner, mysteries of generation, causes and cures of sterility, abuse and economy of the generative organs, effects of*

excessive indulgence, consequences of total abstinence from coition, &c. &c.: Also, useful hints to lovers, husbands and wives.

10. I take seriously Britt Rusert's important critique that "the deployment of *pseudo-science* tries to imagine a scientific present unencumbered by an embarrassing scientific past." In this case, however, Alphonse Broussais's work was inconsistent with its contemporary medical thought. As will be discussed shortly, this work was not a good-faith contribution to scientific discourse; it was a forgery. Rusert, *Fugitive Science: Empiricism and Freedom in Early African American Culture* (New York: NYU Press, 2017), 6 (emphasis in original). Other works that explore the relationship between race and health in early America include Rana A. Hogarth, *Medicalizing Blackness: Making Racial Difference in the Atlantic World, 1780–1840* (Chapel Hill: University of North Carolina Press, 2017); Deirdre Cooper Owens, *Medical Bondage: Race, Gender, and the Origins of American Gynecology* (Athens: University of Georgia Press, 2017); Marie Jenkins Schwartz, *Birthing a Slave: Motherhood and Medicine in the Antebellum South* (Cambridge, MA: Harvard University Press, 2006); Kathleen M. Brown, *Foul Bodies: Cleanliness in Early America* (New Haven, CT: Yale University Press, 2011); Stephen Jay Gould, *The Mismeasure of Man* (1981; repr., New York: Norton, 1996). Works that center the scientific value of enslaved people's knowledge and praxis of healing include Rusert, *Fugitive Science*; Pablo Gómez, *The Experiential Caribbean: Creating Knowledge and Healing in the Early Modern Atlantic* (Chapel Hill: University of North Carolina Press, 2017); James H. Sweet, *Domingos Álvares, African Healing, and the Intellectual History of the Atlantic World* (Chapel Hill: University of North Carolina Press, 2013); Sharla M. Fett, *Working Cures: Healing, Health, and Power on Southern Slave Plantations* (Chapel Hill: University of North Carolina Press, 2002).

11. "Under the institution of racial slavery," Martha Hodes writes, "Southerners could respond to sexual liaisons between white women and black men with a measure of toleration; only with black freedom did such liaisons begin to provoke a near-inevitable alarm, one that culminated in the tremendous white violence of the 1890s and after." Hodes, *White Women, Black Men: Illicit Sex in the Nineteenth-Century South* (New Haven, CT: Yale University Press, 1997), 1.

12. April R. Haynes, *Riotous Flesh: Women, Physiology, and the Solitary Vice in Nineteenth-Century America* (Chicago: University of Chicago Press, 2015), 25; Manion, "Historic Heteroessentialism."

13. Siobhan B. Somerville, *Queering the Color Line: Race and the Invention of Homosexuality in American Culture* (Durham, NC: Duke University Press, 2000); George Chauncey, *Gay New York: Gender, Urban Culture, and the Makings of the Gay Male World, 1890–1940* (New York: Basic Books, 1994).

14. Stephanie M.H. Camp, "The Pleasures of Resistance: Enslaved Women and Body Politics in the Plantation South, 1830–1861," *Journal of Southern History* 68, no. 3 (August 2002): 533–72. There is a larger debate about the possibilities of sexual pleasure in the context of chattel slavery. See Treva B. Lindsey and Jessica Marie

Johnson, "Searching for Climax: Black Erotic Lives in Slavery and Freedom," *Meridians* 12, no. 2 (2014): 169–95.

15. *New Orleans Daily Picayune*, March 15, 1840, 3 (emphasis in original).

16. On reproduction, "increase," and slavery, see Morgan, *Laboring Women*; Daina Ramey Berry, *The Price for Their Pound of Flesh: The Value of the Enslaved, from Womb to Grave, in the Building of a Nation* (Boston: Beacon, 2017); Daina Ramey Berry, *"Swing the Sickle for the Harvest Is Ripe": Gender and Slavery in Antebellum Georgia* (Urbana: University of Illinois Press, 2007); Sasha Turner, *Contested Bodies: Pregnancy, Childrearing, and Slavery in Jamaica* (Philadelphia: University of Pennsylvania Press, 2017).

17. Appendix to Newton M. Curtis, *The Black-Plumed Riflemen: A Tale of the Revolution* (New York: Burgess, Stringer, 1846), 126–28.

18. Obituary for William Brisbane Dick, *Publishers' Weekly*, no. 1546, 434, http://googlebooks.com; John Strausbaugh, "When Barnum Took Manhattan," *New York Times*, November 9, 2007, www.nytimes.com.

19. Claudia D. Johnson, "That Guilty Third Tier: Prostitution in Nineteenth-Century American Theaters," *American Quarterly* 27, no. 5 (December 1975): 582.

20. Elizabeth Alexander, "The Venus Hottentot (1825)," *Callaloo* 32, no. 3 (2009): 725–28.

21. Sharla M. Fett, *Recaptured Africans: Surviving Slave Ships, Detention, and Dislocation in the Final Years of the Slave Trade* (Chapel Hill: University of North Carolina Press, 2017), 63. See also Benjamin Reiss, *The Showman and the Slave: Race, Death, and Memory in Barnum's America* (Cambridge, MA: Harvard University Press, 2001).

22. Raymond Corbey, "Ethnographic Showcases, 1870–1930," *Cultural Anthropology* 8, no. 3 (August 1993): 354. On the connection between display, difference, and ethnology, see Juliet Hooker, *Theorizing Race in the Americas: Douglass, Sarmiento, Du Bois, and Vasconcelos* (New York: Oxford University Press, 2017), 6–11; Andrew Curran, *The Anatomy of Blackness: Science and Slavery in an Age of Enlightenment* (Baltimore: Johns Hopkins University Press, 2013).

23. Strausbaugh, "When Barnum Took Manhattan."

24. Burgess, Stringer & Co. advertisement, *National Police Gazette* 1, no. 43 (July 4, 1846): 367. The number of advertisements is based on a keyword search of ProQuest Historical Newspapers. The *Police Gazette*—which owed its rise to the increasing popularity of the "sporting press" that emerged in urban areas in the 1830s and 1840s, paperbacks, and the penny press—"could arguably proclaim to have been one of the country's most sensational—and influential—journals of the late nineteenth and early twentieth centuries." At its peak, the New York–based publication's "regular readership included an estimated half a million or more men. On sale at most urban newsstands and available to be read gratis in almost every barbershop, hotel, pool hall, fire company, and street-corner saloon, each issue passed through dozens of hands, virtually all of them male." Howard P.

Chudacoff, *The Age of the Bachelor: Creating an American Subculture* (Princeton, NJ: Princeton University Press, 1999), 187.

25. Benedict R. O'G. Anderson, *Imagined Communities: Reflections on the Origin and Spread of Nationalism* (1983; repr., London: Verso, 2006); Kirsten Silva Gruesz, *Ambassadors of Culture: The Transamerican Origins of Latino Writing* (Princeton, NJ: Princeton University Press, 2002), chap. 4.

26. *Daily Picayune*, August 13, 1840, 2.

27. *Daily Picayune*, December 24, 1840, 2.

28. *Daily Picayune*, December 26, 1840, 3 (*Truth Teller*); *Daily Picayune*, January 1, 1841, 3 (Goshen butter).

29. *Daily Picayune*, April 21, 1842, 2.

30. For reference to 18 Exchange Place, see *Daily Picayune*, May 21, 1842, 2. On the second branch, see *Daily Picayune*, January 18, 1843, 2.

31. *New York New World*, October 7, 1843. On race and literacy in the antebellum South, see, among others, Beth Barton Schweiger, *A Literate South: Reading before Emancipation* (New Haven, CT: Yale University Press, 2019); Michael O'Brien, *Conjectures of Order: Intellectual Life and the American South, 1810–1860* (Chapel Hill: University of North Carolina Press, 2004). On literacy among the free people of color, see Elizabeth McHenry, *Forgotten Readers: Recovering the Lost History of African American Literary Societies* (Durham, NC: Duke University Press, 2002). On literacy among *gens de couleurs libres* in New Orleans, see Rodolphe Lucien Desdunes, *Our People and Our History: A Tribute to the Creole People of Color in Memory of the Great Men They Have Given Us and of the Good Works They Have Accomplished*, ed. and trans. Dorothea Olga McCants (1911; repr., Baton Rouge: Louisiana State University Press, 1973). Finally, on print culture in New Orleans, see Gruesz, *Ambassadors of Culture*.

32. Frederic Cople Jaher, *A Scapegoat in the New Wilderness: The Origins and Rise of Anti-Semitism in America* (Cambridge, MA: Harvard University Press, 1996), 162.

33. "New Orleans Literary Depot," *Daily Picayune*, February 28, 1844, 2.

34. F. J. V. Broussais wrote *Histoire des phlegmasies ou inflammations chroniques* (1808), *Examen des doctrines medicales et des systèmes de nosology* (1816), and *De l'irritation et de la folie* (*On Irritation and Insanity*, 1828). J. D. Rolleston, "F. J. V. Broussais (1772–1838): His Life and Doctrines: (Section of the History of Medicine)," *Proceedings of the Royal Society of Medicine* 32, no. 5 (March 1939): 408. For a reference to Broussais in a New Orleans–based medical journal, see Samuel G. Armor, "On the Use of Purgatives in the Treatment of Bilious Fevers, and Other Bilious Affections of the South and West," *New Orleans Medical and Surgical Journal* 9, no. 5 (March 1853): 623. On the basis of the records consulted, scholars did not cite Alphonse Broussais in scholarly literature, and today the world's preeminent libraries do not hold copies of his tome. The obscure copy cited here is held at the Library Company of Philadelphia, the city where the unnamed coauthor was allegedly based.

35. Broussais, *Self-Preservation*, iii.

36. Haynes, *Riotous Flesh*, 21–22.

37. Samuel Auguste Tissot, *L'Onanisme* (1832), quoted in Broussais, *Self-Preservation*, 14–15.

38. Broussais, *Self-Preservation*, 16–23, 38, 23.

39. Broussais, 56.

40. Broussais, 105.

41. Jann Matlock, *Scenes of Seduction: Prostitution, Hysteria, and Reading Difference in Nineteenth-Century France* (New York: Columbia University Press, 1994), 2.

42. Broussais, *Self-Preservation*, 104–5.

43. Broussais, 165.

44. Broussais, 106.

45. "Application for Divorce," *Daily Picayune*, February 28, 1844, 2. See also Loren Schweninger, *Families in Crisis in the Old South: Divorce, Slavery, and the Law* (Chapel Hill: University of North Carolina Press, 2012).

46. "The territory's first civil digest, compiled in 1808, unambiguously required 'free white persons,' 'free persons of colour,' and slaves to marry endogamously, thus using the regulation of sex to define the tripartite system's three castes." Jennifer M. Spear, *Race, Sex, and Social Order in Early New Orleans* (Baltimore: Johns Hopkins University Press, 2009), 217.

47. Tera W. Hunter, *Bound in Wedlock: Slave and Free Marriage in the Nineteenth Century* (Cambridge, MA: Harvard University Press, 2017).

48. Alexander Walker, *Intermarriage; or, The Natural Laws by Which Beauty, Health and Intellect Result from Certain Unions, and Deformity, Disease and Insanity, from Others* (London: John Churchill, 1838). It was by the same printers in 1841 and then in Philadelphia by Lindsay and Blakiston in 1853. It is unlikely that the average reader would have known the chapter was plagiarized, so here I use "Broussais" as the author.

49. Broussais, *Self-Preservation*, 124. See also Sharon Block, *Rape and Sexual Power in Early America* (Chapel Hill: University of North Carolina Press, 2006).

50. Hogarth, *Medicalizing Blackness*; Ibram X. Kendi, *Stamped from the Beginning: The Definitive History of Racist Ideas in America* (New York: Nation Books, 2016); Gould, *Mismeasure of Man*.

51. Broussais, *Self-Preservation*, 139.

52. Broussais, 142.

53. Broussais, 145.

54. Broussais, 143–44.

55. Broussais, 144.

56. Dale W. Tomich, *Through the Prism of Slavery: Labor, Capital, and World Economy* (Lanham, MD: Rowman and Littlefield, 2004); "The Second Slavery: Mass Slavery, World Economy and Competitive Microhistories," ed. Dale Tomich and Michael Zeuske, special issue of *Review* 34, nos. 1–2 (2008).

57. José Vasconcelos, *The Cosmic Race: A Bilingual Edition*, trans. Didier T. Jaén (Baltimore: Johns Hopkins University Press, 1997); José F. Buscaglia-Salgado, *Undoing*

Empire: Race and Nation in the Mulatto Caribbean (Minneapolis: University of Minnesota Press, 2003).

58. Walter Johnson penned an enduring critique of this pernicious use of agency to obscure the specific predicaments of chattel slavery: "the term 'agency' smuggles a notion of the universality of a liberal notion of selfhood, with its emphasis on independence and choice, right into the middle of a conversation about slavery against which that supposedly natural (at least for white men) condition was originally defined." Johnson, "On Agency," *Journal of Social History* 37, no. 1 (Autumn 2003): 115.

59. Broussais, *Self-Preservation*, 144; Walker, *Intermarriage*, 364–65.

60. Haynes, *Riotous Flesh*, 15.

61. After competition between American and French Creole elites led to the city's 1836 partitioning into three units, the Third Municipality, which included Faubourg Marigny, became the political unit for free émigrés of color from Saint-Domingue; French, Irish, and German immigrants; Americans from the Eastern Seaboard; and enslaved persons from across the African diaspora. The *Daily Orleanian*, which was published between 1847 and 1858, generally consisted of four pages, two in French and two in English. Richard Campanella, *Bienville's Dilemma: A Historical Geography of New Orleans* (Lafayette: University of Louisiana-Lafayette Press, 2008); Linda Schneider and Sheila Lee, comps., "Louisiana Newspaper Project: Parish Indexes," Louisiana State University Special Collections, Baton Rouge, 2012, www.lib.lsu.edu.

62. David T. Gleeson, *The Irish in the South, 1815–1877* (Chapel Hill: University of North Carolina Press, 2001), 63.

63. Walter Johnson, *River of Dark Dreams: Slavery and Empire in the Cotton Kingdom* (Cambridge, MA: Harvard University Press, 2013); Matthew Karp, *This Vast Southern Empire: Slaveholders at the Helm of American Foreign Policy* (Cambridge, MA: Harvard University Press, 2016); Robert E. Bonner, *Mastering America: Southern Slaveholders and the Crisis of American Nationhood* (New York: Cambridge University Press, 2009); Matthew Pratt Guterl, *American Mediterranean: Southern Slaveholders in the Age of Emancipation* (Cambridge, MA: Harvard University Press, 2008).

64. Haynes, *Riotous Flesh*, 7.

65. Calvin Schermerhorn, *The Business of Slavery and the Rise of American Capitalism, 1815–1860* (New Haven, CT: Yale University Press, 2015); Edward E. Baptist, *The Half Has Never Been Told: Slavery and the Making of American Capitalism* (New York: Basic Books, 2014); Sven Beckert, *Empire of Cotton: A Global History* (New York: Vintage Books, 2014); W. Johnson, *River of Dark Dreams*; Scott P. Marler, *The Merchants' Capital: New Orleans and the Political Economy of the Nineteenth-Century South* (New York: Cambridge University Press, 2013); Richard Follett, *The Sugar Masters: Planters and Slaves in Louisiana's Cane World, 1820–1860* (Baton Rouge: Louisiana State University Press, 2005).

66. *Daily Orleanian*, February 12, 1849, 2.

67. Baptist, "'Cuffy,' 'Fancy Maids,' and 'One-Eyed Men,'" 1640.

68. L. A. Caldwell, "Ten Dollars Reward," *Daily Orleanian*, January 7, 1851, 2.

69. Clark, *Strange History of the American Quadroon*. Clark challenges the idea that these quadroon balls were as common as popular representations suggest.

70. *Daily Orleanian*, February 12, 1849, 2.

71. *Daily Orleanian*, February 9, 1849, 2. Deborah Sampson was perhaps the most famous example, but there were many other similar ones. See Carol Berkin, *Revolutionary Mothers: Women in the Struggle for America's Independence* (New York: Knopf, 2005).

72. See Block, *Rape and Sexual Power in Early America*.

73. *Daily Orleanian*, February 9, 1849.

74. Angela Y. Davis, *Blues Legacies and Black Feminism: Gertrude "Ma" Rainey, Bessie Smith, and Billie Holiday* (New York: Pantheon Books, 1998); Judith Butler, *Gender Trouble: Feminism and the Subversion of Identity* (New York: Routledge, 1990); George Chauncey, *Gay New York: Gender, Urban Culture, and the Makings of the Gay Male World, 1890–1940* (New York: Basic Books, 1994).

75. *Daily Orleanian*, January 3, 1850, 2.

76. Gleeson, *Irish in the South*, 62.

77. David T. Gleeson, *The Green and the Gray: The Irish in the Confederate States of America* (Chapel Hill: University of North Carolina Press, 2013), 12. Under the Second Party System (mid-1840s to mid-1860s), the Whig Party challenged Andrew Jackson's Democratic Party. The Louisiana Whigs favored protective tariffs to help build domestic manufacturing, a national bank, investment in infrastructure, and protection for political minorities rather than a strict popular sovereignty. The Whigs held power in Louisiana in the late 1830s, but their appeal declined by the mid-1840s. See William H. Adams, *The Whig Party of Louisiana* (Lafayette: University of Southwestern Louisiana Press, 1973). For an analysis of masculinity, the Irish, the Second Party System, and US expansion, see Paul Foos, *A Short, Offhand, Killing Affair: Soldiers and Social Conflict during the Mexican-American War* (Chapel Hill: University of North Carolina Press, 2002).

78. "Wet Nurse," *Daily Orleanian*, January 7, 1851, 2.

79. Elsa Barkley Brown and Gregg D. Kimball, "Mapping the Terrain of Black Richmond," in *The New African American Urban History*, ed. Kenneth Goings and Raymond Mohl (Thousand Oaks, CA: Sage, 1996), 97.

80. "A Recorder's Office," *Daily Orleanian*, May 5, 1849, 2 (emphasis in original).

81. "Frailty, Thy Name Is Waters," *Daily Orleanian*, January 7, 1851, 2.

82. As Christine Stansell argues, "The alarm over prostitution was one response to the growing social and sexual distance that working-class women—especially working-class daughters—were traveling from patriarchal regulation." Stansell, *City of Women: Sex and Class in New York, 1789–1860* (New York: Knopf, 1986), 171–72.

83. Nicolette Severson, "'Devils Would Blush to Look': Brothel Visits of the New York Female Moral Reform Society, 1835 and 1836," *Journal of the History of Sexuality* 23, no. 2 (May 2014): 226–46.

84. In New Orleans, such infections were common enough that advertisements for treatments appeared in the local paper. A February 1849 *Daily Orleanian* advertisement titled "Gonorrhœ Specific" proclaimed one doctor's cure "FOR PRIVATE DISEASES, and all Disorders of the SEXUAL ORGANS." This treatment would "radically cure any case which can be produced"; "its ingredients are entirely vegetable and no injurious effect, either constitutional or local, can be caused by its use," and instructions came "in Spanish, French and English." *Daily Orleanian*, February 8, 1849.

85. Tim Lockley, "Survival Strategies of Poor White Women in Savannah, 1800–1860," *Journal of the Early Republic* 32, no. 3 (Fall 2012): 415–35.

86. Stansell, *City of Women*, 171.

87. William W. Sanger, *The History of Prostitution: Its Extent, Causes, and Effects throughout the World* (New York: Harper and Brothers, 1858), 519–20. See also Judith Kelleher Schafer, *Brothels, Depravity, and Abandoned Women: Illegal Sex in Antebellum New Orleans* (Baton Rouge: Louisiana State University Press, 2009).

88. Richard Tansey, "Prostitution and Politics in Antebellum New Orleans," in *History of Women in the United States: Historical Articles on Women's Lives and Activities*, vol. 9, *Prostitution*, ed. Nancy F. Cott (Munich: K. G. Saur, 1993), 45–75.

89. Martha Hodes terms these "liaisons" rather than "relationships" because, absent sources from the people involved, it is difficult to determine the motivations for and duration of these arrangements. These liaisons took place on a spectrum that included sex work and monogamous relationships. Hodes, *White Women*, 14. For an earlier version of these two references, see Rashauna Johnson, "'Laissez les bons temps rouler!' and Other Concealments: Households, Taverns, and Irregular Intimacies in Antebellum New Orleans," in *Interconnections: Gender and Race in American History*, ed. Alison M. Parker and Carol Faulkner (Rochester, NY: University of Rochester Press, 2012), 19–50.

90. "Snowy White and Sooty," *Daily Orleanian*, January 15, 1852.

91. "Snowy White and Sooty," *Daily Orleanian*, February 12, 1852.

92. *Daily Orleanian*, April 30, 1852.

93. "Ladies of Easy Virtue," *Daily Orleanian*, May 19, 1852.

94. "Lewd Women," *Daily Orleanian*, May 19, 1852.

95. "Amalgamation," *Daily Orleanian*, May 19, 1952.

96. "Amalgamation."

97. "Amalgamation." See also Marisa J. Fuentes, "Power and Historical Figuring: Rachel Pringle Polgreen's Troubled Archive," *Gender & History* 22 (2010): 564–84.

7

Heterosexual Inversions

Satire, Parody, and Comedy in the 1950s and 1960s

MARC STEIN

Historians of heterosexuality, like historians of masculinity and white-ness, often describe their subject as anxious and insecure.[1] The specific character of these anxieties and insecurities, however, has changed over time. In the United States of the 1950s and 1960s, heterosexuality was distinctly popular and powerful, but it also was explored and exhibited in ways that imagined its deconstruction and destabilization. In some respects, heterosexuality had been challenged as never before during the previous two decades, when economic hardship, military mobiliza-tion, and gender instability during the Great Depression and World War II undermined dominant sexual norms. After the war, much of North American culture idealized normative heterosexuality as the key to economic affluence, family happiness, social success, and national secu-rity. Careful observers, however, saw signs of trouble lurking beneath the platitudes of the Baby Boom years: divorcing spouses, unmarried parents, interracial couples, rebellious youth, sexual revolutionaries, feminist critics, lesbian reformers, and gay dissidents.[2] This chapter uses a dystopian short story published in *Playboy* magazine in 1955, two parodies of a 1964 *Life* magazine essay about homosexuality, and a 1967 *Esquire* magazine play about a gay man who plays straight to consider how and why heterosexuality became the butt of queer jokes in Cold War America.

The title character of Charles Beaumont's "The Crooked Man," which appeared in Hugh Hefner's *Playboy*, is a straight man struggling against persecution in a futuristic society dominated by homosexuals.[3] Guy Strait's "Heterosexuality in America," published by the San Francisco gay periodical *Citizens News*, parodied *Life*'s "Homosexuality in America."

Drum, the Philadelphia-based "gay *Playboy*," also featured an essay titled "Heterosexuality in America," this one by "P. Arody."[4] Three years later, *Esquire* published Paddy Chayefsky's *The Latent Heterosexual*, a play about a gay writer who marries for financial reasons and finds, initially at least, that he likes the straight life.[5]

This chapter examines the authors, editors, and publishers who queered heterosexuality in these works; the texts and contexts in which they did so; and the letters, reviews, and other comments that responded to these inversions of heterosexual hegemony. On one level, all of these works destabilized and deconstructed heterosexuality. On another level, they each did very different social, cultural, and political work. "The Crooked Man" tried to promote sympathy and compassion for homosexuals, but the story's stereotypical depictions of gay men, sexist representations of straight people, and problematic portrayals of sexuality and heterosexuality as presumptively male undermined this effort. Both versions of "Heterosexuality in America" more radically challenged heterosexual hegemony, but their subversive potential was undercut by their arguments about the fundamental similarities of gay and straight cultures, their failure to consider lesbian critiques of heterosexuality, and their racially insensitive photographs. *The Latent Heterosexual* included critical language about heterosexuality, which the plot linked to insanity, inhumanity, and death, but the play was strikingly antigay, profoundly misogynist, and distinctly conservative in presenting unattractive straight men as inevitable objects of desire for straight women and gay men. Together, these texts suggest that it was becoming increasingly possible to question heterosexual hegemony in the 1950s and 1960s, but there were also historically determined limits on the possibilities of queer critique.

"The Crooked Man"

Charles Beaumont's "The Crooked Man" imagines a future world in which homosexuals oppress heterosexuals. The story is set in the Phallus, a gay bar where Jesse, the protagonist, has arranged to meet his girlfriend, Mina, who cross-dresses as a man to evade hostile surveillance. In the middle of the story, Jesse offers Mina a lesson about the origins of their inverted world: "Years ago it was *normal* for men and women to love each other. . . . It's only been since the use of artificial insemination—not even five hundred years ago. . . . I don't know exactly how it happened—maybe, maybe as women gradually became equal to men in every way—or maybe solely because of the way we're born." More recently, the situation had deteriorated: "Before, it hadn't been so bad. . . . You were laughed at and shunned and fired from your job, and sometimes kids lobbed stones at you. . . . Now—it was a crime. It was a sickness." While Jesse blamed women's equality and assisted reproduction for the emergence of homosexual hegemony, he attributed the recent increase in antiheterosexual animus to Senator Knudson, who had declared, "The perverts who infest our land must be flushed out, eliminated *completely*, as a threat not only to public morals but to society at large. These sick people must be cured." This had inspired "frenzied mobs" to demand, "*Wipe out the heteros!*" and "*Kill the Queers!*"[6] In a fictional world where homosexuality was normative, it was natural to see heterosexuals as queer.

In the context of these hysterically historical developments, Jesse had begun life in the usual way: "tube-born and machine-nursed." Children in this world were assumed to have same-sex desires, but at some point Jesse had realized that he was "terribly different." His suspicions crystallized on a date with a "frighteningly handsome" man for whom he felt no attraction. After this, there were "bad days" filled with "black desires." Jesse had searched for friends at "the Crooked Clubs," but apparently he was afflicted with internalized heterophobia at this stage of his life: "There was a sensationalism, a bravura to these people that he could not love. The sight of men and women together . . . disgusted him."[7] Raised in a culture that despised cross-sex desires, Jesse had rejected the flamboyant heterosexuals he met and distanced himself from underground heterosexual communities.

"The Crooked Man" does not reveal much about Mina's history, but halfway through the story she arrives in the secluded booth where Jesse has been waiting. Dressed in a "loose man's shirt" and wearing a hat that hides her "golden hair," Mina is fearful about being discovered, but the two touch, kiss, and talk. After Mina says, "I've tried to be strong, just like you told me to be. But they wouldn't leave us alone. They wouldn't stop. Just because we're qu—" Jesse snaps back, "*Mina!* I've said it before—don't ever use that word. . . . *We're* not the queers."

It is at this point that Jesse shares his history lesson, but after realizing that Mina has accepted society's judgments, he reassures himself, "She's a woman, a very satisfying, desirable woman, and she may think you're both freaks, but you know different." Unfortunately for Jesse and Mina, the vice squad has been observing their rendezvous. As the story comes to a close, they are taken into custody. One policeman says to Jesse, "They've got it down pat now—couple days in the ward, one short session with the doctors; take out a few glands, make a few injections, attach a few wires to your head, turn on a machine: presto! . . . It'll make a new man of you." Medical "treatment" promises to "cure" Jesse's and Mina's deviant heterosexuality.[8]

As a satirical work that upends the sexual hierarchies of Cold War America, "The Crooked Man" can be read in multiple ways. On one level, the story critiques heterosexual hegemony. It does this by suggesting that it is unjust to persecute individuals on the basis of their sexual orientation; by provoking heterosexual readers to think about what it would be like to have their desires labeled sinful, criminal, and diseased; and by reversing some of the ways in which heterosexuals oppressed homosexuals in this era. In Jesse's world, heterosexuals are plagued by childhood bullying, physical violence, employment discrimination, scientific "treatment," and political scapegoating, the latter by a figure modeled on US Senator Joseph McCarthy, who had attacked communists and homosexuals in the Red and Lavender Scares. *Playboy* promoted this sympathetic interpretation, responding to a critical letter to the editor by saying, "We saw it as a kind of plea for tolerance—shoe-on-the-other-foot sort of thing." In an earlier issue, *Playboy* had previewed "The Crooked Man" by noting that the story was "so unique and terrifying that another men's magazine was actually afraid to print it." The other magazine was *Esquire*, and *Playboy*'s competitive boast can be read as implying that self-confident straight men had little to fear from a fantasy of homosexual hegemony.[9]

In many respects, "The Crooked Man" was aligned with *Playboy*'s ethos of sexual tolerance. From its founding in 1953, the magazine had aggressively promoted heterosexuality, but *Playboy* and its publisher also defended gay rights. In the 1960s, the magazine featured extensive discussions about homosexuality, including contributions by gay people. Beginning in 1962, Hefner's "Playboy Philosophy," published in regular installments, emphasized the rights of consenting adults to do as they pleased in private. The Playboy Foundation, founded in 1965, supported challenges to "laws and policies that discriminated on the basis of sexual orientation."[10] The magazine's publication of Beaumont's story and its response to the critical letter suggest that already in the 1950s the magazine and its publisher saw themselves as heterosexual supporters of homosexual rights.

Biographer Lee Prosser echoes *Playboy*'s sympathetic interpretation in his assessment of Beaumont (1929–1967), a successful writer for film and television (including *The Twilight Zone*) in the 1950s and 1960s. According to Prosser's 1996 book, "Beaumont shattered many editorial taboos . . . and helped make possible the honest discussion of such vital social topics as homosexuality." In an interview with Prosser, *Psycho* author Robert Bloch praised Beaumont as "a keen observer and social commentator—perhaps a little ahead of his time and the tastes of the general public." Bloch explained, "When he tackled homosexuality . . . , it was still a hush-hush subject for 'popular' fiction." Prosser says this about the message of Beaumont's story: "Society is the murderer of the right to have personal dreams. . . . The right to be different has been replaced with conformity." In universalizing the message of "The Crooked Man," Prosser downplays its specific critique of heterosexual hegemony, but his depiction of Beaumont as a homosexually tolerant heterosexual is strengthened by his description of the author as a "sexual athlete and a ladies' man." For Prosser in the 1990s as for Hefner in the 1950s, self-confident heterosexual men were powerfully positioned to advocate for homosexual tolerance.[11]

There are, however, more critical ways to interpret "The Crooked Man." The letter referenced earlier, by Saul Rosenthal of Washington, DC, described his reasons for feeling "sad" after reading the story: "Not at the hypothetical doom, persecution, or disintegration of the hero and heroine, but that so splendid a talent . . . has expended such vitriol, sardonicynicism (if I may coin such a word), satire and maliciousness on an opponent that has already been subjected to the most inhumane derisions." Rosenthal acknowledged that "exaggeration" and "ridicule" were "properly within the domain of the satirist" but argued that "to be a great or good critic there must be a great or good cause for criticism." From his perspective, the "plight of his heterosexual hero" was "such outlandish tomfoolery" that no one could be "moved to compassion" and the "absurd hypothetical topsy-turvydom" suggested that Beaumont had been "twisted into full-scale warfare with a paper-tiger."[12] For Rosenthal, "The Crooked Man" represented an unjustified attack on gay culture, which was an inappropriate target of satire given the pervasive nature of antihomosexual persecution in US society.

For some critics, the key problem with Beaumont's story may have been its depictions of gay men. Beaumont could have presented heterosexuals as lasciviously promiscuous and homosexuals as respectably restrained. Or he could have modeled his homosexuals on the suavely sophisticated men presented as masculine icons in *Playboy*. Instead, he aligned his gay men with popular stereotypes of homosexuality. At the story's beginning, the "barboy" is wearing "gold-sequined trunks," and "his greased muscles seemed to roll in independent motion, like fat snakes beneath his naked skin." Other men grope the "handsome athlete," but Jesse is not interested. The next man we meet, also attracted to Jesse, is "small, chubby, bald" and has "predatory little eyes." He is "bare to the chest" and "his white, hairless chest drooped and turns in folds at the stomach." Before the story concludes, we learn that the grotesque fat man works for the vice squad; he is the one who initiates the arrests of Jesse and Mina.[13]

"The Crooked Man" also can be interpreted as antigay in the support it offered to those who feared gay power. While Beaumont and Hefner may have viewed the idea of homosexual hegemony as far-fetched, others were not so sure. Another letter to the editor in *Playboy*, this one by Herbert Tuthill of Sunol, California, noted that the story "may well be more prophetic than we think," since "the hypocritical heritage of Blue Laws and Puritanical ideologies which permeates our era is certainly giving us a decided push in that direction."[14] Tuthill seemed to be suggesting that sexual repression, rooted in law and religion, was distinctly antiheterosexual and could give rise to homosexual hegemony. Others may have linked Beaumont's story to other frightening evidence of gay gains. The historian Michael Sherry argues that an influential group of post–World War II heterosexuals developed a powerful sense that gay artists constituted "a vast homintern—a homosexual international conspiracy in the arts parallel to the Comintern, or Communist International, in politics." He explains that "'homintern,' a word probably in-

vented in jest by gay men but seized upon by their enemies, alternated
with terms like 'homosexual mafia' to conjure up a queer menace" in
cultural production, which helped produce a "Lavender Scare in the
arts." David Johnson has similarly explored perceptions of gay influence
in government during this era.[15] For some readers, the dystopian future
of "The Crooked Man" may have resonated because it played into Cold
War anxieties about gay power in US culture.

"The Crooked Man" can also be interpreted as sexist and antifemi-
nist. As noted earlier, Jesse partially blames the past emergence of gay
power on the rise of women's equality. As he moves closer to the present,
he attributes the intensification of antiheterosexual animus to Senator
Knudson but also recalls, "The Women's Senator had taken Knudsen's
lead and issued a similar pronunciamento." "The Crooked Man" also refers to the all-powerful state as "Mother," which can be read as a play on
Phillip Wylie's 1942 denunciation of "Momism" in *A Generation of Vipers*
and the subsequent rise of mother-blaming after World War II. When
Jesse is remembering his first date with a man, for example, he recalls
that "'Mother' had arranged it, the way he arranged everything, carefully,
proving and re-proving that he was worthy of the Mother's uniform."
In this case, "Mother" in quotation marks appears to be Jesse's "real"
mother, who is a man, while Mother without quotation marks appears
to represent the state. Given the common stereotype of homosexual men
as excessively close with their mothers, there are homophobic and sexist
logics at play in the depiction of the dystopian state as Mother.[16]

Beaumont's story also can be interpreted as sexist in its depictions of
male and female heterosexualities. While Beaumont presented Jesse as a
tragic hero, he portrayed Mina as weak and wavering. At one point she
tells Jesse, "I can't go on like this." Jesse thinks she has always seemed to
"fight her instincts." At the end of the story, when they are taken into
custody, Jesse notices that Mina does not resist. Then he realizes, "She
had been trying to tell him something all evening, but he hadn't let her.
Now he knew . . . that even if they hadn't been caught, she would have
submitted to the Cure." In fact, while "The Crooked Man" presents Jesse
as a tragic heterosexual hero, the text can be read against the grain to
suggest that he has been imposing himself on Mina. When she first arrives in the bar and he kisses her, she says, "Don't do that, please don't."
When Jesse takes off her hat so he can enjoy her "long tresses of blonde

hair," she says, "We mustn't." Jesse acknowledges that her "affection for him" had never been quite right, "since that first time when he made her admit it, pried it loose from her," but he had thought "this could be conquered." Toward the end of the story, when Jesse tries to save Mina, he tells the police, "I forced her." While the reader is meant to interpret this as chivalrous, it also captures a truth: the story presents male heterosexuality as aggressive, coercive, and strong, while it portrays female heterosexuality as responsive, submissive, and weak. Consistent with common straight male self-representations in the 1950s, Jesse thinks he needs to overcome Mina's resistance to have his way with her.[17]

More generally, Beaumont's tragic hero may have much to tell us about the gendering of heterosexuality in this period. Within the terms of the couple's relationship, Jesse desires and Mina is desired. Jesse pursues and conquers; Mina resists and is conquered. Jesse is profoundly disturbed when he is the object of male desire. The barboy, for example, "made him want to take a knife and carve unspeakable ugliness into his own smooth, aesthetic face." When he thinks back on his first date with a man, he recalls the terror he felt when the "big man" put his arm around him. For Mina, in contrast, terror seems to come when she is the object of heterosexual desire. Insofar as "The Crooked Man" presents Jesse as more heterosexual (and sexual) than Mina, the text portrays heterosexuality (and sexuality) as more male than female.[18]

Beaumont's story also offers gendered depictions of male heterosexual embodiment. In contrast to the gay men who are excessively muscled, grotesquely fat, or frighteningly handsome, Jesse has a "light thin-boned handsomeness" with a "smooth" and "aesthetic" face. In fact, he generally does not experience hostile public scrutiny because he does not "look like a hetero." The story explains, "They said you could tell one just by watching him walk—but Jesse walked correctly. He fooled them."[19] Jesse, in other words, passes as gay because of his looks, walk, and face. This may have resonated with many *Playboy* readers given the types of masculinity that the magazine celebrated: bourgeois, educated, sophisticated, and oriented to consumption, leisure, and pleasure.[20] As queer as this may sound, were it not for the heterosexuality that was relentlessly performed in *Playboy*, the masculinities it promoted might have seemed pretty gay. In this sense, Jesse embodied some of the complicated contradictions of male heterosexuality in Cold War America.

"Heterosexuality in America"

While *Playboy* presented itself as a magazine by and for straight men, *Citizens News* and *Drum* presented themselves as periodicals by and for gay men. Founded in San Francisco by Guy Strait (1920–1987), *Citizens News* began publication in 1963, but in many respects it was the continuation of *LCE News* (named for the League for Civil Education), which Strait established in 1961. According to the historian Martin Meeker, Strait's full name was Elmer Guy Strait, an incredibly appropriate name for the author of "Heterosexuality in America." *Drum*, founded by Clark Polak (1937–1980) and published by the Janus Society in Philadelphia, first came out in 1964; its "Heterosexuality in America" was similar to the one published in *Citizens News* and may have been produced with or without Strait's permission. Both periodicals were at the forefront of the new gay politics of the 1960s, quickly displacing the homophile magazines founded in the 1950s—*ONE*, *Mattachine Review*, and the *Ladder*—as the country's most popular gay movement publications. They did so in part by promoting gay sexual culture, profiting from the commercialization of sex, and embracing fun, pleasure, and humor. They did not have the millions of readers that *Life* and *Playboy* did, but they reached thousands of LGBT people.[21]

Life magazine's "Homosexuality in America," the feature story parodied in *Citizens News* and *Drum*, was not the earliest media exposé of its kind but was distinctly influential. It had four components. The introduction declared in its headline, "A secret world grows open and bolder. Society is forced to look at it—and try to understand it." The main story, authored by the journalist Paul Welch, was titled "The 'Gay' World Takes to the City Streets." After this came a shorter essay by the journalist Ernest Havemann that was headlined "Scientists search for the answers to a touchy and puzzling question: why?" The fourth component consisted of photographs by Bill Eppridge and associated captions.[22]

"Homosexuality in America" was literally an exposé—it purported to expose the "sad" and "sordid" gay world to the gaze of presumptively straight society. While the introduction mentioned in passing that "for every obvious homosexual, there are probably nine nearly impossible to detect," its main point was that "today, especially in big cities, homosexuals are discarding their furtive ways and openly admitting, even flaunting, their deviation." The article offered an introduction to gay geographies (including bars, parks, and streets, primarily in New York, Los Angeles, and San Francisco), an overview of gay male genders (ranging from leather-oriented masculinity to flamboyant femininity), and a guide to gay sexual practices (focusing on cruising, hustling, and sadomasochism). There was also substantial coverage of antigay policing, gay activism, and law reform. Welch's conclusion noted that legal change was not likely to modify "society's basic repugnance to homosexuality." While this seemed to treat antigay animus as inevitable, Havemann's conclusion presented homosexuality itself as inevitable: "We may someday eliminate poverty, slums, and even the common cold—but the problem of homosexuality seems to be more akin to death and taxes." Paraphrasing the Kinsey Institute's Paul Gebhard, Havemann explained, "Even if every present-day American with the slightest trace of homosexuality could be deported tomorrow . . . , there would probably be just as many homosexual men in the U.S. a few generations hence as there are now."[23] Taken as a whole, these articles and the accompanying photographs portrayed homosexuality as an unavoidable "problem" confronting heterosexual Americans.

Reactions to "Homosexuality in America" varied in the gay and lesbian movement, with more established homophile groups tending to offer more positive assessments. According to Meeker, the Mattachine Society leader Hal Call, who had assisted *Life*'s journalists, was "ecstatic" about "introducing the organization to millions." East Coast Homophile Organizations praised *Life* for its "pioneering" article and presented it with an award at its 1964 conference. *Mattachine Review* noted that "there was criticism galore" and "many felt that 'exposure' of the bars and cruising haunts . . . was a bad thing," but the magazine asked, "Do these same people believe for an instant that their own daily living conditions can be improved by keeping these things out of the limelight?" It saw the article as "knowledgeable" and "fair." The *Ladder* objected to the "sensationalism," the "male-oriented" focus, and the failure to emphasize "quiet" homosexuals but praised the article for being "surprisingly objective."[24]

Citizens News and *Drum*, the young upstarts in the gay press, were more critical. The former complained that the "break-thru" was "unoriginal," objected to the depiction of gay men as hyperfeminine or hypermasculine, and added, "No good reason was put forth to change any existing injustice." *Drum* published a letter that Polak had sent to *Life*, which similarly rejected the focus on "the 15 percent of homosexuals who are obvious," the privileging of antigay scientific perspectives, and the failure to support law reform. *Drum* also published the response Polak received from Patricia Hines on behalf of *Life*'s editors. According to Hines, "space limitations" had prevented the magazine from publishing his letter. In defense of the article, she asserted that its intention was to present "a balanced and fair account," noted that it "stated clearly . . . that the large majority of homosexuals are unidentifiable in society," and explained that since the magazine "chose to treat the growing openness of homosexual society," the article focused on "the identifiable minority."[25]

In the same issues in which *Citizens News* and *Drum* presented their serious criticisms, they published their parodies. In so doing, both magazines reversed *Life*'s gaze to expose "heterosexuality in America." *Life*'s first paragraph, for example, had stated, "These brawny young men in their leather caps, shirts, jackets and pants are practicing homosexuals, men who turn to other men for affection and sexual satisfaction. They are part of what they call the 'gay world,' which is actually a sad and often sordid world. On these pages, L I F E reports on homosexuality in America, on its locale and habits . . . , and sums up . . . what science knows." *Citizens News* began its parody by noting, "These healthy young men and women in their gray flannel suits and cocktail dresses are practicing heterosexuals. They are part of what they call the 'straight' world, which is actually not so straight and narrow, but often crooked and twisted, sordid and sadistic. On these pages *Strife* reports on heterosexuality in America, on its locale and habits and sums up what science knows." With minor variations on but major reversals of *Life*'s second paragraph, the parody continued, "Heterosexuality shears across the spectrum of American life—the professions, the arts, business and labor. It always has. But today, especially in big cities, heterosexuals are discarding their furtive ways and are openly admitting, even flaunting, their challenge to sexual conventions. Heterosexuals have their own bars, their special assignation streets, even their own organizations. And for every obvious heterosexual, there are probably ninety nearly impossible to detect. This social disorder, which society tries to suppress, has forced itself into the public eye."[26]

Citizens News and *Drum* parodied "Homosexuality in America" by exposing the characteristics and conventions of heterosexuality, many of which paralleled the aspects of homosexuality that *Life* had highlighted. To attract partners, for example, the heterosexuals described in *Citizens News* wore "tight pants" and "sexy dresses"; drank and danced "suggestively"; "cruised" and "hustled"; and searched relentlessly for "bed-partners." They congregated at private parties and in particular neighborhoods, bars, and other "flagrant" meeting places. "Cocktail lounges," which were "notorious" for heterosexual "assignations," and "Playboy Rooms," which were a new phenomenon, were distinctly popular. In these and other locations, especially in large cities, straight people publicly flaunted their sexualities. Among the specific straight cultures that Strait exposed were those that featured prostitutes and their clients, others that facilitated "wife-swapping," and some that represented the "far-out fringe," including S&M bars, with S standing for "sadism" or "single" and M standing for "masochism" or "married." (*Drum* added an ambiguously feminist comment about "confusing" advertisements for "submissive females interested in discipline and bondage.") Strait's "Heterosexuality in America" also echoed *Life* by mentioning, but only in passing, the "'respectable' heterosexuals who pair off and establish a 'marriage.'" In general, however, the parodies presented heterosexuality as a transgressive culture that was rebelling against conventional morality.[27]

As was the case with *Life*'s article, the parodies paid significant attention to legal matters. According to Strait, heterosexuals recklessly pursued one another, though there were "laws against their conduct" and they had to avoid the "anti-heterosexual police." Strait then made a distinction that echoed one made by *Life*: "Actually there is no law in any state against being heterosexual. The laws which police enforce are directed at specific acts. For the most part these laws make it a crime for two people to engage in any sex activity if they have not previously made a contract of marriage. Even then they must perform the sex act in such a way as to beget children, alimony, and child support." *Drum* added, "It is estimated that 95 percent of all heterosexual men are sex criminals and . . . the overwhelming majority of heterosexual marrieds also consistently violate the law." This was because the law punished "anything other than direct sexual intercourse," meaning that "anal and oral contacts" were prohibited. Strait concluded this discussion by noting that there had been recent calls for more "tolerance of heterosexuals"; the British Wolfenden Commission, for example, favored the decriminalization of prostitution and supported the notion that "sexual behavior between consenting adults in private should no longer be a criminal offense."[28] In these passages, *Citizens News* and *Drum* positioned homosexuals and heterosexuals as similarly oppressed by repressive sex laws, while also highlighting the hypocrisy of discriminatory sex-law enforcement, which more frequently targeted homosexual transgressions.

The parodies did more than just expose heterosexuality as a culture that paralleled its homosexual counterpart; they exposed heterosexuality's failure to see itself, its obtuse objectification of homosexuality, and its hateful hypocrisy. At one point, when referring to a bar where heterosexuals could proposition one another by telephone, Strait commented that in this new type of enterprise, a patron could observe the "desires and reactions" of others "without ever being seen or recognized as a heterosexual."[29] In a sense, this observation captured the larger indictment made in the parodies: that heterosexuals observed and ogled "others" but never looked at themselves. They thus did not recognize that they, like homosexuals, had distinct sexual cultures and that these, too, looked odd from alternative perspectives. They also did not seem to recognize (even after the Kinsey Institute and *Playboy* had highlighted this point) that most heterosexuals, like most homosexuals, were sexual criminals and that they, too, suffered because of repressive policing.[30]

Reactions to the two versions of "Heterosexuality in America" were mixed. In a published letter to the editor, A.E.B. of Holicong, Pennsylvania, congratulated *Drum* for its "clever parody": "For years upon years the homophile movement has taken the defensive, but now he [*sic*] should take the offensive. There is no weapon better than satire, holding up the perversities of the heterosexual world to ridicule." Strait, however, told the *San Francisco Chronicle* columnist Merla Zellerbach, who reported on the parody, that he was "disappointed by the reaction." "A lot of homosexuals didn't dig it," he told Zellerbach. "They thought I was being serious. One fellow even said to me, 'Honestly—ALL heterosexuals aren't like that!'"[31]

While some readers objected to the depictions of heterosexuals, *Citizens News* and *Drum* presented heterosexuals as fundamentally similar to homosexuals, with the differences more superficial than substantive. Straights and gays might wear different clothing, frequent different bars, and establish different organizations, the parodies suggested, but they both pursued sex, love, and happiness; their efforts in doing so were often sad and sordid; they were disciplined and punished by antisexual policing; and they were organizing to fight back. Beyond the parody, *Citizens News* emphasized similarities between heterosexuals and homosexuals in its introductory comments about *Life*'s "Homosexuality in America": "In the homosexual world we have found every facet of life is represented in just about the same proportion as is found in everyday America." Along similar lines, Polak's unpublished letter to *Life* criticized the magazine for ignoring the 85 percent of homosexuals "who are unidentifiable in society." *Drum*'s parody concluded by declaring, "Heterosexuals do form a separate and distinct class of persons in many respects and they have adopted customs which seem perverse and sometimes even sinister to the average homosexual. However, the mainstream of heterosexual life is not much different from the mainstream of homosexual life." These arguments may have been effective in challenging the "otherness" of homosexuality, but they came with a cost. As John D'Emilio has argued with respect to an earlier moment in homophile history, undue emphasis on the similarities of heterosexuals and homosexuals could undermine the radical potential of arguments about the distinctive politics and priorities of gay cultures and communities.[32] They could also undermine the radical potential of gendered arguments about the distinctive politics and priorities of lesbian cultures and communities.

Another troubling aspect of the parodies was the racial politics of their visual images. *Life*'s "Homosexuality in America" featured a set of provocative photographs, the first of which was an image of masculine white gay men with a caption that noted, "A San Francisco bar run for and by homosexuals is crowded with patrons who wear leather jackets, make a show of masculinity, and scorn effeminate members of their world." Strait parodied this with an image taken from a different article in the same issue of *Life*, a photograph featuring four white-robed members of the Ku Klux Klan. The caption referred to them as "practicing heterosexuals who wear white robes and make a show of masculinity and scorn effeminate members of their world." *Drum* similarly used an image of white policemen at an African American civil rights protest and described them as "steel-helmeted young men with billy clubs and vicious dogs"; they were presented as exemplars of "the heterosexual world."[33] While most of the other photographs and captions were consistent with the main text in leaving heterosexuality racially unmarked, the KKK and police images presented heterosexuality as white, male, racist, and brutal. These images suggested that African Americans were not the only community that experienced violent legal and extralegal repression; gay people did as well. A generous reading might suggest that these images also parodied the whiteness of *Life's* homosexuals. More critically, they failed to represent African American people as participants in gay or straight cultures. Moreover, one of the points of the parodic photographs seemed to be that it was as ridiculous to associate heterosexuality with the KKK or the police as it was to associate homosexuality with the hypermasculine gay men of the San Francisco bar. In parodies otherwise devoid of commentary on the racialization of heterosexuality, the attempt to mobilize antiracist and pro-civil-rights sentiments to promote (white) gay rights was potentially alienating to people of color and contributed to the production of heterosexuality as white.

Notwithstanding the limitations of the parodies of heterosexuality, they contributed to the success of the new gay politics of the 1960s. After presenting "Heterosexuality in America" in 1964, *Drum* published other parodies of straight culture over the next several years; these helped the magazine become the most widely circulating gay-movement periodical for much of the decade. "Franky Hill: Memoirs of a Boy of Pleasure," for example, parodied John Cleland's eighteenth-century novel *Fanny Hill*. "Harry Chess: That Man from A.U.N.T.I.E." was a send-up of the 1960s television series *The Man from U.N.C.L.E.* "I Was a Homosexual for the FBI" riffed on the 1951 film *I Was a Communist for the FBI*. "Tropic of Crabs" was a takeoff on Henry Miller's 1934 novel *Tropic of Cancer*.[34] Strait also found that sex and humor were a good combination for a gay periodical. In 1965, he began alternating *Citizens News* with *Cruise News & World Report*, whose title was a campy adaptation of the name of the popular newsmagazine *U.S. News & World Report*.[35]

In the end, however, neither Polak nor Strait had the last laugh. In 1966, *U.S. News & World Report* sued Strait for copyright infringement.

According to the *San Francisco Chronicle* columnist Herb Caen, when the attorney for *U.S. News* expressed confusion about *Cruise News* because "there's nothing in it about cruises," Strait responded, "You're using the King's English. I use the Queen's!" In 1967, Strait stopped publishing *Citizens News* and *Cruise News*; he later became a major producer of pornography and served time in prison for having sex with a teenager.[36] As for Polak, in 1964 government officials began examining *Drum* to determine if it was violating obscenity laws. In 1965, threatened with prosecution, Polak ordered the removal of "Tropic of Crabs" from newsstand copies of the magazine. Around the same time, postal inspectors forwarded "I Was a Homosexual for the FBI" to the FBI. State repression escalated after Polak began including nude photographs in *Drum* and expanded his gay and straight porn businesses, the profits of which he used to support sex-law reform. Government repression ultimately forced Polak to stop publishing *Drum* in May 1969, just weeks before LGBT people revolted on the streets of New York in the Stonewall riots. In 1980, Polak committed suicide.[37] While the demise of *Citizens News*, *Drum*, Strait, and Polak cannot be attributed directly to their publication of "Heterosexuality in America" parodies, many straight people did not like being the butt of queer jokes in the 1960s. The parodies can be criticized for their conservative gender, racial, and sexual politics, but critics of *Citizens News* and *Drum* in the 1960s were more concerned about their subversive radicalism.

The Latent Heterosexual

If the two versions of "Heterosexuality in America" can be seen as the queer progeny of "Homosexuality in America," Paddy Chayefsky's 1967 play *The Latent Heterosexual* deserves recognition as its long-lost bastard child. Best known as the winner of screenwriting Academy Awards for *Marty* in 1955, *The Hospital* in 1971, and *Network* in 1976, Chayefsky (1923–1981) wrote for film, television, and theater in this era. Critics have long noted that *The Latent Heterosexual*, a tragic tale of tax evasion, was inspired by Chayefsky's difficulties with the Internal Revenue Service; they have paid less attention to its sexual politics. The play began life as a mystery novella; multiple drafts, the earliest dated August 1964, survive in Chayefsky's papers at the New York Public Library. Alongside those drafts, in a file labeled "research material," can be found a copy of "Homosexuality in America." There is no way to know whether *Life's* essay, published in June 1964, directly influenced Chayefsky's play, but it is notable that, as mentioned earlier, the magazine's exposé concluded with comments about the inevitability of death, taxes, and homosexuality.[38]

Published originally as an *Esquire* cover story, *The Latent Heterosexual* is a play about the New York novelist John Morley, an apparently gay man who has failed to pay his federal taxes and is advised by financial consultants to pursue a set of tax-avoidance schemes; otherwise he faces a lengthy prison term and expensive fines. With Morley's cooperation, his tax advisers have him declared incompetent by a psychiatrist, set up a publishing company and charitable foundation to absorb his profits, encourage him to write off his narcotics spending as research and development, and facilitate his participation in money laundering. As Irving Spaatz, his main tax man, explains in the first scene, "We're going to turn you into a corporation."[39] More reluctantly, Morley also agrees to get married so he can split his income with his wife.

As the plot unfolds, the schemes work all too well: Morley becomes certifiably insane, fantastically wealthy, and energetically heterosexual. In particular, he embodies the advice to become a corporation, working with his tax men to exploit all available opportunities for financial gain. As he becomes less human and more corporate, he descends into insanity. Later in the play, when his consultants advise him to divorce his wife because it has become financially advantageous to do so, Morley makes a final effort to save himself and his humanity by urging them to liquidate the corporation. But after seeing his wife have sex with one of the consultants, he agrees to the divorce. Ultimately, when it becomes clear that Morley identifies completely with his incarnation as a corporation, Spaatz, in a compassionate gesture to put his client out of his misery and as the logical culmination of the advice he has been providing all along, persuades him that liquidating the corporation and killing himself would be financially advisable; the play ends with Morley's suicide.

On one level, Chayefsky's play presents heterosexuality as a performance, which is seen most clearly in Morley's sexual transformation. At the beginning of the play, he is stereotypically gay. When the reader first meets him, he is an "enormous" and "grotesque" man in his forties; his friend Henry Jadd refers to him as a "fruitcake." After noting that they had met when Morley "came swishing in with a sheaf of short stories, spinsterly things about sensitive Cincinnati schoolboys whose English teachers turn out to be faggots," Jadd explains that Morley's most recent novel, *A Corporation of Cadis*, focuses on "the homosexual community in Tangiers" and features "hot sperm spurting and smooth-skinned Arab boys." Jadd tells Spaatz and his colleague Arthur Landau, "This fecaloid pile of prose is presented to us as man's search for serenity, a search presumably conducted with a proctoscope." In the second scene, Spaatz reports to Landau that Morley is wearing lipstick and rouge. The stage notes describe him as a "frightened, painted schoolboy of a man."[40]

Chayefsky also presents Morley as stereotypically homosexual in his unstable mental state. In the first scene, Morley "breaks into a sob" when Jadd tells Spaatz that the government has blocked his access to thousands of dollars in book and film payments. After Morley reveals that a lien has been placed on his house, he moans softly. Jadd then explains that Morley is a miser, a hoarder, and a junkie. He had learned about the writer's tax troubles when Morley's boyfriend, Richard, called "hysterically" with the news that his partner was having a breakdown. Jadd describes what he discovered after driving to their suburban home, explaining, "If you've ever seen a faggot junkie poet caparisoned in a yellow caftan, green-striped izar and a fringed cashmere girdle, slashing at his wrists with a letter opener—well, now you know what I've been through." In the second scene, Morley proudly reports to Spaatz, in a foreshadowing passage, on the psychiatric assessment he has received: "I'm an instance of character corrosion. . . . I've gone mad before. . . . I defend myself . . . by all these theatrical excesses! I play mad so even my madness will seem a deceit! But I'm terrified it may be my only incontrovertible fragment of reality!" The play paradoxically presents Morley's insanity as a performance but one that is based in reality.[41]

The play similarly portrays Morley's corporatization as a reality-based performance, this one based on his love of money. When Spaatz suggests turning him into a corporation, Morley flirtatiously responds, "May I call you Irving." When Spaatz outlines the plan to have him declared incompetent, Morley replies, "Call me John." The proposal to write off his narcotics expenses as research leads Morley to declare, "I'm going to come." After listening to Spaatz and Landau's advice, he states, "I'm hopelessly in love with both of you." Summarizing these developments in another foreshadowing passage, Morley says, "I came into this office a shattered soul, and in a matter of minutes, you people have incarnated me into a publishing house, a charitable foundation, and even a married man. It's the most goddam transcendental thing."[42]

Performing heterosexuality, however, presents a unique set of challenges for Chayefsky's protagonist. In contrast to Morley's performance of insanity and corporatization, he seemingly cannot draw on a prior truth for his performance of heterosexuality, even though the title of the play, *The Latent Heterosexual*, might suggest otherwise. In the second scene, when Spaatz recommends that he get married, Morley asks, "Do you mean to a woman?" Morley then "swishes prettily" over to Spaatz's desk and declares, "I'm a flaming faggot. . . . I don't go around waving the flag, of course, and I definitely do not proselytize. Homosexuality is, to me, an inner satisfaction, a pride in a heritage of greatness. To marry a woman would be an inadmissible rejection of my identity." When told, however, that marriage would save him $15,000 in 1960 taxes, Morley reverses himself: "In that case, dig something up for me."[43]

The woman whom Spaatz and Landau propose for consideration is Christine Van Dam, a twenty-three-year-old "high-priced whore," who has tax reasons of her own for wanting to get married. Morley calls the idea "radiant," though he insists on the "technical nature of the marriage." He looks "petrified" when facing the prospect of meeting her, but after they are introduced, he draws on his mastery of femininity to critique her outfit and instruct her about how to behave when she moves into his home. Making clear that his love for the feminine only extends so far, Morley says, "I don't want stockings, brassieres and garter belts dangling from the shower rods. . . . During your menstrual weakness . . . , you will simply stay out of the house." He adds, "Above all, stay away from the boy who lives with me. He's mine. Resist that vanity common to all women that makes each think she alone can straighten out a homosexual."[44] The scene thus leaves the impression that Morley's greed has induced him to marry a woman for financial reasons but that his erotic desires are unchanged.

When the third scene opens six months later, however, Morley is a happily married heterosexual. As Landau explains to a colleague, "Apparently, Mr. and Mrs. Morley have fallen dementedly in love." When the colleague responds, "He was a howling faggot, wasn't he?" Landau responds, "Well, perhaps not." He then describes a recent visit to the happy couple's home, where Morley was "wearing a red-checked lumberman's mackinaw and smoking a cigar." His wife was "hanging on her husband's arm" with "a questionable excess of affection." When Landau asked Morley what was going on, he replied, "I'm in love with her. I'm deliriously happy." In fact, Morley recently had asked his friend Jadd to lie about his whereabouts to his partner, Richard, because Morley was having an "affair" with his wife. Landau further revealed that Morley's psychiatrist had expressed doubts about whether he really was gay, claiming instead that "a few shattering adolescent experiences" had led Morley to confuse impotence with homosexuality. Morley's homosexuality turned out to be a "pretense"; he was a latent heterosexual after all.[45]

At this point, we meet the newly heterosexual Morley, who is described as "noticeably different." According to the stage directions, "He is neatly groomed in a dark-blue suit. . . . Most striking perhaps is the ten-gallon Stetson hat. . . . All traces of effeminacy have disappeared." After sharing the exciting news that his wife is pregnant, Morley "extracts a cigar from his jacket pocket" and gives Landau "a manly thump on the shoulder." He then narrates his transformation, beginning with the psychiatric report, which he says revealed, "I'm not the accomplished faggot I thought I was." After describing his wife's sexual pursuit of him, he asks, "Do you know what it's like to find out after forty years the damn thing works?" Morley now claims that he and Richard "had never been anything more than companions," but because of the latter's jealousy, Morley and Christine initially behaved as though she were his "mistress," meeting for secret "trysts" and acting like "illicit lovers." After Morley slipped up and, in his boyfriend's presence, "wacked her affectionately across the ass," Richard's suspicions were confirmed. He killed himself shortly thereafter.[46]

Notwithstanding Richard's death, Morley seems to be doing well. But toward the end of the third scene, after agreeing to go along with the money-laundering scheme, he undergoes another transformation. After experiencing a "frightening sensation," Morley tells Landau, "I've just felt the strangest mythopoeic feeling. Do you know how, in Greek myths, heroes are forever being turned into trees and nymphs into waterfalls? Well, I swear to you, Arthur, I have the feeling as I sit here that some sort of physical reconstruction is going on in me."[47] In the remainder of the play, Morley increasingly acts like an embodied corporation, focusing obsessively on financial gain and losing his grip on reality as he suffers the loss of his child, which is stillborn, and his wife, whom he divorces. In the fourth scene, Christine tells Landau that only the corporation seems real to Morley. Landau responds, "To any good businessman, a corporation is a living thing. All of us are very fond of Morley Associates. . . . As a corporation, it even has a sense of humor, having been born in ludicrous circumstances and having matured as something very close to a travesty on the American business structure."[48]

In the final two scenes, Morley twice tries to save himself. When Spaatz and Landau advise him to divorce Christine, they assure him that he and Christine can continue living together and later remarry. Now the marriage has become real and the divorce a performance. Morley, however, cries out, "No! . . . She's my last sensation of sanity!" He continues, "I'm being reified, disincarnated and converted into an abstract. I'm surrendering my human identity." Soon he announces to Spaatz that he wants to liquidate Morley Associates: "This monstrous deformity is devouring me." After Spaatz and Landau resist, the plot takes another turn. Looking offstage, first Landau, then Spaatz, and finally Morley become aware that Christine is having sex with the lawyer Jimmie Churchill. Morley faints, Spaatz revives him with corporate talk, and as the scene ends, Morley agrees to the divorce plan.[49]

In the sixth and final scene, Morley is barely sentient, but he manages to whisper to Spaatz, "I want to die." The stage directions tell us that "a stinging sensation of compassion shivers through Spaatz." He then explains to Morley that, because of the way they have structured his pension and insurance, he "could make a hell of a tax savings" if he "were to die." Morley whispers his thanks. After Spaatz exits, Morley "disembowels" himself with "pruning shears."[50]

As most critics have noted, the primary message of The Latent Heterosexual is anticorporate, but the play also has much to say about heterosexuality.[51] In many respects, the text destabilizes and deconstructs heterosexuality, presenting it as a performance, depicting it as disabling, and linking it to capitalist dehumanization. In the middle of the play, Chayefsky presents his audience with a caricature of masculine heterosexuality in the form of a cigar-smoking, ass-whacking, and "cheating" husband. In a distinctly critical passage that apparently referenced President Lyndon Johnson, Morley's psychiatrist offers further reasons for condemning male heterosexuality: "In America, a country whose national lunacy is virility, where a man's measure is the multiplicity of his erections—and where a high officer of our government is said to have interrupted councils of state to unzipper his pants, unleash his beef and flop it on the conference table, saying: 'Has Mao Tse-tung got anything like that?'—in such a society, impotence is far more of a stigma than homosexuality." Male heterosexual virility is portrayed here as homosocial competition, pathetic performance, and national joke.[52]

Comments that Chayefsky made in 1956 about his television play *Marty*, a heterosexual "love story" that implicitly addressed "the latent homosexuality of the middle class," support this interpretation. According to Chayefsky, "Most American men have decided homosexual impulses. . . . We are for the most part an adolescent people; and adolescence is a semihomosexual stage. . . . Latent homosexuality is perfectly normal; but so much stigma is attached to it that it provokes fears and anxieties." He continued, "The man who proudly claims how virile he is could very well be a man who is so unsure of his virility that he needs to re-establish it over and over again. The married man who chases other women might well be doing this to confirm his manliness in his own mind. He is probably being driven by a fear of homosexuality."[53] More than a decade later, some of these critical perspectives on male heterosexuality made their way into Chayefsky's new work.

In other respects, however, Chayefsky's play depicts heterosexuality as authentic and real and homosexuality as artificial pretense and hysterical performance. The play, after all, is called *The Latent Heterosexual*, and the audience eventually is told that Morley was straight all along. Inverting the psychoanalytic concept of latent homosexuality, the notion that unconscious same-sex desires exist in those who identify as heterosexual, Chayefsky presents us with the idea that unconscious cross-sex desires exist in those who identify as homosexual. Just as his comments on *Marty* invoked the notion that exaggerated performances of heterosexuality might suggest unresolved latent homosexuality, Chayefsky's depiction of Morley promoted the novel idea that exaggerated performances of homosexuality might suggest unresolved latent heterosexuality.

In fact, notwithstanding the critical perspectives on heterosexuality highlighted earlier, the play's sexual politics were strongly pro-heterosexual. For instance, in the middle of the play, when Morley is at his most wholly heterosexual, he is also at his happiest and healthiest. In the final scenes, Morley does not see his heterosexualization and corporatization as linked; he sees his marriage to Christine as his final hope for humanization. On this level, the play presents heterosexuality as the potential (though ultimately inadequate) cure for the corporate ills that ail the doomed hero. Alternatively, the play can be read as revealing the ruin that results when homosexuals attempt to perform heterosexuality: in this sense, the authentic heterosexuality of the tax men is "normal," and the fake heterosexuality of Morley is disastrous.

Comments that Chayefsky made in 1955 about television directors and observations that *Esquire* published in a "backstage" interview support these readings of the play as heterosexist and homophobic. According to Chayefsky, "the homosexual director cannot have an accurate understanding of either the relationship between two men or that between a young man and a young woman." He apparently did not see the irony in asserting that gay directors could not understand relationships between men (presumably he meant straight men).[54] As for "Backstage with Esquire," this included comments by Carl Fischer, whose photographs on the cover of the magazine and the pages of *The Latent Heterosexual* featured the boxer Rocky Graziano as Morley, the actor Jack Palance as his boyfriend, and the actress Raquel Welch as Christine. Fischer was quoted as telling Graziano and Palance why they were selected: "we didn't want real fags for the parts, and with the two of you everybody's got to know we're kidding."[55]

The first stagings of *The Latent Heterosexual*, with Burgess Meredith (perhaps best known for playing the Penguin on the 1960s *Batman* television series) as director and Zero Mostel (perhaps best known for playing Tevye in the 1960s Broadway production of *Fiddler on the Roof*) as Morley, repeated this dynamic. Morley's evolution within the play and the performance of the actor who played him suggested to audiences that straights could play gay but gays could not play straight.[56] In a *New York Times* review of the 1968 world premiere in Dallas, Clive Barnes praised Mostel for "the humor of the shriekingly heterosexual actor pretending camp, with grotesquely exaggerated mannerisms that are funny simply through their very distance from reality." Herbert Lawson's more negative review in the *Wall Street Journal* noted that "Mostel injects what vigor he can into this plot, though some may find his homosexual clowning offensive." Bart Cody's critical review of the 1968 Los Angeles production in the *Los Angeles Advocate* (a gay newspaper) noted that "Mostel's camp is fun, but at all times one is conscious of the fact that he is acting."[57] Whether one liked it or not, much of *The Latent Heterosexual*'s humor was derived from the campy, heterosexist, and homophobic performances of gay-acting straight men.

There is another way to think critically about the sexual politics of Chayefsky's play, but this requires focusing more on Christine. Doing so provides an opportunity to consider what *The Latent Heterosexual* says about both female and male heterosexualities. Surely it is significant that the play's one female character is a young and beautiful "whore." According to the stage directions, "There is something predatory in Miss Van Dam's beauty. She looks at Spaatz when introduced the way a man looks at a woman, seeing him naked on the first glance." (Spaatz is described as short, bespectacled, and in his fifties.) When she meets Morley, "She smiles boldly back at him; her eyes rake him up and down with the most shamelessly wayward interest." Later, when Landau reports to his colleagues on a tax agent's visit to Morley's home, he notes, "Mrs. Morley apparently reached over and fondled him." After the tax men have a good laugh, Morley arrives and tells the story of his transformation: "I'm not the accomplished faggot I thought I was. Lord knows, all that crumbled the first moment my wife unzipped my corduroy trousers." He continues, "She was the aggressor, of course. I just stood there, mute and trembling like a fawn. . . . My wife is a predatory lady. Like so many women who are constantly told how desirable they are, my wife distrusts her beauty and can affirm herself only with the love of incompetent men." In the fifth scene, Christine refuses to let go of Spaatz's hand, "trains a look of a barely repressed rapture on him," and "shamelessly if briefly fondles him." After Christine is seen having sex with Churchill, she observes, "I have this compulsive attraction to impotent men. . . . It's the only way I can affirm my femininity."[58]

In *The Latent Heterosexual*, women are sexually active, aggressive, and insatiable, while straight men, regardless of their ages, bodies, looks, or personalities, are objects of female desire. Christine, depicted as a predatory whore in desperate need of male affirmation, is simultaneously presented as an agent of male heterosexualization. This inverts the presentation of straight gender roles in "The Crooked Man," but in both cases, straight men are the objects of male homosexual desires. In short, *The Latent Heterosexual* offers its campy critique of capitalist and corporate culture in the form of a misogynist and homophobic male heterosexual fantasy, one in which straight women and gay men view even the least appealing straight men as objects of desire.

Conclusions

Historians of sexuality have demonstrated that heterosexuality was subjected to new forms of criticism in the 1970s, 1980s, and 1990s, when feminist, LGBT, and queer radicals denounced "compulsory heterosexuality" and declared, "I hate straights."[59] This chapter has shown that in an earlier period—the 1950s and 1960s—straight and gay writers were already beginning to ask penetrating questions about heterosexual hegemony. Comedy, satire, and parody offered unique challenges and opportunities when asking these questions. Works in these genres had the potential to appeal to large audiences, which made them useful for querying a much-loved system of categorizing, classifying, and organizing sexual desires. At the same time, comedy, satire, and parody could offend, and audiences might conclude that it was all just a big joke.[60]

All four of the works examined in this chapter deconstructed and destabilized the existing social order by inverting heterosexual hegemony. "The Crooked Man" did so by imagining a dystopian future world in which homosexuals oppress heterosexuals. The story's apparent intent was to promote sympathy and compassion for sexual dissidents, suggesting that if it is unjust to persecute heterosexuals, it is equally unjust to persecute homosexuals. Both versions of "Heterosexuality in America" inverted the straight gaze by parodying *Life* magazine's "Homosexuality in America." They offered radical critiques of heterosexuality by exposing it to the types of comments and observations that heterosexuals had long made about homosexuals. *The Latent Heterosexual* inverted the notion of latent homosexuality by imagining what would happen if a gay man came out as straight. In this case, heterosexuality was presented as a performance that even apparent homosexuals could perfect. In important respects, all of these works subversively questioned whether the existing sexual order and apparent sexual identities were fixed, natural, and inevitable.

In other respects, however, the sexual politics of these works were quite conservative. *The Latent Heterosexual* reproduced antihomosexual discourses about gay men, sexist representations of straight women, and positive depictions of male heterosexuality. "The Crooked Man" had more liberal intentions; but it, too, relied on antigay and sexist stereotypes, and it presented sexuality and heterosexuality as presumptively male. The two versions of "Heterosexuality in America" were more deeply critical of straight culture, but their subversive potential was limited by the fact that their gaze was more gay than lesbian, by the race politics of their representations of heterosexuality, and by their suggestion that, in the end, homosexuals and heterosexuals are more similar than different.

If Charles Beaumont were to rise from the dead and reimagine my chapter as an episode of *The Twilight Zone*, he might foreground the unfortunate fates of the four authors examined here. Beaumont died in his thirties (undisclosed illness), Polak in his forties (suicide), and Chayefsky in his fifties (cancer). After serving time in prison in the 1970s, Strait died in the 1980s when he was in his sixties. In the fantasy universe of "the twilight zone," we might imagine that all four of these men died prematurely because of what they wrote about heterosexuality in the 1950s and 1960s. The lesson would be clear: it can be perilous to pillory heterosexuality. In our far less interesting world, which exists beyond "the twilight zone," these works of satire, parody, and comedy live on as historical artifacts of destabilizing decades when heterosexuality was distinctly popular and powerful but also problematically questioned and queered.

NOTES

1. I dedicate this chapter to my undergraduate and graduate mentors, Henry Abelove and Carroll Smith-Rosenberg, who taught me much about reading, writing, history, humor, and heterosexuality. See especially Henry Abelove, "Some Speculations on the History of Sexual Intercourse during the Long Eighteenth Century in England," *Genders* 6 (Fall 1989): 125–30; Carroll Smith-Rosenberg, "Davey Crockett as Trickster: Pornography, Liminality and Symbolic Inversion in Victorian America," *Journal of Contemporary History* 17, no. 2 (April 1982): 325–50. This

chapter is also informed, influenced, and inspired by Jorge Olivares's approach to textual analysis and sexual humor in *Becoming Reinaldo Arenas: Family, Sexuality, and the Cuban Revolution* (Durham, NC: Duke University Press, 2013).

2. On heterosexuality in this period, see John D'Emilio and Estelle Freedman, *Intimate Matters: A History of Sexuality in America* (New York: Harper, 1988), 239–343; Jonathan Ned Katz, *The Invention of Heterosexuality* (New York: Dutton, 1995), 83–138; Beth Bailey, *Sex in the Heartland* (Cambridge, MA: Harvard University Press, 1999); David Allyn, *Make Love, Not War: The Sexual Revolution* (Boston: Little, Brown, 2000).

3. Charles Beaumont, "The Crooked Man," *Playboy*, August 1955, 6–8, 10, 14. See also Beaumont, *The Hunger and Other Stories* (New York: Putnam, 1957), 139–48. For a post-Stonewall essay based on a similar concept, see Richard Young, "50 Years of Gay Life in America: Gay Times Are Coming," *Queens Quarterly*, Fall 1970, 9, 52–53.

4. Guy Strait, "Heterosexuality in America," *Citizens News*, July 20, 1964, 5–8; P. Arody, "Heterosexuality in America," *Drum*, October 1964, 18–21. Strait, the editor of *Citizens News*, was not identified as the author of the former, but Martin Meeker indicates he was; see Meeker, *Contacts Desired: Gay and Lesbian Communications and Community, 1940s–1970s* (Chicago: University of Chicago Press, 2006), 176. See also "Homosexuality in America," *Life*, June 26, 1964, 66–80.

5. Paddy Chayefsky, "The Latent Heterosexual," *Esquire*, August 1967, 49–56, 113–22. See also Chayefsky, *The Latent Heterosexual* (New York: Random House, 1967). I thank Rebecca Davis for calling Chayefsky's play to my attention.

6. Beaumont, "Crooked Man," 8, 10.

7. Beaumont, 8, 10.

8. Beaumont, 10, 14.

9. *Playboy*, November 1955, 6; *Playboy*, July 1955, 54. See also Carrie Pitzulo, *Bachelors and Bunnies: The Sexual Politics of "Playboy"* (Chicago: University of Chicago Press, 2011), 110–11; Jeremy Kinser, "Only Hugh," *Advocate*, July 30, 2010, www.advocate.com. In the latter, Hefner is quoted as saying, "I published it first and foremost because I thought it was a good story, but I was well aware of the fact that it would be perceived as controversial because *Esquire* had already turned it down. . . . I was obviously aware of the fact that it would be controversial and, as we discovered, in some corners misunderstood. Some people felt it was homophobic."

10. "Annual Report: The Playboy Foundation," *Playboy*, January 1973, 57. See also Marc Stein, *Sexual Injustice: Supreme Court Decisions from* Griswold *to* Roe (Chapel Hill: University of North Carolina Press, 2010), 246–47; Pitzulo, *Bachelors and Bunnies*, 108–17.

11. Lee Prosser, *Running from the Hunter: The Life and Works of Charles Beaumont* (San Bernardino, CA: Borgo, 1996), 16, 21, 26, 69. Beaumont's fiction includes other instances of gender and sexual inversion and transgression; see *The Hunger*.

12. Saul Rosenthal, letter to the editor, *Playboy*, November 1955, 5–6.

13. Beaumont, "Crooked Man," 6, 8.

14. Herbert Tutill, letter to the editor, *Playboy*, November 1955, 5.

15. Michael S. Sherry, *Gay Artists in Modern American Culture: An Imagined Conspiracy* (Chicago: University of Chicago Press, 2007), 1; David Johnson, *The Lavender Scare: The Cold War Persecution of Gays and Lesbians in the Federal Government* (Chicago: University of Chicago Press, 2004). See also Gregory Woods, *Homintern: How Gay Culture Liberated the Modern World* (New Haven, CT: Yale University Press, 2016). For a recent discussion that argues that some elements of "The Crooked Man" have come true, see Mark Judge, "When Heterosexuality Is Outlawed," RealClearReligion, August 18, 2014, www.realclearreligion.org.

16. Beaumont, "Crooked Man," 8; Philip Wylie, *Generation of Vipers* (New York: Farrar, 1942). See also Molly Ladd-Taylor and Laurie Umansky, eds., *Bad Mothers: The Politics of Blame in Twentieth-Century America* (New York: NYU Press, 1998).

17. Beaumont, "Crooked Man," 10, 14. Alternatively Mina can be reimagined as a transman who resists Jesse because Mina is not attracted to cisgender men.

18. Beaumont, "Crooked Man," 8.

19. Beaumont, 6, 8.

20. See Barbara Ehrenreich, *The Hearts of Men: American Dreams and the Flight from Commitment* (New York: Anchor, 1983), 42–51. My discussion of *Playboy* masculinities is also informed by the unpublished work of Elizabeth O'Gorek.

21. On Strait and *Citizens News*, see John D'Emilio, *Sexual Politics, Sexual Communities: The Making of a Homosexual Minority in the United States, 1940–1970* (Chicago: University of Chicago Press, 1983), 188–89; Rodger Streitmatter, *Unspeakable: The Rise of the Gay and Lesbian Press in America* (Boston: Faber and Faber, 1995), 65, 78, 111–12; Nan Alamilla Boyd, *Wide Open Town: A History of Queer San Francisco to 1965* (Berkeley: University of California Press, 2003), 220–32; Meeker, *Contacts Desired*, 175–78, 208–17. On Polak and Drum, see Marc Stein, *City of Sisterly and Brotherly Loves: Lesbian and Gay Philadelphia, 1945–1972* (Chicago: University of Chicago Press, 2000), 226–302; Stein, "Canonizing Homophile Sexual Respectability: Archives, History, and Memory," *Radical History Review* 120 (Fall 2014): 52–73. For another homophile magazine parody, see Rita Laporte, "The Causes and Cures of Heterosexuality," *Ladder*, September 1967, 2–5.

22. I cite the four as "Homosexuality in America," *Life*, June 26, 1964, 66–67; Paul Welch, "The 'Gay' World Takes to the City Streets," *Life*, June 26, 1964, 68–74; Ernest Havemann, "Scientists Search for the Answers to a Touchy and Puzzling Question: Why?" *Life*, June 26,1964, 76–80; Bill Eppridge, photographs, "Homosexuality in America," *Life*, June 26, 1964, 66–80.

23. "Homosexuality in America," 66; Welch, "'Gay' World," 75; Havemann, "Scientists Search," 80. See also Meeker, *Contacts Desired*, 151–95.

24. Meeker, *Contacts Desired*, 186; ECHO Minutes, August 8 and September 19, 1964, ECHO Papers, John J. Wilcox Jr. Archives, William Way LGBT Community Center, Philadelphia, PA; "Breakthrough: When Will It Come?" *Mattachine Review*, April–September 1964, 4–24; "Cross-currents," *Ladder*, July 1964, 23.

25. "LIFE," *Citizens News*, July 20, 1964, 1–2; Clark Polak, letter to the editors of *Life* and response by Patricia Hines for the editors of *Life*, reprinted in *Drum*, October 1964, 22. For later critiques of *Life*'s exposé, see "The Opposition Is Organized," *Citizens News*, February 15, 1965, 5, 8 (apparently by Harry d'Turk); and "LIFE Bigotry," *Citizens News*, ca. June–July 1965, 1, 2 (the issue is numbered vol. 4, no. 14).

26. Welch, "'Gay' World," 66; Strait, "Heterosexuality in America," 5. See also Sloan Wilson, *The Man in the Gray Flannel Suit* (New York: Simon and Schuster, 1955), which was the basis of a 1956 film, directed by Nunnally Johnson, with the same name.

27. Strait, "Heterosexuality in America," 5–8; Arody, "Heterosexuality in America," 20–21.

28. Strait, "Heterosexuality in America," 5, 7–8; Arody, "Heterosexuality in America," 20–21. For a related discussion, see Andrew Bradbury, "The Heterosexual Minority," *ONE*, June 1965, 6–9.

29. Strait, "Heterosexuality in America," 5.

30. See Alfred Kinsey, Wardell Pomeroy, and Clyde Martin, *Sexual Behavior in the Human Male* (Philadelphia: Saunders, 1948); Alfred Kinsey, Wardell Pomeroy, Clyde Martin, and Paul Gebhard, *Sexual Behavior in the Human Female* (Philadelphia: Saunders, 1953).

31. A.E.B., letter to the editor, *Drum*, December 1964, 34; Merla Zellerbach, "Odd News about Heterosexuals," *San Francisco Chronicle*, July 22, 1964, 39.

32. "LIFE," 1; Polak, letter to the editor, 22; Arody, "Heterosexuality in America," 21; D'Emilio, *Sexual Politics*, 75–91.

33. "Homosexuality in America," 66; Strait, "Heterosexuality in America," 5–6, 8; Arody, "Heterosexuality in America," 19. The KKK photograph was taken from George McMillan, "The Klan Scourges Old St. Augustine," *Life*, June 26, 1964, 21.

34. "Franky Hill: Memoirs of a Boy of Pleasure," *Drum*, December 1964, 6–7, 26; "Harry Chess: That Man from A.U.N.T.I.E.," *Drum*, March 1965, 7–10; P. Arody, "I Was a Homosexual for the FBI," *Drum*, March 1965, 14–15; P. Arody, "Tropic of Crabs," *Drum*, April 1965, 11–12, 31–32.

35. See Streitmatter, *Unspeakable*, 65.

36. Herb Caen, "Kiddin' on the Keys," *San Francisco Chronicle*, December 22, 1967, 27. See also *Citizens News*, ca. July 1966, 12 (the issue is numbered vol. 5, no. 7): 12; *ARC News*, February 1967, 1; Streitmatter, *Unspeakable*, 111–12; Clifford Linedecker, *Children in Chains* (New York: Everest, 1981), 227–42.

37. Stein, *City of Sisterly and Brotherly Loves*, 231–40, 251–58, 282–85, 299–302.

38. See Shaun Considine, *Mad as Hell: The Life and Work of Paddy Chayefsky* (New York: Random House, 1994), 251–67. The Paddy Chayefsky Papers (PCP) can be found in the Billy Rose Theatre Division of the New York Public Library for the Performing Arts, New York, NY. For the drafts, see Boxes 82–87 and 118, PCP. For "Homosexuality in America," see Box 82, Folder 2.

39. Chayefsky, "Latent Heterosexual," 50.

40. Chayefsky, 49, 51.
41. Chayefsky, 49–52.
42. Chayefsky, 50.
43. Chayefsky, 52.
44. Chayefsky, 52–53.
45. Chayefsky, 54.
46. Chayefsky, 55.
47. Chayefsky, 56.
48. Chayefsky, 113–14.
49. Chayefsky, 117–18.
50. Chayefsky, 122.
51. Perhaps the first historian to notice this was Jonathan Ned Katz; see Katz, *Invention of Heterosexuality*, 109. For early comments on the play's anticorporate politics, see Arthur Best, letter to the editor, *Esquire*, October 1967, 10. See also John Clum, *Paddy Chayefsky* (Boston: Twayne, 1976), 83–88.
52. Chayefsky, "Latent Heterosexual," 54. For the Johnson story referenced here, see Robert Dallek, *Flawed Giant: Lyndon B. Johnson and His Times, 1961–1973* (New York: Oxford University Press, 1998), 491.
53. Paddy Chayefsky, *Television Plays* (New York: Simon and Schuster, 1955), 173–75. See also Scott Balcerzak, "Authoring and Performing 'Latency': Postwar Sexual Discourse in the Two Versions of Marty," *Quarterly Review of Film and Video* 34, no. 1 (2017): 18–36.
54. Chayefsky, *Television Plays*, 260, 262.
55. Fischer, quoted in "Backstage with Esquire," *Esquire*, August 1967, 37.
56. On early productions, see Box 87, Folders 6–15, PCP; Box 209, Folders 7–15, PCP; Box 210, Folders 1 and 5, PCP.
57. Clive Barnes, "Theater: 'The Latent Heterosexual,'" *New York Times*, March 22, 1968, 52; Herbert Lawson, "The Theater: Off, Way Off, Broadway," *Wall Street Journal*, March 22, 1968, 12; Bart Cody, "The Latent Heterosexual," *Los Angeles Advocate*, June 1968, 7.
58. Chayefsky, "Latent Heterosexual," 54–55, 116–18. Considine notes that Christine was based on the consolidation of two distinct female characters in earlier drafts of the play—a white divorcée whom he marries and a black woman who becomes his "mistress" (*Mad as Hell*, 253–55).
59. See, for example, Adrienne Rich, "Compulsory Heterosexuality and Lesbian Existence," *Signs: Journal of Women in Culture and Society* 5, no. 4 (Summer 1980): 631–60; Queers, "Queers Read This: I Hate Straights," June 1990, available at the Queer Resources Directory, www.qrd.org.
60. As Smith-Rosenberg argues, "The function of humor is to challenge order but not to overthrow it. Humor is possible only because author and audience are secure in the knowledge that social order is not endangered." Smith-Rosenberg, "Davey Crockett as Trickster," 345.

PART III

Embracing and Contesting Legitimacy

8

Holding the Line

Mexicans and Heterosexuality in the Nineteenth-Century West

ZURISADAY GUTIÉRREZ AVILA AND PABLO MITCHELL

For ethnic Mexicans in the United States, heterosexuality has historically offered a mixed set of blessings at best. In the nineteenth-century US Southwest, for instance, ethnic Mexican women's decisions to delay marriage or otherwise stray from a strictly heterosexual marital path could easily draw the sharp criticism of their community. Spanish-language newspapers, an indispensable resource for ethnic Mexicans throughout the Southwest, were also a powerful force in defining norms of heterosexual behavior and denouncing those individuals, especially women, who failed to follow those norms. A poem published in the newspaper *Sancho Panza* from El Paso in the early 1890s warned a woman named Enriqueta, "la muchacha más coqueta / de toda la capital" (the most flirtatious girl / in the whole capital), to cease her "necia conquetería" (ridiculous flirting). "Hoy es tiempo todavia, / mañana acaso seria ya muy tarde" (Today there is still time, / tomorrow might be too late), the poem continues, urging Enriqueta to marry before she is too old. "Y ya que casarte quieres / deja locuras pasadas, / y cumple tus deberes / imitando a las mujeres / recatadas" (And since you want to marry / leave behind the craziness of the past / and fulfill your obligations / following the lead of demure women), the poem ended. For Mexican women pursuing a life without marriage and a husband, the author made clear, the consequences would be dire.[1]

Stereotypical images of Mexican women as mothers and as confined to the home and family also circulated widely in the Spanish-language press. The historian Doris Meyer notes that "the mother figure is described as the moral and emotional foundation of the Hispanic social structure." This idealized woman, Meyer continues, "was supposed to practice self-abnegation and total dedication to the duty of nurturing her children and caring for the hearth." Meyer points to an essay from an 1892 Albuquerque, New Mexico, newspaper titled "La madre" (The mother), which described mothers as the "mensajera de Dios en el hogar" (messenger of God in the home). Declarations of love and devotion aside, the effect of such soaring rhetoric, Meyer suggests, was to restrict Mexican women "to the emotional realm of the home and family" and ultimately to constrain and restrict their lives and experiences.[2]

Such costs and afflictions of heterosexuality (and the heterosexual practices that make up heterosexuality, such as courtship, marriage, marital reproductive sex between husband and wife, child rearing in heterosexually organized households, clearly defined and studiously maintained differences between men and women) are well documented by historians, including the chapters in this collection. Scholars of settler colonialism have also identified heterosexuality and the damages it has caused. Although heterosexuality rarely appears in more traditional accounts of US expansion, the creation and maintenance of heterosexual families was, in fact, critical to American settler colonialism. At the center of Anglo-American settler colonialism was a profound belief in the inferiority of Native and Mexican (as well as African American and Asian American) gender relations and sexuality. Settlers repeatedly insisted that Anglo-American heterosexuality, exemplified by marital, reproductive, heterosexual sex and by supposedly more clearly differentiated gender roles, elevated Anglo newcomers far above the inhabitants of the lands they entered. For centuries, Anglo-Americans had ridiculed Native men as lazy and "womanish," while Native women often appeared in Anglo accounts as overworked, masculine drudges. Non-Anglo groups, in general, endured widespread criticism about their ostensibly bewildering array of nonprocreative, nonmarital sexual acts. Newly animated science-based distinctions between heterosexuality and homosexuality during the late nineteenth century only amplified these attacks. Indeed, emergent notions of homosexuality as a medical condition were deeply racialized as well as sexualized. Nonwhites appeared as particularly prone to a pathological homosexuality, while Anglo women and men predominantly engaged in "healthy" heterosexuality.[3]

The deviancy associated with non-Anglo families stood in stark contrast to the dominant culture's celebration of the heterosexual Anglo household. In the nineteenth-century US West, as the historian Kelly Lytle Hernández notes, Anglo families were "the building block of the new social order in the conquered territories." Focusing on Los Angeles, Lytle Hernández highlights Anglo "homeseekers" and their characteristics: "middle-class, mid-western, hetero-patriarchal, and nuclear Anglo-American families moving farther west to acquire the land recently opened by the end to the nation's brutal wars with Indigenous peoples on the plains and southwestern territories claimed by the United States." Sarah Carter offers a similar example from Anglo-Canadian settler colonialism in the nineteenth century. "'Proper' marriage," she notes, "would help maintain the new settlers' social and sexual distance from the Aboriginal population, and it would forge the new settler identity." Heterosexuality, in other words, served many purposes, among them the conquest and subjugation of Indigenous and other non-Anglo peoples in developing US and Canadian settler-colonialist regimes.[4]

Political cartoons, illustrations, and engravings offer even more dramatic evidence of this paired celebration of Anglo heterosexual homes and demonization of non-Anglo households. One image from the 1870s, for example, created a stark contrast between Chinese immigrant homes and Anglo domesticity. "A Picture for Employers" placed side by side an image of Chinese American living quarters and an Anglo household (figure 8.1). The Chinese home was exclusively male, and the men were nearly indistinguishable from each other. Men smoked opium or slept in bunk beds, and rats swarmed throughout the room. The image even went so far as to portray two Chinese men as *eating* rats. The Anglo household, on the other hand, exemplified happiness, cleanliness, and heterosexual order. The father, presumably gainfully employed, returned from work to a wife/mother who cheerfully greeted him while holding their infant child. Other children, a boy with a baseball bat in his hand and girl in a dress, eagerly welcomed their father home, while a cat (animals in the Anglo home were pets, not, as in the Chinese boarding house, either vermin or potential food) serenely lapped milk. Above the doorway was a placard stating, "God Bless Our Home," adding religious piety to the Anglo home and reminding readers that Asian immigrants were mostly non-Christians and supposedly practiced "heathen" religions. The proliferation of such charged images undoubtedly fueled anti-immigrant attacks, including nativist legislation like the Page Act of

Figure 8.1. "A Picture for Employers—Why *They* can live on 40 cents a day, and *They* can't," 1878 (Courtesy of the Department of Special Collections and University Archives, Stanford University Libraries)

1875 and the Chinese Exclusion Act of 1882, and helped provide a justification for claims of Anglo superiority and conquest in the nineteenth-century US West.[5]

While scholars have continued to explore such deep and enduring *costs* of heterosexual practices, the *benefits* of heterosexuality have received less scholarly attention. This inattention has persisted, in part, because the advantages and rewards of heterosexuality seem so self-evident and its historical traces so numerous and commonplace. Although the actual term would not emerge in full force until the twentieth century, heterosexuality, one of the most powerful organizing principles in US society, shares a tendency with other powerful concepts, like whiteness, normality, middle-classness, and masculinity, to recede from historical analysis. Heterosexuality can also flex and morph its many features, expanding and contracting based on particular times and locations, different contexts, and contingencies. Below the seemingly unchanging, eternal, "natural" quality of heterosexual relations is in fact a fluid, flexible heterosexuality that could be shifted and adapted to new historical contexts and circumstances. The capacity of heterosexuality to contort itself to changing times has been critical to its ability to maintain its central social and cultural space.

This chapter examines the role of heterosexuality among Mexicans in the US Southwest between the end of the Mexican-American War and the Treaty of Guadalupe Hidalgo in 1848 and the beginnings of large-scale Mexican migration to the region around 1900.[6] We argue that nineteenth-century Mexicans sustained a deep commitment to hetero-sexuality and heterosexual practices and suggest that this commitment may have offered Mexican women and men a source of stability and comfort during an especially traumatic period in the group's long history in what is now the United States.

* * *

Ethnic Mexicans, like Native Americans, were primary targets of US settler colonialism. Throughout what would become the US South-west, from Texas to New Mexico to California, the marginalization of Mexicans included political disenfranchisement, land dispossession, and increasingly violent and widespread attacks. Over the course of the nineteenth century, Mexican-origin communities in the United States experienced profound dislocation and loss. Chicana/o historians have documented this loss over the past several decades. David Montejano points, for example, to a dramatic drop in Mexican political leadership in San Antonio, where Mexicans represented two-thirds of the aldermen around 1850; by the 1870s, they represented less than 10 percent, and there were zero Mexican aldermen in 1900. In Ventura County, California, as Tomás Almaguer notes, Mexicans experienced catastrophic land loss and were increasingly limited to manual labor. Almaguer calculates that by 1900, nearly 80 percent of the unskilled workers and farm laborers in Ventura County were of Mexican descent.[7]

Building on such scholarship, Miroslava Chávez-García has recently observed that Mexicans in California were disproportionately imprisoned during the period as well. "Californio and Mexicano immigrant youth—all of them male"—she notes, "were more likely than young-sters of all other ethnic and racial backgrounds to be tried, convicted, and imprisoned in the state penitentiary in the nineteenth century."

In an important reminder that the horrific rise in US lynchings in the late nineteenth century targeted ethnic Mexicans as well as African American men and women, Ken Gonzales-Day has uncovered over 120 "lynchings or summary executions" of Mexicans in the US Southwest between 1850 and 1900. Chicana historians have provided further proof of the gendered dimensions of this Anglo onslaught. Erika Pérez, for instance, has recently described Mexican women's vulnerability under Anglo settler-colonialist rule. "The violence that women and children experienced were not isolated incidents," she writes, "but were embedded within the macroscopic contexts of Mexican political instability, American imperialism, and conquest that turned the bodies of local women and children into sites of contestation." In raw numbers, by 1900, Mexicans found themselves a distinct minority in the Southwest, as the percentage of Mexicans in major states like Texas and California plummeted to single digits (5 percent in Texas and 3 percent in California).[8]

While Chicana/o historians have thus described many aspects of the devastating effects of Anglo settler colonialism, rarely have scholars focused specifically on heterosexuality and the formation and maintenance of sexual and gender norms within Mexican communities. The lives of ordinary Mexicans typically left few traces in the historical record. Accounts by ordinary Mexicans describing their courtships, marriages, home lives, and other intimacies during the period are rare. Spanish-language newspapers, which we turn to later in the chapter, offer one valuable type of source. Other sources are the US Census records, which provide significant, though still partial, glimpses of Mexican life. The US Census, of course, was produced by and largely for the purposes of US state formation and was committed to re-creating gendered and racialized hierarchies. In this respect, the census records highlighted and even encouraged heterosexual identification. Married couples were listed first in census records of individual homes, followed by children, other relatives, and people boarding at the households. Census enumerators prioritized husbands over wives and listed the married man, not the wife, as the head of household. Women would only appear as heads of household when they were single, divorced, or widowed. The inclusion of marital status as a separate census category further accentuated the importance of marriage and heterosexuality in powerful government documents like the US Census.

Census records from predominantly Mexican neighborhoods and locales across the Southwest reveal that Mexicans married, formed families, and raised children through this period. On one level, this fact should come as little surprise. At the same time, the great power of normative and unmarked categories and social forces like heterosexuality is to hide in plain sight and naturalize as unremarkable and banal those practices and experiences and dispositions that might otherwise merit historical analysis and contextualization. So it is worth noting and perhaps even reflecting a bit on the very presence of heterosexuality and heterosexually organized households in Mexican communities in the United States in the second half of the nineteenth century.

The censuses of predominantly Mexican neighborhoods in cities such as Los Angeles and San Antonio reveal home after home filled with Mexican families. In one Los Angeles neighborhood in 1860, there were thirty-six Mexican-origin households and eleven non-Mexican households. Of the thirty-six ethnic-Mexican homes, twenty were headed by heterosexual couples. Married couples predominated in one stretch of largely ethnic-Mexican homes. Ana Sanchez and her husband, Bautista Moreno, who worked as a "saddler," headed one household with their three boys (Francisco, Bautista, and Jacobo), while Jesus Villanueva, a "cigarmaker," and his wife, Maria Maldonado, headed the household next door, with two children, Consolacion and Agustin. With the exception of two female-headed households next door to the Villanueva-Maldonado home (the families of Adeliza Dominguez and her two children and Balvanada Peru and her three children), the households that were located farther down the street were also headed by heterosexual couples. These homes included the families of Matias Fernandez and Angela Leon, Manuela and Jesus Lujan, and Agustin and Refugio Olvera and their five children.[9]

The neighborhood also contained two homes with mixed Mexican-Anglo families. One of the two mixed families was the household of Rosario and William Osborn. Rosario Osborn was born in Mexico, while William Osborn was a New York–born physician. The family also included two of William Osborn's sons, both probably born of a previous marriage (Rosario Osborn was listed as thirty years old, and the two young men were twenty-two and nineteen years old, respectively, and both had been born in New York State). The other mixed family was the household of Henry and Feliciana Lewis, both in their thirties; Henry was a coffee manufacturer from New York, and Feliciana was a native of Mexico.[10]

Forty years later, the Anglo population of Los Angeles had grown dramatically; however, Mexicans continued to be a major presence in certain areas of the city. In one neighborhood in 1900, there were nearly 140 total households, with 66 ethnic-Mexican homes and 77 non-Mexican households. Two-thirds (44) of the Mexican households contained both husband and wife, and many of those included at least one child as well. Rita and Andrew Lopez, married thirteen years, lived in one home with their five daughters and two stepsons. Two houses down the street lived Federico and Carolina Arismandez, married five years, and their three children, as well as Luz Guerrero, Carolina Arismandez's mother. Encarnacion and Frank Laterio—along with Encarnacion's mother, Carlita Polanco—lived in the next home and had been married for thirty years. A nearby stretch of homes included the families of Panfilo and Carmen Morello, married eight years; Simona and Jose Rivera, married two years; and Juan and Juana Tapia, married twelve years. Two couples (Joaquina and Juan Meza and Placentino and Marcella Leon), each married over thirty years, lived on the next block.[11]

This enduring presence of heterosexuality and heterosexual practices such as marriage in Mexican communities during the second half of the nineteenth century appears in the composition of individual households in other major southwestern cities as well. In 1860s San Antonio, for instance, one neighborhood of forty-three households and three hundred individuals, contained thirty-four ethnic Mexican households (as well as nine non-Mexican homes). In one stretch of homes, John and Trinidad Rodriquez lived with their four children (Martin, eleven; Elizabeth, ten; Antonio, eight; and Francisca, five). The Rodriguezes lived next door to John and Policarpia Ivaria and their children (Martina, five; Jesus, three; and Gregoria, one). Also listed as residing in the Ivaria household was the family of Dolores and Sipriano Sandoval with their four children ranging in age from three to twelve years old. Two widowed women, Juanita and Luz Garcia, lived next door to the Rodriguez family, with Luz raising four children (Jesus, seven; Carlos, five; Refugio, two; and Julia, one). Juanita and Luz Garcia were exceptions in this stretch of families in that they, as women, both appeared as heads of household.

Next to the Garcias, who seem to have been either sisters or sisters-in-law, were several additional families headed by heterosexual Mexican couples.[12]

By 1900, fourteen thousand ethnic Mexicans lived in San Antonio, about 25 percent of the city's population of nearly fifty-five thousand. In one area of the city's First Ward, 45 of the 122 households were Mexican-origin homes. There was also one mixed household, that of Charles and Ygnacia Stevens, who had been married eight years and had two children. The remainder of the households (76) was composed of non-Mexican families. While the proportion of Mexican households organized around a heterosexual couple was smaller in this neighborhood (19 households of the 45), it was still significant. In one stretch of homes on South Laredo Street, Manuel and Leona Olivares, married two years with two children, lived two doors down from Maria and Antonio Saenz and their six children. Benito and Juana Castanero lived nearby, as did Maria and Ignacio Hernandez (married thirty years with three children) and Francisco and Adela Diaz (married twenty-one years with five children). Beyond signaling the continued presence of ethnic Mexicans in the Southwest, such Mexican enclaves in San Antonio and elsewhere in the Southwest, though at times small, could also provide the space for heterosexual mingling within the Mexican community. In these neighborhoods, children of Mexican families, nieces and nephews, lodgers, widows and widowers, and even women and men simply visiting friends and family could potentially socialize and perhaps even find partners or spouses.[13]

Though muted, the presence of heterosexuality is also apparent in the Mexican-origin households headed by widows and widowers, who, after all, had once been married and to an extent were still defined by their status as a husband or wife whose spouse had died. Widows or widowers, in fact, made up a significant portion of the Mexican-origin households led by a single person in both Los Angeles and San Antonio. For instance, in San Antonio in 1900, Luis Cardenas was a forty-four-year-old widower, living with his sixteen-year-old son and sixty-six-year-old father, also a widower. Florentina Ybarra, widowed and seventy-two years old, lived with her son Andrew, himself a widower, on High Street in Los Angeles in 1900. Around the corner from the Ybarras, on Buena Vista Street, lived Juana Gutierrez, a widow with her three-year-old daughter and her teenage nephew. In other cases, a married man or woman was listed as a head of household in the census, but the spouse did not appear in the census. In Los Angeles, Francisca Bracaneida was listed as married in 1900 despite the fact that her husband did not appear in the household. Living with Bracaneida were her five children, ranging from eleven years old to newly born, and her widowed mother. In San Antonio, Cleofas Muñoz Cadena appeared in a similarly constituted household in 1900; she was listed as married for twenty-four years alongside her seven children and a sixty-year-old widow who boarded with the family. As previously married women and men, such widows and widowers had been active participants in heterosexual marriage, one of the cornerstones of heterosexuality, and many had raised, or were raising, children as well, another important feature of heterosexuality—especially for women.

From another perspective, the presence in the census of married Mexican women as heads of households might suggest an additional component of heterosexually organized Mexican families: a sharp division of labor between men and women. Like members of many marginalized communities, Mexican men in the nineteenth-century Southwest were at times forced to migrate in search of jobs in industries such as mining or railroad construction. Mexican women with husbands engaging in such labor migrations most frequently did not themselves migrate but instead remained in their home communities. As is so often the case with attempts to reconstruct the lives of ordinary people (and even more so with the lives of ordinary people of color), archival sources offer limited evidence of how Mexican women and men understood and managed their gendered forms of labor and labor migration. Nevertheless, records like the US Census can provide a glimpse of this additional, more labor-oriented, facet of heterosexuality, namely the possibility that Mexican men and women may have approached the decision to leave family in search of work, even temporarily, in sharply different ways.[14]

As the forced migration of men, either permanently or temporarily, in search of work suggests, Mexicans often struggled mightily in the nineteenth-century Southwest. Of the Mexicans enumerated with occupations in the census, most list manual-labor jobs, reflecting the widespread loss of Mexican wealth during the period and the creation of a Mexican population that was largely working class and poor. Within this upheaval, it is again worth noting that which can easily pass unmarked and unremarkable: the fact that tens of thousands of ethnic-Mexican women and men became engaged to each other, entered heterosexual marriages, and raised children in predominantly heterosexual families in the US West in the second half of the nineteenth century. As mentioned earlier, Kelly Lytle Hernández, Sarah Carter, and others have noted the critical place of heterosexual practices in settler colonialism in North America, and US Census records confirm the widespread presence of heterosexually organized Anglo households through the West during the period. For Mexican communities, the archival record is far less rich than for Anglos; however, it is clear from census records that heterosexual practices were also widespread and enduring among Mexicans. Other historical records can potentially provide more detail on Mexicans' own views of courtship, marriage, and household formation during the nineteenth century. Legal records, such as wills, divorce cases, and other civil and criminal proceedings can offer such perspectives, as can the few existing archival collections of letters and personal memoirs of Mexican women and men (though both sets of sources are beyond the scope of this chapter). Spanish-language newspapers, many of them newly available in digital formats, are similarly valuable, and it is clear from these sources that heterosexuality continued to play a significant role in the lives of Mexicans in the nineteenth-century Southwest.

The Spanish-language press in the Southwest served as a critical space for political activism and community formation for Mexican communities throughout the nineteenth century. A. Gabriel Meléndez notes in his study of Spanish-language newspapers in nineteenth-century New Mexico that Mexicans used newspapers "to voice sociohistorical concerns and to represent themselves as a determinant group of communities in Nuevo México—a particularly resilient corner of the Chicano homeland."[15] Emerging from besieged communities from Texas to California, the newspapers covered local, national, and international news and commented in their editorials on important political developments. Advertisements for local products and businesses also regularly appeared, as did brief announcements of births, engagements, weddings, and deaths, along with the occasional joke or tongue-in-cheek aside. Spanish-language newspapers also offer a wealth of information on the lives of ordinary Mexicans in the Southwest. The continued importance of heterosexuality, especially courtship and marriage, regularly appears in these accounts from nineteenth-century Spanish-language newspapers.

Newspapers, for instance, frequently published articles on marriage, courtship, and the proper relationship between women and men. In an 1846 article from the *Californian*, titled "To Curb This Appetite," young Mexican men were advised to avoid lust and the damages that lust could inflict on individual men and their communities. While women were not mentioned as susceptible to this trap of lust, the article suggested that even marriage could fall short in fighting lust's powerful forces. Despite the presence of delicately appointed tables, fine clothes, and romantic conversations, the author continued, social refinement could not prevent men from falling into patterns of lust and lustful behavior. Even joining the military and participating in war, according to the article, failed to shield men from the dangers of excessive desire. In drawing a comparison to something as deadly as war, the author highlighted the devastating consequence that lust could inflict on society. Lust could even go as far as "the total ruin of the nation."[16]

While the article did not give a great deal of advice on how to avoid or escape lust, the author did advise young men to find ways to contribute to their country. They must go and learn how to work in the fields, and only then, after exercising their strength, should men turn to courtship and find a woman to marry. Undergoing physical discipline, the author counseled young men, would prepare them to marry a hardworking woman. Although "To Curb This Appetite" sounded multiple alarms about the perils of young men's lustful designs and actions, the ultimate goal for men and women remained heterosexual marriage. Curbing lustful appetites, though difficult, according to the author, was not impossible, and the belief that even men inflamed by lust would eventually find a woman to marry remained a bedrock assumption of the article.[17]

The notion that marriage was basic to the fabric of society appeared in another Spanish-language newspaper article from mid-nineteenth-century California. "Galant Literature: Ceremony of the Antique to Celebrate Their Matrimonies" presented marriage as a "serious and important act that decides the fate of the partners for life." This "contract" and "reciprocated consent from the man and the woman," the author explained, received its legitimacy and strength from its foundation in "ancient times." While disparaging the "ridiculous" traditions of older times, the author noted that current marriage practices had their roots in these older traditions. For the author, purity and fidelity were the foundation of society; marriage, as the principal agent of purity and fidelity, thus played a major role in creating society. Turning to a more symbolic level, the author likened water to purity (water's ability to cleanse) and fire to fidelity (fire's refining of metals) to emphasize their elemental roles in society. Marriage's role in promoting purity and fidelity, according to the author, had led to a widespread and long-lasting recognition of the value of marriage.[18]

Another article, from early 1850s Santa Fe, offered an overview of marriage and its societal benefits. "Principios generales acerca del matrimonio" (General principles regarding marriage) argued that individual men, as well as society in general, were much better served by men finding a spouse, marrying, and diligently raising children. "No se debe considerer el matrimonio simplemente como una sociedad que se termina solo en la union de dos personas de diferente sexo por su provecho particular o por su placer," the author stated, "sino que al contrario es preciso mirarla como una sociedad relativa, y por decirlo asi preparatoria al sociedad paternal y a la familia" (We should not consider marriage as a society as only the union of two people of different sexes based on their own benefit or pleasure; but on the contrary it is important to view marriage from a broader perspective as fundamental to paternal society and to the family). Marriage, the article continued, was the union of "un hombre y de una mujer que se obligan a amarse, a socorrerse, y que se prometan reciprocamente favorecerse, con el fin de tener hijos y de educarlos de una manera conveniente a la naturaleza del hombre, al beneficio de la familia y al bien de la sociedad" (a man and a woman that obliges them to love each other, support each other, and endow favors on each other with the goal of bearing children and educating them according to human nature for the benefit of the family and society's well-being). Married women had certain obligations ("el matrimonio se oblige la mujer a someterse a la direccion de su marido para los negocios de la familia, y a socorrerle, en cuanto pueda, con todo el esmero de que es capaz y con la dulzura de su trato" [marriage obliges a wife to submit to her husband's will in matters of family business and to help him when possible with all the care and sweetness that she can provide]), while married men were exhorted in relation to their spouse "amarla, protegerla, tratarla bien" (to love her, protect her, treat her well). Marriage, according to the author, was a heterosexual bond ("the union of two people of different sexes") with discrete and separate responsibilities for wives (submission, helpfulness, sweetness) and for husbands (love, protection, good treatment). Marriage was also, in the author's view, critical to both family and social stability.[19]

In contrast to the praise that the article showered on proper marriage, the author heaped criticism on unions that ran contrary to heterosexual, reproductive, monogamous marriage. Following a short discussion of polygamy and a reminder about the supposed advantages of monogamy, the article next turned to divorce, outlining the handful of circumstances under which divorce might have been acceptable. In addition to "adulterio y la disercíon maliciosa" (adultery and malicious desertion), the author added other justifications for seeking a divorce, "como por ejemplo una sentencia de muerto o un destierro perpetuo por algun crimin capital" (like for example a death sentence or a life sentence for some capital crime). In the end, the article suggested, only proper marital unions could truly ensure the success and well-being of both an individual and society. While matters of social class and differences of wealth and status were not addressed explicitly in the piece, the date of publication (1852) hints at larger issues potentially at stake in the emphasis on the importance of marriage for broader "paternal" society. When the article appeared, less than five years had elapsed since the end of the Mexican-American War and the beginning of US occupation of the formerly Mexican Southwest. It is therefore worth speculating whether the "broader perspective" that the author asked couples to consider when deciding to marry may have included the ongoing transfer of power from Mexican authorities and elites to Anglo political and economic newcomers. In the midst of persistent social turmoil, in other words, heterosexual marriage might have carried an added significance, potentially helping to reinforce a community undergoing dramatic transformations. Moreover, in such settings, husbands and wives who failed to follow the expectations and norms of proper marriage might have faced even sharper criticisms for their perceived personal, and societal, failings.[20]

In addition to articles extolling the virtues of marriage and rallying young men and women to marry for the good of their families and society, Spanish-language newspapers celebrated local engagements and weddings. The marital union of men and women, of course, was a cornerstone of heterosexuality, and thus it is not surprising that newspaper announcements of weddings sharply differentiated the bride and the groom, highlighting, for instance, the beauty of the bride or the details of her dress while emphasizing the groom's social standing and respectability. In the fall of 1879, for instance, *La Gaceta* of Santa Barbara, California, announced that a judge "unió en matrimonio á Sr. Abram Ontiveros y á la señorita Maria Dalariza Adelmira Vidal" (united Mr. Abram Ontiveros and Miss Maria Dalariza Adelmira Vidal in marriage). Two months later, three weddings appeared on one page of *La Gaceta*. Two sets of newlyweds had English surnames, while one bride and groom had Spanish surnames. Francisco Moreno and Biviana Garcia were married, according to the announcement, the previous week, and "la boda fué espléndida y reinó alegría, cangeándose bríndis análogos á la ocasion, todos aludiendo á la buena conducta y amabilidad de la señorita Garcia, quien por sus méritos los merece igualmente el jóven Moreno" (the wedding was splendid and happiness reigned, toasts were exchanged appropriate to the occasion, everyone alluding to the good conduct and kindness of Miss Garcia, who for her gifts deserved similar treatment from young Moreno). "Les deseamos á los nuevos esposados larga vida, salud y prosperidad" (We wish long life, health and prosperity to the newlyweds), the article ended. Echoing the advice given in articles on proper marriage, wedding announcements in Spanish-language newspapers touted the virtues of marriage and the valued features of exemplary wives ("good conduct and kindness") and beneficent husbands ("young Moreno" was advised that his wife deserved to be treated as well as she treated him).[21]

Another Spanish-language newspaper, *El Fronterizo*, announced the union of a leading member of Tucson's Mexican community with a woman from Nogales (the article does not specify either Nogales, Arizona, or Nogales, Mexico) in May 1889. Society "celebrará dignamente la boda de ese caballero que es uno de sus mas distinguidos miembros" (will celebrate in a dignified manner the wedding of this gentleman, who is one of the most distinguished members) of the community, the paper stated, and his bride-to-be, "una bella y muy estimable señorita de Nogales" (a beautiful and highly esteemed young woman from Nogales).

The praise bestowed on the couple and their wedding implied that a marriage was also a communal celebration, and while the announcement was brief, the admiring tone communicated the approval of what the newspaper considered to be a rightful union. On the same day, the newspaper also published the announcement of the wedding of Wenceslao Felix and Adela Garcia. The couple was married in the Catholic Church, and Felix was described as "nuestro querido amigo y muy recomendable jóven" (our good friend and commendable young man), while his bride was praised as "la simpática [the delightful] Srita Adela Garcia." The article ended by noting the attendance of godparents: "sus padrinos el Sr. Mariano Samaniego y Da. Doloritos A. de Samaniego." Below the news of the Felix-Garcia nuptials was an announcement of a wedding conducted by a local magistrate, Judge Meyer, between "el Sr. A. L. Stahl y la apreciable [the esteemed] Srita Clara Foster," in the home of Frank Proctor. While more archival research would be needed to confirm the class status of these married couples, such "splendid" affairs probably involved mostly well-to-do members of the ethnic-Mexican community.[22]

As one of the hallmarks of heterosexuality, marriage and newspaper descriptions of engagements and weddings often drew a bright line between women and men, male attributes and female ones, masculinity and femininity. These accounts also offer a counternarrative to depictions, as mentioned earlier in the chapter, of Mexican (and other non-Anglo) households as chaotic and inferior that were common in both the Southwest and the wider nation in the nineteenth century. Even brief wedding announcements often mentioned the married parents of the bride and groom as well as the godparents of the couple, emphasizing the family and social network that stood in support of newlyweds as they embarked on their life together as well as highlighting a broader sense of community stability. Faced with a determined and aggressively expanding Anglo settler society in the nineteenth century, ethnic-Mexican communities and their Spanish-language newspapers drew on many resources and strategies of endurance and resistance. While scholars have tended to give little thought to the role of heterosexuality and marriage and assorted "dignified wedding celebrations" in the process of resisting settler colonialism and occupation, such accounts and the emphatically heterosexual families and households they represent perhaps deserve more careful consideration.[23]

Like heterosexuality, religious institutions, the Catholic Church in particular, played an important role in stabilizing and supporting the Mexican community during a tumultuous and unsettling time. Religion in fact appeared with some frequency in articles about marriage in Spanish-language newspapers in the Southwest. Religion was a prominent feature of "El matrimonio Cristiano" (The Christian marriage), published in *Revista Católica* in Las Vegas, New Mexico, in 1888.[24] The writer discussed three "consequences," or rules, that should ideally guide the matrimony celebration among the faithful. The suggestion that the faithful should follow the three consequences communicated the notion that those who did not adhere to the laws were unfaithful and therefore were not Christians. Essentially, the author opined, a truly Christian individual would abide by these guidelines and recommendations. The first consequence framed marriage as a contract and a sacrament. Though mundane in the sense that it was controlled by local government, a contract was still serious. A marriage contract, however, was only valid when it was made in conjunction with the sacrament, that is, when it was drafted by the church. The author added that those couples who failed to incorporate the sacrament into their marriage did not have a true marriage.[25]

The second consequence or law addressed the church's primary role in marriage, endowing the church with the responsibility for dictating all that occurred within a marriage. In prioritizing the church in one's marriage, the author informed readers that constant communication with and understanding of the church was essential if a marriage was to be correct under the eyes of God. The third consequence or law turned to the wedding celebration itself. The author stated that the celebration of matrimony did not refer to civil laws but strictly followed church laws. Moreover, the article emphasized that the wedding celebration united a couple in their faithfulness to each other, hinting that readers should perhaps also evaluate their own faithfulness and religious commitments. The audience, the author warned, might want to go as far as to consider (and perhaps reevaluate) how Christian their marriages were at their conception. Whether celebrating marital fidelity or admonishing those who have strayed from the flock, Spanish-language newspapers thus affirmed the continued centrality of heterosexual marriage in the lives of their readers.[26]

While many articles on courtship and marriage focused on local events, nineteenth-century articles also commented on marriage practices in other countries. The commentary at times demonstrated astonishment or mockery. An article from *El Fronterizo* in 1884 described the story of Adelina Patti, a woman who had managed to have two living husbands. Although she was still, in theory, married to her previous husband, Patti had entered a new marriage and, the article stated, would be enjoying the "privilege" of having two husbands. A similar sense of astonishment about a married woman's sexual proclivities emerged when *El Fronterizo* shared a story in 1887 of a woman who apparently managed to have three marriages as a serial monogamist. According to the article, after Annie Towers divorced her husband Charles Tato and obtained a new husband in New York, she eventually made her way to Ontario, Canada, and found a third husband. The article focused on the complexities that could arise during divorce, such as the proof required during divorce proceedings of a spouse's adulterous behavior. Neither story took place near the newspaper's base in Tucson, Arizona, pointing to the broader national and international interests that often emerged in Spanish-language newspapers.[27]

Other articles similarly offered readers accounts of heterosexual courtship and marriage drawn from beyond the US Southwest. Another story in *El Fronterizo*, hailing in this case from 1880s Germany, described a young medical student in Berlin who needed financial assistance to complete his training. The student promised that he would marry the daughter of his debtor and guaranteed that he would make a formal marriage promise in exchange for monetary support. In one respect, the article demonstrated that in other locales, even those far removed from the desert Southwest, marriage was considered equally serious and worthy of protracted negotiation. The article also suggested that, whether in faraway Berlin or in hometown Tucson, standard forms of courtship could occasionally fall short. If traditional courtship did not suffice or matrimony agents proved untrustworthy or unsuccessful, the article seemed also to say, *tucsoneses* inclined to marry could perhaps announce their availability and marital interests in newspapers like *El Fronterizo*. Implicit in the account was the suggestion that successful heterosexual marriage was so important that dramatic steps could be in order if traditional means of courtship did not suffice.[28]

Articles about unhappy marriages could at times also emphasize the importance of heterosexual marriage. An 1892 article from *El Fronterizo* detailed the story of the near divorce of Arturo and Juliana (the article did not specify whether the couple lived in Tucson or outside the region). Desperate after two unhappy years of marriage, the couple turned to divorce court, where Don Facundo de Soncillo, a court official, questioned the couple about their marital troubles. De Soncillo's intervention, which was, according to the article, made possible by the older man's wisdom and knowledge of the human heart, saved their marriage. In the beginning of the article, "Cada uno en su casa" (Everyone in their own house), the author dedicated time to describing the process by which de Soncillo moderated the delicate conversation between Juliana and Arturo. De Soncillo first asked questions, the answers to which revealed that the couple had been married for less than two years. Arturo explained that while he loved his wife, it was becoming increasingly difficult to reside with Juliana's mother and sisters. Juliana responded by stating that she planned to leave Arturo rather than leave her family. Arturo cited the Bible ("la mujer deje á su padre y á su madre por seguir al marido" [the woman ought to leave her father and mother to follow the husband]) to condemn Juliana's action when she prioritized her mother, whom she was supposed to leave upon marrying, over her own husband.[29]

As Don Facundo continued to hear both sides, he informed them that the divorce would be granted, at which point Juliana admitted that she did not think the divorce would come so soon. Interpreting Juliana's admission as a sign that love was still present, Don Facundo commanded the couple to hug because they both clearly loved each other, and their marriage presumably was saved. The article concluded with a quotation, "Cada uno en su casa, y Dios en la de todos" (Everyone in their house and God in everyone's). The ending of the article reminded readers about what seemed to be a wider, community belief in God's significant role in a successful marriage and household. Arturo's reference to the Bible when describing his mother-in-law also suggested a certain familiarity among readers with biblical references and acknowledged the Bible's, and the Catholic Church's, role in identifying and remediating incorrect actions by individuals and couples. While underscoring both the religious and societal value of remaining in and rehabilitating a heterosexual marriage, the article also sharply critiqued households that were not primarily organized around a husband and wife. Nuclear households, in other words, not households filled with in-laws and other extended family, were integral, the piece suggested, to the proper functioning of ethnic-Mexican society.[30]

In addition to highlighting the link between heterosexual marriage, domesticity, the Catholic Church, and overall social stability, the article presented Mexicans as knowledgeable of and committed to proper civic participation. The magistrate and government official Don Facundo de Soncillo was depicted as well trained and capable of discerning whether divorce was necessary or whether changes in a marriage could be implemented in the hopes of saving the marriage. Divorce also appeared as deeply undesirable in the Mexican community and acceptable only as a last resort. El Fronterizo's account of Arturo and Juliana's visit to the courthouse in order to obtain a legal divorce and their extended conversation with a government official suggested that Mexicans could be relied on to conform to a proper governmental process, a subtle but important intervention, given widespread Anglo denunciations during the late nineteenth century of Mexican communities as supposedly lawless and crime-ridden.

Indeed, the judicious Don Facundo and law-abiding Arturo and Juliana were far removed from accounts like the following, fairly representative, report from an English-language newspaper in Arizona of the murder of an Anglo man by "two Mexicans." According to the 1873 Arizona Sentinel, "Edward Lumley was butchered, probably first tortured," in his home; "one of the assassins is believed to be 'Sanchez,' the Mexican who helped murder Reid and others at Mission Camp in 1871, and he is also the murderer of a boy in Altar Sonora, several years ago." The Sentinel reported that the other man, "his companion in crime, also a Mexican, is not known by name." Like the chaotic images of non-Anglo families that began this chapter, such accounts of Mexican criminality and violence circulated widely in both the Southwest and the nation in the English-language press in the nineteenth century. For ethnic-Mexican readers of Spanish-language newspapers, articles that celebrated weddings as "splendid affairs" and showcased stable, civic-minded Mexican communities were strong counterimages, providing positive accounts of Mexican life to place alongside, and subtly challenge, predominantly negative Anglo views of ethnic Mexicans in the United States.[31]

* * *

While much more research needs to be undertaken on the place of heterosexuality in Mexican communities during the nineteenth century
(exploring, for instance, Mexican legal records and individual accounts
of courtship, marriage, and family life), archival evidence from Spanish-
language newspapers and census records suggest that as they faced the full
force of US settler colonialism, Mexican people also extolled the virtues of
heterosexual marriage and reproduction and continued to form heterosexually based families in large numbers. Following the work of historians
such as Anne Hyde and Erika Pérez, we suggest that this persistence of
heterosexuality might be viewed as attempts by besieged Mexican women
and men to create stability and some semblance of order in a tumultuous
and deeply unsettled world. Heterosexuality certainly played an integral role in justifying and supporting Anglo settler colonialism. Properly
understood, however, heterosexuality could also be viewed as a key source
of resistance and an important strategy for survival.[32]

NOTES

1. "A una coqueta" (To a flirt), *Sancho Panza* (El Paso, TX), November 28, 1891.
   While men could also be subject to strong societal sanction for avoiding marriage
   and proper heterosexual behavior, clear differences between women and men
   characterized gender relations in Mexican-origin communities in both Mexico
   and the United States. As we argue in this chapter, the history of heterosexuality
   in ethnic Mexican communities in the nineteenth-century US Southwest is deeply
   intertwined with the acute presence of US settler colonialism in the region.
2. Doris Meyer, *Speaking for Themselves: Neomexicano Cultural Identity and the
   Spanish-Language Press, 1880–1920* (Albuquerque: University of New Mexico
   Press, 1996), 134–35; "La madre" (The mother), *La Opinión Pública* (Albuquerque,
   NM), July 16, 1892, quoted in Meyer, *Speaking for Themselves*, 135. See also A. Ga-
   briel Meléndez, *Spanish-Language Newspapers in New Mexico, 1834–1958* (Tucson:
   University of Arizona Press, 2005); and Kirsten Silva Gruesz, *Ambassadors of
   Culture: The Transamerican Origins of Latino Writing* (Princeton, NJ: Princeton
   University Press, 2002).
3. There are many excellent discussions of the linking of race with nonnormative sexu-
   ality and domesticity. Some important works are Gail Bederman, *Manliness and
   Civilization: A Cultural History of Gender and Race in the United States, 1880–1917*
   (Chicago: University of Chicago Press, 1995); K. Tsianina Lomawaima, "Domestic-
   ity in the Federal Indian Schools: The Power of Authority over Mind and Body," in
   Deviant Bodies: Critical Perspectives on Difference in Science and Popular Culture, ed.

Jennifer Terry and Jacqueline Urla (Bloomington: Indiana University Press, 1995), 197–218; Kevin J. Mumford, *Interzones: Black/White Sex Districts in Chicago and New York in the Early Twentieth Century* (New York: Columbia University Press, 1997); Mary Ting Yi Lui, *The Chinatown Trunk Mystery: Murder, Miscegenation, and Other Dangerous Encounters in Turn-of-the-Century New York City* (Princeton, NJ: Princeton University Press, 2005); Margaret D. Jacobs, *White Mother to a Dark Race: Settler Colonialism, Maternalism, and the Removal of Indigenous Children in the American West and Australia, 1880–1940* (Lincoln: University of Nebraska Press, 2009); David Wallace Adams, *Education for Extinction: American Indians and the Boarding School Experience, 1875–1928* (Lawrence: University Press of Kansas, 1995). For the relationship between sexuality and race and emerging modern science, see John D'Emilio and Estelle B. Freedman, *Intimate Matters: A History of Sexuality in America* (Chicago: University of Chicago Press, 1997); Siobhan B. Somerville, *Queering the Color Line: Race and the Invention of Homosexuality in American Culture* (Durham, NC: Duke University Press, 2000); Lisa Duggan, *Sapphic Slashers: Sex, Violence, and American Modernity* (Durham, NC: Duke University Press, 2000); Jennifer Terry, *An American Obsession: Science, Medicine, and Homosexuality in Modern Society* (Chicago: University of Chicago Press, 1999).

4. Kelly Lytle Hernández, *City of Inmates: Conquest, Rebellion, and the Rise of Human Caging in Los Angeles, 1771–1965* (Chapel Hill: University of North Carolina Press, 2017), 14, 49; Sarah Carter, *The Importance of Being Monogamous: Marriage and Nation Building in Western Canada to 1915* (Edmonton, AB: Athabasca University Press, 2008), 6. For other valuable discussions of settler colonialism and gender and domesticity, see Jacobs, *White Mother to a Dark Race*; Adele Perry, *On the Edge of Empire: Gender, Race, and the Making of British Columbia, 1849–1871* (Toronto: University of Toronto Press, 2001); Anne F. Hyde, *Empires, Nations, and Families: A History of the North American West, 1800–1860* (Lincoln: University of Nebraska Press, 2011); Katrina Jagodinsky, *Legal Codes and Talking Trees: Indigenous Women's Sovereignty in the Sonoran and Puget Sound Borderlands, 1854–1946* (New Haven, CT: Yale University Press, 2016). Largely drawn from settings outside the US Southwest, *Haunted by Empire: Geographies of Empire in North American History* (Durham, NC: Duke University Press, 2006), edited by Ann Laura Stoler, offers additional examples of historical approaches to settler colonialism that focus on sexuality, marriage, and gender relations. The contributions by Gwenn Miller, Nayan Shah, Damon Salesa, Linda Gordon, and Catherine Hall provide especially useful points of comparison to our chapter.

5. "A Picture for Employers," *Puck*, August 21, 1878, courtesy of the Department of Special Collections and University Archives, Stanford University Libraries, http://web.stanford.edu, accessed May 26, 2018.

6. Energized by US expansionists who sought to extend the country westward into new territory in the 1840s, the Mexican-American War began in 1846 over a border dispute in Texas between the United States and Mexico. The United States defeated Mexico in 1848, and the countries signed the Treaty of Guadalupe Hidalgo.

In the treaty, the United States acquired millions of acres of land in the region that would become the states of California, Nevada, and New Mexico and parts of the states of Colorado, Arizona, and Utah.

7. David Montejano, *Anglos and Mexicans in the Making of Texas, 1836–1986* (Austin: University of Texas Press, 1987), 41; Tomás Almaguer, *Racial Fault Lines: The Historical Origins of White Supremacy in California* (Berkeley: University of California Press, 1994).

8. Miroslava Chávez-García, *States of Delinquency: Race and Science in the Making of California's Juvenile Justice System* (Berkeley: University of California Press, 2012), 33; Ken Gonzales-Day, *Lynching in the West: 1850–1930* (Durham, NC: Duke University Press, 2006), 206; Erika Pérez, *Colonial Intimacies: Interethnic Kinship, Sexuality, and Marriage in Southern California, 1769–1885* (Norman: University of Oklahoma Press, 2018), 166; Pablo Mitchell, *Understanding Latino History: Excavating the Past, Examining the Present* (Santa Barbara, CA: ABC-CLIO, 2018), 73. Some of the many important works in nineteenth-century Chicana history are María Raquél Casas, *Married to a Daughter of the Land: Spanish-Mexican Women and Interethnic Marriage in California, 1820–1880* (Reno: University of Nevada Press, 2007); Miroslava Chávez-García, *Negotiating Conquest: Gender and Power in California, 1770s to 1880s* (Tucson: University of Arizona Press, 2004); Deena J. González, *Refusing the Favor: The Spanish-Mexican Women of Santa Fe, 1820–1880* (New York: Oxford University Press, 1999); Nicole M. Guidotti-Hernández, *Unspeakable Violence: Remapping US and Mexican National Imaginaries* (Durham, NC: Duke University Press, 2011).

9. United States Census, "Population, Los Angeles County, California, 1860."

10. United States Census.

11. United States Census, "Population, Los Angeles County, California, 1900."

12. United States Census, "Population, Bexar County, Texas, 1860."

13. Raquel R. Márquez, Louis Mendoza, and Steve Blanchard, "Neighborhood Formation on the West Side of San Antonio," *Latino Studies* 5 (2007): 301; United States Census, "Population, Bexar County, Texas, 1900."

14. United States Census, "Population, Los Angeles County, California, 1900"; United States Census, "Population, Bexar County, Texas, 1900." The 1860 US Census did not include marital status as one of its categories; however, it is likely that many of the single women living with children in both Los Angeles and San Antonio had also been married at some point and were either widows or separated from their spouses.

15. Meléndez, *Spanish-Language Newspapers*, 3.

16. "To Curb This Appetite," *Californian* 1, no. 9 (October 10, 1846).

17. "To Curb This Appetite."

18. "Galant Literature: Ceremony of the Antique to Celebrate their Matrimonies," *Los Angeles Star*, November 12, 1853.

19. "Principios generales acerca del matrimonio" (General principles regarding marriage), *Santa Fe Weekly Gazette*, December 4, 1852.

20. "Principios generales acerca del matrimonio."

21. *La Gaceta* (Santa Barbara, CA), September 20, 1879; *La Gaceta*, November 8, 1879.

22. A notice in *Revista Católica* from Las Vegas, New Mexico, in 1888 announced, for instance, "José Lopez, hijo de Federico Lopez y Juliana Ruiz, casó con Candelaria Romero, hija de Perfecto Romero y de Trinidad Montoya." *Revista Católica* (Las Vegas, NM), September 23, 1888.

23. *El Fronterizo* (Tucson, AZ), May 25, 1889.

24. While Anglo settlement in Texas and California accelerated rapidly in the 1850s after the conclusion of the Mexican-American War (especially in California, where the discovery of gold in 1848 sparked the rapid arrival of tens of thousands of gold seekers), New Mexico did not experience widespread Anglo population growth until the appearance of the transcontinental railroad in the early 1880s. Settler colonialism tended to operate differently in New Mexico, with its continued presence of an ethnic-Mexican elite class and the enduring strength of Native American communities; however, the effects of Anglo occupation were nonetheless profound in New Mexico as well. By 1888, the year that the article was published in New Mexico, the territory was beginning to experience many of the political and economic dislocations that Mexicans in states like California and Texas had been suffering for several decades.

25. "El matrimonio Cristiano," *Revista Católica* (Las Vegas, NM), April 29, 1888. The article appears to be part of a series of articles on the topic of marriage; the author states, "como se dijo en el artículo antecedente" (as stated in the preceding article). Like heterosexuality, religion has received less than robust attention from historians of ethnic Mexicans in the United States. See Mario T. García, *Católicos: Resistance and Affirmation in Chicano Catholic History* (Austin: University of Texas Press. 2008); Anthony P. Mora, *Border Dilemmas: Racial and National Uncertainties in New Mexico, 1848–1912* (Durham, NC: Duke University Press, 2011); Adrian A. Bautista, "Vatos Sagrados: Exploring Northern Ohio's Religious Borderlands" (PhD diss., Bowling Green State University, 2013); Anne M. Martínez, *Catholic Borderlands: Mapping Catholicism onto American Empire, 1905–1935* (Lincoln: University of Nebraska Press, 2014); and Felipe Hinojosa, *Latino Mennonites: Civil Rights, Faith, and Evangelical Culture* (Baltimore: Johns Hopkins University Press, 2014).

26. "El matrimonio Cristiano."

27. *El Fronterizo* (Tucson, AZ), November 7, 1884; *El Fronterizo*, May 14, 1887.

28. *El Fronterizo* (Tucson, AZ), August 1, 1884.

29. "Cada uno en su casa," *El Fronterizo* (Tucson, AZ), January 23, 1892.

30. "Cada uno en su casa."

31. "Edward Lumley Murdered at Kenyon Station," *Arizona Sentinel* (Tucson), August 30, 1873.

32. Hyde's magisterial *Empires, Nations, and Families* (2011) offers a powerful description of the role of families and women in shielding endangered communities from the violences and dislocations of settler colonialism, while Pérez's *Colonial Intimacies* (2018) is a more finely grained account of the strategic use by ethnic Mexicans of familial strategies like godparentage and interethnic marriage to fend off and endure the rise of Anglo culture in California.

9

Suburban Swing

Heterosexual Marriage and Spouse Swapping in the 1950s and 1960s

CAROLYN HERBST LEWIS

In July 1957, the editors of *Mr. Magazine*, a bimonthly publication, offered the results of their recent reader sex survey. In between advertisements for hair rejuvenation products, men's corsets, and women's lingerie, as well as several pieces of short fiction outlining supposedly erotic scenarios, editor B. F. Shelton's headline boasted, "We cast for minnows but hooked a killer whale." Shelton explained that the editors had inaugurated a "Sex Survey Department" a few months earlier "in an effort to get more specific, localized reports on the behavior of men and women in the United States than can be found in the averages worked out by large-scale studies such as the Kinsey Reports." Much to their surprise, the editors received numerous responses from readers detailing married couples' "wife-swapping" activities. Using these reader letters as a rough sample, Shelton estimated that the number of "swappers . . . is now in the millions. They appear evenly distributed throughout the country, from Maine through the Midwest, down to Texas and on out to California."[1] Shelton included letter excerpts that supported his assertion that most respondents were affluent, suburban, married couples with children. Exchanging spouses, the authors of these letters insisted, was an activity that helped to cement their marriages.

In the absence of the actual letters, it is difficult to know whether the editors of *Mr. Magazine* truly received this startling response to their reader survey or whether this is yet another example of the outrageous sexual scenes they fabricated for readers' amusement. Even if the letters were available, they certainly would not constitute a representative sample. Recognizing these limitations, when University of Arizona anthropology graduate student Gilbert Bartell's classmate showed him the *Mr. Magazine* article, he was skeptical. "I had heard rumors that wife-swapping goes on in married students' housing," Bartell later recalled. "I had also heard reports that in some suburbs couples get together for parties that center around 'key exchanges.'" But, he continued, "The article in *Mr.* seemed titillating but none too credible. . . . We therefore dismissed the subject . . . [as] an amusing topic to discuss informally, but not to be taken seriously from a scientific point of view."[2]

Bartell's skeptical response to *Mr. Magazine*'s proclamations reflects a broader discordance surrounding the recreational exchange of spouses throughout the 1950s and 1960s. On the one hand, sensationalist accounts in magazines, novels, and eventually film and television suggest at least a prurient national interest in spouse swapping. On the other hand, despite reports of mate sharing in more respectable venues, such as mainstream newspapers and even *Redbook* women's magazine, there seemed to be widespread dismissal of these accounts as not something that "normal" couples really do.

By the late 1960s, this attitude had changed. Scholars, including the now-tenured Gilbert Bartell, had begun to study heterosexual mate swapping seriously. Bartell's 1971 book *Group Sex: An Eyewitness Report on the American Way of Swinging* became and remains one of the leading sources on married swinging in the United States. But Bartell definitely was not alone in his new interest. Between 1967 and 1973, a cluster of sociologists and anthropologists began writing about spouse swapping. Their professed impetus was both the growing visibility of swinging in popular culture and the belief that the era's sexual revolution had fomented change in the sex lives of Americans across demographic lines. Whether calling it swinging, spouse swapping, mate sharing, wife swapping, or group sex, these academics concluded that the sexual exchange of spouses indicated that the nation's sexual morality had been thoroughly and irrevocably altered.[3] In the future, they predicted, swinging would be a common practice among married heterosexual American couples.

This chapter considers the history of spouse swapping through the lens of the academic studies written between 1967 and 1973. These years mark both a growing cultural visibility of swinging and a sudden surge in academic publishing on the practice. While a proliferation of films, books, and other popular representations of swinging suggested that the sexual revolution had reached the bedrooms of white, middle-class suburbia, academic conference panels and special issues of academic journals devoted to mate swapping highlight how seriously anthropologists, sociologists, marriage counselors, and others were taking these and other accounts. Of course, swinging itself predated this academic interest. The couples under study actually engaged in mate swapping *earlier* in the decade, given the time that research, writing, and actual publication took. Even when authors do not explicitly identify the time span of their research, references to political and social events as well as statements made by the subjects themselves about when they started mate swapping further confirm that suburban swinging occurred on the eve, rather than in the wake, of the sexual revolution.

My goal here is not to argue that married swinging was a pre- rather than post-sexual-revolution phenomenon. Instead, my interest is in how married heterosexual swingers throughout the 1960s—and perhaps even in the 1950s—helped perpetuate a particular heteronormative ideal. Swingers, while seemingly defying the gender and sexual constraints of heteronormative marriage, in practice and in intention, actually reinforced them. The suburban swingers who caught the attention of academics between 1967 and 1973 formed subcommunities throughout the nation that were racially and ethnically exclusive, that maintained strict standards of hygiene and appearance reflective of cultural ideals, and that operated according to codes of conduct that reinforced patriarchal marital and gender structures. Although the scholars writing about swingers in this period celebrated the practice as evidence of a permanent revolution in heteronormative marriage, a closer reading of their work reveals that they, just as much as the swingers themselves, contributed to the maintenance of a white, heteronormative, marital ideal well into the 1970s.

Firm statistics on how many heterosexual, married couples participated in mate swapping in this period are difficult to ascertain. In 1953, the sex researcher Alfred Kinsey noted that 40 percent of the women who reported having coitus with a man other than their husband did so with their husband's knowledge or consent. "A not inconsiderable group" of these cases, Kinsey elaborated, included couples who engaged in "wife swapping."[4] Later estimates range anywhere from one million to ten million individuals exchanging mates in 1970.[5] Even at the most liberal estimate, then, swinging involved a minority segment of the married population. To the anthropologists and sociologists who began studying swinging couples and communities in the mid-1960s, the critical question was not how many couples participated or even what they did when they got together. What mattered most in their estimation was *which* couples engaged in swinging. They were especially interested in mate swapping among a particular demographic.

Across disciplines, the consensus was that the most active swingers were not sophisticated, hedonistic urbanites of the Hugh Hefner and Helen Gurley Brown variety, but rather they were the residents of the nation's suburbs—white, middle class, politically conservative, PTA-leading and Little League–coaching parents. In other words, swingers were "average" Americans of the Silent Majority, the embodiments of Cold War domesticity.[6] This fact, the era's academics insisted, was what made their sexual practices so revolutionary. If the couples who were meant to uphold the nation's most cherished values and produce the citizens who would carry these values forward into the future were engaging in a sexual culture that defied the most basic norms regarding fidelity and morality, then how could we expect to see anything but a social revolution on the horizon?

Ironically, the very factors that convinced anthropologists, sociologists, and other academic observers that spouse swapping was inaugurating a marital revolution instead served to reinforce a conservative, patriarchal, and perhaps even monogamous marital institution. Swinging undeniably departed from generally held expectations about sexual fidelity and monogamy. But the ability to participate in swinging depended on access to a community of similarly inclined couples. Whether advertising in lifestyle magazines, meeting at a club, or getting an introduction to an exclusive group, access depended on conforming to the community's norms. As a result, as early as the 1950s, swinging involved seemingly well-adjusted individuals who had outwardly happy marriages, men and women who conformed to, rather than challenged, the era's gender expectations. In order to swing, couples had to perform the exterior trappings of the postwar domestic ideal. They were inherently invested, then, in maintaining, rather than disrupting, the status quo when it came to the economic, gender, and political basis of the marriage institution. Scholars, attempting to emphasize how "normal"

swingers and swinging were, reinforced the defining facets of heteronormative marriage at midcentury.

The creation of *Mr. Magazine*'s sex-survey department reflects a
larger national interest in cataloging the sex lives of ordinary Americans. In 1948 and 1953, Alfred Kinsey's reports on Americans' sexual
behavior had shocked the nation with higher than expected incidences
of premarital, extramarital, and even homosexual encounters. Scientists
like Kinsey were not the only ones heightening their scrutiny of citizens'
sex lives in the postwar decades. From physicians recommending sexually instructive premarital consultations to federal policies barring suspected homosexuals from employment, a variety of authorities sought to
mandate specific heterosexual prescriptions.[7] The era's films, novels, and
women's magazines further modeled the social rituals regarding heterosexual dating and marriage that dictated gender-appropriate behaviors,
appearances, and roles. Feminine, nurturing, and passive women were
coupled with masculine, authoritative, and financially successful men.
United in marriage, heterosexual couples would create the familial environments that would serve as the building blocks of the nation.[8] The
foundation of these successful marriages was a passionate and mutually
satisfying sex life. Sex, multiple experts promised heterosexual couples,
was the key to marital happiness and stability. Without it, husbands
might become bored and stray, marriages would collapse, the divorce
rate would climb, and social chaos would ensue. In contrast, a satisfying
marital sex life kept a man's attention and resources focused at home.
Books and articles encouraged wives to keep the spark alive with lingerie and candles, while *Playboy* and comparable publications, including
Mr. Magazine, permitted men a respectable form of titillation that could
be channeled into the home as well. Swinging embraced this newfound
emphasis on marital sexuality but rejected the underlying expectation
of monogamy.

In American cultural memory, swinging is synonymous with the
1970s. After all, this was the decade when the sexual revolution seemed
to have reached all segments of US society, and when, post-pill, post-
Roe, and pre-AIDS, heterosexual intercourse seemed to have the fewest
consequences. Films of the era, such as *Bob and Carol and Ted and Alice*,
certainly suggested that something new was afoot in American marriages. Starring Natalie Wood, Dyan Cannon, Elliott Gould, and Robert

Culp, this "wife-swapping" film became the fifth-highest-grossing film of 1969 and garnered four Academy Award nominations.[9] More recent examples of the link between suburban swinging and the 1970s include Ang Lee's 1997 film *The Ice Storm* and CBS's 2008 series *Swingtown*. Taken as a whole, these and other cultural productions reinforce the belief that the 1970s was the decade in which the new sexual morality made its way into the bedrooms of married couples.

Swinging's cultural visibility has not translated to scholarly attention. The cultural historian Peter Braunstein notes that mate sharing was a theme in many so-called adult films of the 1970s, but historical accounts of the decade mention swingers only in passing, if at all.[10] Sociologists and psychologists have written about contemporary swingers within their broader accounts of group sex and polyamory. For example, the psychologist Deborah Anapol positions mate sharing as a sort of entry into polyamorous arrangements for some couples.[11] None of these scholars attempt a serious consideration of the history of swinging.[12]

Swinging seems to have made its national news debut in 1954. That summer, a murder investigation in Amesbury, Massachusetts, made national headlines when papers reported that the district attorney had informed the press that the primary suspect's confession "contained 'lurid' details which allegedly involved 'wife-swapping parties.'"[13] Lorraine Clark, a young mother and housewife, was convicted a few months later for the murder of her husband, Melvin. No further information on the alleged spouse-swapping parties ever was released to the press, and an article in the *American Weekly* by Ellery Queen, famed author of true-crime and detective fiction, noted that everyone involved in the case vehemently denied that such parties ever took place.[14] Nevertheless, it is noteworthy that newspapers used the term in such a way that indicates that readers were already familiar with its meaning.

After 1954, references to spouse swapping in American newspapers and magazines could refer either to cases involving two couples seeking a permanent trade or to parties in which multiple couples participated. Overall, these publications demonstrated a growing public awareness of the existence of groups of married heterosexual couples who exchanged sexual partners as recreational activity. In 1956, *Redbook* magazine, regular reading for the nation's housewives, printed an anonymously written article in which a woman included swinging in her litany of complaints about life in the suburbs.[15] For those who might have thought that this detail was mere exaggeration and not any indication of actual activities, in1958, a Chicago postal inspection into suspected pornography uncovered an interstate "wife-swapping ring." Run by brothers-in-law Ronald Grisby and William Duncan, the ring allegedly circulated "lewd" photographs and ran advertisements for couples seeking interested partners.[16]

Although mate swapping became the subject of shock and ridicule in the mainstream press, other publishing venues took a much different tone. "Gentleman's" magazines such as *Mr.* depicted a vibrant swinging culture. By the mid-1960s, publishing houses also were capitalizing on the growing interest—both actual and prurient—in mate swapping. William and Jerrye Breedlove's 1964 Sherbourne Press *Swap Clubs* offered the first glimpse into alleged nationwide networks of mate-swapping clubs and promised to introduce readers to the swinging scene as the participants themselves "feel it and live it."[17] Matt and Kathleen Galant, former owners of Club Rebel, an infamous swingers' club in Atlanta and publishers of the newsletter *The Rebel*, wrote a series of six books in the mid- to late 1960s exposing the swinging scene. With such titles as *Sex Rebels*, *Mate Swapping Syndrome*, and *Swinging Bi-sexuals*, the Galants' small press volumes offered an insider perspective with explicit details on masturbation, oral sex, and other sexual activities that could be instructive whether or not the reader participated in swinging.[18]

While these magazines and books might have appealed most to those who were already interested in swinging, by the end of the 1960s, a broader audience was consuming cultural representations of spouse swapping. For example, several films featured story lines that depicted some elements of swinging. In addition to *Bob and Carol and Ted and Alice*, moviegoers in 1969 also may have seen *All the Loving Couples*, which the reviewer Roger Ebert described as "the most innocent of the recent skin-flicks, and so socially redeeming you'll walk out thinking wife-swapping is second only to scouting in making our nation strong."[19] A few years later, the 1971 series *Doctors' Wives*, starring Dyan Cannon, brought swinging into American households via their television sets.[20] By the end of the 1960s, then, we see evidence that a range of Americans were, at the very least, aware of swingers.

Scholars took note. Sociologists and anthropologists began to study mate swapping as a unique sociocultural phenomenon. Unlike Abigail

Van Buren, who reassured a "Dear Abby" reader in 1969 that suburban key parties were not real, these scholars accepted that spouse-swapping clubs and communities were more than rumors or the product of a sensationalist press.[21] Charles Varni declared in the introduction to his 1970 sociology master's thesis, "I know very little about the phenomenon I am about to investigate other than it exists and has some sort of structure."[22] Cherie Schupp was more familiar with the prevalence of swinging. In her 1970 dissertation on human sexual relations, she explained, "This new pattern of sexual conduct has become so prevalent that it is of interest to find [out] what it is these people are doing, what are their reasons, and how it is affecting the pattern of family relationships." After all, she continued, "the swinging phenomenon shows no sign of disintegrating."[23] American sociologists and anthropologists had decided it was time to pull swinging out of the shadows and consider what mate sharing meant to the state of the nation's marriages.

Scholars incorrectly assumed that there would be much to set these sexual nonconformists apart from their peers. Much to Gilbert Bartell's surprise, there was little to differentiate swingers from their nonswinging contemporaries.[24] An anthropologist at Northern Illinois University, Bartell was renowned for his work on Native American cultures. Like the entomologist Alfred Kinsey, his interest in contemporary American sexual behaviors marked a departure from his usual research field. In 1967, Bartell began working with his wife, Ann, to investigate the swinging "way of life." Presenting themselves as a couple considering joining a swinging club, the Bartells used a combination of advertisements in swinging magazines and the snowball effect of relying on introductions to meet other active couples. Although they spoke with swingers in Louisiana and Texas, most of their informants came from a two-hundred-mile radius of the city of Chicago.[25] Their results were published solely under Gilbert's name in various academic venues, as well as a trade-press book from Signet.

The Bartells found that the couples they met were not the radicals that they expected them to be. Most lived in the suburbs, with the husbands' incomes ranging from $6,000 to $75,000 annually.[26] The men worked in a variety of white-collar fields, but 90 percent of the women were housewives.[27] Politically, the couples tended both to identify as conservatives and to voice conservative opinions. During the 1968 election season, for example, the GOP emerged as the party of choice, although 60 percent of the individuals the Bartells met declared themselves to be supporters of the American Independent Party candidate, George Wallace.[28] Bartell surmised that this political allegiance reflected both their shifting economic status from blue to white collar as well as their stance on civil rights. "These people were anti-Negro," Bartell wrote. "They were less antagonistic to Puerto Ricans and Mexicans. They were strongly anti-hippie, against the use of any and all drugs, and would not allow marijuana in their homes or people who use it."[29] In other words, he concluded, "Informants overall reflect generalized white suburban attitudes as outlined in almost any beginning sociological text."[30]

Other scholars echoed Bartell's observations about swingers' demographics and affiliations. Another husband-and-wife team, James and Lynn Smith, were Berkeley graduate students in behavioral sciences. They described the five hundred respondents to their questionnaire as a "socially stable group of persons."[31] "Generally speaking," they wrote in an article in the *Journal of Sex Research*, "our data and our observations indicate that this sub-culture, at least in California, is composed of relatively mobile, educated, affluent, mostly Caucasian, upper-middle class persons."[32] The anthropologists Paul and Rebecca Palson's eighteen-month study of 136 swingers in eight states also found that most were middle class.[33] In a study that included single participants as well as married couples, the anthropologists George and Nena O'Neill likewise found that their sample included "mainly middle-class business and professional people spanning the occupational range from academia to the entertainment world."[34]

So many of the scholars mentioned thus far worked as husband-and-wife teams because they had to position themselves as normatively heterosexual in order to gain entry into swinging communities. Most of the early scholars writing about swinging indicated that the participants would only talk to them when it was clear that they were not hostile to the practice. Many of the scholars found that they had to portray themselves as "virgins" curious about entering the world of mate sharing. All of them needed a research partner to lend credibility to this portrayal, and most involved their own spouse or sexual partner in their research. Some wives were credited equally as authors, while in other cases, only the husband's name made it into print. If both spouses were not scholars, then, without exception, the husband was the academic. Only three authors were women writing alone; none of them mentioned the presence of a male research partner. Unlike their male colleagues, these women did not indicate that their professional interest in swinging was accompanied with a personal curiosity. Most male- or couple-authored articles, however, indicated that, while their academic fields prompted them to question the significance of swinging in contemporary US society, they also felt drawn to the practice on a more intimate level. Some of these authors hinted that they had participated in spouse-swapping activities after completing their research or that they intended to do so in the future. Only one couple, Charles and Rebecca Palson, confessed, "it seemed to us that the only way to find out what we wanted to know was to participate ourselves."[35]

Performing a feigned or hidden interest in joining a swinging community may have been the only way for researchers to gain access to a relatively clandestine subculture. Suburban swinging communities were especially secretive. In urban areas, swingers could advertise in lifestyle magazines or visit clubs to meet new partners. The city's population density and spatial patterns shielded them from any censure in their daily lives. Cities thus offered both anonymity and community. In contrast, suburban couples seemed to feel simultaneously more isolated and less anonymous. They could neither tap into a preexisting swinging scene nor risk outing in their daily life. Suburban spouse swappers understood that their recreational sexual activities set them apart from their nonswinging neighbors. As a result, they tended to rely on carefully considered invitations to home-based swinging parties. These small groups of like-minded couples tended to form very exclusive clusters. Whereas urban swingers might never repeat partners, suburban cohorts exchanged partners with the same couples on a regular basis. Members of these swinging "clubs" depended on each other not only for sexual recreation but for secrecy and friendship as well. Cherie Schupp, one of the few scholars who worked without a partner, asserted in her 1970 dissertation that mate-swapping groups based on neighborhood proximity might be longer lasting and more stable than other groups: "Neighbors are tied together by many common interests, much more so than school friends or business or civic friends who may be in completely different circumstances, economically, temperamentally, or similar circumstances."[36] Swinging reinforced cohesion among couples who might otherwise feel out of step with their suburban communities. Other scholars, such as the Bartells, worried that the insularity went too far, isolating swingers from their larger communities. Bartell wrote, "The suburbanite is usually involved in community affairs, numerous sports, and family centered activities. These people do nothing other than swing and watch television."[37]

Bartell's assessment was not accurate. In fact, suburban swingers were involved in their careers and communities, and they pursued a range of leisure activities similar to their nonswinging neighbors, such as venturing into a nearby city for an evening out or traveling on vacations and cruises. The difference was that swingers sought venues that also incorporated recreational sex. They invested a great deal of time, energy, and money in building or seeking communities that catered to their sexual interests. Relying on data from Matt and Kathleen Galant's *Wife Swapping: The People*, Cherie Schupp underscored the fact that swinging not only required a financial commitment but also created an economy of its own: "the average couple spends fifty dollars a month in swinging," while some spent twice that amount. The Galants estimated that in 1966 the more than eight million people participating in swinging spent over $50 million on their hobby and that the numbers were growing each year.[38] In 1967, the Galants indicated, there were forty correspondence clubs for swingers nationwide, two travel agencies catered to swingers, and multiple cities boasted cocktail lounges and restaurants that offered special treatment for the swinging set.[39] Charles Varni found that the cover charge at one swing club was three dollars per person, about twice the cost of an average movie ticket.[40] Swingers without a local community—or perhaps those who were seeking new partners—frequently traveled in order to check out swinging venues in other cities. "Down here," explained one San Diego woman, "you have to worry about meeting someone you know, but up there [in the San Fernando Valley] nobody knows anybody else!"[41] While many of these clubs were open to the public, others required membership that included joiners' fees as well as monthly dues. Swinging required ample resources of time and money, and many of these venues screened admission based on perceived race, class, ethnicity, and religion.

Suburban swingers therefore built community within the confines of a remarkably homogeneous demographic. They exchanged partners only within their own economic, racial, ethnic, and, to some extent, religious cohort. The sexual radicalism that spouse swapping seemed to reflect was not matched by an openness to crossing other lines. Perhaps this was due to anxiety about attracting attention within their homogeneous suburban neighborhoods or an indication that participants understood the need to project a certain degree of white, middle-class respectability. Or perhaps they were elitist, racist, and xenophobic. In any case, suburban mate swappers maintained standards for inclusion that reflected the era's ideals and practices regarding marriage, family, gender, and even sexuality that were closely tied to whiteness and other markers.[42] For example, Gilbert Bartell found that when he arrived at one party with long hair and a beard, none of the other attendees would speak with him.[43] On another occasion, the unexpected arrival of a mixed-race couple caused tension at a suburban house party.[44] The swingers who spoke with Charles Varni indicated that their groups would not accept "weirdos," whom they defined as "all those persons who exhibit gross character aberrations such as sadism, masochism, or other, not necessarily sex related, deviance."[45] While most subcultures seek to challenge the larger culture's expectations and norms, swingers primarily reinforced the era's race- and class-based heteronormative ideals. The suburban swinging community was almost an exaggerated version of mainstream heteronormative domesticity. The one exception, of course, was their rejection of monogamy.

Scholars expressed surprise that spouse swappers were not more unconventional in their sexual views and practices. Charles Varni observed, "Swingers, as a group, do not appear to have been atypical in their sexual attitudes or behavior before they started swinging," although they may have been more accepting of premarital sex than their contemporaries were.[46] Descriptions of the sexual scenes at a typical suburban mate-swapping party centered on a range of heteronormative activities—for example, kissing, penile-vaginal intercourse, oral sex, fondling—with the added titillation of multiple partners and a few group activities. A closer reading of these scholarly accounts, however, reveals the unwritten rules of swinging that fostered certain additional expectations regarding female desire, pleasure, and sexual performance that turned much of the era's heterosexual prescriptions on their head.

First, swingers made female sexual pleasure central to each encounter. To a certain extent, this was true of larger cultural expectations regarding healthy female heterosexual desire and pleasure. Medical professionals throughout the 1950s and 1960s asserted that female sexual response was an important part of psychosexual health, reproductive success, and marital satisfaction.[47] But these and other experts emphasized that the only healthy female sexual response was a vaginal orgasm induced by penile penetration. They also insisted that morally virtuous women only engaged in such activities with their legal husbands. Swingers, of course, disagreed with them on this latter point. Moreover, most swingers expected to engage in a wide range of activities beyond "missionary-style" intercourse. They would participate in threesomes, daisy chains, and other group-sex arrangements.[48] Couples performed oral sex not simply as a form of foreplay but as an activity in itself. In order to ensure that men would be able to service as many women as possible, the Bartells found that female-performed fellatio was unlikely to continue to the point of male orgasm, whereas "every attempt is made by the male to bring the female to climax by cunnilingus."[49] Men were expected to pleasure women whether or not they themselves experienced orgasm. Since the parties generally went all night, men might expect to have sexual encounters that did not culminate in male orgasms but that also did not involve penile-vaginal intercourse or perhaps even an erection at all. The men Varni interviewed reported "two to five orgasms an evening while some women reported experiencing upwards of fifteen."[50] Charles and Rebecca Palson interviewed one woman who recalled having sexual contact with eleven or twelve men in three hours.[51] Other scholars reported similar statistics. Clitoral stimulation and clitoral orgasms, then, were normalized sexual outlets for swinging women.

Second, the primacy of nonvaginal, nonpenetrative female orgasms also supported and was supported by expectations regarding female same-sex behavior. Same-sex activity was commonplace among women in all of the studies published. The Bartells found that 75 percent of the group-sex activities they studied included two women engaging in cunnilingus. "Sixty-five per cent of the female respondents," Bartell wrote, "admit to enjoying their homosexual relationships with other females and liking it to the point where they would rather 'turn on' to the female than to males."[52] Some of this was performative and observed by men who found watching their wives with other women arousing. But women also engaged in sexual acts with each other without any men watching. As one woman told Bartell, "It was a great party! All the guys passed out and we girls had a wonderful time."[53] By comparison, few swinging communities welcomed male same-sex activity. The Bartells estimated only 1 percent of their cases included two or more men performing fellatio or other same-sex activities.[54] Similar figures on the difference between female and male same-sex encounters were reported elsewhere.[55] Quite possibly men did engage in same-sex activities but did not report this to the scholars. Generally, however, swinging provided men with the opportunity to showcase their heterosexual prowess. For women, the group-sex scene offered instead a somewhat wider range of sexual outlets and partners.

Finally, active female consent was imperative. Legally, American wives consented to sex with their husbands upon taking their marriage vows. Moreover, prescribed heteronormative roles required women to take a responsive sexual role.[56] The passivity demanded of women within conventional gender and marriage roles did not, however, continue during swinging. The unofficial swinging code of conduct placed female consent at the center of each sexual encounter. Women were empowered to accept or refuse a man's interest.[57] Each group had its own system of cues and responses that signaled mutual interest in sexual activity or permitted one of the individuals to politely but clearly decline an invitation. Most parties required that everyone present participate in some sexual activity, but anyone who took offense or became aggressive when an offer was declined would not be invited back. The anthropologists George and Nena O'Neill succinctly observed in their survey of fifty swingers, "Nobody does anything they don't want to do."[58] Charles Varni made a similar observation, adding, "The complementary expectation, that no one should coerce or force anyone to do anything he does not want to, is a check on any man who may feel so inclined."[59] Key parties, then, were out, as assigning sexual partners through the random selection of key rings would have eliminated the ability to accept or reject an individual partner, particularly for the women. The Smiths guessed that the myth of the suburban key party was based on a mix of "fear and fantasy" that protected a man who worried he might be rejected as a sexual partner.[60]

Although the expectation of multiple clitoral orgasms, women having female partners, and an emphasis on active female consent defied the era's heteronormative prescriptions for women, scholars made little comment on this reality. Instead, they dismissed these female-centered practices as clever tricks to ensure men's access to multiple partners. Entry into swinging communities required that both partners be willing and eager to join in the spouse exchange. Scholars attributed this emphasis on female desire, pleasure, and consent to men's efforts to persuade their wives of the benefits of mate swapping. Wives anxious about sharing their husbands, scholars assumed, could be placated once they realized how attractive and desirable they were to other men. Attention to female desire and pleasure thus became a by-product of appealing to women's vanity.

Scholars were far more intrigued by the husbands' initial and ongoing willingness to share their wives with other men. They did not expect men's anxieties to be as easily assuaged as wives' apprehensions. Scholars marveled at the ability of so many couples to integrate swinging into their marriages without jealousy, anger, or disruption. This, not the actual sexual practices of swingers, was what made spouse swapping so revolutionary in the estimation of the (mostly male) academics.

Many of the observed couples had indicated to incredulous scholars that trading sexual partners had improved their relationships. As Varni observed, "It was as if the swinging experience had become proof and validation of their love for one another."[61] Moreover, many couples reported integrating techniques learned from swinging—such as oral sex and greater attention to female orgasms—into their marital sex lives. As couples reported the positive effects of swinging on their marriages, scholars embraced the notion that this move away from monogamy was beneficial not only to individual couples but also to the institution of marriage itself. As an economic, political, and social convention, marriage was dependent on the linked commitment to sexual fidelity and reproductive exclusivity. Deviation from this expectation, scholars asserted, historically had been tolerated only among the highest and lowest socioeconomic groups, while the middle class remained stodgily respectable. The sociologist Mary Lindenstein Walshok thought that the increasing prevalence of swinging was a result of the upward mobility of less puritanical lower classes: "The rapid decline of traditional values, the development of instant communities in the suburbs, and the new-found affluence among many heretofore rural, uneducated populations, characterize the ever-increasing middle-class."[62] Watching as the era's sexual revolutions chipped away at other gender and sexual conventions, most scholars celebrated the evidence that the last bastion of American sexual conservativism—the middle-class, white, suburban married couple—was now joining the party.

To some of the sociologists and anthropologists studying swinging, this revolution was not so much a step forward as it was a return to a more natural state. Sexuality, they argued, had become so contained and regulated by various social strictures that people had lost touch with any genuine sense of pleasure and desire. Schupp, for instance, suggested that mate sharing was simply part of a much longer history of human evolution and social development and therefore had both biological and psychological functions.[63] As Walshok noted, "What makes contemporary co-marital behavior sociologically interesting is its preponderance among basically middle-class, and essentially conventional people, and its somewhat bureaucratized and decidedly unfestival-like quality."[64] In her estimation, swinging had become so respectable that it was almost boring.

Other researchers suggested that mate swapping would continue to grow in popularity and visibility as society as a whole became more accepting of the importance of variation in human sexuality. Charles Varni predicted that "older couples, seeking excitement and fun, relief from boredom, or perhaps new relationships will begin swinging," while younger people "will continue to expand the traditional values of marriage" so that monogamy would no longer be an expectation.[65] The behavioral scientist James Ramey agreed. He surmised that swinging, like other contemporary marriage variations, such as free love and communal living, reflected changes in individual self-esteem, which enabled couples to build "more dynamic and more solid bonded-pairs."[66] As a result, sexuality could become a form of self-expression that could be nurtured and explored independent of the marital bond.

All of the researchers who celebrated the expansion of swinging credited the sexual emancipation of women and the normalization of more egalitarian marriages as essential steps in this process. They concluded that mate sharing among the white, suburban middle class reflected the sexual liberalism that was becoming endemic to US society. Swingers, they assumed, would join the increasingly visible demands for gay and lesbian civil rights, for lifting of abortion restrictions, and for greater acceptance of both heterosexual premarital intercourse and nonmarital cohabitation, as part of the great sexual awakening of the latter half of the twentieth century.[67]

Interpreting suburban swinging as a marital revolution, however, dismisses all the ways that swingers ultimately reinforced the era's marital, gender, and sexual conventions. None of the researchers gave evidence that swingers had any interest in disrupting marriage as an institution. Indeed, swingers were rather heavily invested in maintaining the marital status quo. Some couples had been quietly swinging for decades.[68] Mate swapping was a supplement to their marriage, not a means of transforming it. When couples emphasized all the positive ways that swinging had improved their marriages, they were not seeking to escape the institution. In fact, marital stability was requisite. While there were some urban swingers who permitted single people to join their groups, suburban communities deliberately excluded nonmarried couples and individuals. Performing a happy marriage, then, was the key to entering the swinging world.

Perhaps swinging enabled some couples to find the era's marriage conventions more tolerable. The "togetherness" demanded of postwar couples could become suffocating.[69] At the same time, the move to suburban nuclear family arrangements could be isolating. One researcher found that swingers expressed an intense loneliness. They despaired that they had "no close married friends, . . . friends who you can turn to for help, comfort, and assistance—friends whom you love."[70] Swinging could provide otherwise-isolated suburban couples with a family-like community rooted in mutual trust and need. Bartell even went so far as to describe suburban swinging groups as "fictive kin."[71] Closeted lesbians and bisexual women might have found some solace in the encouragement of female same-sex activity.[72] But all of this was about making conventional marriage tolerable, not turning the era's heteronormative domesticity on its head.

This certainly was the conclusion of those scholars who interviewed swinging "dropouts." Duane Denfeld's nationwide survey of over 2,000 marriage counselors yielded 473 who reported working with a total of

1,175 swinging clients.[73] The counselors reported that, despite the belief that swinging emphasized sexual equality, particularly for wives, couples found themselves unable to escape the era's double standards. For example, 109 couples reported that they resumed a monogamous relationship because the husbands became jealous, especially if their wives were popular partners or if they "feared that their wives were having more fun than they were."[74] More often, though, the wives initiated the "dropping out" because they had not been enthusiastic about mate swapping in the first place. "Swinging," Denfeld observed, "was a way for some of the men to have sexual variety, but they needed their wives to accomplish it."[75] Despite the talk of egalitarian marriages, the prevalence of men talking their wives into swinging reinforced conventional patterns of male status and dominance within the relationship.[76]

The sociologist Anne-Marie Henshel's study about how couples made the decision to swing offered similar conclusions about the ways that mate swapping reinforced patriarchal marriage patterns.[77] Henshel pointed out that the researchers who were so enthusiastic about new egalitarian marriages always reported that the idea of mate sharing had been initiated by the husband and was followed by sometimes-lengthy efforts to persuade the wife to give it a try.[78] Henshel's survey of a group of Toronto women revealed that, even among swingers, marriage continued to reflect a male-dominant, not egalitarian, model. "In the context of decision making," she wrote, "swinging can be viewed as a male institution, and confirmations of the advent of a 'sexual revolution' and of the abolition of the double standard should be reconsidered."[79] Henshel's critique of mate sharing anticipates arguments later made by feminists that the sexual revolution was not particularly liberating for women.[80] Despite new methods of contraception and a greater expectation for female pleasure, many heterosexual women found that the sexual double standard simply took new and yet familiar forms. The emphasis on female consent described earlier thus took place within a context in which women may have felt coerced to participate in the first place. Swinging, it seems, was another example of how the promise of greater sexual liberation met disappointing ends.

No matter why couples decided to swing—out of desire for sexual adventure, to make their relationship tolerable, because they believed sex and love were distinct—their participation in mate swapping served to reinforce the era's marital conventions. Charles and Rebecca Palson, the only set of researchers to admit openly to participating in mate swapping, concluded, "Swinging often succeeds in solidifying a marriage. It does this by re-romanticizing marriage, thereby making it tolerable, even enjoyable to be married. In a very important way, then, swinging is a conservative institution."[81] So, too, was the scholarship that depicted it. Again and again, scholars celebrated the ways that swinging strengthened individual marriages and, by extension, the institution as a whole.

The conservative nature of suburban swinging stands in sharp contrast to the portrayal of mate swapping in American popular culture since the 1970s. Swingers have been depicted in movies and novels as either bitter spouses seeking simultaneously to injure and escape from each other or mistakenly confined hedonists, finally awakening to their true sexual passions. The reality was—and probably remains—far more complex. The couples who shared their swinging lifestyles with academic researchers in the 1960s and early 1970s offered a glimpse into a suburban sexual culture that was rooted in upholding the era's heteronormative ideals and practices. Conformity and conservatism, both social and political, were the hallmarks of this crowd. Although swinging gave the appearance that American couples had been liberated from old-fashioned sexual mores, in actuality, the practice did little to disrupt the era's marital and sexual conventions.

NOTES

1. B. F. Shelton, "Wife Swapping: Exclusive Reader Reports," *Mr. Magazine* 1, no. 6 (July 1957): 28.

2. Gilbert D. Bartell, *Group Sex: An Eyewitness Report on the American Way of Swinging* (New York: Signet Books, 1971), 7–8.

3. The terms "swinging" and "wife swapping" tend to be used interchangeably in common conversations. Scholars cited in this chapter used a variety of terms, most often "swinging" and "wife swapping." I have chosen to avoid using the term "wife swapping," as it reinforces patriarchal and heteronormative conventions.

4. Alfred C. Kinsey, Wardell B. Pomery, Clyde E. Martin, and Paul H. Gebhard, *Sexual Behavior in the Human Female* (Philadelphia: W. B. Saunders, 1953), 434–35.

5. Gilbert Bartell, "Group Sex among Mid-Americans," *Journal of Sex Research* 6, no. 2 (May 1970): 114. There were over eighty-seven million married individuals over age fourteen in the United States in 1970. "Marital Status and Family Status: March 1970" (US Census Bureau, Washington, DC, 1971), 9, www.census.gov.

6. For more on the era's domesticity and the demographic that would become known as the Silent Majority, see Elaine Tyler May, *Homeward Bound: American Families in the Cold War Era* (New York: Basic Books, 1988); Lizabeth Cohen, *A Consumers' Republic: The Politics of Mass Consumption in Postwar America* (New York: Knopf, 2003); Lisa McGirr, *Suburban Warriors: The Origins of the New American Right* (Princeton, NJ: Princeton University Press, 2001); Matthew D. Lassiter, *The Silent Majority: Suburban Politics in the Sunbelt South* (Princeton, NJ: Princeton University Press, 2007).

7. Miriam Reumann, *American Sexual Character: Sex, Gender, and National Identity in the Kinsey Reports* (Berkeley: University of California Press, 2005); Carolyn Herbst Lewis, *Prescription for Heterosexuality: Sexual Citizenship in the Cold War Era* (Chapel Hill: University of North Carolina Press, 2010); David K. Johnson, *The Lavender Scare: The Cold War Persecution of Gays and Lesbians in the Federal Government* (Chicago: University of Chicago Press, 2004); Jennifer Terry, *An American Obsession: Science, Medicine, and Homosexuality in Modern Society* (Chicago: University of Chicago Press, 1999); Margot Canaday, *The Straight State: Sexuality and Citizenship in Twentieth-Century America* (Princeton, NJ: Princeton University Press, 2009).

8. For more on the expectations surrounding postwar marriages, see Stephanie Coontz, *The Way We Never Were: American Families and the Nostalgia Trap* (New York: Basic Books, 2000).

9. *Bob and Carol and Ted and Alice*, dir. Paul Mazursky (Columbia Pictures, 1969). Despite the promotional image that featured the four characters in bed together, the film was not actually about spouse swapping but rather was an exploration of the seemingly inevitable influence of the new sexual morality on conventional marriages. Throughout the film, the two couples navigate within their marriages and their friendships their newfound awareness of the distinctions between love and sex and marital fidelity. While Bob and Carol embrace an open marriage, Ted and Alice struggle with affection and fidelity. In the final sequence, the characters determine that swapping partners in a predinner "orgy" is the natural next step in their friendship. The characters ultimately do not trade partners. Nevertheless, the film was linked in headlines and in cultural memory with "wife swapping." Roger Ebert, review of *Bob and Carol and Ted and Alice*, December 22, 1969, www.rogerebert.com (accessed August 9, 2017); Emerson Batdorff, "'Bob and Carol' Is Wife-Swapping Farce," *Cleveland Plain Dealer*, December 22, 1969, 20; Foster Hirsch, review of *Bob and Carol and Ted and Alice*, *Film Quarterly* 23, no. 2 (Winter 1969–70): 62.

10. Peter Braunstein, "'Adults Only': The Construction of an Erotic City in New York in the 1970s," in *America in the 70s*, ed. Beth Bailey and David Farber (Lawrence: University Press of Kansas, 2004), 129–56. For general histories of the decade, see Bruce J. Schulman, *The Seventies: The Great Shift in American Culture, Society, and Politics* (Cambridge, MA: Da Capo, 2001); Alice Echols, *Hot Stuff: Disco and the Remaking of American Culture* (New York: Norton, 2010).

11. Deborah Anapol, *Polyamory in the 21st Century: Love and Intimacy with Multiple Partners* (Lanham, MD: Rowman and Littlefield, 2010), 21–23.

12. Present-day swinging communities assert an origin myth rooted in fighter-pilot communities of the Second World War. For example, Annalee Newitz, "Swinging in the Suburbs," *Metroactive*, January 20–26, 2000, www.metroactive.com; Liberated Christians, www.libchrist.com. This account seems to have emerged from the journalist Terry Gould's 1999 book *The Lifestyle: A Look at the Erotic Rites of Swingers* (Buffalo, NY: Firefly Books, 1999) and is repeated by other journalists and academics in various venues. For example, Katherine Frank, *Plays Well in Groups: A Journey through the World of Group Sex* (Lanham, MD: Rowman and Littlefield, 2013); Christopher Ryan and Cacilda Jetha, *Sex at Dawn: The Prehistoric Origins of Modern Sexuality* (New York: Harper, 2010); Christopher Ryan, "Not All Military Adultery Results in Scandal: Can Military Adultery Support Unit Cohesion?," *Psychology Today*, November 16, 2012, www.psychologytoday.com; Merissa Nathan Gerson, "At Group Sex Parties, Strict Rules Make for Safe Spaces," *Atlantic*, September 24, 2014, www.theatlantic.com.

13. "Clark Case Said Nearly Complete," *Springfield Union*, July 7, 1954, 6.

14. Ellery Queen, "The Dream Cottage Murder," *American Weekly*, November 14, 1954. The *American Weekly* appeared in newspapers across the country.

15. N.A., "'I Live in a Development . . . and Hate It!,'" *Redbook* 107, no. 3 (July 1956): 76.

16. "Wife Swapping Ring Linked to Lewd Pictures," *Chicago Tribune*, September 10, 1958, B6.

17. William Breedlove and Jerrye Breedlove, *Swap Clubs* (Los Angeles: Sherbourne, 1964), 9.

18. See Matt Galant and Kathleen Galant, *Sex Rebels: A True Expose of Wife Swapping Clubs* (El Cajon, CA: Publishers' Export Company, Inc., 1964); and Galant and Galant, *The Mate-Swapping Syndrome* (Los Angeles: Triumph, 1967).

19. *All the Loving Couples*, dir. Mark Bing (Cottage Films, 1969); Roger Ebert, "All the Loving Couples," December 11, 1969, www.rogerebert.com.

20. *Doctors' Wives*, dir. George Schaefer (Frankovich Productions, 1971). The following year, Archie and Edith Bunker found themselves in an awkward mate-swapping scene. *All in the Family*, season 3, episode 7, "The Bunkers and the Swingers," dir. Bob LaHendro and John Rich, writ. Norman Lear, Michael Ross, Bernie West, and Lee Kalcheim, CBS, October 28, 1972.

21. Abigail Van Buren, "Dear Abby," *Springfield Union*, June 4, 1969, 23.

22. Charles A. Varni, "An Exploratory Study of Wife Swapping" (master's thesis, San Diego State University 1970), 3.

23. Cherie Evelyn Schupp, "An Analysis of Some Social-Psychological Factors Which Operate in the Functioning Relationship of Married Couples Who Exchange Mates for the Purpose of Sexual Experience" (PhD diss., United States International University, 1970), 5.

24. Bartell, "Group Sex among the Mid-Americans," 124.

25. Bartell, *Group Sex*, 13.

26. Bartell, "Group Sex among the Mid-Americans," 122. Median household income in 1970 was $9,870; see US Census Bureau, "Median Family Income Up in 1970 (Advance data from March 1971 Current Population Survey)," May 20, 1971, 1, www.census.gov.
27. Bartell, "Group Sex among the Mid-Americans," 121.
28. Bartell, 123.
29. Bartell, 123. Similar attitudes on race were observed by other scholars, such as Varni, "Exploratory Study of Wife Swapping," 87.
30. Bartell, "Group Sex among the Mid-Americans," 123.
31. James R. Smith and Lynne G. Smith, "Co-marital Sex and the Sexual Freedom Movement," *Journal of Sex Research* 6, no. 2 (May 1970): 135.
32. Smith and Smith, 134.
33. Charles Palson and Rebecca Palson, "Swinging in Wedlock." *Society*, February 1972, 29.
34. George C. O'Neill and Nena O'Neill, "Patterns in Group Sex Activity," *Journal of Sex Research* 6, no. 2 (May 1970): 104.
35. Palson and Palson, "Swinging in Wedlock," 29.
36. Schupp, "Analysis of Some Social-Psychological Factors," 34.
37. Bartell, "Group Sex among the Mid-Americans," 122.
38. The Galants, quoted in Schupp, "Analysis of Some Social-Psychological Factors," 38.
39. The Galants, quoted in Schupp, 38.
40. Varni, "Exploratory Study of Wife Swapping," 79. For movie-ticket cost, see the Internet Movie Database's Box Office Mojo, www.boxofficemojo.com (accessed August 9, 2007).
41. Varni, "Exploratory Study of Wife Swapping," 80.
42. Schupp, "Analysis of Some Social-Psychological Factors," 66.
43. Bartell, *Group Sex*, 34.
44. Bartell, 144–45.
45. Varni, "Exploratory Study of Wife Swapping," 88.
46. Varni, 93.
47. Lewis, *Prescription for Heterosexuality*; Reumann, *American Sexual Character*.
48. Varni, "Exploratory Study of Wife Swapping," 103.
49. Bartell, "Group Sex among the Mid-Americans," 118.
50. Varni, "Exploratory Study of Wife Swapping," 82.
51. Palson and Palson, "Swinging in Wedlock," 30.
52. Bartell, "Group Sex among the Mid-Americans," 118.
53. Bartell, *Group Sex*, 142.
54. Bartell, "Group Sex among the Mid-Americans," 118.
55. Palson and Palson, "Swinging in Wedlock," 30, 37; O'Neill and O'Neill, "Patterns in Group Sex Activity," 107.
56. On the history of consent and marital rape, see Jill Elaine Hasday, "Contest and Consent: A Legal History of Marital Rape," *California Law Review* 88, no. 5 (October 2000): 1375–1505.
57. Palson and Palson, "Swinging in Wedlock," 35.
58. O'Neill and O'Neill, "Patterns in Group Sex Activity," 106.

59. Varni, "Exploratory Study of Wife Swapping," 77.

60. Smith and Smith, "Co-marital Sex and the Sexual Freedom Movement," 139.

61. Varni, "Exploratory Study of Wife Swapping," 101.

62. Mary Lindenstein Walshok, "The Emergence of Middle-Class Deviant Subculture: The Case of the Swingers," *Social Problems* 18, no. 4 (Spring 1971): 490.

63. Schupp, "Analysis of Some Social-Psychological Factors," 26, 28.

64. Walshok, "Emergence of Middle-Class Deviant Subculture," 490.

65. Varni, "Exploratory Study of Wife Swapping," 113.

66. James W. Ramey, "Emerging Patterns of Behavior in Marriage: Deviations or Innovations?," *Journal of Sex Research* 8, no. 1 (February 1972): 30.

67. For more on these movements and changes, see David Allyn, *Make Love, Not War: The Sexual Revolution, an Unfettered History* (Boston: Little, Brown, 2000); Beth Bailey, *Sex in the Heartland* (Cambridge, MA: Harvard University Press, 1999); Leslie J. Reagan, *When Abortion Was a Crime: Women, Medicine, and the Law in the United States, 1867–1973* (Berkeley: University of California Press, 1997); Marc Stein, *Sexual Injustice: Supreme Court Decisions from* Griswold *to* Roe (Chapel Hill: University of North Carolina Press, 2010); Elizabeth H. Pleck, *Not Just Roommates: Cohabitation after the Sexual Revolution* (Chicago: University of Chicago Press, 2012).

68. Varni, "Exploratory Study of Wife Swapping," 66–67.

69. The stifling aspects of togetherness, especially for men, is discussed in Elizabeth Fraterrigo, *"Playboy" and the Making of the Good Life in Modern America* (New York: Oxford University Press, 2009); Carrie Pitzulo, *Bachelors and Bunnies: The Sexual Politics of "Playboy"* (Chicago: University of Chicago Press, 2011); Ralph LaRossa, *The Modernization of Fatherhood: A Social and Political History* (Chicago: University of Chicago Press, 1997).

70. LaRossa, *Modernization of Fatherhood*, 111.

71. Bartell, *Group Sex*, 42–43.

72. Bartell, 120–21.

73. Duane Denfeld, "Dropouts from Swinging," *Family Coordinator* 23, no. 1 (January 1974): 45–49.

74. Denfeld, 46.

75. Denfeld, 47.

76. Denfeld, 47–48.

77. Anne-Marie Henshel, "Swinging: A Study of Decision Making in Marriage," *American Journal of Sociology* 78, no. 4 (January 1973): 885–91.

78. Henshel, 886.

79. Henshel, 890.

80. See Sheila Jeffreys, *Anticlimax: A Feminist Perspective on the Sexual Revolution* (New York: NYU Press, 1991); Beth Bailey, "Sex as a Weapon: Underground Comix and the Paradox of Liberation," in *Imagine Nation: The American Counterculture of the 1960s and '70s*, ed. Peter Braunstein and Michael William Doyle (New York: Routledge, 2002), 305–26.

81. Palson and Palson, "Swinging in Wedlock," 37.

10

Race, Sexual Citizenship, and the Constitution of Nonmarital Motherhood

SERENA MAYERI

The 1965 Moynihan Report, formally known as *The Negro Family: The Case for National Action*, reinforced the reigning consensus among policy makers that racial progress and social peace required a traditionally gendered division of family labor in a two-parent family headed by a male breadwinner and a female homemaker. "Matriarchal" family structures, Assistant Secretary of Labor Daniel Patrick Moynihan argued, aggravated unemployment, poverty, and violence in black communities. Though his reasoning proved controversial, Moynihan's analysis reflected the conventional wisdom that African Americans should emulate a white patriarchal family structure in order to rescue their families from the "tangle of pathology" that fed growing rates of "illegitimacy," "welfare dependency," and "juvenile delinquency."[1] Moynihan's conclusions proved to be both galvanizing and misleading. Not only would African American feminists, welfare activists, and their allies fight back against his disparaging portrait of "the Negro Family," but within the decade, Moynihan's presumptions about white families would be upended as well.

African American feminists and their allies responded to Moynihan by calling for the passage and vigorous enforcement of laws against sex discrimination in employment, education, and jury service. Leaders such as Pauli Murray and Eleanor Holmes Norton built coalitions with white feminists to lobby Congress, courts, and administrative agencies to extend civil rights protections to women. They also promoted an alternative vision of African American marriage: an egalitarian partnership in which both spouses pursued careers, cared for children and elderly relatives, and respected each other as moral, political, and intellectual equals. Rather than holding up the white, middle-class, male-breadwinner-female-homemaker ideal as a model for black families, black feminists suggested that white couples could learn from their black counterparts. Instead of condemning female "dominance" as pathological, feminists urged that black women's high rates of labor-force participation and assertive leadership had laid the groundwork for the gender equality that a predominantly white women's movement now sought.[2] By the end of the 1970s, the African American feminist vision of marriage had come to fruition as a matter of formal legal doctrine, if not social reality. In a series of cases challenging sex-specific allocations of government benefits, this campaign, led by the American Civil Liberties Union (ACLU) attorney and professor Ruth Bader Ginsburg, largely succeeded in rendering marriage formally gender neutral. In the eyes of the law, husbands and wives were mostly fungible spouses; the government could no longer overtly penalize nontraditional divisions of family labor.[3]

The obstacles that unmarried African American mothers faced challenged both the Moynihan Report's assumptions and the egalitarian marriage remedies that legal activists proposed. For many African American and low-income women and men, an egalitarian marriage between two well-employed partners remained out of reach.[4] As welfare-rights activists such as Johnnie Tillmon highlighted, the most that many poor black women could hope for was a Hobson's choice between back-breaking, low-wage labor and a stingy welfare allotment conditioned on the relinquishment of privacy and dignity. Before the 1960s, many policy makers, social workers, lawyers, and judges encouraged young, white, unwed mothers who could not marry their partners to leave their parents and siblings and enter maternity homes as soon as pregnancy became visible, give birth, and surrender their children for adoption by presumptively white, two-parent, marital families. Unmarried African American girls and women, by contrast, rarely had access to maternity homes or adoption services; instead, they usually kept and raised their children, often with the help of their parents or other extended family.[5] The legal treatment of nonmarital parents reflected the white middle- and upper-class ideal: for example, nonmarital fathers had few rights or responsibilities for their offspring, in part because courts and other state actors assumed that swift adoption by strangers served "illegitimate" children's—and their mothers'—best interests.[6] Moreover, laws,

policies, and practices penalized nonmarital childbearing, often targeting African American families.

While educated, professional black and white women challenged
sex roles within marriage, poor and working-class African American
women used emerging constitutional equality principles to fight discrimination based on family status. Between 1967 and 1979, African
American women brought lawsuits attacking what I have called "illegitimacy penalties." They challenged laws that excluded "illegitimate"
children from government benefits such as Social Security or workers'
compensation, and they disputed policies that deprived nonmarital
children of private rights such as the ability to inherit from their fathers. Women also brought lawsuits fighting employment discrimination against unmarried women who became pregnant or raised their
nonmarital children. They battled efforts to withhold public-assistance
benefits from women who gave birth to children outside of marriage,
engaged in intimate relationships with nonmarital partners, or refused
to disclose the identity of their children's biological fathers.

Efforts to redefine normative sexuality through constitutional litigation enjoyed mixed success. Courts often framed discrimination based
on birth status primarily as an injustice visited upon "hapless" and "innocent" children unfairly punished for the "sins" of their parents. Judges
largely ignored advocates' arguments that penalizing nonmarital families
violated constitutional equal protection principles by targeting Americans
based on race, gender, sexual behavior, and poverty. Plaintiffs were most
likely to prevail when their claims coincided with state efforts to privatize
the costs of childbearing and child rearing within the nuclear family and
to promote what scholars would later call neoliberal sexual citizens: those
who managed to earn a living and care for their children with minimal
help from the state. American jurisprudence began to acknowledge that
nonmarital sex could be compatible with normative sexuality, but it still
held that responsible sexual citizenship required unmarried mothers to
find private sources of support and care for their families.

In the wake of the US civil rights movement, black women challenged
the vision of normative heterosexuality embedded in the law's treatment
of unmarried mothers. They largely succeeded in establishing a right not
to be excluded from jobs because of nonmarital childbirth—the right to
work outside the home. Unmarried mothers did not win compensation

for their caregiving work for their own families, however. Those who could not earn a living ceded their right to privacy and autonomy as reproductive and family decision-makers. The vision of normative heterosexuality that prevailed permitted women to bear children outside of marriage and head households without male partners—but only if they could serve as breadwinners themselves.

* * *

Constitutional challenges to illegitimacy penalties had their roots in Louisiana's passage of a "suitable home" law in August 1960, which immediately terminated public assistance to more than twenty thousand African American children whose mothers engaged in nonmarital sexual relationships. Part of a larger backlash against civil rights, the Louisiana purge was the most notorious of many state and local efforts to punish nonmarital childbearing and enact morals regulations targeting African Americans in the aftermath of *Brown v. Board of Education* (1954).[7] Such laws, for example, excluded children from white-identified schools on the basis of their parents' marital status; denied public assistance to unmarried mothers in intimate relationships with men; and, in some states, even mandated sterilization or other criminal penalties for women who gave birth to nonmarital children.

Civil rights lawyers recognized these illegitimacy penalties as massive resistance by another name and immediately challenged them as racial injustice. A young ACLU lawyer, Mel Wulf, wrote a brief to the Department of Health, Education, and Welfare, attacking Louisiana's policy as racially motivated, "a punitive step to deter [the state's] Negro citizens from pursuing their goal of equality." Wulf also suggested that discrimination against "out-of-wedlock" children itself was "invidious and likely unconstitutional." Wulf's brief stopped short of suggesting that the state had no interest in nonmarital childbearing; he did not deny that illegitimacy penalties might deter nonmarital sex and "promiscuity." Even if these penalties created conditions of such physical deprivation that they deterred other women and men from conceiving children out of wedlock, Wulf called it "clearly unreasonable to attempt to improve a home's moral climate by starving its occupants to death."[8]

Antipoverty and civil rights lawyers who joined Wulf in challenging these laws emphasized their detrimental impact on children's well-being. The foremost proponent of this child-focused approach was the University of Illinois law professor Harry Krause, a leading legal authority on illegitimacy, a "psychic catastrophe," in the words of a 1945 study that Krause often quoted. Krause cannily perceived that children's innocence could be "successfully exploited," much like images of brave yet vulnerable children enduring hostile, hysterical mobs resisting school integration spoke more eloquently than any legal brief ever could.[9] But his focus on children also stemmed from genuine conviction. He expressed frustration that "well-intentioned people have lavished disproportionate effort on the welfare mother," declaring that it was "time that the matter be considered from the standpoint of the child!"[10] ACLU and National Association for the Advancement of Colored People (NAACP) Legal Defense Fund lawyers contended that illegitimacy penalties unfairly discriminated against children on the basis of race, poverty, and birth status, highlighting the injustice of punishing blameless children for their parents' ostensible transgressions. In cases challenging the exclusion of illegitimate children from wrongful-death recovery, paternal inheritance, and workers' compensation, they argued that illegitimacy-based legal exclusions violated the Fourteenth Amendment's equal protection and due process provisions.[11]

The leading Supreme Court case, *Levy v. Louisiana*, epitomized the child-focused approach of the early litigation. In 1964, a local attorney filed a lawsuit in Louisiana seeking damages on behalf of Louise Levy's five nonmarital children for their mother's wrongful death as a result of malpractice by doctors at a New Orleans hospital. Court submissions depicted Louise Levy as a model mother and citizen: she worked hard, attended Catholic Mass regularly, and inculcated moral values in her children. Notably, Levy depended on the state for neither public assistance nor education, scraping together money from domestic work to avoid welfare and send her children to parochial school. Lawyers emphasized that the Levy children's inability to recover damages under Louisiana's wrongful-death statute—which excluded illegitimate children from the definition of "child"—would burden public coffers. The "sins of the parents are being visited upon the children," the attorney Adolph Levy (no relation to plaintiffs) stressed, "who had absolutely nothing to do with their status."[12] The Levy children's allies were careful not to question directly the state's legitimate interest in promoting marriage and discouraging illicit sex. Apart from the "sin" of nonmarital childbearing, court papers depicted Louise Levy as a responsible, self-sufficient parent and citizen; legal recognition of her children's right to recover from a private actor would place lesser burdens on government funds. Lawyers were wary of accusations that they sought to "destroy" marriage and the nuclear family, arguing instead that discrimination against illegitimate children was highly unlikely to deter illicit sex or promote marriage.

By contrast, Mrs. Sylvester Smith's contemporaneous attack on Alabama's "substitute father" law entailed a more direct challenge to sexual respectability. When told that her family would be ineligible for Aid to Dependent Children (ADC) benefits if she did not disprove rumors of her intimate relations with a family friend, the married father of another woman's nine children, Smith adamantly refused to confirm or deny the affair. "I told [the caseworker] it was none of her business," Smith later recalled, adding that she had every intention of "going with" whomever she wished as long as she was young enough to enjoy the company of men. Smith, who worked daily eight-hour shifts as a cook in Selma for less than twenty dollars per week to support her four children and one grandchild, valued her social and sexual autonomy enough to risk losing the stingy but significant ADC benefit for which her family was eligible.[13] With her lawyer, Martin Garbus, Smith translated her defiant declaration of sexual independence into a robust vision of sexual privacy and autonomy. By requiring mothers to disclose their "most intimate relationships" and conditioning government benefits on marriage or celibacy, Smith contended, Alabama violated her rights to privacy and freedom of association. ACLU lawyers who litigated the early illegitimacy cases made supportive arguments outside of court, arguing for an expansive interpretation of the 1965 ruling in *Griswold v. Connecticut* to "include [all] private sexual activity between consenting adults" and suggesting that "the right of government to prohibit or discourage 'immoral' conduct which damages no other public interest has been seriously challenged."[14]

Smith's challenge was the opening salvo in a more radical feminist critique of illegitimacy penalties and of the Court's constitutional approach. The Court decided *Levy v. Louisiana*, *King v. Smith* and several other illegitimacy-related cases in the plaintiffs' favor but reaffirmed the state's prerogative to promote marriage and to regulate adults' nonmarital sexual activity.[15] Justice Lewis F. Powell's influential 1972 opinion in *Weber v. Aetna Casualty*, a challenge to the exclusion of illegitimate children in Louisiana's workers' compensation statute, embraced the idea that birth-status-based classifications were unconstitutional because they punished "hapless" children for the "irresponsible liaisons" of their parents.[16] According to the Court, punishing illegitimate children was an ineffective means of achieving the state's (perfectly legitimate) goals of deterring illicit adult sex and privileging marital relationships.[17]

* * *

Mrs. Smith's challenge to Alabama's substitute-father law prefigured an alternative, feminist approach to illegitimacy that emerged more fully in the late 1960s and early 1970s. As unprecedented numbers of women graduated from law school and became advocates, they acquired the tools to translate the claims to equality, autonomy, and dignity articulated by African American women and their families into legal and constitutional arguments. The feminist challenge to illegitimacy penalties targeted a wide range of laws and policies. Feminists emphasized how illegitimacy penalties forced women to shoulder most or all of the burden of supporting and caring for nonmarital children when fathers died or deserted their families. These laws, they contended, shamed and punished women for illicit sex while allowing men to escape consequences with impunity. They argued that denying jobs, child-support payments, government benefits, and inheritance rights to nonmarital families restricted women's reproductive autonomy by penalizing their decision to bear and raise nonmarital children rather than giving up the children for adoption or terminating their pregnancies. Women of color and their allies protested how the state invasively patrolled poor women's personal lives by conditioning sustenance on the disclosure of sexual relationships or paternity.[18]

Feminist lawyers and commentators sharply critiqued the child-centered approach to illegitimacy cases promoted by Krause and embraced by the Court. The recent law-school graduates Patricia Tenoso and Aleta Wallach wrote in 1974 of the need to abolish illegitimacy as a legal category. Instead, they insisted, the law must embrace "the right of women to self-determination . . . free from all forms of male domination."[19] Wallach and Tenoso criticized reformers such as Krause who accepted the premise that nonmarital childbearing was inherently undesirable. "Illegitimacy," they argued, was only a "problem" because law and social norms made it so; patriarchy and poverty were the true culprits. They resisted Krause's focus on determining paternity and extracting child support from biological fathers, contending instead that state policy should "treat the mother as an economic resource" by "eliminat[ing] barriers to employment" for unmarried mothers and guaranteeing "adequate government support of all unmarried mothers and their children."[20]

The theory of illegitimacy advanced by Wallach and Tenoso echoed tenets of welfare-rights activism in its most feminist guise,[21] questioning the foundational premises of American family and social welfare law: the two-parent nuclear family's superiority, the undesirability of nonmarital childbearing, and the privatization of dependency through marriage—or, in the absence of marriage, through paternity determination and child-support enforcement. Others mounted more limited challenges, seeking to redefine rather than eschew sexual respectability; to rehabilitate single mothers as responsible, productive citizens, independent from men but not reliant on the state; or to gain access to remunerative employment as a path to economic self-sufficiency.

In the 1970s, unmarried African American mothers explicitly and implicitly challenged these assumptions, asserting their right to bear and raise children outside of marriage. Lois Fernandez, a black community activist, later achieved local fame as the founder of Odunde, an annual African cultural festival that is now a Philadelphia institution. Less well-known is Fernandez's crusade against Pennsylvania's illegitimacy laws, launched a few years after the birth of her first child. Fernandez recalled lying in the maternity ward in 1967, joyful about becoming a mother but chagrined to realize—shortly after being told that maternity health benefits only covered married women—that her newborn son, Adeyemi, would not be issued a birth certificate because she was not married.[22] Instead, she could pay two dollars for a short form that confirmed his birth but listed neither mother nor father.[23] Fernandez refused to purchase such a form on principle and began to research the legal status of illegitimacy. She discovered that under state law, a child born to

unmarried parents could only become "legitimate" if the parents married each other—a recent reform of a law that had previously required
a mother's husband to adopt the child.[24] In 1971, Fernandez launched a
letter-writing campaign that spurred state representatives to introduce
legislation formally abolishing the distinction between "legitimate" and
"illegitimate" children. "To give birth is human, not illegitimate," Fernandez insisted.[25]

Fernandez, one of ten surviving children of an African American
mother and a Bahamian-immigrant father who admired black nationalist Marcus Garvey, saw her crusade against illegitimacy as part of a
larger commitment to racial justice and cultural pride. Her mother, a
South Philadelphia Democratic committeewoman who had migrated
from Alabama as a child, had been aghast when Lois—inspired by the
South African singer Miriam Makeba and awakening to a lost African heritage—had stopped straightening her hair and wearing "high-
fashion" clothing.[26] Mrs. Fernandez was a clerk at the Bureau of Vital
Statistics who issued the very birth certificates that her daughter ab-
horred and raised her children as "high-church" Episcopalians. Though
she had also encouraged her children to "take a stand," Mrs. Fernandez
expressed skepticism that Lois could "change that white man's law" after
"200 years." But after seven years and much litigation, lobbying, and
local TV and radio appearances by Fernandez and her allies at the National Urban League's Child Advocacy Project, Governor Milton Shapp
signed a bill in 1978 providing that "all children shall be legitimate regardless of the marital status of their parents" and should enjoy "the
same rights and privileges."[27]

Meanwhile, with the help of Community Legal Services and the
Women's Law Project, Fernandez also challenged the constitutionality
of Pennsylvania's discriminatory laws in court.[28] Fernandez's lawyers—
eventually including the prominent feminist attorney and professor
Ann Freedman—argued that state laws preventing children "born out
of wedlock" from inheriting from fathers who died intestate (without
a will) and taxing bequests to nonmarital children at a higher rate was
unconstitutional sex discrimination. Such laws, Freedman and her colleagues argued, exacerbated women's economic disadvantage, for "as
sole surviving parent," mothers of nonmarital children were "burdened
with the far more onerous task of supporting a child who has no claim

against his or her father's estate . . . requiring [her] to replace the support previously provided by the father."[29]

Outside of court, Fernandez and her allies fought against the sexual double standard that stigmatized unmarried mothers as well as their children, even as nonmarital children began to escape ignominy. She later recalled, "The thing that bothered me the most was that . . . the question of the fathers never came up. . . . There were the mothers, who were considered 'whores,' or 'illicit women,' and then there were the children, who were considered 'bastards,' 'illegit.' I just couldn't accept that."[30] She resented "the stereotype of mothers of out-of-wedlock children as promiscuous" and recoiled when family and friends expected her children to have their fathers' surnames rather than her own.[31] Fernandez considered her decision to become a single mother a deliberate step of which she was proud, not an unfortunate, inadvertent, or shameful fate. "To have a child without a husband was my choice," she said in 1979. "I made the decision with pride; I did not worry about societal pressures. To give birth is one of the most beautiful experiences I have ever had."[32]

Fernandez celebrated single motherhood as a valid, voluntary lifestyle choice, even as her status as a worker, property holder, and taxpaying citizen provided a weapon she could wield against demeaning ideas about "unwed mothers" as "lazy" "welfare chiselers."[33] As a *Philadelphia Inquirer* reporter observed in 1971, "That picture hardly fits Lois. She has only one child and she works as hard as anyone else to support him," as a "gang worker" for the youth conservation service of the public welfare department. She was also attending college in pursuit of a degree in library technology. With a war raging in Vietnam, Fernandez observed that her son had "no birth certificate and no inheritance rights, [but] he can still be drafted." As a "working mother" and a "homeowner," Fernandez insisted that she and her family deserved better.[34] Emphasizing the dignity of her hard work and self-sufficiency allowed Fernandez to reconfigure normative heterosexuality to include mothers who chose to raise children on their own.

* * *

Katie Mae Andrews's 1973 challenge to a Mississippi school district's exclusion of unmarried mothers from teaching positions sought to redefine heterosexual respectability in the strikingly different context of the rural Deep South. Andrews's case struck at the heart of long-simmering racial, cultural, and economic tensions, highlighting how arguments about heterosexual respectability often served to reinforce white supremacy. Battles over voting rights and school desegregation had rocked Andrews's tiny Delta community in the 1960s and early 1970s. Residents of Drew recognized the ban on unmarried parents—nicknamed the "Pettey Rule" after the school superintendent George F. Pettey—as the latest skirmish in an ongoing campaign of white resistance to civil rights activism: all five of the women who were turned away from teaching jobs because of the ban were African American.

When twenty-three-year-old Andrews knocked on the door of the newly minted lawyer Charles Victor McTeer, the twenty-eight-year-old Baltimore native and protégé of the civil rights lawyer Morty Stavis of New York's Center for Constitutional Rights had just arrived in Mississippi. The cast of characters who assembled in Judge William Keady's federal district courtroom in nearby Greenville reflected the past, present, and future of Mississippi politics. Judge Keady, a Mississippi native, had ascended the bench in 1968, the day after the assassination of Dr. Martin Luther King Jr., and immediately confronted the daunting task of presiding over school desegregation. Representing the school district was Champ Terney, son-in-law of staunch segregationist Senator James O. Eastland. McTeer enlisted the support and testimony of the local civil rights icon Fannie Lou Hamer, as well as Mae Bertha Carter, a mother of thirteen whose children had single-handedly integrated the Drew schools a few years earlier. Testifying via deposition from New York were the social psychologist Kenneth Clark, the author with his wife, Mamie Phipps Clark, of the "doll studies" cited by the Supreme Court in *Brown v. Board of Education*, and Ernest van den Haag, a Dutch-born former communist who survived imprisonment in fascist Italy and became a conservative defender of racial segregation and genetic theories of intelligence in his adopted country.[35]

McTeer set out to show that although the Pettey Rule had been designed ostensibly to stem the rising tide of "schoolgirl pregnancies" among Drew's now majority-black student population, its purpose and effect, like that of many civil-rights-era anti-illegitimacy policies, was to exclude and stigmatize African American families. An estimated 30 to 40 percent of black children in Drew were born to unmarried parents, and even more-open-minded white teachers and school officials warned that allowing mothers of "illegitimate" children to become teachers would deal a death blow to already-sagging white support for the public schools.[36] Superintendent Pettey justified the rule as crucial to maintaining high standards of moral character among teachers and other adults who had daily contact with children, particularly given the "alarming number of school girl pregnancies" in Drew.[37] He insisted that the restriction applied equally to men and women, black and white; he conceded that ferreting out male teachers with illegitimate children was difficult, whereas "the unwed mother is stuck with the result."[38] Mrs. Fred McCorkle, a white woman charged with making hiring recommendations in the district, acknowledged that, in practice, the exclusion affected only black women.[39]

Drew's black community initially divided over the wisdom of opposing the Pettey Rule, with some preferring not to air "dirty laundry" in public for fear of reinforcing damaging stereotypes and undermining a fragile racial peace.[40] Women who had been rejected or dismissed from employment because of their status as unmarried parents also held various views about sexual morality. Violet Burnett, a teacher's aide who had lost her job because of the policy, was almost defiant in her embrace of sexual freedom. "Do you personally feel that it's moral or immoral for an unmarried person to have sexual intercourse?" asked the school district's lawyer on cross-examination. "I feel like as an individual a person can do whatever they want to, they has the freedom to do anything they want to as long as it's not hurting anyone," Burnett replied. Would she advise a teenage student in her charge to have sexual intercourse with her boyfriend? "I would tell her if that's what she wanted . . . go right ahead."[41] Did she plan to have any more children outside of wedlock? No. Why? "Because taking care of one is hard enough."[42] Plaintiff Lestine Rogers, too, saw nonmarital sex as an individual decision: "I can't say it's right and I can't say it's wrong. Because I think it's left up to you as long as you are not hurting anyone else. I think you should do whatever you feel is right." Did she intend to have more children outside of marriage? "I don't know," Rogers candidly replied.[43]

Katie Mae Andrews presented herself as an upstanding citizen, a religious, churchgoing woman who had become pregnant outside of marriage not because of any moral deficiency but because of a lack of knowledge of and access to contraception. "During the time I became pregnant [early 1968] . . . black people wasn't aware of the many things that the white person would use in order to keep from getting pregnant. So if I had had all this counseling . . . maybe a parent that knew more about this, as a white person did, then . . . I wouldn't become pregnant at that time and no other time."[44] Her lawyers emphasized that Andrews and her compatriots "had never attempted to 'publicize their status' or to proselytize students," actions that in other cases involving school-teachers' sexual morality had often been determinative.[45] "Moreover," they contended, "it is well known that the status of unwed parenthood is not something which is affirmatively sought but rather imposed by force of circumstance." The blame instead rested with the "lack of in-formation and realistic understanding about the risks of pregnancy, and the lack of access to effective contraception, which falls heaviest on the poor." "Abortional services," they noted, "are virtually unknown in Mississippi"—and would have been unlawful in any event.[46]

Andrews valued marriage, largely drawing from her Christian faith to explain her understanding of sexual sin, repentance, and morality. She did not defend single parenthood or nonmarital sex per se. She consid-ered premarital sex "a sin" but insisted, "The Bible says repent. . . . You can repent for your sin and be forgiven." Andrews did not intend to have any more children until she got married: "I didn't plan this one." But she also refused to apologize for her decision to give birth outside of mar-riage. "I mean, God put us here on earth and if it came up to that I feel that we should have them. . . . If we try to get rid of it, as most people do, that's killing it. Well, you know where we would wind up then."[47] And she defended her prerogative to marry when she met "the right person to marry" and not before.[48]

Andrews and her supporters sought to rehabilitate the image of single mothers and to frame single mothers' exclusion from employment—not nonmarital childbearing—as morally wrong as well as unconstitutional. Andrews had managed to graduate from Mississippi Valley State College and earn money as a factory worker in Cleveland, Mississippi, while raising her son with the help of her mother and siblings, with whom she lived. Hamer, who gained an unusual dispensation from Judge Keady to testify as an expert on the social mores of Sunflower County's black community, emphasized the impact of employment exclusions on unmarried mothers who sought gainful employment rather than relying on public assistance. "I know so many young women that after having one child, go back to school, finish school and yet not marry, but try to better theirselves by getting a good job so they can support their children without becoming a ward of the welfare."[49] The exclusion of unwed mothers from employment, applied writ large, she said, would "be a terrible blow to all of us . . . across the country. . . . People are trying . . . [to] bring theirselves up to a level where they can support theirselves and their child."[50]

The plaintiffs' allies emphasized that access to decent jobs in education would alleviate nonmarital families' dependence on public assistance. Denying a mother employment in the Drew school system would mean that she "must uproot herself and travel to a distant community," or, "more likely, she is consigned to unemployment or welfare or relegated to marginal employment, often available only at a distance from her home and child."[51] The rule not only contradicted "federal policy as evidenced in Congressional enactment of the Work Incentive Program, but it serves to perpetuate the cycle of poverty from which these women have struggled so arduously to escape."[52] An amicus brief from the Child Welfare League of America noted the vast gulf between salaries for Drew teachers and aides, on the one hand, and the paltry Aid to Families with Dependent Children (AFDC) and food-stamp benefits for which impoverished Mississippi families were eligible, on the other. "An absolute bar to employment," especially in a time of economic recession and job scarcity, "almost inevitably will result in forcing reliance on public assistance benefits—benefits which do not even approach meeting a family's needs."[53]

Hamer testified that the black community viewed the choice Andrews and her compatriots made—to keep, care for, and support their children—as evidence of strong moral character, the opposite of immorality or irresponsibility. Hamer highlighted the Catch-22 that employment restrictions created for unmarried mothers who wished to avoid depending on AFDC. "You always tell us . . . we have got so many kids on the welfare roll, 'Why don't you get up and do something?' And then when we start doing something, 'You don't have any business being that high.'"[54] Hamer exposed the hypocrisy of those who would condemn young women for engaging in nonmarital sex. "If justice was really done," Hamer declared, "it wouldn't only be black women in here, it would be a whole lot of young white folk in here too." When Terney pressed her on whether evidence of teachers engaging in nonmarital sex would lead students to infer that such conduct was acceptable, Hamer replied that if all faculty were held to the same standard, "You know what you have to do . . . ? When you get back to Drew this evening, lock up the doors. There won't be any school."[55]

Kenneth Clark's deposition testimony provided scholarly support for Andrews and her allies. He confirmed that nonmarital childbearing "has nothing to do with morality, . . . has nothing to do with sexual behavior," but rather "reflects the inability or lack of knowledge . . . as to how to avoid unwed parenthood, if it is undesired."[56] To him, it was Drew school officials who acted immorally by "pry[ing] into the personal or sex life of other individuals" and "impos[ing] their personal sexual patterns or gratifications upon others."[57] Clark stated repeatedly his belief that the right to individual and personal privacy should shield teachers from any inquiry into their sexual activities unless those activities involved the exploitation or abuse of a student. He scoffed at the notion that a teacher who bore a child out of wedlock would be an influential factor in schoolgirl pregnancies: "I am sorry, I just can't take that seriously. I think that young girls become pregnant through sexual behavior. They don't become pregnant in a classroom."[58] Notably, Clark's conviction that private sexual conduct was irrelevant to teaching ability extended to homosexual as well as heterosexual behavior, a live question in contemporaneous lawsuits challenging the exclusion of gay and lesbian teachers from public employment.[59]

An amicus brief from the ACLU Women's Rights Project and Equal Rights Advocates bolstered the argument at the center of Andrews's constitutional challenge: that excluding unmarried parents from employment unjustly discriminated against women. The brief explained how the Pettey Rule "vindicat[ed] 'the double standard' of sexuality morality, under which women must remain virginal and uninformed about sexual matters until marriage, obedient and ignorant of matters such as contraception within marriage, . . . and generally ashamed and displeased about sexual intercourse."[60] Under Mississippi law, only fathers could unilaterally "legitimate" their children, further reinforcing the operation of the sexual double standard.[61] And, the brief pointed out, "unwed fathers in this society do not generally rear their children," further insulating men from the policy's operation.[62] In sum, Pettey's policy "represents an unwarranted return to times during which stigmatization of unwed mothers was a tool, along with forced pregnancy, compulsory marriage, and deprivation of birth control information, by which women were kept in their legal and societal place."[63] Not only feminist legal organizations but also respected social scientists—Clark foremost among them—argued that illegitimacy penalties subordinated women.

An informal coalition of young feminist attorneys seized on the case as an opportunity to advance expansive claims about reproductive freedom, which they defined as the right to carry an unintended or nonmarital pregnancy to term as well as the right to obtain an abortion. Rhonda Copelon, Nancy Stearns, and Elizabeth Schneider of the Center for Constitutional Rights (CCR) argued that young women subject to the Drew school-district policy faced an impossible decision: abort or abandon their children or give up their "aspirations to enter the teaching profession or to work in the school system."[64] Pettey's policy "encourage[d] abortion," they charged, "a practice that offends the moral sensibility of a significant segment of American society" and, more specifically, the personal moral and religious code to which Andrews and Hamer adhered.[65] These arguments resonated with reproductive-justice arguments advanced in contemporaneous challenges to involuntary sterilization. As the CCR's Jan Goodman told the Women's Rights Law Reporter, "We are arguing that all women should have the freedom to choose, and that they not be penalized whatever the choice is—to bear the child or to abort."[66] Hamer, for her part, had drawn national attention to punitive reproductive control years earlier when she spoke of her own nonconsensual hysterectomy and popularized the term "Mississippi appendectomy" to refer to the coercive surgeries imposed on poor women of color, often as a condition of receiving medical care or public assistance.[67] The vision of normative heterosexuality advanced by Andrews and Hamer valorized the choice *not* to end a pregnancy, even in the face of considerable hardship.

The plaintiffs also emphasized how laws that excluded unmarried parents harmed the children of those families: indeed, Andrews's lawyers gave the parent-child relationship top billing in their brief to the

Supreme Court. "The ineluctable impact of Mr. Pettey's rule is both to infringe and to punish the fundamental right of nurturance" recognized in the 1972 decision in *Stanley v. Illinois*, which struck down a state law that denied parental rights to Peter Stanley, an unmarried father who had lived with his children since their birth.[68] The "denial of employment here," they argued, was "functionally indistinguishable" from the illegitimacy-based discrimination that the Court had found unconstitutional.[69] Banning unmarried parents from employment stigmatized and shamed nonmarital children, "thereby branding them as inferior to their 'legitimate' classmates."[70] The Child Welfare League drove home these points. The Drew policy directly deprived nonmarital children of "adequate food, shelter, clothing, and medical care," increasing the likelihood that children would be removed from their parents for "neglect" and that unmarried mothers would relinquish their children to adoption—or, more likely, foster care—rather than raise them.[71] Investigations of birth status might cause "the stigma of illegitimacy" to be "attached to an innocent child where no stigma previously existed."[72]

The plaintiffs emerged victorious from their lawsuit against the Drew school district. The remedy they won—the right to apply for teaching jobs on equal terms—did not impose any additional financial burden on the state and indeed provided gainful employment to mothers who might otherwise depend on public assistance. As in the Fernandez case, the mothers in *Andrews* successfully framed their constitutional claims as consonant with their children's well-being. Fernandez and Andrews ultimately prevailed, though without vindicating any of their more radical arguments about race, gender, privacy, and sexual citizenship in court: their aspirations to gainful employment, economic self-sufficiency, and improving their children's life prospects won the day.

* * *

A Connecticut law that compelled poor, unmarried mothers to disclose the names of their children's fathers on pain of a contempt fine or imprisonment posed a more daunting challenge to feminist lawyers and their clients. *Roe v. Norton*, a lawsuit challenging the state's mandatory paternity-disclosure law, reached the US Supreme Court around the same time as Katie Mae Andrews's lawsuit. Many state officials and judges saw the interests of unmarried mothers and children as diametrically opposed when mothers resisted identifying fathers and thereby deprived the state of a potential private source of child support.

Efforts to identify fathers and pursue child-support claims against them intensified in the 1960s as anxiety about welfare expenditures and the changing racial composition and family structure of public-assistance recipients grew. When "suitable home" and "substitute father" laws confronted statutory and administrative barriers, "man in the house" rules and "midnight raids" often replaced them. States also began to condition AFDC receipt on mothers' cooperation with paternity determinations, but courts ruled—as they had in *King v. Smith*—that needy children could not be deprived of benefits because of their parents' conduct.[73] In order to circumvent these rulings, some states enacted statutes that did not withhold benefits from children whose mothers refused to identify fathers but instead imposed penalties directly on mothers themselves.[74]

Though Connecticut's law technically applied to married women whose children were "found not to be issue of the marriage" and to unmarried mothers regardless of eligibility for public assistance, everyone concerned understood that the primary targets of the law were poor, unmarried mothers, disproportionately African Americans.[75] The Connecticut Civil Liberties Union brought a class-action lawsuit on behalf of these women in 1973, claiming that the law violated their right to privacy, due process, and equal protection. The state defended the law as necessary to protect not only the state's financial resources but also the interests of children who would otherwise be deprived of a relationship—affective, financial, and otherwise—with their fathers. Connecticut's attorney general charged that mothers who refused to disclose paternity "cast their children into the eternal caverns of illegitimacy," selfishly withholding information that could transform the lives and prospects of their offspring. Officials described unwilling mothers as "recalcitrant," "obstinate," and "primarily concerned with their own welfare," framing women's actions and interests as contrary to their children's well-being.[76] Federal district court judge M. Joseph Blumenfeld decried the "anguish suffered by illegitimate children denied the satisfaction of knowing their paternity." Not only did he reject the mothers' arguments that the statute discriminated against nonmarital families; he also opined that the statute "operates prophylactically against the adverse differential treatment which the unwed mothers would impose on their children."[77] If law could not deter low-income women from bearing children outside of marriage, at least it could compel their cooperation in identifying a potential source of child support.

Mothers who declined to disclose paternity insisted that it was their very concern for their children's welfare that prompted them to oppose the law. Affidavits explained mothers' refusal as the product of legitimate concerns about their families' safety and well-being. Rena Roe (a pseudonym) of Willimantic averred that the father of her child "has threatened [her] with physical harm if she divulges his name. He has never shown any interest in his child and has consistently denied fathering the child."[78] Mildred Walter of Rockville explained that she had divulged the name of her child's father to the welfare department but had declined to initiate paternity proceedings herself because she lived in "fear of this man . . . due to the beatings and physical abuse he inflicted" on her, including dragging her by the hair and kicking her down the street while she was nine months pregnant. On pain of losing welfare benefits for herself and her daughter, Walter declared, "I cannot testify or sign papers that may place my life and that of my child in danger."[79] Unlike the law's defenders, some mothers described biological fathers not as potential providers but as severe hazards to family safety.

Other mothers feared that disclosure would undermine or destroy their relationships with their children's fathers or with other potential father figures. Sharon Roe of New Haven testified that her daughter's father "has started to develop a good relationship with her; he plays with her": "If I were to give his name he would leave the state and break off the relationship."[80] A woman named only as "A" in court records explained that she planned to marry her child's father and was "afraid if she discloses his name, subsequent legal action could jeopardize their relationship and the possibility of marriage."[81] Several mothers further pointed out that the likelihood of recovering any financial support from the fathers of their children was, at best, low—and even if support could be collected, it would benefit the state, not poor mothers and their children.[82]

The plaintiffs placed women's right to privacy at the center of their challenge. As the mothers' lawyers put it in their brief to the Supreme Court, "Even if successful, [a paternity suit] may not be worth the price" of a severed relationship between father and child, cessation of any financial or emotional support, and the public humiliation of invasive questioning about sexual conduct in open court.[83] Like Mrs. Sylvester Smith, who declared her intimate life none of the caseworker's business, the plaintiffs in *Roe v. Norton* asserted that mandatory paternity disclosure infringed on their right to sexual and personal privacy. Sharon Roe listed "first" among her reasons for silence, "the question of with whom I have had sexual intercourse is private; I don't feel I should be forced to tell any government agency that."[84] Pressed repeatedly by a judge to "stop playing games," Rosalyn Carr replied that she did not know the father's name, and even if she did, she "would consider it a gross intrusion of [her] privacy to have to give the name": "Even having to be here is a gross intrusion of my privacy."[85] Lawyers for the mothers invoked a "constitutional zone of privacy" violated by the state's intrusive inquiries into women's sexual histories and decision-making autonomy.[86]

The plaintiffs' attorneys also secured the deposition testimony of child-welfare experts to counter the state's contention that involuntary paternity disclosure served children's best interests. The prominent pediatric psychiatrist Albert Solnit, coauthor of the influential *Beyond the Best Interests of the Child*, testified that forcing an unwilling mother to identify her child's father would cause material and psychological harm to the child that would rarely, if ever, be outweighed by the often illusory financial or psychic benefits of a legal paternal relationship. Incarcerating a mother, usually the "primary" or "psychological" parent, could be "catastrophic." Children "cannot escape the devastating impact of the loss of the person who has taken care of them since they were born, helpless as an infant into this world." Solnit also provided support for mothers' assertion that initiating a paternity action would probably destroy any existing positive relationships between fathers and children.[87] Mothers, he argued, should be considered champions, not enemies, of their children's well-being.[88] Solnit testified, "the one who has the care and the responsibility and the loving affectionate bond" with a child should be the one to determine that child's best interests.[89] Like the exclusion of unmarried mothers from employment, the incarceration of mothers for failure to disclose paternity violated the constitutional sanctity of the parent-child relationship.[90]

As in Mrs. Sylvester Smith's and Katie Mae Andrews's cases, in *Roe v. Norton*, the Supreme Court punted on the constitutional questions presented, sending the case back to the lower courts after a new federal regulation preempted the challenged state law. Though the plaintiffs in each of these cases enjoyed some success in persuading courts to invalidate the state laws and policies they challenged, unmarried mothers' expansive visions of sexual citizenship prevailed in none of the litigation. As a result, unmarried mothers often won temporary victories subject to retrenchment when the political winds shifted. And triumphs couched in terms of protecting innocent children from punishment for their parents' sins hardly vindicated the rights of unmarried mothers to sexual privacy, reproductive freedom, and decisional autonomy regarding their families' welfare.

* * *

Plaintiffs in the cases described here shared a vision of sexual citizenship that prized intimate privacy shielded from government intrusion. Their expansive definition of family autonomy included the right of mothers to make decisions they believed to be in their own and their children's best interests. While the perceived opposition between children's and mothers' welfare seemed most acute in cases like *Roe v. Norton*, plaintiffs in *Andrews* and *Fernandez* also challenged, sometimes implicitly, an ideal of normative nonmarital sexuality that privileged adoption by married strangers over care by birth mothers, grandparents, and extended kin networks. In *Roe*, some of the plaintiffs used prevailing ideas about the marital family's superiority against the state, claiming in effect that the paternity-disclosure requirement would frustrate their efforts to establish a married household, either with their child's father or with another man.

Although all of their lawsuits challenged marital supremacy to varying degrees, unmarried mothers and their allies held a range of views about marriage as an institution and an ideal. The long-married Fannie Lou Hamer implied that a marital household with a male breadwinner remained her normative preference; in the absence of marriage, though, mothers deserved access to good jobs at decent wages all the same. Katie Mae Andrews found "the right man" to marry even before her case reached the Supreme Court and, as Mrs. Katie Peacock, enjoyed a thirty-five-year career as a beloved teacher and librarian in Mississippi public schools. Lois Fernandez never married. A venerated community activist, she later recalled that growing up, "You had to find a husband. So you didn't have to work. He had to be the provider. . . . [Other women] were husband-hunting. My thing was to get a job, make some money, and travel and buy me some clothes."[91] Many of the plaintiffs in *Roe v. Norton* questioned, sometimes indirectly, the notion that unmarried mothers should be compelled to rely on their children's fathers for financial support. Mothers' insistence on protecting their personal and sexual privacy and their invocation of the right to choose whether to cooperate with efforts to collect child support translated the welfare-rights movement's most feminist claims into constitutional language.

Fernandez and Andrews may have enjoyed greater success, in part, because their claims helped the state to shift responsibility for children's care and support from the state to private individuals and households. Vanquishing discrimination against nonmarital children and fathers in inheritance laws and opening new jobs to unmarried mothers meant that children and their mothers would have greater access to private resources and be less likely to call on the state for assistance. In contrast, disallowing state coercion of paternity disclosure or implementation of substitute-father laws impeded states' efforts to limit or deter welfare receipt and nonmarital childbearing.

African American feminists confronted not only legal barriers to equality but also a political culture that mourned the perceived decline of (white) male supremacy and resisted efforts that appeared to undermine the legal and economic hegemony of heterosexual marriage. The rising tide of nonmarital childbearing, single-parent households, and women's workforce participation that Moynihan identified in mid-1960s black America increasingly became features of American life more generally. By the early 1970s, many more young, white, unmarried women kept their babies, and unmarried fathers, once written off as hopeless deadbeats, attracted new interest from lawyers and social workers.[92] In 1978, Christopher Lasch lamented that white "middle-class society has become a pale copy of the black ghetto."[93]

By the end of the decade, advocates like Harry Krause, who emphasized child-support enforcement against fathers, had prevailed over those who took a feminist approach that prioritized mothers' sexual freedom and economic independence from men. Just as judicial and legislative decisions that favored plaintiffs in the early welfare-rights and illegitimacy cases emphasized that needy, innocent children should not be made to suffer for their parents' "sins," successful efforts to find private sources of support for those children often invoked not only fiscal responsibility but also children's well-being as primary rationales. Although plaintiffs won some of their cases, the more capacious visions of sexual citizenship advanced by unmarried mothers and their allies in and out of court never found their way into constitutional law or judicial reasoning. As a result, many of unmarried mothers' gains were partial, temporary, and vulnerable to reversal. To this day, mandatory cooperation with paternity determination remains a cornerstone of welfare policy, and unmarried mothers maintain a mixed record in holding employers responsible for discrimination based on sex and marital status. And on the broader question of equality for nonmarital families in the age of marriage equality for same-sex couples, the jury is still out.

NOTES

1. Daniel Patrick Moynihan, *The Negro Family: The Case for National Action* (Washington, DC: US Department of Labor, Office of Policy Planning and Research, March 1965), 8–9, 12, 14, 29–31, 38–40.

2. Serena Mayeri, *Reasoning from Race: Feminism, Law, and the Civil Rights Revolution* (Cambridge, MA: Harvard University Press, 2011), chap. 2.

3. Serena Mayeri, "Historicizing the 'End of Men': The Politics of Reaction(s)," *Boston University Law Review* 93 (2013): 729, 736–37.

4. Margot Canaday, "Heterosexuality as a Legal Regime," in *The Cambridge History of Law in America*, vol. 3, ed. Michael Grossberg and Christopher Tomlins (New York: Cambridge University Press, 2008), 460.

5. Regina G. Kunzel, *Fallen Women, Problem Girls: Unmarried Mothers and the Professionalization of Social Work, 1890–1945* (New Haven, CT: Yale University Press, 1993); Rickie Solinger, *Wake Up Little Susie: Single Pregnancy and Race before Roe v. Wade* (New York: Routledge, 1992).

6. Serena Mayeri, "Foundling Fathers: (Non-)Marriage and Parental Rights in the Age of Equality," *Yale Law Journal* 125 (2016): 2182; Serena Mayeri, "Marital Supremacy and the Constitution of the Nonmarital Family," *California Law Review* 103 (2015): 1277.

7. See Anders Walker, *The Ghost of Jim Crow: How Southern Moderates Used* Brown v. Board of Education *to Stall Civil Rights* (New York: Oxford University Press, 2009).

8. Memorandum from the ACLU on Louisiana Plan for Aid to Dependent Children, Filed with the Department of Health, Education, and Welfare, at 2 (November 22,

1960), Folder 11, Box 32, Norman Dorsen Papers, Tamiment Library and Robert F. Wagner Archive, Elmer Holmes Bobst Library, New York University, New York, NY; quoted in Mayeri, "Marital Supremacy," 1286–87.

9. Mayeri, 1289.
10. Harry D. Krause, *Illegitimacy: Law and Social Policy* (New York: Bobbs-Merrill, 1971), 294–95.
11. Mayeri, "Marital Supremacy," 1292.
12. Petition for Writs of Certiorari and Review to the Court of Appeal, Fourth Circuit, State of Louisiana at 4, Levy v. State (La. 1967) (No. 48518), Folder 14, Box 32, Dorsen Papers; quoted in Mayeri, 1290.
13. Serena Mayeri, "Intersectionality and the Constitution of Family Status," *Constitutional Commentary* 32 (2017): 377.
14. John C. Gray Jr. and David Rudovsky, "The Court Acknowledges the Illegitimate: *Levy v. Louisiana* and *Glona v. American Guarantee & Liability Insurance Co.*," *University of Pennsylvania Law Review* 118 (1969): 1, 16.
15. Levy v. Louisiana, 391 U.S. 69 (1968); King v. Smith, 392 U.S. 309 (1968). For more on *King v. Smith*, see Mayeri, "Marital Supremacy," 1297–1300; Rickie Solinger, "The First Welfare Case: Money, Sex, Marriage, and White Supremacy in Selma, 1966, a Reproductive Justice Analysis," *Journal of Women's History* 22, no. 3 (Fall 2010): 13–38.
16. Weber v. Aetna Casualty, 406 U.S. 164, 175–76 (1972).
17. Mayeri, "Marital Supremacy," 1309–10.
18. Mayeri, "Intersectionality and the Constitution of Family Status."
19. Patricia Tenoso and Aleta Wallach, "A Vindication of the Rights of Unmarried Women and Their Children: An Analysis of the Institution of Illegitimacy, Equal Protection, and the Uniform Parentage Act," *University of Kansas Law Review* 23 (1974): 23, 25.
20. Patricia Tenoso and Aleta Wallach, review of *Illegitimacy: Law and Public Policy*, by Henry Krause, *UCLA Law Review* 19 (1972): 845, 950.
21. Premilla Nadasen shows how black female welfare-rights leaders "went one step further" than "other Black feminists," attempting "to debunk the notion that single motherhood was a sign of cultural deficiency and challeng[ing] the assumption that poor single mothers needed a male breadwinner." These women "rejected traditional notions of female respectability—and all of its class trappings—as a condition for their political demands." They vocally asserted their right to sexual freedom and countered the perception that wage work was the sine qua non of liberation. Nadasen, "Expanding the Boundaries of the Women's Movement: Black Feminism and the Struggle for Welfare Rights," *Feminist Studies* 28, no. 2 (Summer 2002): 281, 296.
22. In another recollection, Fernandez traced her realization to a later point—when she did not receive notification of her son's birth in the mail as her married friends had. Lois Fernandez, "Legitimate," Cowbird, November 26, 2013, http://cowbird.com. See also Fernandez, *Recollections (Part One)* (San Francisco: Blurb, 2016), 49.

23. Pamela J. Smith, "Lois Fernandez: Because of Her There Are No More 'Illegitimate Children,'" *Philadelphia Tribune*, January 2, 1979, 1; Kendall Wilson, "A Mother's War on 'Illegitimate,'" *Philadelphia Tribune*, December 9, 2003.
24. Sarah C. Casey, "He Has No Father . . . That Makes Him 'Different,'" *Philadelphia Inquirer*, December 4, 1971, 6.
25. Casey.
26. Garland L. Thompson, "26 Years of ODUNDE: One Woman's Vision Fulfilled," *Philadelphia Tribune*, June 12, 2001.
27. Wilson, "Mother's War; Smith, "Lois Fernandez."
28. Fernandez and several coplaintiffs had also challenged the exclusion of nonmarital children from workers' compensation benefits after a father's death. "Unwed Mothers Disclose Reasons for Court Fight over Rights of 'Illegitimate' Kids," *Philadelphia Tribune*, March 8, 1975.
29. Plaintiff's Memorandum of Law in Support of Cross-Motion for Summary Judgment at 28, No. 74-2959, Fernandez v. Schapp (E.D. Pa. 1976), in Folder 11, Box 34, Dorsen Papers.
30. Fernandez, "Legitimate."
31. Stephen Franklin, "Mother Wins Fight to End Stigma of Illegitimacy," *Bulletin*, December 10, 1978.
32. Smith, "Lois Fernandez."
33. Wilson, "Mother's War."
34. Casey, "He Has No Father."
35. For more on van den Haag, see Nancy MacLean, *Freedom Is Not Enough: The Opening of the American Workplace* (Cambridge, MA: Harvard University Press, 2006).
36. See, for example, Testimony of Ruby Nell Stancill, Joint Appendix at 142, Drew Municipal School District v. Andrews, 425 U.S. 559 (1976): "The white community just does not approve of such. It is against the community's values. And morally the unwed mother situation is just not an accepted situation." "Question: What effect do you feel it would have on the white students in the Drew schools if unwed parents were allowed to teach? Answer: I think we would lose the ones we have."
37. Joint Appendix, 32–35.
38. Joint Appendix, 39.
39. Joint Appendix, 54.
40. Charles Victor McTeer, personal communication, August 2012.
41. Joint Appendix, *Andrews*, 84.
42. Joint Appendix, 84.
43. Joint Appendix, 88.
44. Joint Appendix, 96.
45. Brief for Respondents, *Andrews*, 5.
46. Brief for Respondents, 47.
47. Joint Appendix, *Andrews*, 94–95.
48. Joint Appendix, 94.

49. Joint Appendix, 104.
50. Joint Appendix, 104.
51. Brief of Respondents, *Andrews*, 54.
52. Brief of Respondents, 55.
53. Brief Amicus Curiae Child Welfare League of America, *Andrews*, 8–9.
54. Joint Appendix, *Andrews*, 109.
55. Joint Appendix, 109.
56. Joint Appendix, 192.
57. Joint Appendix, 195.
58. Joint Appendix, 196.
59. Joint Appendix, 196.
60. Brief of Amicus Curiae ACLU Women's Rights Project and Equal Rights Advo-cates, *Andrews*, 10–11.
61. Brief of Amicus Curiae, 28.
62. Brief of Amicus Curiae, 33.
63. Brief of Amicus Curiae, 46.
64. Brief of Respondents, *Andrews*, 53.
65. Brief of Respondents, 40.
66. Interview with Nancy Stearns, Rhonda Copelon Schoenbrod, and Janice Good-man, *Women's Rights Law Reporter* 1 (1974): 20, 35.
67. Mayeri, "Intersectionality and the Constitution of Family Status," 393.
68. Brief of Respondents, *Andrews*, 53; Stanley v. Illinois, 405 U.S. 645 (1972).
69. Brief of Respondents, *Andrews*, 55–56.
70. Brief of Respondents, 58.
71. Brief Amicus Curiae of Child Welfare League of America, *Andrews*, 11–12.
72. Brief Amicus Curiae, 14–18. There could be "little debate that the public proc-lamation of a child's illegitimacy causes grave damage to his or her reputation." Brief Amicus Curiae, 19.
73. See, for example, Doe v. Shapiro, 302 F. Supp. 761 (D. Conn. 1969).
74. In 1973, a federal regulation explicitly allowed states to withhold benefits from parents who failed to comply, though not from their children.
75. Mayeri, "Intersectionality and the Constitution of Family Status."
76. Brief of the Appellee at 10, Roe v. Norton, 422 U.S. 391 (1975) (No. 73-6033), 1974 WL 186124.
77. Doe v. Norton, 356 F. Supp. 202, 206 n.6 (D. Conn. 1973).
78. Roe felt that the "father's character [was] such that he would be a detrimental influence on his child and on the mother/child relationship." Affidavit, Joint Ap-pendix, *Roe v. Norton*, 37.
79. Affidavit, 41; see also Affidavit, 51.
80. Affidavit, 51.
81. Affidavit, 39. See also Affidavit of "M," Joint Appendix, *Roe v. Norton*, 45; Affidavit of Donna Doe, Joint Appendix, *Roe v. Norton*; Affidavit of Mary Brown, Joint Ap-pendix, *Roe v. Norton*.

82. See Affidavits of Sharon Roe, Linda Loe, Rena Roe, Dorothy Poe, *Roe v. Norton*; Brief for Appellants, *Roe v. Norton*, 43.

83. See Affidavits of Dorothy Poe, "D.," *Roe v. Norton*.

84. Affidavit, Joint Appendix, *Roe v. Norton*, 51.

85. Appendix of Brief of Children of Appellants, *Roe v. Norton*, 14a.

86. Brief for the Appellants, *Roe v. Norton*, 10–11. See also Affidavit of Katherine Lopes, Joint Appendix, *Roe v. Norton*.

87. Deposition of Albert J. Solnit, M.D., Appendix, *Roe v. Norton*, 69.

88. Deposition of Solnit, Appendix, *Roe v. Norton*, 62–71.

89. Deposition of Solnit, 69; Mayeri, "Marital Supremacy," 1321.

90. Brief of Appellants, *Roe v. Norton*, 39–47.

91. Fernandez, *Recollections*, 36.

92. On the legal treatment of unmarried fathers, see Mayeri, "Foundling Fathers."

93. Christopher Lasch, *The Culture of Narcissism: American Life in an Age of Diminishing Expectations* (New York: Norton, 1978), 67; quoted in Natasha Zaretsky, *No Direction Home: The American Family and the Fear of National Decline, 1968–1980* (Chapel Hill: University of North Carolina Press, 2007), 13.

PART IV

Discourses of Desire

11

Restoring "Virginal Conditions" and Reinstating the "Normal"

Episiotomy in 1920

SARAH RODRIGUEZ

In late May 1920, the Chicago obstetrician Joseph DeLee presented a paper called "The Prophylactic Forceps Operation" during the annual meeting of the American Gynecological Society in Chicago. During the talk, he argued for prophylactically performing an episiotomy, using forceps to deliver the baby, and then repairing the episiotomy. DeLee, a prominent physician both locally and nationally, called childbirth "pathogenic" in his talk; because childbirth had the potential to cause disease, laboring women needed attending by the expert hands of a trained physician. Such physicians, by administering interventions like his proposed prophylactic forceps operation, he argued, reduced the likelihood that women would suffer during or after labor from lacerations of the perineum.[1]

DeLee "freely" admitted that his proposal to cut prophylactically was "a revolutionary departure from time-honored custom" of only performing an episiotomy when it seemed indicated during labor. He claimed, however, that his prophylactic forceps operation shortened labor and saved women from "the debilitating effects of suffering in the first stage" of labor as well as from "a prolonged second stage" that could often result in tearing.[2] DeLee proposed to reduce tearing of the perineum (the area between the anus and the vulva / lower vaginal opening), a common occurrence during labor, by instead widening the vaginal opening by cutting it and then using forceps to hasten the delivery of the baby. This cut, an episiotomy, was developed during the eighteenth century, but when DeLee presented his paper, most physicians only performed it during difficult births.[3] DeLee, however, was concerned that many women experienced the damage of perineal tearing during labor, and he believed a physician could mitigate tearing by making a controlled cut. This controlled cut, DeLee asserted, would then be easier for the physician to repair.[4] As one of DeLee's contemporaries noted, it was a "fable to think that torn, jagged wounds heal better, or even as good as clean-cut wounds."[5] Instead, performing a careful repair of an episiotomy, DeLee argued, resulted in a woman "as anatomically perfect as she was before" childbirth: indeed, "virginal conditions," he wrote, "are often restored."[6]

DeLee is considered one of the "titans" of American obstetrics, sometimes even called the father of modern obstetrics, and his talk—published that fall in the inaugural issue of the *American Journal of Obstetrics and Gynecology*—is often credited with the routine uptake of episiotomy in normal labors. A previously rarely used procedure, episiotomy became increasingly common by the 1930s and a standard part of hospitalized birth by the 1950s in the United States.[7] It became one of the means by which physicians moved birth from a normal occurrence to an event that necessitated medical intervention to manage. DeLee is a major figure in the history of American obstetrics, and his 1920 paper is still considered groundbreaking.[8] As the historian Judith Walzer Leavitt pointed out, his prophylactic procedure "represented the new move in the 1920s and 1930s to make obstetrics scientific, systematic, and predictable by putting it under the control of the specialist."[9] Both historians and obstetricians have discussed the historical significance of DeLee's 1920 paper; his comment about the restoration of virginal conditions as one of the benefits of the prophylactic procedure, however, has gone almost entirely unexamined.[10]

By the 1970s, feminists concerned with the medicalization of childbirth in the United States began to critique this kind of approach to childbirth as a means of reinforcing male heterosexual privilege in sex.[11] Writing about episiotomy and its repair in general, and not explicitly about DeLee, the feminist author Suzanne Arms argued in her 1979 book *Immaculate Deception: A New Look at Women and Childbirth*, for example, that doctors believed that following birth, "husbands will be unable to enjoy sexual intercourse with their wives if an episiotomy has not been performed, because the vagina will be permanently enlarged and misshapen."[12] But feminists concerned with the medicalization of childbirth, especially the effects of episiotomy, also worried about women; the British birth activist Sheila Kitzinger addressed concerns about women's sexual pleasure following episiotomy in the early 1980s.[13]

One can read DeLee's comment, however, as Arms did regarding episiotomy generally, as a concern for male sexual pleasure, that such pleasure necessitated a tight vaginal opening and that surgically restoring a smaller vaginal opening was an underlying intention of the procedure both in the 1970s and in the 1920s. DeLee's advice about restoring virginal conditions can be read, then, as medical privileging of heterosexuality— especially for men. To unpack his comment initially a bit more, although Thomas Lathrop Stedman's 1918 medical dictionary defined a virgin as "a woman (or a man) who has never had sexual intercourse," virginity, as Hanne Blank has pointed out in her history of it, has most often been gendered female.[14] Further, when DeLee made this statement, physicians as well as other professionals were also increasingly turning their attention to marital sexual behavior, particularly among white, middle-class couples, and the importance of mutual sexual pleasure within such relationships as an area of concern and intervention.[15] But whereas there was increasing focus on mutual sexual pleasure among married couples by the time DeLee presented this paper, men were still seen as the sexually active members of marriage, with women responding to them, thus reinforcing male responsibility for, and privilege in, marital sexual relations.[16] DeLee's comment needs to be seen within a cultural context that defined virginity as most often female, and if there was recognition of the importance of sexual pleasure to both men and women in marriage within this context, men were regarded as the primary sexual actors.

DeLee's comment is certainly about enabling sex, and of the heterosexual penetrative kind. This enabling, though, existed not just in a context that privileged heterosexuality but also in the context of the clinical practice of restoring normalcy to bodily functions, which here includes not just vaginal intercourse but childbirth as well. Medical theories of the normal body began to accumulate during the late nineteenth century, displacing previously held ideas about a *woman's* bodily norms for ideas about *women's* bodily norms—that is, displacing ideas that focused on the specifics of the individual person in favor of the specifics of the individual condition. Birth disrupted this normal female body, and medical practice called for the restoration of physiological normalcy to the body, here its sexual and reproductive functions. DeLee's comment, then, provides us not just a view of how heterosexuality was medically supported but also an opportunity to see how a physician applied medical theory about bodily norms in clinical practice. This application of theory to practice is something not well covered in the historical literature; as the historian and physician Christopher Crenner has noted, "we understand the concept 'normal' in medicine better in theory than in practice."[17] Closely reading DeLee's comment on restoring a woman to anatomical perfection provides a lens to examine the concept of normal as understood and acted on in clinical practice in the early twentieth century—both as a reflection and reinforcement of normative heterosexual behavior *and* as a reflection and reinforcement of the normative basis for medical interventions on the body—meaning for DeLee to restore a woman's body to its capacity for normative sexual and reproductive functions.[18] And to enable this capacity, a normal female body, per DeLee, was one with an intact perineum.

Perineal Lacerations and the Disruption of the Female Body

To understand why DeLee considered perineal lacerations to be a common and concerning disruption of the body caused by labor, I begin by discussing the state of maternal mortality during the early twentieth century in the United States, a rate considered to be "abysmal," per the historian Jacqueline Wolf. To illustrate, Wolf noted that of the "20 countries that tracked maternal mortality in the early twentieth century, the United States ranked 19th—ahead of only Chile." Even as infant deaths began to decline in the early twentieth century, maternal deaths actually increased between 1900 and 1921: per 100,000, the rate increased from 13.3 to 16.9.[19] Importantly, one of the reasons more women were dying while giving birth was probably a result of women increasingly giving birth in a hospital, exposing them to a higher risk of puerperal infection.[20] As Leavitt and Wolf have shown, middle- and upper-class white women began going to the hospital in the early twentieth century because the pain of childbirth could be managed better in this institutional setting than in their own homes.[21] But, as Leavitt writes, "if pain relief represented the greatest improvement in women's childbirth experiences in the second half of the twentieth century, continuing postpartum problems and puerperal fever illustrated how much of this experience remained unchanged and dangerous."[22] Though the pain could be better managed in the hospital, women incurred risks by going there as well.

Women had long feared dying or being harmed in childbirth, and early twentieth-century evidence, as Leavitt has shown, revealed how "women, rich and poor, suffered in childbirth, died in childbirth, and were at risk of a multitude of health problems that potentially affected their childbearing and may have shortened their lives."[23] Women during the first decades of the twentieth century feared childbirth because of the risk of death but also because women, as Leavitt has observed, "continued to have horrible birth experiences that left them debilitated for the rest of their lives, and continued to fear the event as probably the most dangerous physical trial of their lives."[24]

Women feared death as well as complications following birth if they lived through the experience. As the physician John Williams of Boston noted in 1919, the women whom physicians saw at their clinics showed how childbirth often left women in poor health and unable "to take part in the world as well as before [their] confinement."[25] DeLee himself said during a 1916 talk before his fellow obstetricians that "the procession of women passing through our dispensaries and private consulting rooms, repeating monotonously the statement, 'Doctor, I have never been well since my baby was born,' should draw our attention to the fact that things are not right in obstetric practice." Having looked at his clinical notes "carefully," DeLee found that "the majority of women who have borne children suffer from physical damage due to childbirth."[26] As DeLee presented it here, he also claimed to have learned about the problem of lacerations from women's experiences, with women telling him that they had long-term impairment from their childbirth experiences.[27] For many women, physicians believed, this impairment was the result of a torn perineum.

Physicians considered damaging tears to the perineum during childbirth to be one of the most common maternal morbidities in the late nineteenth and early twentieth centuries, especially for women delivering for the first time. Often these physicians considered it so common as to be a normal occurrence: H. V. Sweringen, a physician in Fort Wayne, Indiana, wrote in 1885, "a woman never lived whose perineum was not more or less lacerated in giving birth to her first child."[28] Similarly, in

1905, the physician Claude Holland, a practitioner in West Virginia, wrote that during his "short experience as a practitioner of medicine," few things had impressed him "more than the great number of perineal lacerations in women."[29] In 1918, the physician Ralph Pomeroy of Brooklyn, New York, stressed, "Every primipara [first-time laboring woman] incurs a permanent modification of the pelvic floor in the course of delivery of her full-term child."[30] In 1920, the New York physician James Harrar estimated that 44 percent of all women giving birth for the first time in the New York Lying-In Hospital experienced perineal lacerations.[31] Walter Levy, a physician in New Orleans, said for physicians doing obstetrics, "the delivery of a primipara without a tear, either anteriorly or posteriorly, is considered quite an accomplishment."[32] Physicians discussing these tears often lamented how they were both common and inevitable.[33] As early as 1876, Montrose Pallen, a professor of gynecology in New York, wrote, "under certain conditions nothing can be done by the obstetrician to prevent the accident."[34]

Although physicians regarded women tearing during childbirth as common—and, some physicians believed, inevitable—there was no clear standard of care for how to deal with the tears.[35] Some physicians advocated leaving the tears to heal on their own. Others called for enabling better natural healing by confining a woman to bed and having her lie on her side with her legs tied together for up to six weeks.[36] Others advocated for sewing up the tears. In 1885, for example, R. B. Bontecou, a physician in Troy, New York, recommended sewing up the tears, writing that he could not understand "how the vulvar fissure is to regain its normal condition unless the surfaces, while raw, are coapted and retained in a surgical manner by sutures or pins."[37] And still others called for the "IMMEDIATE operation for repair" following a birth in which the woman tore.[38]

Despite debate about how to handle lacerations, by the early twentieth century some clinicians claimed that repairing fresh or old perineal lacerations constituted a major part of their obstetric work. Indeed, "modern obstetric surgery" mostly involved "the repair of injuries occurring at labor," especially laceration, stated E. P. Davis, a physician from Philadelphia, in 1916.[39] According to another physician, writing four years later, "Except for curettage [using a tool called a curette to scrape or scoop out tissue in, for example, the uterus], secondary perineorrhaphy [suturing the perineum] is the most frequent operation performed on the child-bearing woman." This secondary surgery occurred most often, he asserted, because the initial repair had not been done adequately.[40]

The effects on women from these commonly acquired perineal lacerations were regarded as very serious within the obstetric literature. In 1885, Bontecou stressed to his peers the importance of not leaving the "accident untreated" and thus leaving women "deformed," as women who were left with tears "suffer a great variety of evils in consequence thereof," evils that were "unnecessary to specify."[41] Although Bontecou felt it "unnecessary to specify" them, the "evils" may have included not just pain during a woman's everyday activities but also perhaps pain during the sexual activity of penetrative intercourse. In 1905, Holland wrote that "no impression has been more profound than that made by the untold suffering endured and the physical and nervous wrecks found as a direct result of perineal lacerations." The injuries also affected the "general constitution" of women, some of whom, he claimed, became invalids following unrepaired lacerations, and he called on his peers to immediately repair any tears directly after birth to prevent a patient from becoming "a semi-invalid who might have been one of health and vigor."[42] Another physician wrote that unrepaired tears resulted in great "suffering" by women and that their "future usefulness in life is often impaired by serious traumatism of the pelvic floor."[43]

One of the "evils" of perineal tears was (and is) pain. Perineal tears can vary in severity. Less serve lacerations consist of a small tear at the entrance to the vagina along the surface of the perineum, and such a tear may be mildly painful or sting, especially when a woman urinates. More serious tears can extend from the vaginal entrance into the muscle of the perineum, and the most serious tears involve the vaginal entrance, the muscle of the perineum, and/or the entrance of the anus. And while all tears may be painful, complications from a tear into the anal opening can include leakage of feces or fecal incontinence.[44] Severe tears can also lead to rectovaginal fistulas (a hole between the vagina and the anus), resulting in feces passing through the vagina—with the possible attending infection complications.[45]

In order to prevent women from experiencing pain—and, in the less common but the most serious form of tearing, infection, smell, and incontinence—from lacerations, physicians in the late nineteenth century began considering how tears occurred, how to repair them, and how they could prevent them from even occurring.[46] However, what DeLee proposed to his obstetrician peers with his prophylactic forceps operation was new to the specialty: to cut *before* an indication to do so presented. But despite such a proposal being new to obstetrics, his preemptive operation, as Leavitt argues, "was compatible with many other contemporaneous attempts to combine medical practice and prevention."[47] DeLee agreed with his peers who asserted the commonness of lacerations and of the problems that such lacerations inflicted. And just as importantly, or perhaps more importantly, he then called for obstetricians to consider such lacerations as not needing to occur, as being preventable. DeLee argued for making a controlled cut with the belief it would be less invasive than a tear, and thus the repair would be easier to make. This procedure would then provide the physician with the best opportunity to restore the disrupted body to normal following childbirth.

Prophylactically Saving the Perineum

In DeLee's 1920 paper, he set up his argument for preventive intervention using episiotomy and forceps by asserting that labor should no longer be considered "a normal function." DeLee (in)famously compared childbirth to falling on a pitchfork—with the handle driven through the perineum, asserting that no one would consider that normal—to provide an analogy for why childbirth should not be considered normal, as it similarly drives a baby through the pelvic floor. As DeLee argued, "in both cases, the cause of damage, the fall on the pitchfork, and the crushing of the floor, is pathogenic, that is disease producing, and in the same sense labor is pathogenic, disease producing, and anything pathogenic is pathologic or abnormal." Perhaps, he challenged his peers, they considered it normal that women should suffer and "be used up in the process of reproduction," and lacerations, too, were "natural to labor and therefore normal." If they accepted this view, DeLee continued, "I have no grounds to stand on." But if they believed "that a woman after delivery should be healthy" and "as anatomically perfect as she was before," then, he argued, "you will have to agree with me that labor is pathogenic, because experience has proved such ideal results exceedingly rare."[48]

DeLee was by no means the first to argue in favor of episiotomy.[49] Although physicians began using the procedure during the eighteenth century, it was only in the 1870s, when the Philadelphia physician Anna Broomall introduced episiotomy at the Women's Hospital, that American physicians began to show interest in the procedure.[50] Broomall noted that she recognized the objections and appreciated the risks of the procedure. However, she considered episiotomy "a safe and justifiable procedure, when the perineum is threatened"; and "where the danger of deep laceration is imminent," she thought it the "proper and indispensable" means of "diverting the risks of labor from what may possibly be a horrid permanent mutilation to a harmless temporary lesion."[51] Other physicians similarly advocated for making the cut in laboring women when it seemed that a tear was imminent. The physician Charles Child wrote in 1919, "Though many good authorities give episiotomy a low rating, I warmly approve of it, and can heartily recommend it as a most valuable operation for the general practitioner as well as specialist."[52] Others, however, opposed the use of episiotomy—or at least did not feel the need to perform it. During a 1904 symposium on injuries of the perineum, the physician Edwin Cragin asserted that "the indications for [performing an episiotomy] are very seldom, if ever, present."[53] Henry Thomas, a physician from Ohio, stated during a similar discussion in 1919 among his fellow obstetricians, "it is seldom necessary to cut the parts." Instead, he thought physicians should pay attention to the laboring woman's condition.[54] As the New York physician James Harrar, an episiotomy proponent, noted in 1919, "there is a conflict of opinion" regarding the benefits of performing an episiotomy.[55]

By the time DeLee proposed his prophylactic forceps operation in May 1920 as a means of preventing lacerations and of best enabling a physician to return a perineum to normal physiological function, there had already been considerable disagreement regarding when—or if— to perform an episiotomy for decades. DeLee presented his paper before other physicians, and a few, such as the Brooklyn physician John Polak, were "convinced that episiotomy is a prophylactic procedure" and agreed with DeLee.[56] For the most part, however, those in attendance reacted with hostility—although not (as far as what was publicly recorded) to DeLee's comment regarding restoring virginal conditions.[57] Rather, the disagreement concerned an intervention being made without an indication of need. John Whitridge Williams, equally as prominent an obstetrician as DeLee, worried that if DeLee's "practice were to become general and widely adopted, women would be worse off eventually than had their labors been conducted by midwives."[58] Williams was not the only one to express caution regarding DeLee's suggestion for routine intervention. According to Leavitt, DeLee "was looking for preventive techniques to save women before they suffered damage during labor and delivery; his fellow obstetricians felt more comfortable acting to obvert a dangerous situation once it presented."[59] In contrast to his peers—who believed in waiting to see if an intervention was needed before intervening—DeLee argued that it was better to prevent the laceration than deal with it after it occurred. Although DeLee stated that he had sewn "up thousands of lacerations after delivery," he had never been "fully satisfied" with the results of the repair.[60] A controlled cut enabled a more satisfactory repair and, DeLee asserted, greater likelihood of returning a woman's disrupted body to normal function.

Restoring Normality to the Perineum

Physicians, both those who agreed and those who disagreed with DeLee regarding the clinical usefulness of an episiotomy, regarded perineal tears as a significant maternal morbidity, and not just because of the pain such tears caused. Medical concern also centered on the functionality of the perineum, since labor changed the perineum: "where lacerations have occurred, gaping of the parts begins as soon as the muscles have regained their tone."[61] Others concurred, writing that lacerations could result in a "relaxed perineum."[62] These "gaping parts," the result of tearing, were considered difficult to repair.

For DeLee, a clean cut made by a physician would be easier to repair than lacerations, and, despite the tepid response at best to his 1920 paper by the physicians in the audience, he was not the only one to regard this as true. Harrar noted that by performing an episiotomy, "we avoid a jagged or transverse slitting, or butterfly tear, by making a single straight clean-cut incision."[63] Similarly, Pomeroy stressed the following in 1918: "the natural and usual tear of the perineal structure is asymmetrical in detail, wandering indecisively on one side or other of the median line."[64] Others noted that the repair of a laceration—"far more complex" than a cut—meant that the "restoration of the perineum to its original integrity after a laceration is a by no means simple operation."[65]

The purpose, then, of avoiding lacerations by making a controlled cut was to better enable the satisfactory repair of the perineum and to restore the perineum following labor to "its original integrity." Some physicians writing about lacerations of the perineum noted the importance of restoring the woman to her "original condition," as the Cincinnati physician William Porter wrote in 1920. The physician Henry Bernstein expressed a similar idea in 1918: "no lacerated perineum unaided and of its own accord ever can be restored to its original intact condition."[66] As the sociologist Ian Graham notes in his analysis of how episiotomy became routinized in the twentieth century, physicians who argued for the uptake of the procedure contended that it returned the perineum to its "prepregnancy state."[67] This intention, then, was what restoring the perineum to normal meant: as Pomeroy wrote in 1918, following an episiotomy and repair, "when healed the conditions reproduce nullipara" (a woman who has never given birth).[68] As DeLee said in 1920, his prophylactic procedure would result in a woman "as anatomically perfect as she was before" labor. Episiotomy and its repair, physicians asserted, restored a woman to normal, and normal was a perineum as it existed before pregnancy; pregnancy was thus seen as disrupting the normal body, leaving not just tears but also "gaping parts." An implication of such a view—perhaps unintended, perhaps not, given the desire by some physicians to medicalize birth—is that pregnancy, then, is an *abnormal* state. Regardless, one needs to place this conceptualization within larger ideas of a normally functioning body and the importance of the restoration of "normality" as an objective of medical practice.

Normality in Medicine

Standard bodily norms as a medical concept originated in the nineteenth century.[69] For much of the nineteenth century, medical practice had incorporated all aspects of a specific person's life into explaining his or her presenting condition—family history, the season, where the person lived. All of the idiosyncrasies of a person, as Charles Rosenberg argued, mattered in determining a condition and a treatment. In such an environment, disease specificity played little role. But during the nineteenth century, medical ideas about how to understand, and thus treat, the body changed, moving from a theory of medicine that necessitated treating the individual specificities of a patient to one influenced by the standardization of conditions and a uniformity of treating patients with specific conditions. In other words, within medicine the individual was no longer unique and thus requiring a unique therapy. Rather, the diseases were now unique, and the specific disease—regardless of who had it—was treated in the same manner.[70] Supporting this change, clinical practice moved from an emphasis on understanding an *individual* patient's body to a professional commitment to understanding a *standard* body—understood regardless of the individual attributes of the patient. Importantly, standard (or normal) bodies were seen (and tacitly assumed) to be white, increasingly so during the early twentieth century.[71]

Theorists looking at this change have argued that, during the nineteenth century, medicine began to search for and create uniformity within clinical understandings of the body and, thus, of the clinical care of bodies. Nineteenth-century research in physiology—the study of how living beings function—radically changed how physicians understood the body, moving the view of the body from a focus on its structure to a focus on its functions.[72] Physiology became a separate discipline during the late nineteenth century, and it grew in importance to clinical practice.[73] This increased role of physiology in medicine meant that the functions of the body became increasingly relevant. Notably, this attention to physiology was part of a growing belief that clinical treatment should be based on a universal understanding of bodies.[74] This claim of the universality of bodies for therapeutics relied on an understanding, then, of how "normal" bodies functioned.

The philosophers Michel Foucault and Georges Canguilhem argued that nineteenth-century medicine—as a discipline—began distinguishing between the normal and the pathological. And the historian Mary Tiles has noted, in her discussion of these two philosophers, how physicians became "interested in diagnosis and cure, where curing is taken to mean restoring a function or an organism to the norm from which it has deviated."[75] This restoration of the body to normal functions following a deviation became the particular purview of surgery.[76] Surgery especially embraced physiological thinking, and this affected its practice, as surgeons very consciously began thinking of the body in terms of function and of restoring the patient to normal functioning.[77] Physiological conceptions of how the body worked, and of how the body could be repaired, were the impetus for surgical interventions.[78] The restoration of normality was a fundamental goal within medicine generally, and the emphasis on the restoration of bodies to normal functioning was particularly strong within surgery.

Reinstating the Normal Function of Vaginal Intercourse

What, then, constituted a normally functioning perineum? Because some physicians believed that the perineum included the opening of the vagina, a "normally functioning perineum" would mean that the vaginal opening had not succumbed to "relaxation" or become "stretched to the extent that it will not regain its normal tone."[79] Labor risked altering the perineum from normal, through either tearing or stretching. A perineum with a "normal tone" was, as the earlier comments by physicians asserted, a prepregnancy perineum, one that had not been stretched or torn as a result of labor. Dale Martin, a San Francisco physician, wrote that a "careful restoration of the urogenital septum restores the non-parous [a woman who has not given birth] appearance of the vulva and prevents a gaping introitus," a gaping of the entrance to the vagina.[80] There are two functional implications regarding the presentation of a relaxed, stretched, and/or torn perineum: childbirth and vaginal intercourse. First, I look at the restoration of the capacity for vaginal intercourse as a medically envisioned normal function of the female body.

As Martin noted, since the perineum involves the vaginal opening, vaginal birth itself—whether tearing occurred or not—alters the perineum, implied perhaps when physicians like Martin discussed the "gaping parts" or relaxed "tone" of the area. Although, for the most part, the implications for vaginal intercourse were only implied, some doctors, such as the St. Louis physician Francis Reder in 1919, explicitly connected perineal stretching and tearing to sexual intercourse: "What we want is a perineum that fulfills the function of former days. It is a very common thing to have a woman come to us suffering every time she has sexual intercourse because nature has not been imitated. The parts have

not been restored as an elastic, small, perineal body, but there is a perineal body about three times as big as nature made it."[81] A perineum, per
Reder, needed to be restored to the "function of former days" to prevent
a woman from "suffering every time she has sexual intercourse"—an
indication that physicians at the time knew (here suggested by Reder as
a knowledge gained from his female patients) that in addition to being
generally painful, a torn perineum made penetrative vaginal sex especially painful.[82] Vaginal intercourse thus resulted in "suffering." Whereas
no formal studies were conducted (or at least published) during this
time regarding painful intercourse following perineal tearing, recent
studies have found that many women find intercourse painful following
childbirth and that perineal damage—from either tearing or an episiotomy—is associated with high rates of postnatal dyspareunia, meaning
difficult or painful intercourse.[83] Although it is difficult to read clinical
information backward, one can, I think, safely assume that women in
1920 similarly found postchildbirth intercourse sometimes painful—and
that lacerations were often a reason; as Reder wrote, it was a "very common thing to have a woman come to us suffering every time she has
sexual intercourse." Presumably, Reder was not the only physician who
knew this was one of the reasons women complained about lacerations:
intercourse could hurt postbirth, especially if there had been tearing.

    But in addition to acknowledging pain from vaginal intercourse, Re-
der's comments regarding the need to restore the function of former
days necessitates the restoration of an "elastic, small, perineal body." The
perineum, and, importantly, the entry of the vagina, was, according to
Reder, looser and larger than prior to birth. The male partner, one assumes, would be sexually affected by this change, based on the idea that
a penis needs to have friction within the vagina for sexual stimulation
and that the fit between vagina and penis must be tight for this friction to occur. This idea about the importance of a tight vagina is one of
those concepts with wide cultural circulation within the United States
but rarely formally recorded, so tracing its historical path and meaning
is difficult. That said, that it existed in concept during the first decades
of the twentieth century can be seen from a comment by one of the
New York gynecologist Robert L. Dickinson's patients, who told him
that following childbirth, "her husband complains that she is completely
relaxed," that she is "too large and therefore [he] can have no gratifica-

tion."[84] The size of the vaginal opening had been enlarged from child-birth to a size larger than "nature made it." Childbirth disrupted the normal state of the perineum—and thus disrupted vaginal intercourse, in particular, perhaps, for men.

These descriptions of the postpartum perineum, then, suggest that what was considered the normal state of the perineum was its state *before* childbirth. DeLee's 1920 comment that a benefit of episiotomy and its repair was the restoration of virginal conditions seems to suggest that a virginal perineum/vagina was normal. According to the 1918 edition of Stedman's *A Practical Medical Dictionary*, "normal" was the "typical, usual, healthy, according to the rule or standard."[85] This definition reveals a tension that existed regarding the idea of the normal in medicine: Was normal an existing state or an ideal one? For "normal" could also mean the ideal, or "corresponding to the perfect type in all respects," per the first definition of "normal" from the 1915 *Appleton's Medical Dictionary*.[86] So, did the restoration of normal function mean returning the body to the average, to the typical, or did it mean intervening to improve on the function of the body, to create an ideal body?[87] As the historian Ian Hacking puts it, normal can be used to "say how things are, but also to say how things ought to be." The "magic of the word," according to Hacking, is that it can be used to "do both things at once."[88] The tension between the normal and the ideal can be seen here in DeLee: Was a normal female perineum one that had never experienced birth and an ideal perineum one that had never experienced sexual intercourse? Or, per Hacking, was it both? DeLee's comments that an episiotomy could restore "virginal conditions" suggest restoring the female body to a normal state, a virginal state, though it is not clear whether such a state was how it was or how it ought to be. Regardless of whether the normal, virginal perineum was the typical or ideal one, the idea of tightness is central to what constitutes a virginal vagina; it is what supposedly makes a virginal vagina different from a vagina that has experienced penetrative intercourse.[89] It has not been stretched or, less delicately put, used.

The gynecologist Robert L. Dickinson—who was president of the American Gynecological Society when DeLee presented his paper—had a concern regarding his female patients' sexual lives; he regarded mutual sexual enjoyment to be a fundamental base of solid, happy marriages.[90] As part of this concern, Dickinson measured the sizes of his female patients' vaginas in the 1920s in order to ensure the possibility of vaginal intercourse; he did not publish this information until later. Dickinson noted the average sizes of 109 women he considered to be a "sample." The vaginas of women he labeled as "virgin" allowed "one finger" (indeed, Dickinson called the admittance of only one finger "verifiable virginity"), indicating a greater degree of tightness especially at the vaginal entrance area, the perineum.[91] Married women who had not yet borne children—but who presumably had engaged in sex with their husbands—allowed "two full fingers."[92] Such measurements reflected, Dickinson wrote, "the increased elasticity and size of the vagina after marriage," indicating the women's vaginas had been stretched as a result of penetrative sex.[93] A woman who had given birth showed the greatest widening of all, allowing "three fingers."[94]

Dickinson's measurements do not reflect the capacity of the vagina, as an organ, to swell and tighten. Regardless, his data supported the idea that the vagina changed depending not just on maternal experience but also on sexual activity and that both reduced the tightness of the organ. He believed his measurements reflected a measurable difference among vaginas, a difference between an organ that had not engaged in intercourse and one that had, as well as one that had also given birth—that a vagina could be differentiated and routinized as normal and fall into one of these categories.[95] These measurements supported the clinical idea of different normal vaginas, and they supported the contention that there was a change, or disruption, of the female body because of birth or sexual activity.

The purpose of the intervention that DeLee advocated—both the episiotomy and its repair—was meant to restore a disrupted perineum, especially the vaginal entrance, to the typical female body, or possibly to the ideal body, for the function of normal sex.[96] It was meant, then, to ensure the capacity to have penetrative, vaginal sex—essentially to restore the capacity of the organ's ability to engage a penis—by restoring tone/tightness of the perineum, the structural functionality of the vagina.[97] For when DeLee was arguing for his prophylactic forceps operation in 1920, normal sexual behavior most often meant vaginal penetrative intercourse between a man and a woman.[98]

Although the term "heterosexual" was perhaps not being widely used within medical discourse in 1920—the first indexed use of the word in the *American Journal of Obstetrics and Gynecology*, for example, was not until 1926—the idea of heterosexuality as normal sexual behavior certainly existed.[99] To illustrate, in a 1925 medical dictionary, heterosexuality was defined as "love or sexual desire toward persons of the opposite sex," while homosexuality was defined as "sexual perversion toward those of the same sex," with "perversion" defined as "a turning from what is right or normal."[100] Heterosexual behavior was seen as medically normal by the early 1920s, then, and such views would only continue and deepen. The nurse and birth-control advocate Margaret Sanger, for example, wrote in her 1926 book *Happiness in Marriage*, "any *normal* woman may be enabled to share with her husband the fullest joy of sex communication."[101] For Sanger and others, a normal woman could, and presumably would (or was at least expected to) experience pleasure during intercourse with her husband—and, as other historians have shown, this expectation became more paramount during this decade.[102]

Although some physicians argued that because masturbation was a "rather average experience among women," women's "auto-erotic practices," so long as they were "moderate," "may be called a normal sex experience," Sanger was far from the only medically trained person of this time who, writing about sex, considered heterosexual, vaginal sex to constitute what was normal.[103] To illustrate, the physician Gilbert Hamilton gathered information from one hundred married men and one hundred married women—fifty-five of whom were married to each other—about marital life, including their sexual lives, in the 1920s.[104] But to be enrolled, "of course, the two hundred had to be *normal men and women*," meaning they engaged in, or desired to engage in, penetrative intercourse with their spouse, a member of the opposite sex.[105] DeLee's proposal for using episiotomy sought to surgically restore a woman's body to "normal" (or ideal) function, that being vaginal sex. And his framing of why one needed to do so also suggests how physicians—or at least this particular physician—sought to apply the concept of normal to their clinical practice.

The Function of the Perineum

DeLee's proposal to prevent lacerations by making and then repairing a surgical cut was intended to restore the female body to functional normality. The point I want to emphasize is that DeLee's call for the use of episiotomy is a story not just about the reflection and reinforcement of heterosexual norms but also about norms within clinical medicine about restoring a body that had been disrupted. DeLee saw the female body as disrupted by childbirth, a disruption that included the woman's capacity to engage in penetrative vaginal sexual intercourse with her husband. Her body, specifically her perineum and vaginal opening, needed restoration to normal, a prepregnancy state, or even perhaps to an ideal one, a preintercourse state, because vaginal, penetrative sex was not the only functional disruption that childbirth rendered on the female body: perineal lacerations also potentially disrupted the function of subsequent labors. An unrepaired torn perineum, or an imperfectly repaired perineum, following childbirth lacerations could have negative effects on future births. As a 1926 article in the *American Journal of Obstetrics and Gynecology* noted, "a badly repaired perineum is predisposed to laceration on subsequent deliveries" because the perineum would be unable to support the pressure of the delivering infant's head.[106] Unlike Dickinson, who largely stopped obstetrical work in 1910 to focus on select gynecological concerns, including his patients' sexual concerns, DeLee was an obstetrician: very often, as Judith Leavitt has pointed out, his care for women revolved around their pregnancies.[107] The restoration of "normal" functionality to the perineum might have been defined differently by obstetricians and gynecologists. DeLee's idea, then, of what a normally functioning perineum meant could have been one able to support subsequent pregnancies.

We do not know specifically what DeLee intended by making his comment. Indeed, although DeLee spoke and wrote about episiotomy both before and after his seminal 1920 paper, he only seems to have mentioned the restoration of virginal conditions as a benefit one other time—at least in a publicly accessible forum.[108] But when considering his comment that an episiotomy and its repair could restore virginal conditions as one framed by his practice of obstetrics, perhaps we should see it as about the medically envisioned normal functions of the female perineum: vaginal intercourse but, just as importantly, childbirth. Virginity, per a 1918 medical dictionary, did not just define a woman who had never had sexual intercourse; its second definition was "fresh, unused, uncontaminated."[109] DeLee's comment about virginal conditions can perhaps be read, then, as about restoring the female perineum's sexual function *and* birth function to a state before either vaginal intercourse *or* vaginal birth disrupted it: restoring the female body to its original—its fresh, its unused, its uncontaminated—condition.

NOTES

1. Joseph B. DeLee, "The Prophylactic Forceps Operation," *American Journal of Obstetrics and Gynecology* 1 (1920): 34–44 (quotation on 41).
2. DeLee, 43.
3. Ian D. Graham, "The Episiotomy Crusade" (PhD diss., McGill University, 1994).
4. DeLee, "Prophylactic Forceps Operation."
5. DeLee also discussed as a reason to use episiotomy that it saved "babies' brains from injuries and from the immediate and remote effects of prolonged compression." DeLee, 41, 43. Charles J. Rothschild, "Episiotomy, a Perineal Safety Measure," *Journal of the Indiana State Medical Association*, September 1915, 418.
6. DeLee, "Prophylactic Forceps Operation," 41, 43.
7. In 1974, the obstetrician D. N. Danforth, then the president of the American Gynecological Society, called DeLee and John Whitridge Williams titans. Danforth, "Contemporary Titans: Joseph Bolivar DeLee and John Whitridge Williams," *American Journal of Obstetrics and Gynecology* 120, no. 5 (November 1, 1974), 577–88. The historian Jacqueline Wolf refers to DeLee as the father of modern obstetrics in "Saving Babies and Mothers: Pioneering Efforts to Decrease Infant and Maternal Mortality," in *Silent Victories: The History and Practice of Public Health in Twentieth Century America*, ed. John W. Ward and Christian Warren (New York: Oxford University Press, 2007), 135–60; and in *Deliver Me from Pain: Anesthesia and Birth in America* (Baltimore: Johns Hopkins University Press, 2009), 84. In addition, the historians Judith Walzer Leavitt and Wendy Kline have called him "one of the most influential obstetricians during the first half of the twentieth century." Leavitt, "Joseph B. DeLee and the Practice of Preventive Obstetrics," *American Journal of Public Health* 78, no. 10 (1986): 1353–60; Kline, "Back to Bed: From Hospital to Home Obstetrics in the City of Chicago," *Journal of the History of Medicine and Allied Sciences* 73, no. 1 (2018): 1–23 (quotation on 3). Harold Speert, an obstetrician who wrote about his specialty's history, called him "one of America's most distinguished obstetricians." Speert, *Obstetric and Gynecologic Milestones: Essays in Eponymy* (New York: Macmillan, 1958), 516. DeLee's influence was recognized outside the United States as well: he was called the "world's foremost obstetrician" in his obituary in the *British Medical Journal*. M.P.H., "Joseph B. DeLee, M.D.," *British Medical Journal*, June 6, 1942, 711. On the rise of the routine use of episiotomy, see Graham, "Episiotomy Crusade"; and Ian D. Graham, "Processes of Change in Obstetrics: A Cross-National Case-Study of Episiotomy," *Health* 2, no. 4 (1998): 403–33; as well as David Banta and Stephen B. Thacker, "The Risks and Benefits of Episiotomy: A Review," *Birth* 9, no. 1

(Spring 1982): 25–30. Alongside DeLee's 1920 paper, Banta and Thacker as well as others also often cite Ralph H. Pomeroy's 1918 paper as motivating obstetricians to routinely employ episiotomy. Pomeroy, "Shall We Cut and Reconstruct the Perineum for Every Primipara?," *American Journal of Obstetrics and Diseases of Women and Children* 78 (1918): 211–20. DeLee, however, never intended for this procedure to be used routinely, but, as Carolyn Herbst Lewis noted, his peers took his statements "as a recommendation to employ forceps" and, thus, episiotomy "as standard practice." Lewis, "The Gospel of Good Obstetrics: Joseph Bolivar DeLee's Vision for Childbirth in the United States," *Social History of Medicine* 29, no. 1 (2015): 113. The routine use of episiotomy would continue through the twentieth century, though rates would start to decline as the century came to a close. A systematic review published in 2005, however, showed few benefits in routinely making this cut, and in 2006, the American College of Obstetricians and Gynecologists issued guidelines stating that it should no longer be uniformly performed. Katherine Hartmann, Meera Viswanathan, Rachel Palmieri, Gerald Gartlehner, John Thorp Jr., and Kathleen N. Lohr, "Outcomes of Routine Episiotomy: A Systematic Review," *JAMA* 293 (2005): 2141–48. "Episiotomy: Clinical Management Guidelines for Obstetrician-Gynecologists," ACOG Practice Bulletin 71, *Obstetrics and Gynecology* 107, no. 4 (April 2006): 957–62.

8. Leavitt, "Joseph B. DeLee." Danforth called it a "classic paper." Danforth, "Contemporary Titans," 581.

9. As Leavitt further notes, this move was made as other specialties in medicine were also developing. Judith Walzer Leavitt, *Brought to Bed: Childbearing in America, 1750 to 1950* (New York: Oxford University Press, 1986), 180.

10. For example, Richard J. Wertz and Dorothy C. Wertz, in their history of childbirth in America, just note that he lists this as one of the reasons to perform it but do not discuss it further. Wertz and Wertz, *Lying-In: A History of Childbirth in America* (New York: Schocken Books, 1979), 142. Similarly, Graham lists DeLee's claim that his procedure would restore virginal conditions but then does not discuss what he meant. Graham, "Episiotomy Crusade," 68. Margarete Sandelowski also notes that DeLee provided this as a reason to perform episiotomy but does not discuss beyond noting. Sandelowski, *Pain, Pleasure, and American Childbirth: From the Twilight Sleep to the Read Method, 1914–1960* (Westport, CT: Greenwood, 1984), 41. Others, such as the the physician Harold Speert, do not mention this as one of the reasons DeLee gave for performing an episiotomy. Speert, *Obstetrics and Gynecology in America: A History* (Chicago: American College of Obstetricians and Gynecologists, 1980), 187–88. In a brief discussion of DeLee's article, Jacqueline Wolf also does not bring this up as one of the reasons DeLee recommended an episiotomy. Wolf, *Deliver Me from Pain*, 84.

11. In the book *A Bun in the Oven*, the sociologist Barbara Katz Rothman notes that DeLee gave the potential of restoring virginal conditions as a reason but does not consider the historical context of the comment—though she does briefly ponder whether it was the "forerunner of our modern 'cosmetic surgery' business for

vaginas," indicating a possible connection she sees to contemporary vaginal tightening surgeries. Rothman, *A Bun in the Oven: How the Food and Birth Movements Resist Industrialization* (New York: NYU Press, 2016), 91. On vaginal tightening surgeries in the early twenty-first century, see Virginia Braun, "Female Genital Cosmetic Surgery: A Critical Review of Current Knowledge and Contemporary Debates," *Journal of Women's Health* 19 (2010): 1393–407.

12. Suzanne Arms, *Immaculate Deception: A New Look at Women and Childbirth* (New York: Bantam Books, 1979), 100–101.

13. Sheila Kitzinger, *Some Women's Experiences of Episiotomy* (London: National Childbirth Trust, 1981).

14. Thomas Lathrop Stedman, *A Practical Medical Dictionary*, 5th ed., rev. (New York: William Wood, 1918), 1086; Hanne Blank, *Virgin: The Untouched History* (New York: Bloomsbury, 2007).

15. Kristin Celello, *Making Marriage Work: A History of Marriage and Divorce in the Twentieth Century* (Chapel Hill: University of North Carolina Press, 2009); Christina Simmons, *Making Marriage Modern: Women's Sexuality from the Progressive Era to World War II* (New York: Oxford University Press, 2009); Jessamyn Neuhaus, "The Importance of Being Orgasmic: Sexuality, Gender, and Marital Sex Manuals in the United States, 1920–1963," *Journal of the History of Sexuality* 9 (2000): 447–73.

16. Kevin White, *The First Sexual Revolution: The Emergence of Male Heterosexuality in Modern America* (New York: New York University Press, 1993); Simmons, *Making Marriage Modern*.

17. Christopher Crenner, "Race and Laboratory Norms: The Critical Insight of Julian Herman Lewis (1891–1989)," *Isis* 105 (2014): 477–78.

18. DeLee's recommendation should also be seen alongside other larger changes within medical practice occurring during this time: the work of physicians to consolidate medical practice around allopathic medicine, the growth of specialization, the growth of ideas from both within and outside medicine about standardization, and the changing economics of the practice of medicine. See Paul Starr, *The Social Transformation of American Medicine* (New York: Basic Books, 1984).

19. Wolf, "Saving Babies and Mothers," 146.

20. Leavitt, *Brought to Bed*, 182–83.

21. Leavitt; Wolf, *Deliver Me from Pain*.

22. Leavitt, *Brought to Bed*, 142.

23. Leavitt, 70. Leavitt's study, however, focused on middle- and upper-class (presumably also white) women, not because she thought these groups representational for all women but because she wanted to focus on women's experiences, and the voices of these women were the ones historically available. Leavitt, 8.

24. Leavitt, *Brought to Bed*, 142.

25. John T. Williams, "Present Day Problems in Obstetrics," *Modern Medicine* 1, no. 8 (December 1919): 731.

26. Joseph B. DeLee, "Meddlesome Midwifery in Renaissance," *JAMA* 68, no. 16 (October 14, 1916): 1126.

27. Sally Wilde and Geoffrey Hirst, in their article exploring surgery during DeLee's time, note that surgeons learned from both the laboratory and the bodies on their operating tables: they were "instructed by their interactions with the bodies of the people on the operating table." Here, Wilde and Hirst focus on surgeons learning from the *bodies* of their patients, but I am extending their point to suggest DeLee also learned from his patients' *experiences* of their bodies. Wilde and Hirst, "Learning from Mistakes: Early Twentieth-Century Surgical Practice," *Journal of the History of Medicine and Allied Sciences* 64, no. 1 (2008): 42.

28. H. V. Sweringen, "Laceration of the Female Perineum," *JAMA*, August 15, 1885, 176.

29. Claude L. Holland, "Duty of Physician to Patients with Perineal Lacerations," *JAMA*, July 29, 1905, 326–27.

30. Pomeroy, "Shall We Cut," 201.

31. James A. Harrar, "Median Episiotomy in Primiparous Labors," *American Journal of Obstetrics* 80 (1919): 705.

32. Walter E. Levy, "Prophylactic Incisions of the Vaginal Outlet during Labor," *New Orleans Medical and Surgical Journal* 72 (1919–20): 692.

33. Christine Kettle and Khaled M. K. Ismail, "Perineal Trauma: A Historical and International Perspective," in *Perineal Trauma at Childbirth*, ed. Ismail (Cham, Switzerland: Springer, 2016), 1–15.

34. Montrose A. Pallen, "Perineal Lacerations," *New York Medical Journal* 23 (1876): 466. Physicians did try to do so, however. The British physician J. W. Ballantyne noted that there were three "methods of trying to save the perineum from lacerations." First was to leave the area alone and let nature take its course; the second was at "the other extreme of obstetric practice," and that was to perform an episiotomy; and the third was, he believed, "midway" between these two options, and that was "various plans of protecting, preserving, guarding, supporting, saving, or simply caring for the structures in question." Ballantyne, "The Protection of the Perineum in Labor," *Edinburgh Medical Journal* 23 (1919): 407, 408, 411. Many women, Wertz and Wertz note in their history of childbirth, tore during hospital births, and an increasing number of women were delivering in the hospital. Though observing this, obstetricians did not ask whether the tears were the result of "nature or from hospital practice, which often immobilized a woman on her back with legs raised in stirrups." One technique may have necessitated the other, they argued. Wertz and Wertz, *Lying-In*, 143.

35. Importantly, not all physicians agreed that such tears were inevitable: in 1882, the obstetrician Theophilus Parvin wrote about the difficulty in predicting when lacerations may occur, and even when some of his peers believed them to be inevitable, women ended up not tearing. Graham, "Processes of Change in Obstetrics," 412.

36. Kettle and Ismail, "Perineal Trauma"; Pallen, "Perineal Lacerations."

37. R. B. Bontecou, "Lacerations of the Perineum," *JAMA*, August 29, 1885, 248.
38. William B. Dewees, "Relaxation and Management of the Perineum during Parturition," *JAMA*, December 7, 1889, 845 (emphasis in the original).
39. "Abstract of Discussion on Papers of Drs. Davis and DeLee," *JAMA* 68, no. 16 (October 14, 1916), 1129.
40. William D. Porter, "A Method of Placing Sutures in Immediate Repair of the Perineum," *Transactions of Obstetrics and Gynecology* 32 (1920): 113.
41. Bontecou, "Lacerations of the Perineum," 248.
42. Holland, "Duty of Physician to Patients," 326–27.
43. Charles G. Child, "Episeotomy [*sic*]: Its Relation to the Proper Conduct of the Perineal Stage of Labor," *Medical Record*, July 26, 1919, 142.
44. Mayo Clinic, "Vaginal Tears in Childbirth," March 6, 2018, www.mayoclinic.org.
45. Fistulas are less common in the United States now than they would have been in DeLee's time. "Managing Complications of Perineal Lacerations," *Contemporary OB/GYN*, September 1, 2017, www.contemporaryobgyn.net.
46. Henry T. Byford, "The Production and Prevention of Perineal Lacerations during Labor, with Description of a Unrecognized Form," *JAMA*, March 6, 1886, 253–57.
47. Leavitt, "Joseph B. DeLee," 1354. DeLee was, as Wolf notes, engaged at this time in "increasingly complex and expensive obstetric treatments." DeLee advocated for "aseptic, nonintrusive obstetrics" for his immigrant and working-class patients, but among his wealthier patients, he started practicing more interventions—in part to cover his expenses working with the women who could not afford to pay much for his services. Wolf, "Saving Babies and Mothers," 149–50.
48. DeLee, "Prophylactic Forceps Operation," 40–41.
49. Indeed, Graham dates the "launching of the campaign for prophylactic episiotomy" to the "1915 Annual Meeting of the American Gynecological Society," when one gynecologist "declared 'episiotomy would reduce the physical incapacity following labor'" and reduce maternal morbidities. Graham, "Episiotomy Crusade," 64–65.
50. Leavitt, *Brought to Bed*, 152.
51. Anna Broomall, "The Operation of Episiotomy as a Prevention of Perineal Ruptures during Labor," *American Journal of Obstetrics and Diseases of Women and Children*, 11, no. 3 (July 1, 1878): 525.
52. Child, "Episeotomy."
53. "Discussion of the Symposium on Injuries of the Perineum," *Transactions of the American Gynecological Society* 29 (1904): 223.
54. "Discussion on the Papers of Drs. Porter and Harrar," *American Journal of Obstetrics and Diseases of Women and Children* 80 (January–June 1919): 756.
55. Harrar, "Median Episiotomy in Primiparous Labors," 705.
56. "Discussion—The Prophylactic Forceps Operation," *American Journal of Obstetrics and Gynecology* 1 (1920): 78.
57. And this was the case not just at the meeting itself: of the episiotomy articles I looked at that were published for five years following DeLee's talk, I did not find

any mention of this as a reason to perform episiotomy—either in support or opposed.

58. "Discussion—The Prophylactic Forceps Operation," 77. On Williams's prominence, see Wolf, "Saving Babies and Mothers," 150.

59. Leavitt, "Joseph B. DeLee," 1354.

60. "Discussion—The Prophylactic Forceps Operation," 78–79.

61. Henry A. Bernstein, "The Immediate Operation for Perineal Lacerations," *JAMA*, April 27, 1918, 1217.

62. C. E. Stafrin, "Episiotomy," *Proceedings of the Alumni Association of the Medical School of the University of Oregon* 10 (1922): 58.

63. Harrar, "Median Episiotomy in Primiparous Labors," 707.

64. Pomeroy, "Shall We Cut," 202.

65. Chas. Jewett, "Note on Episiotomy," *Brooklyn Medical Journal*, June 17, 1890, 708.

66. William D. Porter, "A Method of Placing Sutures in Immediate Repair of the Perineum," *American Journal of Obstetrics and Diseases of Women and Children* 80 (January–June 1919): 701; Bernstein, "Immediate Operation for Perineal Lacerations," 1217.

67. Graham, "Processes of Change in Obstetrics," 413.

68. Pomeroy, "Shall We Cut," 205.

69. Crenner, "Race and Laboratory Norms," 477–78.

70. Charles E. Rosenberg, "The Therapeutic Revolution: Medicine, Meaning, and Social Change in Nineteenth-Century America," *Perspectives in Biology and Medicine* 20, no. 4 (Summer 1977): 485–506; Rosenberg, "The Tyranny of Diagnosis: Specific Entities and Individual Experience," *Milbank Quarterly* 80, no. 2 (2002): 237–60.

71. See Julian B. Carter, *The Heart of Whiteness: Normal Sexuality and Race in America, 1880–1920* (Durham, NC: Duke University Press, 2007). See also Crenner, "Race and Laboratory Norms," on how assumption of whiteness was made at the laboratory level. Sometimes, though, it was not assumed but stated: the gynecologist Robert Latou Dickinson, in his 1931 *A Thousand Marriages*, described some of his patients as "European, Oriental, Negro and Jewish," women who differed "among themselves and from the American type which constitutes the *standard*." Dickinson and Lura Beam, *A Thousand Marriages: A Medical Study of Sex Adjustment* (Baltimore: Williams and Wilkins, 1931), 27 (emphasis added).

72. Deborah Brunton, "The Rise of Laboratory Medicine," in *Medicine Transformed: Health, Disease and Society in Europe, 1800–1930*, ed. Brunton (Manchester: Manchester University Press, 2004), 92–118.

73. Jacalyn Duffin, *History of Medicine: A Scandalously Short Introduction*, 2nd ed. (Toronto: University of Toronto Press, 2010), 56–57; John C. Burnham, *Health Care in America: A History* (Baltimore: Johns Hopkins University Press, 2015), 88.

74. John Harley Warner, "Ideals of Science and Their Discontents in Late Nineteenth Century American Medicine," *Isis* 82, no. 3 (1991): 454–78.

75. Mary Tiles, "The Normal and the Pathological: The Concept of a Scientific Medicine," *British Journal for the Philosophy of Science* 44 (1993): 733.

76. Margaret Lock and Vinh-Kim Nguyen, *An Anthropology of Biomedicine* (Malden, MA: Wiley-Blackwell, 2010), 45. For more on the history of the rise of normality in medicine in particular (and for a disagreement about when and where the concept of normal arose), see Peter Cryle and Elizabeth Stephens, *Normality: A Critical Genealogy* (Chicago: University of Chicago Press, 2017).

77. Burnham, *Health Care in America*, 206–7.

78. Wilde and Hirst, "Learning from Mistakes," 71.

79. Lucius E. Burch, "The Etiology and Pathology of Relaxed Vaginal Outlet Following Childbirth," *Southern Medical Journal* 17, no. 5 (May 1924): 343–44.

80. Dale L. Martin, "The Protection of the Perineum by Episiotomy in Delivery at Term," *California State Journal of Medicine* 19, no. 6 (June 1921): 231.

81. "Discussion on the Papers of Drs. Porter and Harrar," 757.

82. Lisa B. Signorello, Bernard L. Harlow, Amy K. Chekos, and John T. Repke, "Postpartum Sexual Functioning and Its Relationship to Perineal Trauma: A Retrospective Cohort Study of Primiparous Women," *American Journal of Obstetrics and Gynecology* 184, no. 5 (April 2001): 881–90; Zeelha Abdool, Ranee Thakar, and Abdul H. Sultan, "Postpartum Female Sexual Function," *European Journal of Obstetrics and Gynecology and Reproductive Biology* 145 (2009): 133–37; Lawrence M. Leeman and Rebecca G. Rogers, "Sex after Childbirth," *Obstetrics and Gynecology* 119, no. 3 (March 2012): 647–55.

83. A study published in 2000 noted that of the 365 women who responded to the question, 20 percent experienced "vaginal looseness / lack of muscle tone" three months after giving birth, compared to 12 women (3 percent of the 403 women who responded to this question) who had experienced this in the year before pregnancy. This study—like, as the authors noted, previous studies—found "high rates of postnatal dyspareunia" following childbirth, with "perineal damage" "associated with higher rates of postnatal dyspareunia." Indeed, they found that women experienced "high levels of sexual morbidity after childbirth, with dyspareunia, vaginal dryness and loss of libido being very common." Geraldine Barrett, Elizabeth Pendry, Janet Peacock, Christina Victor, Ranee Thakar, and Isaac Manyonda, "Women's Sexual Health after Childbirth," *BJOG* 107, no. 2 (2000): 186–95 (quotations on 189, 192).

84. Dickinson and Beam, *Thousand Marriages*, 405.

85. Stedman, *Practical Medical Dictionary*, 669.

86. Smith Ely Jelliffe and Caroline Wormeley Latimer, *Appleton's Medical Dictionary* (New York: D. Appleton, 1915), 595.

87. Lock and Nguyen, *Anthropology of Biomedicine*, 46; Tiles, "Normal and the Pathological," 734; Phillip V. Davis and John G. Bradley, "The Meaning of Normal," *Perspectives in Biology and Medicine* 40, no. 1 (Autumn 1996): 68–77.

88. Ian Hacking, *The Taming of Chance* (1990; repr., Cambridge: Cambridge University Press, 2002), 163.

89. Loss of virginity is often associated with pain. According to Blank, since blood and pain were "considered proof positive of a woman's virginity since the earli-

est documents we have on the subject, pain and bleeding have been so strongly associated with virginity loss that we scarcely speak about first-time sex without talking about them." Blank, *Virgin*, 111. Anke Bernan also briefly notes that pain and bleeding have also long been associated as a sign of virginity. Bernan, *Virgins: A Cultural History* (London: Granta Books, 2007).

90. Robert L. Dickinson, "Premarital Examination as Routine Preventive Gynecology," *American Journal of Obstetrics and Gynecology* 16, no. 5 (1928): 631–41; his presidency is noted in the discussion section to DeLee's 1920 paper. DeLee, "Prophylactic Forceps Operation," 77.

91. Dickinson, "Premarital Examination," 635; Robert Latou Dickinson, *Human Sex Anatomy: A Topographical Hand Atlas*, 2nd ed. (Baltimore: Williams and Wilkins, 1949), fig. 59.

92. Dickinson, *Human Sex Anatomy*, fig. 59.

93. Dickinson and Beam, *Thousand Marriages*, 54.

94. In actual measurements, Dickinson gave averages as 2.5 centimeters for the vaginal opening of the virgin, 4 centimeters for the vaginal opening of the married but childless woman, and 5.5 centimeters for the woman who had given birth. Dickinson, *Human Sex Anatomy*, fig. 59. On this page, he lists the date of the measurements as 1925.

95. Dickinson understood his measurements as also reflecting sexual behaviors; he believed he could discern not only if a woman had engaged in vaginal intercourse but also if it was regular. He also argued that other forms of sexual behavior could be recognized: if the opening of the vagina permitted four fingers "to the whole hand," such a size was "beyond the possibilities of the phallus and suggest prolonged manualization." Dickinson and Beam, *Thousand Marriages*, 439. Dickinson also measured the genitals of women who told him they had sex with other women in an effort to assess if there were recognizable differences on the body from these sexual behaviors, too. Jennifer Terry, "Anxious Slippages between 'Us' and 'Them': A Brief History of the Scientific Search for Homosexual Bodies," in *Deviant Bodies: Critical Perspectives on Difference in Science and Popular Culture*, ed. Jennifer Terry and Jacqueline Urla (Bloomington: Indiana University Press, 1995), 129–69.

96. This was not the first time physicians had interfered with the vagina in order to restore the organ to what was regarded as normal, nor was it the first time they did so for sexual reasons. The American gynecologist J. Marion Sims developed a surgery to correct for vaginismus—vaginal hypersensitivity that resulted in a contraction of the vaginal sphincter muscle—and other physicians, similarly concerned with ensuring that sexual intercourse occurred in a marriage, also performed what became known as the Sims surgery for the treatment of vaginismus. See Peter Cryle, "Vaginismus: A Franco-American Story," *Journal of the History of Medicine and Allied Sciences* 67, no. 1 (2012): 71–93.

97. Indeed, in a 1928 article regarding the construction of a vagina in a case of a congenital absence of the organ, the authors wrote that their patients were "willing to

take the risk of operation rather than continue living with a defect which, for all practical purposes, prevented marriage." Carl Henry Davis and Roland S. Cron, "Congenital Absence of the Vagina," *American Journal of Obstetrics and Gynecology* 15, no. 2 (1928): 197. See also Geertje A. Mak, "Conflicting Heterosexualities: Hermaphroditism and the Emergence of Surgery around 1900," *Journal of the History of Sexuality* 24, no. 3 (2015): 402–27.

98. Mak challenges us to think critically about what heterosexuality meant and not to consider it a single conception. Mak, "Conflicting Heterosexualities."

99. Katherine Bement Davis, "Periodicity of Sex Desire; Part I: Unmarried Women, College Graduates," *American Journal of Obstetrics and Gynecology* 12, no. 6 (1926): 824–38.

100. William Newman Dorland, *The American Illustrated Medical Dictionary* (Philadelphia: W. B. Saunders, 1925), 527, 534, 760.

101. Margaret Sanger, *Happiness in Marriage* (New York: Blue Ribbon Books, 1926), 98 (emphasis added).

102. Celello, *Making Marriage Work*; Simmons, *Making Marriage Modern*; Neuhaus, "Importance of Being Orgasmic."

103. Robert L. Dickinson and Henry H. Pierson, "The Average Sex Life of American Women," *JAMA* 85, no. 15 (October 10, 1925): 1114.

104. Most of those who participated in his study were patients of psychiatrists in New York City or were friends of the patients. Hamilton's study, though funded by the Bureau of Social Hygiene—a creation of John D. Rockefeller Jr.—was regarded as so controversial that the bureau declined to be recognized as funding it. Vern L. Bullough, "Katherine Bement Davis, Sex Research, and the Rockefeller Foundation," *Bulletin of the History of Medicine* 62 (1988): 74–89.

105. G. V. Hamilton and Kenneth MacGowan, *What Is Wrong with Marriage* (New York: Albert and Charles Boni, 1929), 7 (emphasis in original).

106. Antonio Villarama, "The Protection of the Perineum," *American Journal of Obstetrics and Gynecology*, 11, no. 6 (1926): 824.

107. I thank Judy Leavitt, whom I spoke to about this chapter at the American Association for the History of Medicine annual meeting in May 2018.

108. For example, in the 1915, 1918, and 1925 editions of his obstetrics textbook for physicians—the editions published around the time he made the comment—DeLee did not mention virginal conditions in the section on episiotomy or in his discussion of preserving the perineum during labor. Joseph B. DeLee, *Principles and Practice of Obstetrics*, 2nd ed. (Philadelphia: W. B. Saunders, 1915); DeLee, *Principles and Practice of Obstetrics*, 3rd ed. (Philadelphia: W. B. Saunders, 1918); DeLee, *Principles and Practice of Obstetrics*, 4th ed. (Philadelphia: W. B. Saunders, 1925). I did look through the Joseph B. DeLee Papers at Northwestern Memorial Hospital's archives but found nothing indicating his ideas about virginal conditions and episiotomies. The only other time he seems to have mentioned this subject was during a talk he gave in Mankato in December 1919 before the Southern Minnesota Medical Association. There, DeLee provided much of the

same information he would five months later back in Chicago, including that episiotomy and its repair meant that "virginal conditions are often restored." This was, of course, what he would later say in May 1920. But at his talk in Minnesota, he added that "some might say that this is a disadvantage." One could write another chapter exploring just what he possibly meant by this as well. DeLee, "The Treatment of the Second Stage of Labor with Special Reference to the Prevention of Injury to the Child and to the Pelvic Floor," *Minnesota Medicine* 3, no. 7 (July 1920): 322–23.

109. Stedman, *Practical Medical Dictionary*, 1103.

12

How Heterosexuality Became Religious

Judeo-Christian Morality and the Remaking of Sex in Twentieth-Century America

HEATHER R. WHITE

Civil laws that permit only heterosexual marriage reflect and honor a collective moral judgement about human sexuality. This judgment entails both moral disapproval of homosexuality, and a moral conviction that heterosexuality better comports with traditional (especially Judeo-Christian) morality.
—House Report on the Defense of Marriage Act, H.R. Rep. No. 104-664 (1996)

In June 2015, in the weeks leading up to a highly anticipated Supreme Court decision in *Obergefell v. Hodges*, a group of fifty thousand religious conservatives preemptively threatened civil disobedience if the justices ruled to legalize same-sex marriage. Those who signed their names to the online "Pledge in Solidarity to Defend Marriage" signaled that they would continue to enforce the state-level Defense of Marriage ordinances under scrutiny by the Court. These DOMA laws, as they were termed in shorthand, barred various forms of relationship recognition, including legal marriage, to same-sex couples. Rick Scarborough, one of the organizers of the petition, went so far as to suggest the he and fellow signatories were prepared to fight to their deaths in defense of the heterosexual exclusivity of legal marriage. "We are not going to bow; we are not going to bend; and if necessary we will burn," he declared ominously in an interview.[1]

Many of these avowed defenders of marriage did proceed to challenge the Court's ruling in *Obergefell*, which struck down the remaining DOMA laws and made same-sex marriage legal across the nation.[2]

And while none of these dissenters faced anything so drastic as death or burning, they did face municipal fines and, in the highly publicized case of Kim Davis, a five-day stint in jail. Davis, a county clerk whose job included issuing marriage licenses, stopped granting marriage licenses altogether and continued this refusal after being remanded by a federal judge. She was released once her staff began issuing licenses on her behalf.[3] Davis and other dissenters cited their religious beliefs as the reason for their challenge. While most were conservative evangelical Protestants, they claimed a moral foundation that surpassed any one denomination or sectarian tradition and that superseded the temporal laws produced by human courts. "One man, one woman" marriage was an ontological truth, grounded in the shared Christian and Jewish scriptures. This higher, divine law was rooted in a universal civilizational inheritance, a millennia-long Judeo-Christian tradition.[4]

Conservative Protestants are predictable critics of same-sex marriage. But not only social conservatives identify the Judeo-Christian tradition as a historical and cultural force that has traditionally defined marriage as exclusively heterosexual. Indeed, this link was well established in the body of secular law under consideration by the Supreme Court in *Obergefell*. The Federal Defense of Marriage Act, passed by Congress in 1996, identified "traditional (especially Judeo-Christian) morality" as a reason for the "government's interest in defending traditional notions of morality."[5] Through the late 1990s and early 2000s, states followed suit, passing statutory and constitutional bans against same-sex marriage. The text of these laws appealed to history and tradition as rationales for making heterosexuality a newly explicit condition for legal marriage, and lawmakers routinely argued that they represented a national heritage of Judeo-Christian morality.[6] On the other side of the debate, progressive critics of the laws rarely questioned these claims about religious origins. Instead, they tended to focus on how the explicit appeal to religion as a foundation for the law violated constitutional provisions for the separation of church and state. According to these critics, Judeo-Christian morality, whatever its historical influence, should not have proprietary legal standing in a secular democracy.[7] Thus, in all sorts of contexts, the connection between Judeo-Christian religion and traditional heterosexual marriage is so frequently asserted as a plain fact that many readers might not even think to question it.

And yet, from a historical perspective, it is an odd union. This chapter highlights this strangeness by tracing the historical genealogy of these separate terms—Judeo-Christian religion and heterosexuality—with attention to how they came to be so closely associated. This mapping of relations shows that Judeo-Christian morality has little to do with ancient Jewish or Christian origins. Rather, the ideas and values encapsulated by notions of a Judeo-Christian tradition are surprisingly recent. The terms themselves first appeared in American publications at the turn of the twentieth century, a sign of the expanding transnational circuits of social scientific inquiries that originated in western Europe. During the early twentieth century, these academic neologisms came to encompass new vernacular meaning. In the era following World War II, they began to appear in popular rhetoric—in reference to the nation's newly pluralist "Judeo-Christian heritage" and in the growing psychoanalytic discussion of sexual health. It was not until the second half of the twentieth century, however, that significant numbers of Protestants, Catholics, and Jews began to speak and think about their traditions as connected to a Judeo-Christian history. The invocation of an ideal of a common heritage took place amid rancorous disagreement about what these three heterogeneous religious groups actually shared as religious viewpoints on marriage and sexual morality.[8]

This history of the surprisingly recent origins of Judeo-Christian morality typifies what the historian Eric Hobsbawm theorizes as the "invention of tradition," a constructed memory of the past that stabilizes and naturalizes emergent beliefs and practices.[9] However, this invention was not a singular event but a series of transformations, which reflected the ways that twentieth-century Americans—Protestants, Catholics, Jews, and nonreligious people—redrew the boundaries of religious pluralism as they also redefined marriage to encompass ideals of health and pleasure. This new ideal of Judeo-Christian morality was also important to twentieth-century social changes in ethnic assimilation, which other scholars have traced as the progressive "whitening" of various outsider European groups, most notably European Jews and southern and eastern European Catholics.[10] The production of the celebrated midcentury "melting pot" helped to reposition white ethnic Americans as "trifaith" allies. At the same time, the notion of religious unity produced by the Judeo-Christian formulation also colluded in the marginalization of black Americans and nonwhite people of color by deeming their religious practices as existing outside a particular consensus vision of mainstream American religious life. Tracing the formation of Judeo-Christian morality shows how religion has helped to shape and sustain new, often racialized twentieth-century sexual and family norms. While religious communities themselves have certainly been part of these changes, the historical effects of the Judeo-Christian formulation have markedly exceeded the precincts of practicing faith communities. It came to serve as a shorthand reference to a past of religious regulation and a descriptive foil against which Americans broadly—religious and not—would position the companionable progress of secularism and liberated sexuality. This focus on religion as a singular pivot on the arc of sexual change notably obscures a more troublesome past.

Rethinking Jewish and Christian Sexual History

As a claim about historical origins, "Judeo-Christian" would seem, first of all, to convey the textual and scriptural origins of Judaism and Christianity. These traditions, after all, share a set of scriptures, which Jews call the Tanakh or Hebrew Bible and Christians term the Old Testament. Christianity emerged in the first century CE as a splinter sect of dissident Jews and therefore contained beliefs and practices that originated within Judaism. To challenge the historicity of "Judeo-Christian" as a descriptive term is not to deny the overlapping histories of these two major religions. There are indeed important beliefs and practices that have been shared, borrowed, and adapted among diverse movements within Christianity and Judaism. However, this variegated history of cultural and religious interaction is precisely not what is conveyed by most modern American references to Judeo-Christian, in which this phrase nearly always points to *a* tradition and *a* set of beliefs. The scholarship on the history of Christian and Jewish interaction underscores a simple but important point: there is no monolithic tradition or singular relationship between these heterogeneous traditions and their diverse practitioners. Therefore, there can be no one way of depicting the relation between them.[11]

There is also now a rich body of historical work that counters the unitary framework of Judeo-Christian sexual history by focusing instead on how sex and embodiment have been powerful themes of division across Jewish and Christian histories. David Hunter, a scholar of early Christianity, points out that key authors in early Christianity and in rabbinic Judaism ascribed their different views about sex and human origins to what might otherwise seem to be shared scriptures. The rabbis emphasized that God's first commandment was the Genesis 1:28 injunction to "increase and multiply"; the Patristic Fathers of early Christianity, in contrast, came to interpret the Genesis account of Adam and Eve as a story about sexual desire as a result of human rebellion against God. Thus, where Jewish scriptures affirmed the goodness—indeed, the necessity—of procreation, Christian scriptures declared that celibacy was the highest spiritual path. Shared texts took up divergent meanings as their readers interpreted them in ways that supported different moral teachings about sex and procreation.[12]

At the same time, neither Christianity nor Judaism, for most of their long histories, endorsed sexual desire as a good in itself. Historians of both rabbinic Judaism and early Christianity emphasize the formative influence of Greco-Roman asceticism on marriage and sexual practices; teachings in both traditions forbade nonprocreative sexual practice. For rabbinic Judaism, these prohibitions barred intercourse during a woman's menstruation, coitus interruptus, and male masturbation. Christianity took an even more radical approach to the ascetic imperative, resulting in a theology and practice that insistently separated physical pleasure from spiritual devotion. In the Roman Catholic tradition, this orientation to ethereal purity shaped teachings that celebrated celibacy as the higher estate and, by the fourth century, required it for church leaders. While the Protestant Reformation of the sixteenth century reversed this requirement of clerical celibacy, the Reformers remained as adamantly opposed as their Catholic counterparts to nonprocreative sexual behavior within marriage. Thus, for most of the long histories of these three faiths—Judaism, Catholicism, and Protestantism—sexual teachings within their mainstream traditions addressed an imminent moral peril: the perverse and excessive desire of a wife and husband for each other.[13] The notion of heterosexuality—that male-female attraction and pleasure is fundamentally good and healthy—became an organizing principle for religious marriage only in the twentieth century.

More surprising than the twentieth-century development of sex-positive religious teaching was the novel embrace of a multifaith theology signaled by the concept of Judeo-Christian morality. For much of Christianity's history, Christian leaders employed a rhetoric of sexual slander to characterize their theological differences from Jews and to differentiate Protestants from Catholics. Susanna Drake's research on the splintering of early Christians from rabbinical Judaism shows how Christian leaders directed accusations of perversity against Jewish communities, a key justification for anti-Jewish violence.[14] Sexual invective also pervaded the sixteenth-century schisms of the Reformation, as leading Protestant Reformers decried the "popish sodometry" of the Roman Catholic Church.[15]

This discourse of sexualized religious difference did not abate with the founding of modern secular democracies. The founding architects of the US nation-state largely shared the assumption that authentic religion—specifically, Anglo-Protestantism—was a vital guarantor of virtuous citizenship. They generally perceived the American experiment in church-state separation as an aspect of ecumenical Protestantism, defined as the liberal alternative to the "papal tyranny" of Catholicism and to the perceived "theocratic legalism" of Judaism.[16] Protestant moral ideals remained central to the ways that Anglo-Protestant Americans linked Christianity to norms of democratic self-governance and consequently to ways that they portrayed Jews and Catholics as sexual and moral threats. Perpetrators of religious intolerance in the United States, as John Corrigan and Lynne S. Neal show, persistently raised fears about how Catholics and Jews, as well as other religious minorities, "violate the mythical norms of nuclear family—monogamy, heterosexuality, and patriarchy, all upheld through marriage."[17] American nativist movements of the antebellum era produced vicious anti-Catholic propaganda that linked papal tyranny to sexual bondage; under Catholic authority, women were reportedly "prostituted" by "licentious priests," a perception that helped to fuel a series of attacks on Catholic convents.[18] American Jews of the nineteenth and early twentieth centuries also increasingly became the targets of race-based prejudice, which fused Christian anti-Judaism with newer forms of anti-Semitism and presented Jews as a separate and inferior race of so-called Semites.[19] Catholic immigrants from eastern and southern Europe were similarly targeted as racialized outsiders. This race-based thinking fueled worries that interfaith marriage and procreation would lead to degeneracy.[20] In these earlier religious efforts to defend marriage, Protestants castigated Jews and Catholics as perceived threats to the purity and sanctity of the traditional family.

The interfaith sexual consensus that emerged in the twentieth century thus did not derive from a shared past. For most of the millennia-long history of Protestants, Catholics, and Jews—and even for most of their history in the United States—sex and marriage remained at the heart of what seemed to make them different from each other. Sexual teachings were thus not a source of interfaith unity. Nor was heterosexuality a shared value. Indeed, for all three of these broad traditions, the twentieth-century embrace of heterosexuality substantially transformed longer legacies of bodily and sexual discipline. The perception that Jewish and Christian views of sex shared a fundamental religious outlook germinated from a surprisingly modern source: not ancient scriptures but new inquiries into the respective sciences of sex and religion.

Empirical Studies of Sex and Religion

In May 1892, notes the historian Jonathan Ned Katz, the term "heterosexuality" appeared in an American medical journal. The label was pejorative, designating persons who sought "abnormal methods of gratification."[21] Katz shows—as have other historians of sexuality—that this term's particular way of referencing sexual attraction between women and men is not simply a description of timeless, universal biological processes. Rather, it is a historically specific ideology, which first circulated in the authoritative discourses of late nineteenth-century scientific and medical specialists.

The religion scholar Mark Silk offers a parallel account about the emergence of new terminologies for religion: the phrase "Judeo-Christian" first appeared in an American scholarly dictionary in 1899. The reference was to an arcane "continuity theory," which postulated that Jewish practices of the Second Temple influenced the first rituals of Christianity.[22] This coinage of new terms and the theorizing about social and historical connections among the world's religions reflected an empirical, scientific turn in the study of religion that paralleled the contemporaneous study of sexuality. The European experts at the helm of these new scientific endeavors undertook related projects: they sought to develop neutral, empirical tools for investigating and classifying religion and sexuality as universal human phenomena.

On their own terms, these experts sought to replace the inadequate, provincial claims of Christian theology with ostensibly universal and objective facts. Yet neither the science of sex nor the science of religion created an unbiased and universal paradigm. In distinct yet related ways, they expanded the value systems and cultural logic of European and Anglo-American Protestantism as scientific truth.

These intellectual projects converged in a wide-ranging scholarly inquiry into the origins of sexual morality, a question assumed to be central to the emergence and growth of human civilization. These nineteenth-century scholars developed an evolutionary model of religious advancement that fused cultural Darwinism and Protestant supersession. In this model, the development of human societies began with the primitive polytheism of the nonwhite "races" and advanced to the monotheism of civilized northern Europeans.[23] The British Anglican Robertson Smith, one influential chronicler of religion's evolutionary development, positioned Christianity as a liberating harvester of spiritual concepts that first appeared in primordial form—"in a merely physical and mechanical shape"—in what Smith called "the religion of the Semites." This religion was not something that Jewish contemporaries would recognize as their tradition; it was rather something that Smith, following other European Protestant scholars, projected into the Old Testament with the interpretive abandon of an armchair anthropologist. Smith, consequently, perceived Judaism as a rudimentary container for Christian truth. Primitive Semitic rituals, Smith wrote, "wrapped up in the husk of a material embodiment" the kernels of meaning that Christianity would subsequently free, as "spiritual truth from the husk."[24] As the historian Tomoko Masuzawa writes, this intellectual discourse granted to Judaism a germinal and even "supra-historical significance" as "its essence [was] directly connected to the pith of civilization itself, and thus to the present."[25] While Judaism supplied the pith, or the raw materials, of civilization, Protestantism was nonetheless at its pinnacle, the fully evolved exemplar of civilization.

Turn-of-the-century scholars of sexuality elaborated the connections between these theories of religious origins and the evolution of marriage and sexuality. They postulated a similar germinal role for ancient Jewish religion: as originator of sexual regulation, Judaism created an order to family life that subsequently contributed to Christian civilization. However, this inheritance was also a problem. Most of these intellectuals saw religiously based sexual prohibition as irrational and ineffective, and they positioned science and medicine as the perfecting solution. The British sexologist Havelock Ellis, in his widely influential *Studies in the Psychology of Sex* (1897), highlighted the religious lineage of contemporary disgust toward homosexuality, noting that "our modern attitude is sometimes traced back to the Jewish law and its survival in St. Paul's opinion."[26] Ellis pointed out these religious influences in order to argue that what homosexuals needed was not a squeamish moralist but a clear-sighted medical expert. Jewish thinkers also contributed to this intellectual trend. Sigmund Freud, an Austrian secular Jew whose work established the field of psychoanalysis, remixed these narratives of civilizational emergence into theories of the human psyche. In *Totem and Taboo* (1918), Freud contended that ancient Hebrew sexual taboos brought about a new patriarchal social structure and consequently the psychic origins of the Oedipal complex, a form of neurosis that could be alleviated by psychoanalysis.[27] An axiom of the emerging therapeutic sciences of the early twentieth century was that religion—and more particularly the heritage of Judeo-Christian sexual regulation—provided the foundation for Western civilization. This inheritance was also a problem, which the medical approach of therapy stood poised to address. Dogmatic religion fostered guilt, anxiety, and neuroticism, which might disrupt the process by which men and women realized their natural and healthy attraction to each other. The therapeutic approach of psychoanalysis, in contrast, released troubled psyches from religious guilt and ostensibly helped women and men to achieve sexual health.[28]

This critique of Judeo-Christian sexual regulation also supplied bedrock assumptions for American sexual liberals who sought to reform laws governing sex. A version of this thinking appeared in Alfred Kinsey's research reports on the sexual behavior of white American men and women. Published in the decade after World War II, Kinsey's books became unexpected best-sellers, well-read primers that revealed the diversity of Americans' actual sexual behavior. In these books, Kinsey and his coauthors also urged legal reform of US sex laws. The religious influences in US law, they wrote, "go back to the Old Testament philosophy on which the Talmud is based. . . . In many details, the proscriptions of the Talmud are nearly identical with those of our present-day legal codes governing sexual behavior."[29] This comment, which overlooked the significant ways in which Talmudic law differed from Anglo-American legal codes, instead reflected Kinsey's uncritical adoption of a civilizational narrative about the Jewish origins of Western sexual regulation. It positioned Judaism as the historical taproot of cultural stigmas against nonprocreative sex, masturbation, and homosexuality, and it presented this Judeo-Christian inheritance as a problem. From this diagnosis, the argument was that US sex laws needed to shed their putative moralism in order to efficiently and rationally address the problem of sexual deviance. The United States' sin-sick society needed a secular cure to be sexually healthy.

The loudest religious reactions to the Kinsey studies reflected outrage; one conservative Protestant pastor denounced the study of sexual behavior in American women as "a moral Hell-bomb."[30] But amid the protest emerged a more nuanced reaction from a quieter group of religious reformers. While many of these religious leaders criticized aspects of Kinsey's project, they also engaged with the studies in order to initiate a very different conversation about sexuality, health, and Judeo-Christian morality. One of these reformers, Rabbi Morris Max, commented on Kinsey's studies in the Orthodox journal *Jewish Life* in 1954. Max began by asserting Kinsey's ignorance of "the fundamental difference between the traditional Jewish and the traditional Christian concept of sex life. The two cannot be combined and spoken of as similar cases. They are diametrically opposed to each other." Not only were Jewish teachings about sex distinct from Christianity, but those Jewish sources were also remarkably compatible with the outlook that Kinsey himself had to offer. The Talmud, Max argued, offered an uncensored discussion of "normal sex life" that rivaled the sexologists in its "scientific" outlook.[31]

Like this rabbi, other religious liberals of the postwar era sought to challenge religion's bad reputation in the field of sexual health. Their earnest labors helped to produce a new kind of sexual and religious pluralism, which articulated modern medical insights about sex as spiritual values. According to this theory, sexual attraction and pleasure were positive goods—important to one's self-understanding, to selecting a compatible spouse, and to cultivating a happy marriage. A sense of religious unity among religious liberals emerged not from their loyalty to past traditions but from their desire to better adapt their respective faiths to the multiple ills of modernity. They came to view each other as allies as they also increasingly embraced a health-based framework for human sexuality, which in its own terms was set against the unhealthy taboos of religious dogma. The product of this essentially liberal set of reforms was a refurbished ideal of Judeo-Christian morality, which reimagined Jews, Catholics, and Protestants as allies in a shared project of American cultural—and sexual—reproduction.

All Faiths Affirm the Family

Judeo-Christian ideals received a significant rebranding during World War II, when they were counterpoised against Nazi anti-Semitism. After the war, US political leaders repurposed Judeo-Christian rhetoric as a stock phrase to signal an inclusive, God-fearing national identity. During the Cold War, the "Judeo-Christian ethos" was a useful foil to the so-called godless communism of the Soviet Bloc. This language acknowledged, at least rhetorically, that Jews and Catholics were no longer religious outsiders but rightfully part of the American religious mainstream. Post–World War II religious pluralism also reflected a demographic diversity that was by this point a settled fact: the vast influx of immigrant Catholics and Jews who arrived at the turn of the twentieth century had upturned the overwhelmingly Protestant demographics of the United States. Will Herberg's landmark study *Protestant-Catholic-Jew* (1955) influentially captured this trend and argued that assimilated European immigrants had traded in ethnic identities for religious ones as markers of national inclusion. This trajectory of inclusion, of course, was predicated on the experience of European immigrants—Irish Catholics, German Lutherans, Russian Jews—for whom assimilation into unmarked whiteness allowed for an identity characterized by religious rather than ethnic difference.[32]

The postwar rhetoric of Judeo-Christian tradition also implicitly defined a model of family life: the heterosexual nuclear family. Idealized images of white, middle-class domesticity showcased a cultural fiction rather than a demographic norm, but it was a fiction that was made powerfully consequential through a variety of midcentury economic, political, and cultural programs. The historian Margot Canaday, whose work documents the sexualized exclusions of what she calls "the straight state," argues that various forms of government support functioned to "cleave the population into homosexuals and heterosexuals."[33] It was in this context that a group of Protestant, Catholic, and Jewish leaders began to develop resources in the field of family life education, an educational effort that addressed the heterosexual nuclear family as a site in need of spiritual support. These resources fused the values of sexual liberalism and religious pluralism, producing a consolidated religious heteronormativity.

A 1950 gathering of Protestant, Catholic, and Jewish educators showed how they labored—and perhaps failed—to articulate a trifaith foundation for the issue of sexual health. A daylong conference for clergy and social hygiene experts took place in New York City and marked the thirty-seventh annual meeting of the American Social Hygiene Association (ASHA). The conference culminated with three presentations, representing the "Three Major Religious Faiths" of Protestantism, Catholicism and Judaism.[34] ASHA's efforts to build interfaith collaboration had begun in 1933, when the dominantly mainline Protestant leadership of the organization began forging connections to Jewish and Roman Catholic family-life educators under the auspices of the organization's decorously titled Division of Family Relations. In the formative years of its history, the social hygiene movement had often described Catholics and Jews as targets for moral reform rather than as genuine collaborators. By contrast, the 1950 conference indicated the dawning of a new "trifaith" era, even as the dialogue illustrated the tensions that plagued Protestant-led interfaith efforts.[35]

The conference featured three speakers, who represented their respective faith traditions' views toward sexuality, marriage, and family. The Protestant speaker, the Baptist minister and former missionary Leland Foster Wood, led the trio by offering a framing lecture on the "significant areas of agreement" among the "great religions" on the topic of marriage and family life, with source material from Wood's trusted Bible to illustrate this grand thesis.[36] The Bible, Wood argued, holds that "it is not good for man to be alone."[37] Wood was also unequivocal that God's purpose for marriage included sexual pleasure that could not be reduced to procreation, and he urged family planning—meaning birth control—as a similarly shared religious value.[38] From beginning to end, the principles that Wood endorsed as generically religious were typical only of mainline liberal Protestants, making this speech a classic example of sectarian Protestants' universalizing overreach.

Albert Goldman, a Reform rabbi, represented Judaism. He broadly endorsed ASHA's aims and policies but took a very different approach to the question of religion and family-life education.[39] Unlike his Protestant colleague, Goldman claimed a distinct "Jewish point of view" and maintained that this tradition was uniquely different from Christianity.[40] It was also from this vantage point that Goldman endorsed the efforts of family-life education as well as the conclusions of modern psychiatry, urging his audience to face the "insights of the psychoanalysts and sexologists with complete interest and earnestness."[41] Goldman's claims ran notably counter to the stereotype of Judaism as a source of sexual regulation. He argued that moralizing efforts to forbid sexual behavior must confront the new Freudian paradigm and its theories about innate erotic drives. This specialized knowledge made education all the more necessary, as parents and teachers bore great responsibility for teaching children how to channel those drives—not by a "command-into-behavior" approach but instead through a "substratum of security and trust."[42] Goldman's comments reflected a thorough embrace of psychoanalytic theories of sexual development. In his view, education and psychiatry were necessary tools to direct the sexual impulse of children and youth toward the one sanctioned option: heterosexual marriage.

The final speaker, Edward B. Lyman, presented himself as a proud Irish Catholic layman and also "the father of a growing family," a self-disclosure that was probably a subtle jab against the supposed universality of religious support for family planning.[43] Roman Catholic teaching formally forbade all use of contraception, even as contraceptive use was a lively topic of debate among many American Catholic laypeople. While Lyman echoed his counterparts' support for family-life education, he also pugnaciously insisted that ASHA's educational effort must support Catholic values. He urged the organization to revise the language of its mission statement to acknowledge "fundamental belief in God," and he also insisted that family-life education should include explicitly theistic and moral approaches to family life.[44] Lyman's comments further under-

scored the salient religious differences that shaped each of these speakers' approaches to family-life education. Notably, none of these speakers
at the interfaith forum used the phrase "Judeo-Christian." And they also
offered quite different accounts of how their respective faiths informed
the larger project. Not surprisingly, it was the Protestant who was most
willing to speak for "religion" as a generic, encompassing category, while
the Jewish and the Catholic speakers highlighted the particular—and, in
this case, distinctly conflicting—perspectives of their respective faiths.

If ASHA's interfaith efforts brought Protestants, Catholics, and Jews
together, these conversations did not naturally tend toward unity, even
among participants who professed to share support for family-life education. Over the next decade, religious liberals began to more directly
acknowledge their differences as they also determinedly addressed a
much-heralded "sexual revolution," which seemed to demand frank
talk about sexual values.[45] These shifts during the early 1960s were not
a sudden eruption. Rather, many of those trends—including access to
contraception, an emphasis on sexual pleasure, and candid discussion of
sex—had long been championed by sexual liberals, including many religious liberals, who believed these changes would foster healthy, happy
marriages.[46] By the 1960s, as the historians John D'Emilio and Estelle
Freedman have argued, these same trends also supplied new norms and
values for sex, ones that openly challenged its exclusive attachment to
marriage.[47] It was amid these worrisome changes that a group of religious liberals helped to create a new organization, one that would directly intervene in the issue of morals and values while also providing
health-based information about sex.

Sexual Liberalism and Judeo-Christian Pluralism

The Sex Information and Education Council of the United States
(SIECUS) was founded in 1964 as a collaborative effort by a group
of health professionals and religious leaders. From its inception, the
organization worked with leaders across mainstream religious groups
to develop faith-based sex-education curricula. These networks were
surprisingly broad: they included Roman Catholics; Orthodox, Conservative, and Reform Jews; and historically Protestant denominations
that spanned the progressive Unitarian Universalists to the more

conservative Southern Baptists. The effort to encourage conversations across religious difference was one part of the organization's work; another part was to encourage religious leaders to address sexual health within the distinct values of their own communities. This outreach to religious communities was vital to the vision of SIECUS's director, Mary Calderone. A staunch Quaker, Calderone was as committed to spiritual ecumenism as she was to healthy sexuality.[48]

The involvement and support of these religious leaders also came to be of increasing strategic importance as the organization, beginning in the late 1960s, faced a wave of attacks that focused on issues of religion and morality. Leading this opposition was the John Birch Society, a far-right organization, and the Tulsa-based Christian Crusade, which was led by the fundamentalist preacher Billy James Hargis. Working in tandem, these two organizations spearheaded a sweeping disinformation campaign, which presented SIECUS as an atheist, communist organization peddling "raw sex" to corrupt America's youth.[49] Anti-sex-education pamphlets featured spurious reports: of an elementary teacher who disrobed before her classroom; of sex-education curricula that unashamedly relied on pornography; and of a vast conspiracy to undermine American morals.[50] The campaign gained grassroots followers among conservative Christians across the country, who angrily accused their local school boards of taking religion out of school and replacing it with sex.

In the face of these efforts to fuel moral panic against sex education, SIECUS leaders fervently worked to claim religious legitimacy. The "Interfaith Statement on Sex Education," publicly released on June 8, 1968, was part of this strategy. The document presented a Judeo-Christian framework for sex education and was itself the product of formal "trifaith" support. Representatives from the Synagogue Council of America, the United States Catholic Conference, and the National Council of Churches helped to draft the statement, and each of these organizations formally endorsed it.[51] The statement was, at the same time, an important symbolic expression of interfaith unity and a strategic response to the moral attacks led by Christian Crusade and the John Birch Society.

"Human sexuality is a gift of God," the statement began. With this theistic framing, the "Interfaith Statement" countered the charge that sex education was atheistic and immoral; it called for the implementation of curricula "shaped and guided by spiritual and moral considerations which derive from our Judeo-Christian heritage."[52] The liberal religious leaders who drafted the document largely agreed that sex education could not be taught as a list of rules or dictates, but they also stressed the importance of morals and values, calling for a curriculum that "recognized basic moral principles, not as sectarian religious doctrine but as the moral heritage of Western civilization."[53] These authors perceived no conflict between moral principles and SIECUS's naturalistic and health-based framework for sexuality. Indeed, they perceived sexuality as both "a gift of God" and a natural force that was intrinsically gender normative and heterosexual—a "dynamic urge or power, arising from one's basic maleness or femaleness."[54] It was thus for reasons of nature and health, and not extrinsic moral standards, that "sexual intercourse within marriage offers the greatest possibility for personal fulfillment and social growth."[55] This document fused the distinct traditions of Judaism, Catholicism, and Protestantism into a singular Judeo-Christian heritage, which nurtured—rather than regulated—healthy and fulfilling sexuality.

While this document presented heterosexual marriage as a Judeo-Christian value, those who were involved in its drafting knew quite well that there was nothing seamless or given about this ideal. In many ways, the invocation of Protestant, Catholic, and Jewish unity was strategic, created precisely for the purpose of countering conspiratorial attacks against sex-education programs. And it was reportedly a useful document: the Reverend William Genné, a SIECUS board member, recalled one contentious school-board election in which sex-education advocates circulated ten thousand copies of the "Interfaith Statement"—a pamphlet for every home in the school district. "Voters realized that the U.S. Conference of Catholic Bishops could not be called communist dupes for favoring sex ed," Genné reported. "It turned the tide of the election."[56] The statement thus helped to quell community fears that sex education would encourage immorality by showing that influential religious leaders supported these reforms and saw them as a support for—not a challenge to—traditional sexual values.

This symbolic statement of unity was also produced through ongoing expressions of difference and disagreement. The differences among the Protestant, Catholic, and Jewish participants fractured along predictable lines. Protestants seemed consistently the most idealistic about the project of interfaith unity. The key aim of interfaith work, in the urging of more than one Protestant clergyman, was to utilize "resources from Roman Catholic, Protestant and Jewish groups" to "develop a theology of human sexuality."[57] Perhaps predictably, one of the participating rabbis questioned this goal, and he lobbed a loaded question to a Catholic priest: "Father McFadden," the rabbi asked, "do you think the Protestant, Catholic, and Jewish disciplines could really make a theological statement?" The priest replied, "if we never raised concrete issues such as homosexuality or premarital intercourse, yes. But once we get into these questions—well, it's not going to take place this morning."[58] This exchange was just one of many in which participants acknowledged genuine, and perhaps intractable, differences in their ideas about sexuality and morality. Indeed, some of the participants argued that the group should refocus their efforts away from "statements of goodwill" that cloaked their disagreements and work instead to "surface the differences and identify the pluralism."[59] When speaking among themselves, these religious leaders not only frankly disagreed but also openly criticized the project of producing shared values.

But most of the clergy supporters of SIECUS did agree that it was vitally important for religious leaders to address the issue of healthy sexuality. This health-based approach to sexuality was a foundational part of SIECUS's mission, and it was also clearly elaborated as a point of agreement in the "Interfaith Statement." The statement did not address any of the issues that the signatories, in other conversations, noted as points of disagreement, especially masturbation, homosexuality, and nonmarital sex. But it did encourage educators to address and acknowledge "strong difference of opinion . . . on what is right and wrong sexual behavior" without squelching dissent or demanding uniformity. Education should foster "objective, informed and dignified discussion" across these disagreements, and educators should not present their own moral views as "the consensus of the major religions or of society generally."[60] The "Interfaith Statement" thus embodied genuine tensions: while it asserted Judeo-Christian support for healthy—and implicitly heterosexual—sexuality and marriage, it also appealed for pluralism and tolerance in the face of moral disagreement about sex.

The conservative attacks on SIECUS did not halt the implementation of sex-education curricula in public schools; in many places, the opposition inadvertently worked in favor of sex-education reformers. But the sex-education battles had lasting consequences for religious debates about sexual morality. They paved the way for the notorious culture wars of the next decade, as the sociologist Janice Irvine notes, by helping "launch Christian evangelicals and fundamentalists into the realms of sexual politics."[61] Leaders of this emerging Religious Right, as this movement would be termed, defended their ideals about sexuality and social life with traditionalist—even reactionary—claims about preserving the past. The content of these traditionalist ideals, however, were more complex and innovative than this rhetoric implied. The conservative evangelical Protestants at the helm of the Religious Right were changing their own teachings about sex: their traditionalist political vision was shaped and fueled by their adaptive embrace of the modern, health-based framework championed by their liberal opponents.[62]

Judeo-Christian Morality and the Religious Right

The sex-education protests made conservative Protestants look like fearful, antisex reactionaries. This reputation seemed all the more apt as the early skirmishes over sex education opened into a larger battle over feminism, abortion, and homosexuality. Beginning in the late 1970s and gaining force through the 1980s, conservative Protestants joined with like-minded Roman Catholics and some conservative Jews to support "moral values" politics, and they anchored these politics to traditional Judeo-Christian values. While this conservative movement used the rhetoric of tradition, much of what they defended was in fact very new. These ideals, in fact, had been shaped by the liberal religious groups that had earlier fused together therapeutic sexuality and religious pluralism into a shared ideal of Judeo-Christian morality. Evangelical and fundamentalist Protestants at the forefront of these developments were drawing from the medical and scientific resources that had so powerfully influenced ASHA and SIECUS. In ways that might seem contradictory, these medical and scientific resources shaped fundamentalists' and evangelicals' embrace of heterosexuality as a spiritual value.

The embrace of this Judeo-Christian conception of sexual health was also surprising, given the extent to which many evangelical and fundamentalist leaders before the 1960s adamantly criticized the modern celebration of heterosexual pleasure. Early twentieth-century fundamentalist leaders regarded sexual desire as unruly and dangerous, as something that needed to be strictly regulated. As liberal religionists actively developed educational programs to encourage healthy sexuality, fundamentalists doubled down on taboos against unchaperoned "sex-mingling." To many outsiders, these aversions suggested exactly the fear-based mentality that led to unhealthy sexuality. The writing of early twentieth-century fundamentalists looked like a case in point. The Presbyterian bachelor Clarence Macartney, author of the 1931 marital advice book *The Way of a Man with a Maid*, derided sentimental expectations for marriage, which he blamed on romance novels and moving pictures. These worldly sources disseminated "an unnatural, unwholesome sentimental relationship between man and woman; a sort of sex thrill altogether apart from the sober marriage." Men and women should enter marriage with the expectation to suffer. This "garden of labor, denial, and trial" was not designed for happiness; it was created to test and prove one's faith.[63] While conservative Protestants increasingly embraced the ideals of marital happiness, they questioned the value of heterosexual pleasure as late as 1960. The sociologist Pitirim A. Sorokin, writing in the conservative evangelical publication *Christianity Today*, derided "heterosexual love" as a sign of the United States' increasingly "sex-obsessed" culture. This "glamorized . . . model of sex conduct," Sorokin lamented, was obsessive and self-serving—a mere "union of the sex organs" and a "means for self-gratification."[64]

During the middle decades of the twentieth century, this group of stalwart antimodernists overhauled their brand. Beginning in the 1960s, evangelicals began to adopt and adapt the psychoanalytic framework of sexual health. A new openness was apparent in evangelicals' reevaluation of birth control, a permission that went hand in hand with their newfound celebration of love and sexual pleasure in marriage. A 1966 article in *Christianity Today* by John Warwick Montgomery, an evangelical Lutheran theologian and celebrated critic of liberal Christianity, became the authoritative evangelical response to the question of birth control. Marriage, wrote Montgomery, should not be viewed "simply as a procreative function," and birth control could nurture a loving relationship between spouses. Montgomery carefully distinguished his reasoning from "the shackles of legalism" expressed in the Roman Catholic prohibition and the "chaos of libertarianism" found in the liberal Protestant embrace of contraception.[65] Strategically positioned between the extremes of cultural relativism and rigid traditionalism, evangelicals thus continued to stand apart—at least in their theological reasoning—by citing the sole authority of the Bible for questions of human sexual morality.

Conservative Protestant leaders of the 1960s began to authorize sexual pleasure as part of God's design for marriage, but they did this by rearticulating new ideas within a traditionalist and biblicist idiom. The Southern Baptist preacher Billy Graham typified this mode of resignifying sex. A leader in the evangelical realignment and widely hailed as "America's pastor," Graham preached a gospel that linked Christian nationalism to the nuclear family. He also proclaimed what was essentially a therapeutic approach to sexuality, linking sex to pleasure and well-being—in marriage—while also insisting that God's design for sex in marriage was neither primarily nor exclusively about procreation. At the same time, Graham derided the perils of secularism and warned against God's punishment for sexual immorality.[66] Even as evangelical leaders invoked the timelessness of scripture as their authority, they transformed the nature of marital sexuality.[67]

As evangelicals embraced new ideals of heterosexuality, they also forged new connections with conservative Jews and Catholics as "cobelligerents" in a culture war against secular humanism. The idea of cobelligerency was developed by Francis Schaeffer, a conservative theologian and scholar, who used it to argue that evangelicals and fundamentalists should align with socially conservative Catholics and Orthodox Jews, an alliance that Schaeffer saw as especially needed for opposing abortion.[68] This ecumenical cooperation was a groundbreaking development for evangelicals and fundamentalists, whose fierce commitments to doctrinal purity had often made it difficult to work with each other, much less with people who held different doctrines altogether.

The sense of urgency that fueled these new interfaith political alliances was also tied to a changing sense of the cultural enemy. Evangelical and fundamentalist leaders of the 1950s and 1960s routinely warned about the perils of communism; during the mid- to late 1970s, these leaders began to shift their focus to the perceived threat of secular humanism. Francis Schaeffer's immensely popular film series *How Should We Then Live?* (1976), Tim LaHaye's best-selling book *The Battle for the*

Mind (1980), and Jerry Falwell's *Fundamentalist Phenomenon* (1981) warned of a secularizing trend in US culture that infiltrated all but the most stalwart of Bible-believing traditionalists.[69] In this battle between religious and secular worldviews, conservative Protestant leaders spoke increasingly of their political alignment with conservative Jews, Catholics, and Mormons, all of whom shared a foundation of Judeo-Christian and biblically based values.[70] This formulation allowed evangelicals to claim their place as the legitimate heirs to Judeo-Christian morality while interpreting liberal and progressive Jewish and Christian views as secularized and immoral, a form of bad faith that threatened to corrupt the US nation. By claiming the true Judeo-Christian outlook against the essentially secular framework of liberal Catholics, Jews, and Protestants, Judeo-Christian values could become something different—something that allowed evangelicals to claim their own authority as the authentic inheritors of the long history of Judaism and Christianity and of American civilization.

It was not until the 1980s—and new crises over HIV/AIDS—that evangelicals and their "cobelligerent" Catholics and Jews began to routinely present homosexuality as a threat to family values. And it was not until the 1990s that such rhetoric came to focus on marriage and the specifically heterosexual nature of marriage as essential religious teaching that united these three religious traditions. Conservative Protestants, together with like-minded Roman Catholics and some Jews, joined forces to support a "moral values" politics anchored in their own vision of Judeo-Christian values. While this conservative movement used the rhetoric of tradition, much of what it defended was in fact very new. It was exactly this group—the fundamentalist and evangelical leaders of the Christian Right—who most influentially shaped the public meanings of the Judeo-Christian tradition, particularly as they gained political power on the platform of family values.

Conclusion: Which Judeo-Christianity?

This chapter shows that Christian and Jewish investment in the distinct heterosexuality of marriage is a remarkably recent development, one that emerged in the twentieth century. Religious marriage incorporated new conceptions of heterosexuality as leaders and practitioners in US faith communities incorporated the health-based frameworks of the therapeutic sciences into their teachings about marriage and sexuality. As Christians and Jews revised their notions of sexuality and marriage, they also articulated a positive inheritance of "Judeo-Christian" morality. In this new framing, the Judeo-Christian inheritance was not merely a source of regulation and prohibition but a positive resource that nurtured a fulfilling spiritual and sexual relationship between husband and wife. These new expectations for marriage were in some ways a force of sexual liberalism that helped to pave the way for second-wave feminist and gay-rights challenges to patriarchal marriage.[71] At the same time, another consequence of these changes was that among some religious groups—and especially among conservative evangelicals—being religious came to entail a ferocious investment in heterosexuality as right and moral. Indeed, the heteronormative definition of marriage took up increasing importance as a symbol of tradition as norms and practices for marriage changed. Changes within faith communities also proceeded in step with the broader culture, with more marriages ending in divorce, more married women pursuing careers outside the home, and increasing rates of non-marital sex and out of wedlock parenthood.[72] Amid these changes, it seems more apt to interpret the various religious styles of heterosexuality as one of many politicized forms of contemporary sexual identity and not—as often claimed—as the expression of an ancient moral code. To contest the historicity of Judeo-Christian heteronormativity is not to question the sincerity within which such views are embraced as religious values. But it is to deny the proprietary way that "Judeo-Christian values" are often deployed to suggest that there is only one right way for Jewish and Christian practitioners to claim an authentic and adaptive relationship to their traditions.

NOTES

1. Quoted in "Texas Pastor Makes National News with 'We Will Burn' Comments [Update]," KFYO News Talk website, June 25, 2015, http://kfyo.com; Todd Starnes, "'We Will Not Obey': Christian Leaders Threaten Civil Disobedience If Supreme Court Legalized Gay Marriage," Fox News, April 28, 2015, updated May 6, 2015, www.foxnews.com; Jim Forsyth, "U.S. Evangelicals Draw Battle Lines against Same-Sex Marriage," Reuters, June 21, 2015, www.businessinsider.com.
2. Bill Chappell, "Supreme Court Declares Same-Sex Marriage Legal in All 50 States," NPR, June 26, 2015, www.npr.org.

3. Bruce Schreiner, "Kim Davis, Kentucky Clergy Jailed over Marriage Licenses, Loses Re-election Bid," *Chicago Tribune*, January 8, 2019, www.chicagotribune. com.

4. "Religious Leaders Pledge Not to Cross the Marriage Red Line," press release, Liberty Counsel, April 24, 2015, www.lc.org; "Marriage Pledge," accessed January 8, 2019, www.lc.org.

5. US Congress, House of Representatives, House Report on the Defense of Marriage Act, H.R. Rep. No. 104-664 (1996), www.gpo.gov.

6. See, for example, "American Renewal Calls on GOP to Protect Pro-Family Planks in Platform," *PR Newswire*, July 10, 2000; Larry Yudelson, "Why 'Judeo-Christian Values' Should Worry Us," *Jewish News*, October 23, 2008.

7. Jeremy Leaming, "Marriage Proposal: Religious Right, Political Allies Launch Crusade to Alter Constitution," *Church and State*, October 1, 2003, 4–6.

8. The literature on "Judeo-Christian" as a category includes K. Healan Gaston, "Interpreting Judeo-Christianity in America," *Relegere: Studies in Religion and Reception* 2, no. 2 (2012): 291–304; Mark Silk, "Notes on the Judeo-Christian Tradition in America," *American Quarterly* 36, no. 1 (1984): 65–85; Kevin M. Schultz, *Tri-faith America: How Catholics and Jews Help Postwar America to Its Protestant Promise* (New York: Oxford University Press, 2011); K. Healan Gaston, *Imagining Judeo-Christian America: Religion, Secularism, and the Redefinition of Democracy* (Chicago: University of Chicago Press, 2019).

9. Eric Hobsbawm, "Introduction: Inventing Traditions," in *The Invention of Tradition*, ed. Eric Hobsbawm and Terence Ranger (Cambridge: Cambridge University Press, 1983) 1–14; Gaston, "Interpreting Judeo-Christianity," 301.

10. Studies on the history of European nationalities and American whiteness include Nell Irvin Painter, *The History of White People* (New York: Norton, 2011); Noel Ignatiev, *How the Irish Became White* (New York: Routledge, 1995); Karen Brodkin, *How Jews Became White Folks and What That Says about Race in America* (New Brunswick, NJ: Rutgers University Press, 1998); Matthew Frye Jacobson, *Whiteness of a Different Color: European Immigrants and the Alchemy of Race.* (Cambridge, MA: Harvard University Press, 1998).

11. Megan Hale Williams, "No More Clever Titles: Observations on Some Recent Studies of Jewish-Christian Relations in the Roman World," *Jewish Quarterly Review* 99, no. 1 (2009): 37–55; Annette Yoshiko Reed and Adam H. Becker, "Introduction: Traditional Models and New Directions," in *The Ways That Never Parted: Jews and Christians in Late Antiquity and the Early Middle Ages*, ed. Adam H. Becker and Annette Yoshiko Reed (Minneapolis: Fortress, 2007), 1–34.

12. David Hunter, "Celibacy Was Queer: Rethinking Early Christianity," in *Queer Christianities*, ed. Kathleen T. Talvacchia, Michael Pettinger, and Mark Larrimore (New York: NYU Press, 2015), 13–24.

13. Hunter, "Celibacy Was Queer," 13–24; Ann Taves, "Sexuality in American Religious History," in *Retelling U.S. Religious History*, ed. Thomas A. Tweed (Berkeley: University of California Press, 1997), 30–32; David Biale, *Eros and the Jews: From*

Biblical Israel to Contemporary America (Berkeley: University of California Press, 1997).

14. Susanna Drake, *Slandering the Jew: Sexuality and Difference in Early Christian Texts* (Philadelphia: University of Pennsylvania Press, 2013).

15. Harry Cocks, *Visions of Sodom: Religion, Homoerotic Desire, and the End of the World in England, c. 1550–1850* (Chicago: University of Chicago Press, 2017), 146.

16. See David Sehat, *The Myth of American Religious Freedom* (New York: Oxford University Press, 2010), 13–68; Joan Wallach Scott, *Sex and Secularism* (Princeton, NJ: Princeton University Press, 2017), 44–50; Tisa Wenger, *Religious Freedom: The Contested History of an American Ideal* (Chapel Hill: University of North Carolina Press, 2017), 8–10; Chris Beneke and Christopher S. Grenda, introduction to *The First Prejudice: Religious Tolerance and Intolerance in Early America*, ed. Beneke and Grenda (Philadelphia: University of Pennsylvania Press, 2011), 1–20.

17. John Corrigan and Lynne S. Neal, conclusion to *Religious Intolerance in America: A Documentary History*, ed. Corrigan and Neal (Chapel Hill: University of North Carolina Press, 2010), 258.

18. Jenny Franchot, *Roads to Rome: The Antebellum Protestant Encounter with Catholicism* (Berkeley: University of California Press, 1994), 155, also 112–61; for an example of sensationalized anticonvent literature, see Maria Monk, *Awful Disclosures of Maria Monk* (New York: Howe and Bates, 1836).

19. See "Anti-Semitism," chap. 6 in Corrigan and Neal, *Religious Intolerance in America*, 147–80.

20. Anne C. Rose, *Beloved Stranger: Interfaith Families in Nineteenth-Century America* (Cambridge, MA: Harvard University Press, 2001), 123–28.

21. Jonathan Ned Katz, "'Homosexual' and 'Heterosexual': Questioning the Terms," in *A Queer World: The Center for Lesbian and Gay Studies Reader*, ed. Martin Duberman (New York: NYU Press, 1997), 13.

22. Silk, "Notes on the Judeo-Christian Tradition," 45.

23. On the history of European anthropology and so-called primitive sexuality, see Andre P. Lyons and Harriet Lyons, *Irregular Connections: A History of Anthropology and Sexuality* (Lincoln: University of Nebraska Press, 2004); on the history of European anthropology and religion, see Tomoko Masuzawa, *The Invention of World Religions, or, How European Universalism Was Preserved in the Language of Pluralism* (Chicago: University of Chicago Press, 2007).

24. William Robertson Smith, *Lectures on the Religion of the Semites* (New York: D. Appleton, 1889), 418.

25. Masuzawa, *Invention of World Religions*, 300.

26. Havelock Ellis, *Studies in the Psychology of Sex, Volume II: Sexual Inversion* (London: University Press, 1897), 147–48.

27. Freud's later work also further developed these theories. Freud's *Moses and Monotheism*, written as Nazis overcame his native Vienna, renarrated Robertson Smith's myth of civilizational progress as a searing critique of Christian barbarism. Freud transformed Christian supersession into an Oedipal drama in which European

Christians projected their repressed hostility toward God, the father deity, onto contemporary Jews. See Sigmund Freud, *Moses and Monotheism*, trans. Katherine Jones (London: Hogarth, 1939), 206–7, 215. For a history of the writing of the book, see Mark Edmundson, *The Death of Sigmund Freud: The Legacy of His Last Days* (New York: Bloomsbury, 2010).

28. Heather R. White, *Reforming Sodom: Protestants and the Rise of Gay Rights* (Chapel Hill: University of North Carolina Press, 2015), 19–23; Rebecca L. Davis, *More Perfect Unions: The American Search for Marital Bliss* (Cambridge, MA: Harvard University Press, 2010), 153–57.
29. Alfred Charles Kinsey, Wardell Baxter Pomeroy, and Clyde Eugene Martin, *Sexual Behavior in the Human Male* (Philadelphia: W. B. Saunders, 1948) 465, 473, 483, 563. Similar ideas may be found in Derrick Sherwin Bailey, *The Mystery of Love and Marriage; A Study in the Theology of Sexual Relation* (New York: Harper, 1952); Donald Webster Cory [Edward Sagarin], *The Homosexual in America: A Subjective Approach* (New York: Greenberg, 1951); and Herbert Marcuse, *Eros and Civilization: A Philosophical Inquiry into Freud* (1955; repr., Boston: Beacon, 1966).
30. Religious News Service, "Indiana Religious Leaders Attack Kinsey Report," August 24, 1953, 1, Folder 42, Box 62, Record Group 6, Papers of the National Council of Churches, Presbyterian Historical Society, Philadelphia, PA. For further discussion of religious responses to Kinsey, see R. Marie Griffith, "The Religious Encounters of Alfred C. Kinsey," *Journal of American History* 95, no. 2 (September 2008): 349–77; and Rachel Gordan, "Alfred Kinsey and the Remaking of Jewish Sexuality in the Wake of the Holocaust," *Jewish Social Studies: History, Culture, Society* 20, no. 3 (Spring–Summer 2014): 72–99.
31. Gordan, "Alfred Kinsey," 86.
32. Gaston, "Interpreting Judeo-Christianity in America," 292; Wenger, *Religious Freedom*, 167–87.
33. Margot Canaday, *The Straight State: Sexuality and Citizenship in Twentieth-Century America* (Princeton, NJ: Princeton University Press, 2009), 11.
34. "Priest, Scientist Debate Sex Mores: Clergy's Ability to Provide Guidance Also Is Discussed at Social Hygiene Session," *New York Times*, February 2, 1950, 50. The conference proceedings were published in the *Journal of Social Hygiene* 36, no. 5 (May 1950): 179–98.
35. On the history of ASHA and interfaith education, see Jeffrey P. Moran, "'Modernism Gone Mad': Sex Education Comes to Chicago, 1913," *Journal of American History* 83, no. 2 (September 1996): 481–513; Kristy L. Slominski, "Cardinal Gibbons as a Symbol for Early Sex Education" *U.S. Catholic Historian* 34, no. 1 (Winter 2016): 1–25; Christina Simmons, *Making Marriage Modern: Women's Sexuality from the Progressive Era to World War II* (New York: Oxford University Press, 2009), 16–21.
36. Leland Foster Wood, "Religion as a Family Foundation," *Journal of Social Hygiene* 36, no. 5 (May 1950): 181–86. Wood was a Baptist minister and former missionary to the Belgian Congo. He was also secretary of the Committee on Marriage and

the Home of the Federal Council of Churches of Christ in America and former professor of social ethics and religious education.

37. Wood, 181.

38. Wood, 184.

39. Albert A. Goldman, "The Jewish Tradition in Family Life Education," *Journal of Social Hygiene* 36, no. 5 (May 1950): 186–90.

40. Goldman, 186.

41. Goldman, 189–90.

42. Goldman, 189.

43. Edward B. Lyman, "Viewpoint of a Catholic Layman," *Journal of Social Hygiene* 36, no. 5 (May 1950): 192.

44. Lyman, 193.

45. See, for example, Ervin Drake, "The Second Sexual Revolution" *Time*, January 24, 1964, www.time.com; "The Morals Revolution on the U.S. Campus," *Newsweek*, April 6, 1964, 52–53.

46. For more on religion and sexual liberalism, see Griffith, "Religious Encounters," 349–377 and Davis, *More Perfect Unions*, 136–75.

47. John D'Emilio and Estelle B. Freedman, *Intimate Matters: A History of Sexuality in America*, 3rd ed. (Chicago: University of Chicago Press, 2012), 324–25.

48. See Janice M. Irvine, *Talk about Sex: The Battles over Sex Education in the United States* (Berkeley: University of California Press, 2002), 22–24; and R. Marie Griffith, *Moral Combat: How Sex Divided American Christians and Fractured American Politics* (New York: Basic Books, 2017), 155–69.

49. Gordon V. Drake, *Is the Schoolhouse the Proper Place to Teach Raw Sex?* (Tulsa: Christian Crusade, 1968).

50. Irvine, *Talk about Sex*, 40–62.

51. Griffith, *Moral Combat*, 182–83; Interfaith Commission on Marriage and Family Life, "Interfaith Statement on Sex Education," by the National Council of Churches, Synagogue Council of America, and United States Catholic Conference, approved for release June 8, 1969, reprinted in "Appendix: Interfaith Statement on Sexuality Education," in *Sexuality and Human Values: The Personal Dimensions of Sexual Experience*, by Mary S. Calderone (New York: Association Press, 1971), 153–56.

52. Interfaith Commission, "Interfaith Statement," 153.

53. Interfaith Commission, 156.

54. Interfaith Commission, 153.

55. Interfaith Commission, 154, 156.

56. William Genné, "Speaking of Sex," undated pamphlet, Box 23: Sex Education—1969, Christian Life Commission Resource Files, Archives of the Southern Baptist Church, Nashville, TN. The pamphlet advises members of Church Women United on how to counter anti-sex-education campaigns in local schools.

57. "Emerging Issues: A Dialogue," in Calderone, *Sexuality and Human Values*, 128.

58. "Emerging Issues," 129.

59. "Emerging Issues," 127.

60. Interfaith Commission, "Interfaith Statement," 156.

61. Irvine, *Talk about Sex*, 61.

62. White, *Reforming Sodom*, 123–37, 180–84.

63. Clarence Edward Macartney, *The Way of a Man with a Maid* (Nashville, TN: Cokesbury, 1931), 18–19.

64. Pitirim A. Sorokin, "The Depth of the Crisis: American Sex Morality Today," *Christianity Today*, July 4, 1960, 3.

65. Allan Carlson, *Godly Seed: American Evangelicals Confront Birth Control, 1873–1973* (New Brunswick, NJ: Transaction, 2012), 131–32; John Warwick Montgomery, "How to Decide the Birth-Control Question," *Christianity Today*, March 4, 1966, 8–10.

66. Kelsey Burke, *Christians under Covers: Evangelicals and Sexual Pleasure on the Internet* (Berkeley: University of California Press, 2016), 14.

67. See also Susan Friend Harding, *The Book of Jerry Falwell: Fundamentalist Language and Politics* (Princeton, NJ: Princeton University Press, 2000), 168–73; Davis, *More Perfect Unions*, 205–13.

68. See Neil Young, *We Gather Together: The Religious Right and the Problem of Interfaith Politics* (New York: Oxford University Press, 2016).

69. *How Should We Then Live?*, writ. Francis A. Schaeffer (Gospel Films, 1976); Tim LaHaye, *The Battle for the Mind* (Old Tappan, NJ: Revell, 1980); Jerry Falwell, *The Fundamentalist Phenomenon* (Garden City, NY: Doubleday, 1981).

70. George Marsden, *Understanding Fundamentalism and Evangelicalism* (Grand Rapids, MI: W. B. Eerdmans, 1991), 107–9.

71. Simmons, *Making Marriage Modern*, 218–26.

72. On changing marriage practices for evangelicals, see Sally K. Gallagher and Christian Smith, "Symbolic Traditionalism and Pragmatic Egalitarianism: Contemporary Evangelicals, Families, and Gender," *Gender and Society* 13, no. 2 (April 1999): 211–33; Mark A. Smith, "Religion, Divorce, and the Missing Culture War in America," *Political Science Quarterly* 125, no. 1 (Spring 2010): 57–85; and Burke, *Christians under Covers*, 1–28.

13

The Price of Shame

Second-Wave Feminism and the Lewinsky-Clinton Scandal

ANDREA FRIEDMAN

In 1998, Monica Lewinsky became known around the world as the former White House intern whose affair with President Bill Clinton almost destroyed his political career. Almost: Clinton's refusal to admit that he had "sexual relations" with her led to his impeachment by the House of Representatives; yet he was acquitted by the Senate, and his public approval ratings actually went up. It was Lewinsky whose ruin seemed more assured. Her narrative about their sexual relationship—that it was consensual, intimate, and mutually pleasurable—was widely ridiculed, and so was she. During Clinton's Senate trial, only 12 percent of Americans viewed her favorably, and 42 percent expressed "no sympathy" toward her at all. Accusing Lewinsky of stalking, selfishness, greed, and seduction, many blamed her for the whole affair.[1]

In 2014, Monica Lewinsky successfully reinvented herself as a public intellectual and an antibullying activist, drawing links between her experiences in the 1990s and those of contemporary youth victimized by cyberbullying. Her claim that she was "patient zero" of internet shaming found ready support in the media that had once provided the engine for her public humiliation. As the *Time* columnist Jessica Bennett wrote, "Long before slut-shaming was a term, Monica Lewinsky was its original target."[2]

Bennett was wrong in at least one important sense: shaming women for their "excessive" sexual desire is a time-honored practice of exclusion and erasure, and Lewinsky was hardly the first to experience it. A close look at the Lewinsky-Clinton scandal further suggests that "slut-shaming" is too flat a term for understanding the relationship between the scandal and the history of heterosexuality. Slut-shaming disciplines women by placing them in a sexual economy defined by female excess. But as much as Lewinsky was painted as voraciously sexual, she was humiliated for believing that she and the president had an emotionally intimate and mutually satisfying relationship in which her pleasure mattered. Focusing on the story about the affair she told at the time highlights important shifts as well as continuities in the systems of value and exchange that constituted the economy of normative heterosexuality at the end of the twentieth century.

Lewinsky's experience reveals the contradictions within a strand of second-wave feminist activism that sought to place an ethic of mutual pleasure and desire at the core of heterosexuality. This ethic grounded early women's liberationist critiques of the so-called sexual revolution; it mobilized movements against sexual violence and pornography; and it was embedded in sexual harassment law under the rubric of "unwelcomeness." By the 1990s, the normative value of sexual mutuality was widely accepted within American culture, but its meaning was up for grabs. Mutuality necessitated exchange among individuals, but what sorts of sharing or reciprocity were required to constitute such exchange? Did mutuality demand sameness? Was mutuality possible while broader structures of inequality—at the workplace, in the family, in the culture at large—remained?

Monica Lewinsky's affair with Bill Clinton expressed in particularly compelling ways the instabilities at the heart of norms of mutuality. It was an office relationship that became visible only because another woman sued the president for sexual harassment. While other women accused Clinton of exploiting and abusing them, Lewinsky insisted that their relationship was fully consensual and mutually pleasurable. Their access to status and power could not have been more unequal.[3] They told wildly competing stories about the facts and meanings of their intimate behavior. Those stories mattered deeply to the outcome of an ongoing investigation of the Clinton administration being conducted by Kenneth Starr. For all of these reasons, the Lewinsky-Clinton scandal presents a perfect storm for analyzing the impact of and response to feminist reimaginings of heterosexuality at the end of the twentieth century.[4]

Ironically, the feminist-inspired ethic of heterosexual mutuality centered around women's pleasure provided the foundation for Lewinsky's humiliation. Humiliation is, after all, a political technology, intended to shame those who step outside their place in a social order. When Lewinsky asserted that her affair with Clinton was about a "man and a woman and not the president and the intern," she most definitely moved out of her place. With few exceptions, the response to her claims, from Clinton's defenders and his critics, depended on denying the authority of her narrative, ridiculing her interpretations, and silencing her voice. Indeed, she was doubly humiliated, for claiming that her relationship with the president was constituted by meaningful and mutual exchange and for enjoying sex acts (specifically, fellatio) that were broadly understood as the epitome of inequality.

Feminists contributed to Lewinsky's humiliation, although there was no singular "feminist" response to the scandal. Reflecting divisions that had marked feminist organizing since the late 1970s, some advocates of women's freedom and equality supported Lewinsky's claims of mutuality. Others could not and labeled her naïve at best but, more often, a victim of exploitation. One very popular strategy for humiliating Lewinsky was to deride her rendering of her desire for Clinton as a romantic fantasy. According to this logic, she misinterpreted his actions and intentions, convincing herself that Bill Clinton was her Prince Charming and that they had a future together. Many feminists subscribed to this view at the time, and it continues to hold sway as an example of the ways that ideologies of patriarchal heterosexuality overdetermine women's experience. For the sociologist Chrys Ingraham, for example, Lewinsky's self-representation is an example of the heterosexual imaginary, demonstrating the influence of ideologies of romantic love that distract women from the social relations of the heterosexual institution, "mask[ing] or conceal[ing] contradictions in favor of reproducing a reassuring illusion or the promise of well-being and bonding." "Patriarchal heterosexuality," she argues, "makes use of the ideology of romantic love to serve the interests of male dominance and capitalism."[5] While there is undoubtedly truth to this view, it nonetheless dismisses the value of Lewinsky's own testimony while diminishing the historical change, however incomplete, that enabled her to imagine herself something of Clinton's equal. Further, such an interpretation leaves little room for thinking about how we make meaning for ourselves, even if we cannot make it as we please. Rather than viewing Lewinsky as "trapped" by institutionalized heterosexuality, I suggest, we would do better to trace the meanings she made of her experience as Bill Clinton's lover, as well as how those meanings were turned against her. At the end of this chapter, I briefly consider Lewinsky's continued efforts to understand that experience in the wake of #MeToo.

Feminism, Mutuality, and the Meanings of Workplace Sex

The value of mutual pleasure to a well-functioning heterosexuality has been a fixture of American sexual ideology at least since early in the twentieth century. From companionate marriage in the 1920s to togetherness in the 1950s, it was a truism that heterosexual relationships and marriage worked better when women's and men's experiences were somehow "in tune." When activists in the women's liberation movement began thinking and writing about sexuality in the mid-1960s, their foremost contribution was to unmask the notion of heterosexual mutuality as an ideal rather than a reality, even as an ideal that operated to subordinate women to men by making them desire intimacy with those who oppressed them. Most famously, in 1970 Anne Koedt argued that men's construction of the vaginal orgasm as both an anatomic possibility and the sexual standard functioned ideologically to prohibit the creation of an authentic and autonomous female sexuality. While she noted that men maintained the myth in part because they feared women would discover they were disposable—"the recognition of clitoral orgasm as fact would threaten the heterosexual institution"—Koedt's greatest concern was to use knowledge about the possibilities of female sexual pleasure to "create new guidelines which take into account mutual sexual enjoyment." By the 1970s, some feminists shifted their emphasis to emotional intimacy and "bonding" rather than orgasm as the measure of mutuality. Still, they also emphasized reciprocity between partners as the basis of a "feminist" sexuality. Fostering true intimacy through common concern for each other's emotional and physical feelings would revolutionize heterosexuality and make it possible to build a world that valued women's pleasures and desires equally with men's.[6]

Subsequent debates among feminist activists revealed that the meanings and value of mutuality were anything but simple. Antiviolence and antipornography activists maintained that attending to emotional intimacy and mutual desire might operate as a brake on male sexual aggression and dominance, but they questioned the possibilities for real mutuality under the current conditions of a sexuality that was made for the purpose of enacting male supremacy. Those who identified themselves as "sex positive" disputed the very idea that mutuality (especially when equated with something akin to "sameness") ought to be the marker of a feminist sex. For these activists, judging sex against a standard of mutuality and closeness proved an impediment to imagining a universe of possibility for women's sexual self-determination.

Despite these disagreements, feminist reimaginings of mutuality came to reside at the center of the emerging regulatory framework for adjudicating sexual harassment. Women had long struggled to defend themselves against sexual abuse in their workplaces, but in the 1970s and 1980s, working women and their advocates crystallized a specific understanding of the harms of that abuse and the remedies for it, creating a legal schema that was endorsed by federal officials by the mid-1980s. As defined by the Equal Employment Opportunity Commission (EEOC) in 1980, sexual harassment consisted of "unwelcome sexual advances, requests for sexual favors, and other verbal or physical conduct of a sexual nature." Such behavior constituted sex discrimination and was barred by the Civil Rights Act of 1964. Borrowing terms popularized by the feminist legal scholar Catharine MacKinnon, EEOC staffers defined two forms of sexual harassment: "the *quid pro quo*, in which sexual compliance is exchanged, or proposed to be exchanged, for an employment opportunity," and the "hostile work environment," in which sexual conduct in the workplace had "the purpose or effect of unreasonably interfering with an individual's work performance, or creating an intimidating, hostile or offensive working environment." Six years later, in *Meritor Savings Bank v. Vinson*, the US Supreme Court unanimously upheld this approach.[7]

The ruling in *Meritor* revealed how substantially certain feminist approaches to sexuality were being embedded in state processes, even if the court did not fully satisfy anti-sexual-harassment activists. First, *Meritor* offered a nuanced understanding of sexual consent. Rejecting the argument that a woman's "voluntary" or "consensual" participation in workplace sex prohibited a claim of sexual harassment, the justices agreed that the important question in such a claim was whether sexual attention—including advances as well as comments, gestures, or climate—was "unwelcome." The legal category of consent often presumed that women were free actors, even when they were operating within social institutions such as the workforce that were grounded in hierarchy. Welcomeness, on the other hand, began with the assertion that mutual interest and mutual desire were necessary to constituting the conditions under which women could move freely within the marketplace.[8] Second, citing precedent in racial-discrimination law, the court asserted that the harms posed by sexual harassment need not be economic; they could be psychological and emotional. The finding that Title VII of the Civil Rights Act "affords employees the right to work in an environment free from discriminatory intimidation, ridicule, and insult" was critical to the very concept of the hostile work environment.[9]

This emphasis on emotional harm had unintended consequences, buttressing unfortunate connections between female sexuality and notions of shame and humiliation. Feminist antiharassment activists had themselves made the connection. Subjecting women to "sexual slurs and/or the public display of derogatory images of women or the requirement that she dress in sexually revealing clothing," they argued, made women "feel humiliated because of [their] sex."[10] Seeking to highlight the ways that controlling women's *sexuality* was an essential strategy for maintaining the inequality *between the sexes*, activists insisted that harassment constituted a means of defending male supremacy in the face of women's movement into the paid labor market in greater numbers and more diverse sectors.[11] Sexual humiliation was a weapon against the possibility of their economic independence, meant to shore up heterosexuality as a political and social institution that ensured men's dominance over women.

Focusing on humiliation no doubt spoke to many women's experiences in the workplace. For example, when the law professor Anita Hill alleged in 1991 that the Supreme Court nominee Clarence Thomas had created a hostile work environment while he was her boss at the EEOC, some of her most eloquent testimony described her embarrassment and humiliation when he talked explicitly about sex in their workplace. Many women who watched the broadcast of Thomas's confirmation hearings recognized themselves in her testimony. Indeed, as Hill learned, humiliation traveled. Simply speaking about her experience, especially as an African American woman, subjected her to new forms of very public humiliation, ranging from the allegation that she was a "scorned woman" seeking revenge to the charge that she was an uptight prude who misread racialized forms of sociability.[12]

Nonetheless, as long as humiliation was anchored to *unwelcome* sexual attention, there were some limits to the ways it could be used in sexual harassment cases. The passage of the 1994 Violence Against Women Act (VAWA) helped loosen that bond. Part of a broader anticrime effort that vastly expanded government law enforcement capacities, VAWA was promoted as a means of helping women protect themselves from a range of forms of gender violence. Among its sprawling provisions, VAWA incorporated language from the criminal law of sexual assault to define the rules of evidence that applied to sexual harassment proceedings. Most to the point here, the act defined "sexual contact" as "the intentional touching, either directly or through the clothing, of the genitalia, anus, groin, breast, inner thigh, or buttocks of any person with an intent to abuse, humiliate, harass, degrade, or arouse or gratify the sexual desire of any person." Not all "sexual contact" was prohibited, but in designating some contact as harmful and some as gratifying, the law both distinguished "bad" and "good" sex and made each a matter of state surveillance. Further, in a reversal of the normal federal rules of evidence in civil and criminal cases, VAWA allowed evidence of "similar" past acts by an alleged perpetrator to be introduced in order to identify a "pattern" of assault. However, what made acts "similar" was a matter of interpretation. In sexual harassment cases, that past sexual acts occurred *in the workplace* was one potential axis of similarity. As a result, it became possible to introduce evidence relating to a purported harasser's history of workplace sex even if there was no allegation of force, lack of consent, or intent to humiliate, harass, or degrade. Whether that conduct was welcome—and, hence, whether it was relevant to the case—was a matter to be determined through the legal process. Advocates of an expansive definition of sexual harassment viewed such evidence as potentially indicative of a propensity to use one's power in the workplace to exploit one's employees or coworkers. As a result, a wide variety of sexual encounters, even those that might be welcomed by those involved, could be introduced in cases alleging sexual assault, abuse, or harassment.[13]

This ambiguity made Monica Lewinsky's humiliation possible. Lewinsky was twenty-two years old and just completing a stint as a White

House intern in November 1995 when she met President Bill Clinton. Their affair continued, on and off, until May 1997; she was a paid federal employee, first in the White House, then at the Pentagon, for its duration. Lewinsky had promised to tell no one, but she confided in a number of people, including her work friend Linda Tripp. Tripp had a strong distaste for Bill and Hillary Clinton, and she funneled that information to conservative activists, journalists, and ultimately to Special Prosecutor Kenneth Starr, who had been appointed to investigate charges of corruption against the Clintons. She also contacted lawyers for the former Arkansas state employee Paula Jones. Jones was pursuing a suit against the president, claiming that in 1991, then-governor Clinton had invited her to his hotel room, where he exposed his penis and asked her to "kiss" it. She alleged that the incident damaged her career and caused myriad psychological and emotional harms: "embarrassment, humiliation, fear, emotional distress, horror, grief, shame, marital discord and loss of reputation." After hearing from Tripp, Jones's lawyers placed Lewinsky's name on a list of potential witnesses, along with those of other women who were rumored to have had sexual encounters with Clinton while he was an elected official. Lewinsky avoided testifying by filing an affidavit denying a sexual relationship with the president, but Jones's lawyers questioned Clinton about his relationship with Lewinsky in a January 1998 deposition. It was at this moment—about eight months after their physical intimacy had definitively ended—that rumors of the affair surfaced.[14]

Clinton's deposition reveals the ways that the emergent sexual harassment regime blurred the lines between sex that was welcome and sex that was not. Not only was the questioning about his relationship with Lewinsky devoid of any hint that contact between them might have been unwelcome—indeed, Jones's lawyers characterized it as an "affair"—but the entire deposition also relied on a definition of "sexual relations" that selectively drew from VAWA's language regarding "sexual contact." Gone was the language concerned with the "intent to abuse, humiliate, harass [or] degrade." Instead, Clinton was asked if his interactions with Lewinsky included "contact with the genitalia, anus, groin, breast, inner thigh, or buttocks of any person with an intent to arouse or gratify the sexual desire of any person." Jones's lawyers presumed that knowing something about putatively consensual and arguably mutual sex acts that aroused and gratified could produce knowledge about whether Clinton also had a propensity to harass, humiliate, and degrade. Such a move completely elided the question of welcomeness at the heart of sexual harassment law. When Clinton chose to deny that he had had sexual relations with Lewinsky, it ensured that the attention to his sex life, and hers, would not go away.[15]

What Does It Mean to Be a Blow Job Queen? Sexual Pleasure, Mutuality, and Humiliation

Lewinsky and Clinton both denied in January 1998 that they had sexual relations, but by August, when each testified before a grand jury convened by Kenneth Starr, their stories diverged remarkably. The mutuality of the relationship was the key point of difference. Clinton maintained to the grand jurors that, while he may have engaged in "inappropriate intimate contact" with Lewinsky, it did not amount to sexual relations as the term was defined for his deposition. Implying that their contact had been confined to fellatio, he insisted that any touching he might have engaged in was "not with anything on that list, but with the lips of another person."[16] Lewinsky, who had been granted immunity from prosecution in exchange for her willingness to testify about their sex, described ten sexual encounters, all of which involved mutual touching. Almost all of these included fellatio, but they also usually included his touching of her breasts, with his hands and mouth, as well as four occasions when he manually stimulated her genitals and one when he penetrated her with an object (the infamous cigar). Both had orgasms, Lewinsky more often than Clinton, and his occurred only near the end of the affair.[17]

Clinton and Lewinsky may have differed over what body parts were involved in their intimate contact, but in an odd way, they agreed about the importance of mutuality to heterosexual sex. For Clinton, it was not sex if there was no shared interest, concern, or pleasure—or, at least, that was how he interpreted the definition of sexual relations with which he was presented. As he told the grand jury, "I read this [definition] carefully. And I thought about it. I thought about what 'contact' meant. I thought about what 'intent to arouse or gratify' meant." Under questioning, he acknowledged that *if* he had touched Lewinsky's breasts or genitals directly *and if* he had done so "with an intent to arouse or gratify" her, he would have engaged in sexual relations with her, but he maintained, "I do not believe I did anything that I thought was covered." His denial concerned not the touching itself (indeed, he simply refused to answer direct questions about what he and Lewinsky did together) but what he sought to accomplish by the touching: his *own* arousal. Her pleasure was beside the point.[18] In contrast, Lewinsky too insisted on her own arousal, but she emphasized that it was possible only in the context of mutual desire and exchange. Calling Clinton her "sexual soulmate," she described a repertoire of reciprocal touching that created both physical and emotional intimacy.

Most radically, Lewinsky included fellatio as a mutually pleasurable aspect of that repertoire. When asked "how did it come about" that she "perform[ed] oral sex" on February 4, 1996, she replied, "It was a mutual. . . . I mean, it was the course of being intimate. I mean, it was the course of having this kind of a relationship that you—sometimes he initiated it, sometimes I initiated it. . . . I mean, it was, it was the passion of the moment. . . . I always felt that, we sort of just, we both really went to a, to a whole other place together sexually."[19] She countered Clinton's portrayal of their sex as one-sided by placing it in a broader context for the grand jurors:

> M[ONICA LEWINSKY]: From my understanding about what he testi-
> fied to on Monday . . . is that this was a . . . service contract, that all I
> did was perform oral sex on him and that that's all that this relation-
> ship was. And it was a lot more than that to me and I thought it was a
> lot more than that.
> G[RAND] J[UROR]: You said the relationship was more than oral sex.
> I mean, it wasn't like you went out on dates or anything like that like
> normal people, so what more was it?
> M: Oh, we spent hours on the phone talking. It was emotional. . . . Not
> always [phone sex]. . . . I mean, we were talking. I mean, interacting.
> I mean, talking about what we were thinking and feeling and doing
> and laughing.[20]

For Lewinsky, their sex practices could not be extracted from the human interaction that made their relationship "a lot more," an exchange of emotion and intellect, desire and pleasure.[21]

Indeed, as Lewinsky told the story, what would come to be viewed as proof that Clinton lied—her semen-stained blue dress—was a testament to their mutual concern for each other's pleasure. Over the course of their affair, Lewinsky became increasingly disturbed that Clinton would not come during oral sex.[22] As she understood it, this reflected his belief that if he did not ejaculate, it was not really sex. But her concern arose out of a different calculus: his refusal to come served as an impediment to a growing intimacy between them because it represented his unwillingness to "trust" her. His semen would be proof of their emotional exchange, matching her own orgasmic pleasure. She told members of Starr's staff that in February 1997 she pushed Clinton on the issue: "I stood up and I said, you know, I really, I care about you so much; I really, I don't understand why you won't let me, you know, make you come; it's important to me; I mean, it just doesn't feel complete, it doesn't seem right." In her telling, Clinton confessed his fear that, if they went too far, they would become "addicted" to each other; but he was unwilling to disappoint her, so he gave in. The exchange she described was not simply a matter of bodily fluids: it comprised both her desire for his pleasure and, crucially, his care for her feelings.[23]

Ultimately, Lewinsky's description of a relationship that embodied a heterosexual economy of mutual pleasure sustaining emotional intimacy became grist for the mill of her public humiliation. A broad range of commentators and critics found in her claims of mutuality evidence that Lewinsky was delusional, narcissistic, or pathologically naïve. This was an argument readily taken up by many of Clinton's supporters and his legal team. For example, during the Senate impeachment trial, Clinton's attorney Greg Craig showed senators a videotaped excerpt from Richard Davis's testimony before the House of Representatives. (Davis had formerly served as a member of the Watergate Special Prosecution force.) Casting the scandal as a typical he-said/she-said "swearing contest," Davis had told the representatives that the evidence mustered by Starr

> simply does not form the basis for a perjury prosecution. Indeed, in the end, the entire basis for a grand jury perjury prosecution comes down to Monica Lewinsky's assertion that there was a reciprocal nature to their relationship, and that the president touched her private parts with the intent to arouse or gratify her, and the president's denial that he did so. . . .

[Any] prosecutor would understand the problem created by the fact that both individuals had an incentive to lie—the president to avoid acknowledging a false statement at his civil deposition, and Miss Lewinsky to avoid the demeaning nature of providing wholly unreciprocated sex.[24]

Craig used Davis's testimony to suggest that sex acts that existed outside an economy of mutual exchange were so inherently shameful that Lewinsky might invent a fantasy account to make herself feel better.

Craig's defense of the president proved particularly persuasive in the context of long-standing understandings of fellatio as "cocksucking," a degraded act of sexual submission. In the nineteenth century, heterosexual fellatio was associated with female prostitutes, even though many sex workers refused to participate in the practice. By the turn of the twentieth century, both the media and police drew attention to same-sex fellatio as a practice that effeminate "fairies" performed on masculine men and that "gay" or "queer" men engaged in together. Older notions of oral-genital sex as immoral or sinful thus also took on gendered meanings as an act performed by a feminized person, usually for the pleasure of a masculine one. This view persisted even as both fellatio and cunnilingus became increasingly ordinary practices over the course of the twentieth century, particularly for white middle-class Americans who saw them as conducive to marital satisfaction. "Unreciprocated" fellatio, widely understood as fellatio unaccompanied by cunnilingus, interrupted the sexual economy of mutuality within which these practices became normalized heterosexual acts; it stood, instead, for the privileging of phallic pleasure and the domination of women. This critique of fellatio was taken up by feminist antiporn activists in the 1970s and 1980s, particularly in the controversies surrounding the release of the porno-chic film *Deep Throat* and star Linda (Boreman) Lovelace's later allegations of her own sexual abuse during its production.[25]

Most media coverage of the Lewinsky-Clinton scandal echoed this tradition of interpreting unreciprocated fellatio as feminine humiliation, refuting Lewinsky's tale of mutual desire, emotional intimacy, and female pleasure. Clinton was described as inviting fellatio in a brusque and entitled manner: he indicated with gestures that Lewinsky should "perform" oral sex while he was talking on the phone, or he unzipped his pants to "signal" his expectations. The very language of performing oral sex, which was endemic within the scandal (including, it must be noted, Lewinsky's narration) indicated that this was a task to be carried out, even, perhaps, a "command" performance required of a lesser individual for the entertainment of a social superior—a blow *job* in every sense of the word. The notion that Lewinsky might get real pleasure from giving head had no place in this portrayal of unequal heterosexual exchange. The assumption that fellatio could only be reciprocated by an equivalent act of cunnilingus further undermined her assertions. Her explanation that the president *wanted* to go down on her, but "mother nature got in the way" only confirmed that her willingness to give without getting back was shameful.[26]

Special Prosecutor Kenneth Starr was less interested in demonstrating Lewinsky's humiliation than in using her testimony about mutual pleasure to substantiate his case against the president. Nonetheless, his investigation was instrumental in making her an object of ridicule even as it validated some of her claims of mutuality. The report he prepared for members of Congress, popularly known as the "Starr Report" and almost instantaneously distributed globally on the internet, featured her account of her various sexual encounters with Clinton as well as other types of evidence that spoke to their shared experience. It documented exhaustively the many gifts the two exchanged, ranging from coffee mugs, costume jewelry, and neckties to Walt Whitman's *Leaves of Grass*. These, too, were mostly portrayed in the media as tacky and cheap, evidence of the lovers' common lack of class and taste. For Starr, though, this gift economy was crucial evidence of an intimate relationship, supporting Lewinsky's claims of mutuality.[27]

Evidence of mutual touching and female arousal was necessary to prove the case of perjury, yet Starr's investigation perversely hid much of it. The chart of "contacts" between Clinton and Lewinsky that Starr staffers handed out to grand jurors when Lewinsky testified before them and that was later reproduced in the Starr Report was intended to distill Lewinsky's memories of her encounters with the president into a bureaucratic, ostensibly objective document. It listed dates of contact, whether they were in person or by phone, and gifts or notes exchanged. Also included was information on the spaces where contacts occurred and, purportedly, what happened during them: "kissing," "physical intimacy," one instance of "brief direct genital contact," "oral sex," and "oral sex to completion." As Lewinsky's testimony detailed, "physical intimacy" included breast, clitoral, and vaginal play, and so did many of the occasions designated simply as "oral sex." But the chart brought fellatio front and center. Its categories signified whose genitals and whose pleasure mattered: the president's "completion" (the term that was generally used within the discourse of the scandal to signify ejaculation) was highlighted, whereas Lewinsky's orgasms went unmarked.[28] While the technicalities of the case might have required that Starr feature Lewinsky's narrative, the chart's overall effect was to show that, in truth, the only pleasure that mattered was phallic.

The complex nexus between mutuality and humiliation that shaped the entire scandal is particularly clear in the treatment of Monica Lewinsky's semen-stained blue dress. Commandeered by Starr's staff and heralded as the most important piece of physical evidence that Lewinsky and Clinton had sex and he lied about it, the dress testified not only to Lewinsky's desire for mutuality but also to the irrelevance, even the impossibility, of her desire. As a piece of physical evidence, the dress was situated within new technologies of knowledge, surveillance, and punishment that affirmed the fact of male arousal as the sign of heterosexual sex and masked Lewinsky's efforts to situate female desire alongside it. The evidence of the dress worked visually: even though the semen stains were so small that they could not be detected in the grainy black-and-white photos of the dress that circulated publicly, those photos incited the imagination, producing a concrete object on which viewers could project the semen that they could not see.[29] Forensically, the DNA tests used to identify the source of the stains were relatively new. DNA "fingerprinting" techniques, which made it possible to use DNA evidence to identify individuals, were invented only in 1984; not until 1987 was DNA evidence a factor in the conviction of a criminal defendant in the United States, and it remained controversial. In 1995, DNA evidence had failed to persuade a jury that the former football star O. J. Simpson had murdered his ex-wife, Nicole Brown Simpson. The widespread acceptance of the dress as irrefutable evidence of sexual relations owed a good deal to the very recent regularization and normalization of DNA testing as a path to scientific truth. Of course, it also reflected Clinton's original fears: that if he ejaculated, he would have engaged in "real sex."[30]

The forensic uses of the blue dress refocused attention on male arousal. This narrative obscured Lewinsky's descriptions of a mutually satisfying and increasingly intimate heterosexuality in which women's pleasure mattered. Discussions of the dress also hobbled her efforts at self-representation. Even though throughout the affair Lewinsky was a federal employee, she was widely represented as a "bimbo" concerned more with consumption (obsessed with food, with shopping, and with sex) than with production, not really a working woman at all. Consequently, reporters and commentators described the dress in fantastical terms: first, a black silk cocktail dress, then "a navy-blue cocktail dress" or "a little blue dress," and eventually many variations on the theme. Linda Tripp also eroticized the dress when she claimed (against the evidence contained in her taped conversations with Lewinsky) that Lewinsky had kept it as a "souvenir," prompting New York Post staffers to dub it "Monica's Love Dress." Even Starr's assistant Karin Immergut, whom one might expect to know something about the matter, asked Lewinsky about the day she "wore the blue cocktail dress." Lewinsky retorted, with evident irritation, "It's not a cocktail dress. . . . I'm a little defensive about this subject. . . . It's a dress from the Gap. It's a work dress. It's a casual dress." It was a dress she had planned to wear to a family Thanksgiving celebration. As Lewinsky described it, the dress was a utilitarian item, one that situated her in the respectable arenas of work and family. Within the broader spectacle of the hearings, however, the dress confirmed that she was, variously, a seductress, an immature child ("I'll never wash it again!" Tripp claimed she said), a neurotic, or worse.[31]

The dress proved that Clinton ejaculated in Lewinsky's presence (which swayed public opinion and forced the president to change his story but was hardly sufficient to justify a perjury charge), but it doled out humiliation in gendered ways. It humiliated Clinton by calling into question not only his veracity but his masculinity: he seemed both unable to have "real sex" and to control his paramour. It humiliated Lewinsky by using her own desire for shared intimacy and mutuality as evidence that she was nothing but a bimbo. Indeed, the dress took on a life of its own. It stood in for Lewinsky herself, contradicting her own rendering of her experience as a young working woman who happened to have had a frustrating but also pleasurable and exciting relationship with her boss and consolidating her identity as "America's premier blow job queen."[32]

These interpretations of the meanings of the blue dress, and of Lewinsky's sexual life more generally, reveal the instability of a supposedly hegemonic ideal of heterosexual mutuality encompassing women's erotic pleasure at a moment when men's satisfaction was still taken for granted as the measure of sex. In the almost private space of the Oval Office suite, the differences in power and status that undoubtedly shaped Lewinsky's relationship with the president may have felt less significant than her experiences of reciprocity, mutual caring and desire, or even shared ecstasy. Intimacy coexisted with, but also reduced, inequality. But in the context of a public spectacle focused on the legitimacy of one man's power, Lewinsky's interpretation could not hold, and her own oral pleasures provided the most compelling evidence against her. In this end-of-the-century heterosexual economy, Lewinsky was humiliated both by her belief in mutuality and by her (alleged) failure to achieve it.

Sex Wars Redux: Inequality, Mutuality, and Heterosexuality

Contests over the meanings and possibilities of heterosexual mutuality also shaped feminists' responses to Monica Lewinsky's claims. Both at the time and since, it has become a truism that feminists did not weigh in on the affair or, if they did, that they were at best hypocritical, at worst not "feminist" at all. While the scandal was unfolding, commentators from right to left to center posited that feminist leaders sacrificed a critical assessment in order to keep their friend Clinton in office. In reality, as contributors to a *Ms.* forum complained, their critics "seemed to expect 'the feminists' to speak in a single, unified voice," but there was no single feminist position on the dynamics of Lewinsky and Clinton's affair, on the accusations by other women that Clinton had harassed or assaulted them, or even on the very definition of sexual harassment itself.[33] Women who identified as feminists disagreed on a range of issues, from whether Bill Clinton—who had dismantled the welfare system, signed the Defense of Marriage Act, and fired Surgeon General Joycelyn Elders for discussing masturbation as a safe-sex practice—was indeed their friend to whether all of these problems might be avoided if the nation would simply elect a woman president. They also battled over how Lewinsky's affair with Clinton related to complaints lodged by other women, including Paula Jones, Kathleen Willey (who alleged that he had groped her when she approached him about a job), or Juanita Broaddrick (who claimed that Clinton had raped her while he was running for election as governor). Many of Clinton's feminist supporters, as well as some of his critics, charged that the focus on Lewinsky distracted attention from the problem of "real" sexual harassment.[34] Rather than feminist silence or "hypocrisy," then, there was a rancorous cacophony.

These divisions had emerged previously, in the so-called feminist sex wars that began in the late 1970s. Remembered too simply as a contest between "antisex" and "prosex" combatants, the sex wars nonetheless expressed deep disagreement about the possibilities for consent, pleasure, and mutuality under conditions of inequality. On one side were activists who focused their efforts on media and institutions that they believed fostered violence against women, particularly sexualized violence. Intensifying women's liberationist critiques of heterosexuality as the institutionalization of male supremacy, these "radical feminists" imagined men's sexuality to be "violent, genitally focused, and emotionally detached." On the other side was a coalition made up of self-identified "sex radicals" who sought to articulate a more nuanced view of the relationship between sex, power, and pleasure and foes of censorship who mobilized in opposition to the burgeoning feminist anti-pornography movement. The members of this coalition were united by their perception that the antiviolence contingent embraced essentialist understandings of sexuality, overemphasized women's victimization, and had an unsophisticated analysis of power.[35] The Lewinsky-Clinton scandal reinvigorated these differences, becoming a defining moment in the feminist sex wars. The specifics of the case—a younger woman, an older and powerful man, the workplace, and oral sex—highlighted stark contrasts among feminists who sought to dismantle the heterosexual institution.

Some women, especially those who identified themselves as radical feminists, simply could not bring themselves to believe Lewinsky's own narration of her experience. Writing in the feminist publication *Off Our Backs*, for example, Jennie Ruby analyzed the Lewinsky affair as a textbook example of sexual harassment because Clinton used his power to "get sex" from Lewinsky. Asking if, despite the apparent power imbalance between them, this was "actually a relationship of equals because of the great love they felt for each other," she could only dismiss Lewinsky's claims and answer "no." Both the casualness of the sex ("they had sex before there was a pretense of getting to know each other") and the "non-reciprocal" character of the sex acts bothered her. Another article in the same publication argued that a relationship between "a 20-something intern and the 50-something President" could hardly be consensual: "Clearly it is symptomatic of a society where women still have to value themselves according to the men they get and men feel that part and parcel of power is to have sex with any women they want." This view also grounded one writer's argument that Lewinsky was simply one in a long line of women who were victims of Clinton's "womanizing." She defined "womanizing" as "a form of sexual predation where a man views women in terms of how he can 'get' sex from them, without regard for who they are as human beings." She clarified that a man who had sex with many women might not be a womanizer: "If he is truly thoughtful, considers their well-being, listens to them in a respectful way and there is a true sense of mutuality . . . then I would say he is not a 'womanizer.'" But, ignoring Lewinsky's own narrative of mutuality, she concluded that the affair fit a pattern of sexual predation, making it "quite plausible that he might have, on occasion, resorted to rape." All of these interpretations posited a sexual economy of heterosexuality in which a woman's testimony that a relationship was welcome bore no weight.[36]

Clinton's feminist critics also engaged with the broader rhetoric of humiliation, invoking specific sex acts as particularly humiliating and therefore harmful to women. It may come as no surprise that the prominent antipornography activist Andrea Dworkin was an early and vociferous proponent of this view. Writing in the *Guardian* of London in January 1998, Dworkin cast Lewinsky's experience as part of a pattern of abuse of power on Clinton's part, directly relevant to the claims of Paula Jones and others. Although she acknowledged that Lewinsky may have been "consenting," that was beside the point, since Clinton was "guilty of exploitation." She was particularly horrified by what she called Clinton's "fixation" on oral sex, particularly "*non-reciprocal* oral sex," which "consistently puts women in states of submission to him." For her, fellatio was "the most fetishistic, heartless, cold sexual exchange that one could imagine."[37] Even after Lewinsky spoke up for herself, others echoed Dworkin's analysis of the market relations of oral sex, endorsing the view that fellatio could only be reciprocated by an equivalent act of cunnilingus and dismissing Lewinsky's position that it could be part of a broader economy of mutuality.[38]

On the other side were feminists who insisted on taking Lewinsky at her word. In a widely remarked *New York Times* op-ed, *Ms.* magazine's founder, Gloria Steinem, may have gone too far, using Lewinsky's experience to explain why neither Paula Jones nor Kathleen Willey had been victims of sexual harassment. Invoking "the common sense guideline to sexual behavior that came out of the women's movement 30 years ago: no means no; yes means yes," she claimed that, even if Jones's and Willey's allegations of unwelcome advances were true, Clinton had stopped when they expressed their disinterest: he had taken "no" for an answer and had not tried again. This is what distinguished their cases from those of Anita Hill and other women who "had to come to work every day for a long period, never knowing what sexual humiliation awaited them." Lewinsky, on the other hand, was an example of the feminist principle "yes means yes." Steinem's position invited much criticism, but she only slightly altered it in a revision several months later. Although the "imbalance" in their ages as well as "the one-way form that the alleged sex took" might "increase the index of suspicion," she admitted, Lewinsky had insisted that the relationship was one she wanted. "Mutual consent was the primary value and this became the bedrock of sexual harassment. . . . Feminists oppose sex only if it's used to humiliate or hurt someone, or violate their will." Steinem's substitution of consent for welcomeness as the "bedrock" of sexual harassment made for a rather thin understanding of mutuality, but her insistence that respecting women's "free will" was essential to the cause of "sexual freedom" was attractive to a number of feminist commentators. The journalist Katha Pollitt quoted Steinem approvingly on "respect for women's will" and rejected the arguments of "those feminists who see younger women as unable, really, to assert their will with a powerful older man."[39]

Feminist disagreements over these issues were dramatized shortly after the scandal broke, when the Pacifica radio journalist Amy Goodman hosted Pollitt, Catharine MacKinnon, and the lawyer and philosophy professor Linda Hirshman to talk about feminist understandings of the Lewinsky-Clinton scandal on her show *Democracy Now!* The contentiousness of the discussion (Hirshman, MacKinnon, and arguably Goodman lined up against Pollitt) reveals how deeply feminists disagreed about the sexual economy of the relationship as well as its relevance for Paula Jones's and Kathleen Willey's sexual harassment claims. Debate about the first question centered on whether Lewinsky could freely consent to a relationship with, in Hirshman's words, "a notoriously and legendarily persuasive Bill Clinton." While both Hirshman and MacKinnon claimed to respect the idea that it was *possible* that Clinton's attentions were welcome to Lewinsky, they found many ways to contest Pollitt's argument that many women "want to sleep with powerful men" and that they might indeed "get something out of" those relationships. Together, they argued that Pollitt was confusing what was (a patriarchally organized heterosexuality) with what should be (sexuality organized in opposition to status inequalities). Hirshman went further to charge Clinton with serious moral offenses: "I don't think [Lewinsky's] consent . . . takes away his moral responsibility for asking her to do something that was foreseeably damaging to her." MacKinnon also emphasized outcomes that *might* occur in the future: "she may begin to feel that she was used." While there was no evidence that Lewinsky had been sexually harassed, MacKinnon acknowledged, her experience demonstrated the potential dangers of "sex under conditions of unequal power."[40]

Indeed, Hirshman and MacKinnon not only agreed that Lewinsky's experience might be part of a pattern of exploitation but also charged her with engaging in acts that were potentially harmful to herself and to other women. Hirshman was particularly upset about the "lesson" young women would learn from Lewinsky's example: "to dress in a provocative way and hang around the office of a more powerful man, . . . to get a job through questionable channels." When Pollitt suggested that Lewinsky's experience was irrelevant as evidence of a pattern of sexual harassment by Clinton—"This is a different pattern. This is a pattern of having love affairs"—Hirshman dismissed her for offering "the basic sort of free love analysis" that had characterized American society since the late nineteenth century and had exploded in the 1960s. She countered that Lewinsky's relationship with Clinton should be situated as part of a broader pattern of harms to women that emerged from "their lack of resources to live on other than by making an alliance with a male in their world." When young women like Lewinsky "start to mix it up in the big leagues . . . with immensely powerful people with a lot at stake," she concluded, "a lot of damage can occur."[41]

These were the positions that had mobilized the feminist sex wars since their beginnings in the 1970s, and sometimes those origins came into clear view. Linda Hirshman's opening statement that she found herself "unexpectedly in bed with" the Republican senator John Ashcroft, who had, the day before, spoken "movingly" about the "disproportion of power" between Lewinsky and Clinton, invited Pollitt to draw parallels to the dangerous alliances between antipornography feminists and Christian conservatives (alliances that Hirshman denied existed). When MacKinnon argued that the defense of Clinton "by a good many men and some women who support [those men]" amounted to the assertion that "this is the kind of thing that men . . . have a right to do at work," Pollitt tied the issue to the debates over power that had given rise to the sex wars in the first place. "What I fear is what we're saying," she exclaimed, "[is that] 'Oh my goodness, they're not married. Oh my goodness he didn't promise to love her for the rest of her life. This is bad, this is power.' As if marriage wasn't power, . . . as if power isn't deeply sort of a part of everything we do in this society."[42]

As the heated discussion on *Democracy Now!* suggests, the feminist debate about the meanings of Clinton and Lewinsky's sexual relationship turned on the same questions about the economics of intimate exchange that had given rise to the sex wars. Did the inequalities that fundamentally structured social life—inequalities of gender, race, age, class, status—always map directly onto sex? Should sex be authorized only when it operated *outside* and *against* structures of inequality? Did situating sex in the public marketplace intensify the inequalities of sexual exchange? Within the sexual economy of heterosexuality in particular, could women get what they wanted from intimate exchange with men? Was sexual autonomy, self-determination, or mutuality possible under such conditions? If even the validity of a woman's perception that mutual desire could exist within a relationship between unequals was called into question, if even her attraction to a relationship organized around inequality but materialized through mutuality became evidence that her own passions humiliated and harmed her, then it became impossible to sustain the distinctions between welcomeness, consent, and coercion that were at the heart of sexual harassment law.

It also became impossible for many feminists to think about Lewinsky in the terms she thought about herself. A forum in *Ms.* responding to Lewinsky's 1999 television interview with Barbara Walters articulated this problem quite neatly. The writer and humorist Susan Jane Gilman confessed herself "stunned" and "angered" by the narcissism that allowed Lewinsky to insist that the relationship was "about a man and a woman and not the president and the intern." "What can a feminist say," she asked, "about a young woman who feels so entitled that she sees herself as being on equal footing with the president?" The sex radical Susie Bright had a much different response, commenting both on Lewinsky's substantial "erotic appeal" and on her "big IQ." "An ambitious woman," she pointed out, "could be the president rather than blow the president" if her ambitions had not been thwarted by a society that "shamed and condescended to" her "smarts." Bright wanted to denounce the gender inequalities that structured modern America, while honoring Lewinsky's ways of moving through that world. But even here, there was a hint that blowing the president was something to be ashamed of. Abiola Abrams, writing as a woman of Lewinsky's generation, may have come closest to defending her on her own terms: "You were sexually confident enough to say, in essence, 'I wanted and enjoyed it.' . . . Why assume that if a woman declares she welcomes sex and the pursuit of it, either she's young and unstable or somebody else is pulling the strings?" While the term "slut-shaming" had not yet been coined, Abrams, along with other feminists who identified with the "third wave," focused on the ways Lewinsky had been humiliated for her choices and her "in-your-face sexuality." She praised Lewinsky for "moving the discourse of feminism, stagnant for so long, forward" by forcing a national conversation on "women and sex and power."[43]

When Monica Lewinsky spoke her own truth about her affair with Bill Clinton, she acknowledged that the relationship occurred under conditions of unequal power (after all, he was married, he was the one who ended it, and he was the president). She nevertheless refused to flatten the relationship into an example of her shame or his manipulation. Their particular mode of sexual exchange created a new dynamic: rather than "the president and the intern," they were "a man and a woman." She imagined that as a woman, she was not completely enjoined from getting at least some of what she wanted: a lot of bodily pleasure, a bunch of orgasms, emotional intimacy, and the intense excitement of being the president's paramour. Her sense of things was that this exchange was worth it—at least until Linda Tripp, Kenneth Starr, and a host of others used it as capital of their own. Then it suddenly became part of a different sort of economy: one in which her sexual desires, romantic longings, and belief that her pleasure mattered bought public humiliation. Among those who shamed and humiliated her, Lewinsky included feminist leaders who, she remarked in 2014, "failed in articulating a position that was not essentially anti-woman."[44] But this failure, if it was one, betrays both deep divisions among feminists about the possibilities for heterosexual mutuality in a society marked by persistent gender inequality and the ability of powerful men to use feminist ideas to keep women in their place.

* * *

The meanings that we make of our experience are shaped by the times we live in, and Monica Lewinsky's understanding of her "truth" is no exception. For twenty years, she maintained that her relationship with Bill Clinton was intimate and authentic. She acknowledged that the affair was a mistake but insisted that it was consensual. What was not consensual was the theft of her private life for political and economic gain. In a much-praised 2015 Ted Talk titled "The Price of Shame," for example, Lewinsky drew a direct line from her public shaming by Kenneth Starr and members of the media to the creation of an internet marketplace "where public humiliation is a commodity and shame is an industry."[45] But in 2018, in the wake of a renewed movement against sexual harassment, she revisited the question of consent. Given the "vast" power differences between Clinton and herself, she wrote, "I'm beginning to entertain the notion that . . . the idea of consent might well be rendered moot."[46]

Lewinsky is careful to note that the question of consent is "very, very complicated," and she is clear that she is only beginning the process of reassessing her experience as a young woman. But her reconsideration raises several questions for historians. The first concerns the difficulties of studying the recent past: How confident can we be of our interpretations when the history we tell is, as the historian Renee C. Romano puts it, "not dead yet"? The second lies at the center of Joan W. Scott's influential article "The Evidence of Experience," in which she argued that historical subjects' experience ought to be understood not as the "evidence that grounds what is known, but . . . rather that which we seek to explain, that about which knowledge is produced."[47] What, then, can we make of Lewinsky's changing articulations of her own experience?

Some people might interpret Lewinsky's emerging questions about whether her relationship with Bill Clinton was consensual as evidence that she was indeed a young woman trapped by the heterosexual imaginary, duped and delusional. There is a sense in which Lewinsky seems to endorse this view, writing that the pressures of defending herself against untrue accusations that she was a "stalker and Servicer in Chief" rendered her a dweller in the "House of Gaslight," unable to understand fully what happened to her. "An inability to deviate from the internal script of what I actually experienced," she reflects, "left little room for re-evaluation; I cleaved to what I 'knew.'"[48]

But there is room for a different reading, one that foregrounds the multiplicity and complexity of what Lewinsky "actually" experienced. Writing about her struggle with her "own sense of agency versus victimhood," she remembers, "In 1998, we were living in times in which women's sexuality was a marker of their agency—'owning desire.' And yet, I felt that if I saw myself as in any way a victim, it would open the door to choruses of 'See, you did merely service him.'"[49] The binary that Lewinsky posits—agent versus victim—precludes the possibility that women could be both at once. But her effort to break down that binary reminds us that such terms are simply not adequate for capturing the paradoxical experience of some women's pursuit of heterosexual pleasure and desire in a deeply unequal world. It also raises a question that is still with us: When choosing between agent and victim is the only possibility, can we imagine a world in which the price for women's sexuality is not shame?

NOTES

1. Frank Newport, "The Best of Times, the Worst of Times," *Public Perspective*, August–September 1999, 20–25; "CBS Poll: Congress Gets Gonged," CBS News, February 8, 1999, www.cbsnews.com. For an analysis of public opinion polling on the scandal, see Regina G. Lawrence and W. Lance Bennett, "Rethinking Media Politics and Public Opinion: Reactions to the Clinton-Lewinsky Scandal," *Political Science Quarterly* 116, no. 3 (2001): 425–46.

2. Monica Lewinsky, "The Price of Shame," video and transcript of the March 2015 Ted Talk available at www.ted.com; see also Lewinsky, "Shame and Survival," *Vanity Fair*, June 2014; Jessica Bennett, "The Shaming of Monica: Why We Owe Her an Apology," *Time*, May 9, 2014, http://time.com.

3. Race (shared whiteness), class (distinct origins and relationships to upward mobility), and religion (Lewinsky's Jewishness) interacted to mitigate and/or heighten these inequalities.

4. Two comprehensive overviews of the scandal are Ken Gormley, *The Death of American Virtue: Clinton vs. Starr* (New York: Crown, 2010); and Jeffrey Toobin, *A Vast Conspiracy: The Real Story of the Sex Scandal That Nearly Brought Down a President* (New York: Random House, 1999). The essays in Lauren Berlant and Lisa Duggan, eds., *Our Monica, Ourselves: The Clinton Affair and the National Interest* (New York: NYU Press, 2001), remain the most insightful analyses of the affair in the context of the culture wars, and I am indebted to all of the authors for their trenchant interpretations. In that volume, Ann Cvetkovich, "Sexuality's Archive: The Evidence of the Starr Report," 277–82, has been especially influential.

5. Chrys Ingraham, *White Weddings: Romancing Heterosexuality in Popular Culture*, 2nd ed. (New York: Routledge, 2008), 124–26.

6. Anne Koedt, "The Myth of the Vaginal Orgasm" in *Notes from the Second Year* (New York: New York Radical Feminists, 1970), 37–41; Jane Gerhard, *Desiring Revolution: Second-Wave Feminism and the Rewriting of American Sexual Thought, 1920 to 1982* (New York: Columbia University Press, 2001); Christina Simmons, *Making Marriage Modern: Women's Sexuality from the Progressive Era to World War II* (Oxford: Oxford University Press, 2009).

7. Equal Employment Opportunity Commission, "Final Amendment to Guidelines on Discrimination Because of Sex," 45 (219) Fed. Reg. 74677 (November 10, 1980), www.govinfo.gov; Carrie N. Baker, *The Women's Movement against Sexual Harassment* (New York: Cambridge University Press, 2008); Julie Berebitsky, *Sex and the Office: A History of Gender, Power, and Desire* (New Haven, CT: Yale University Press, 2012); Gwendolyn Mink, *Hostile Environment: The Political Betrayal of Sexually Harassed Women* (Ithaca, NY: Cornell University Press, 2000); Reva B. Siegel, "A Short History of Sexual Harassment," in *Directions in Sexual Harassment Law*, ed. Catharine A. MacKinnon and Reva B. Siegel (New Haven, CT: Yale University Press, 2004), 1–39; Catharine A. MacKinnon, *Sexual Harassment of Working Women: A Case of Sex Discrimination* (New Haven, CT: Yale University Press, 1979), 33; *Meritor Savings Bank v. Vinson*, 477 U.S. 57 (1986). On Mechelle Vinson's experience and the history of her case, see Mink, *Hostile Environment*, esp. 64–70.

8. In emphasizing the ways that "unwelcomeness" foregrounded mutuality, my interpretation differs from that advanced by Berebitsky, *Sex and the Office*, esp. 246–47. For critiques of the welcomeness standard, see MacKinnon and Siegel, *Directions in Sexual Harassment Law*, part 2.

9. Attention to the emotional and psychological harms of workplace discrimination originated in cases concerning race. Justice William Rehnquist, who wrote the opinion in *Meritor*, cited *Rogers v. Equal Employment Opportunity Commission*: "One can readily envision working environments so heavily polluted with discrimination as to destroy completely the emotional and psychological stability of minority group workers." *Meritor*, 477 U.S. at 65, 66.

10. Working Women's Institute, "Sexual Harassment on the Job: Questions and Answers," quoted in Krista A. Schoenheider, "A Theory of Tort Liability for Sexual Harassment in the Workplace," *University of Pennsylvania Law Review* 34 (1986): 1461.

11. I use this language advisedly to represent the ways that second-wave feminists understood the relationship between sexual difference and gender.

12. On Hill, see Toni Morrison, ed., *Race-ing Justice, En-gendering Power: Essays on Anita Hill, Clarence Thomas, and the Construction of Social Reality* (New York: Pantheon Books, 1992); Geneva Smitherman, ed., *African American Women Speak Out on Anita Hill-Clarence Thomas* (Detroit: Wayne State University, 1995); Bere-bitsky, *Sex and the Office*, 265–72.

13. Mink, *Hostile Environment*, 104–13. It should be noted that evidence of a "pattern" of assault was to be introduced only in cases of unwelcome sexual touching and not for all allegations of a hostile work environment. In practice, judges had wide discretion over what evidence was deemed relevant in a sexual harassment case, and their decisions were often conflicting.

14. Complaint, Paula Corbin Jones v. William Jefferson Clinton and Danny Ferguson (1994), in "Politics Special Report: Jones v. Clinton," *Washington Post*, 1997, www.washingtonpost.com.

15. Jones's lawyers originally included additional descriptions of sexual relations, also borrowed from the VAWA, but the presiding judge, Susan Wright, excluded these as too broad.

16. In addition, he both implicitly and explicitly contrasted that somewhat-tortured definition to a "commonsense" definition that defined sex as "intercourse," or more accurately as penile penetration of vagina or anus. A transcript of Clinton's and Lewinsky's grand jury testimony, along with other documents that Kenneth Starr submitted to Congress in support of his pursuit of impeachment, is included in Phil Kuntz, ed., *The Starr Report: The Evidence* (New York: Pocket Books, 1998) (hereafter cited as *Evidence*).

17. The Independent Prosecutors' Office threatened Lewinsky with prosecution for lying about her affair in the affidavit she submitted in the *Jones* case. In interrogations and her grand jury testimony, she reported that Clinton's touching of her genitals resulted in orgasms on November 15, 1995 ("an orgasm or two"); on February 4, 1996; and on March 29, 1997 (four to six times). She also said he fondled her genitals on March 31, 1997, but did not say whether she came.

18. *Evidence*, 409, 389, 299.

19. *Evidence*, 299, 302.

20. *Evidence*, 257–58. "GJ" signifies that a grand juror asked the question, not a member of Starr's team.

21. *Evidence*, 302, 299, 306. Maria St. John suggests that Lewinsky "rewrites the history of heterosexual fellatio." St. John, "How to Do Things with the *Starr Report*: Pornography, Performance, and the President's Penis," in *Porn Studies*, ed. Linda Williams (Durham, NC: Duke University Press, 2004), 44. On notions of sexual

servicing and the pleasures of oral sex in the context of the Clinton scandal, see Susan Bordo, *The Male Body* (New York: Farrar, Straus and Giroux, 1999), 294–95. Bordo suggests that sometimes fellatio can be understood as part of an ethic of care, a form of sexual healing.

22. There is a lively online debate about when to use "cum" versus "come." I have chosen to use "come" as a verb and "cum" as a noun, despite the oversimplifications of emotional life that this practice entails.

23. *Evidence*, 308.

24. "Trial of William Jefferson Clinton," 145 Cong. Rec. S818 (daily ed. January 20, 1999).

25. On the history of oral sex, see George Chauncey, *Gay New York: Gender, Urban Culture, and the Making of the Gay Male World, 1890–1940* (New York: Basic Books, 1994); Sharon R. Ullman, "'The Twentieth Century Way': Female Impersonation and Sexual Practice in Turn-of-the-Century America," *Journal of the History of Sexuality* 5, no. 4 (1995): 573–600; Alan Hunt and Bruce Curtis, "A Genealogy of the Genital Kiss: Oral Sex in the Twentieth Century," *Canadian Journal of Human Sexuality* 15, no. 2 (2006): 69–84. On antiporn activists and *Deep Throat*, see Carolyn Bronstein, *Battling Pornography: The American Feminist Anti-pornography Movement, 1976–1986* (New York: Cambridge University Press, 2011). Mandy Merck also discusses *Deep Throat* in the context of the Lewinsky-Clinton scandal. See Merck, *In Your Face: 9 Sexual Studies* (New York: NYU Press, 2000), 180–81.

26. *Evidence*, 127–28.

27. On this gift economy, see Cvetkovich, "Sexuality's Archive," esp. 278–79.

28. *Evidence*, 131. Note, however, that other sex acts, including rimming and Clinton's masturbation, were also absent from the chart. Not everyone was happy with the ways that Lewinsky's arousal was hidden. Robert McCollum, a member of the House Judiciary Committee who went on to present the case for impeachment in the Senate, repeatedly called the attention of his colleagues to Lewinsky's claims that Clinton touched her breasts and genitals. Jeffrey Toobin reports that he was ridiculed for doing so, earning the nickname "Mr. Genitalia" among House staffers (*Vast Conspiracy*, 353).

29. Fedwa Malti-Douglas also suggests that discussions of the stains in the Starr Report invite spectators to imagine "the stains on the dress [as] stains on the female body." Malti-Douglas, *The Starr Report Disrobed* (New York: Columbia University Press, 2000), 109.

30. *Evidence*, 579–92; Gormley, *Death of American Virtue*, 522–27.

31. *Evidence*, 135.

32. Lewinsky, "Shame and Survival." In the 2001 HBO documentary *Monica in Black and White*, she is asked, "How does it feel to be America's premier blow job queen?"

33. For example, Marcia Ann Gillespie, "The Backlash Boogie," *Ms.* 8, no. 6 (May–June 1998): 1; Anne Glusker and the Ms. Editors, "Quote Unquote: On Bill, et al.,"

Ms. 8, no. 6 (May–June 1998): 20–23. Some prominent feminists also argued that feminists were silent about the scandal. See, for example, Barbara Ehrenreich, "The Week Feminists Got Laryngitis," *Time*, February 9, 1998.

34. Ehrenreich, in Glusker and Ms. Editors, "Quote Unquote"; Jennie Ruby, "Maneuvering in the Minefield," *Off Our Backs* 28, no. 3 (March 1998): 13, 24; Jill Nelson, "The Pass on Paula," *Ms.* 8, no. 6 (May–June 1998): 64–65; Marcia Ann Gillespie, "The Penile Code," *Ms.* 8, no. 5 (March–April 1998): 1; Victoria Stanhope, "More on Monica: Where Are All the Real Feminists?," *Off Our Backs* 28, no. 10 (November 1998): 14.

35. On the feminist sex wars, see Bronstein, *Battling Pornography*, chaps. 9 and 10; Whitney Strub, *Perversion for Profit: The Politics of Pornography and the Rise of the New Right* (New York: Columbia University Press, 2011), chaps. 7 and 8; Gerhard, *Desiring Revolution*, 183–95; Claire Bond Potter, "Taking Back Times Square: Feminist Repertoires and the Transformation of Urban Space in Late Second Wave Feminism," *Radical History Review* 113 (Spring 2012): 67–80; Alex Warner, "Feminism Meets Fisting: Antipornography, Sadomasochism, and the Politics of Sex," in *Porno Chic and the Sex Wars: American Sexual Representation in the 1970s*, ed. Carolyn Bronstein and Whitney Strub (Amherst: University of Massachusetts Press, 2016), 249–73.

36. Ruby, "Maneuvering in the Minefield"; Stanhope, "More on Monica"; Karla Mantilla, "Clinton a Rapist? . . . It Could Happen," *Off Our Backs* 29, no. 4 (April 1999): 7.

37. Andrea Dworkin, "Dear Bill and Hillary," *Guardian*, January 29, 1998, www.theguardian.com (emphasis in original). Dworkin was identified for the British readership as "America's most radical and controversial feminist." This article was referenced broadly (and generally positively, even though she also suggested in it that Hillary Clinton should shoot her husband) in mainstream publications such as *U.S. News and World Report* and the *Washington Post*.

38. For example, see Jennie Ruby, "More on Clinton: Until a Woman Is President . . . ," *Off Our Backs* 28, no. 9 (1998): 18.

39. Gloria Steinem, "Feminists and the Clinton Question," *New York Times*, March 22, 1998, 15; Steinem, "Yes Means Yes, No Means No: Why Sex Scandals Don't Mean Harassment," *Ms.* 8, no. 6 (May–June1998): 62–63; Katha Pollitt, "Free Willie," *Nation*, February 16, 1998, 9; see also Jeanne Clark, "Women, Our Agenda, and Zippergate," *Off Our Backs* 28, no. 3 (1998): 12.

40. "Clinton Scandal: A Feminist Issue?," *Democracy Now!*, January 26, 1998, www.democracynow.org. Hirshman was the coauthor, with Jane Larson, of a soon-to-be-published book, *Hard Bargains: The Politics of Sex*, which used game theory to analyze the conditions under which women and men bargained with each other for sex. The book argued for the importance of state regulation as a means of enhancing women's capacity to bargain on their own behalf under conditions of unequal power.

41. "Clinton Scandal."

42. "Clinton Scandal." See also Ellen Willis, "The President and the Prosecutor: Three Views on Politics and Personal Life," *Dissent* 45, no. 2 (Spring 1998): 8–9. This was published in different form as "'Tis Pity He's a Whore," in Berlant and Duggan, *Our Monica, Ourselves*, 237–45.

43. Susan Jane Gilman, "Oral Report," *Ms.* 9, no. 4 (1999): 76–79; Susie Bright, "Monica: The Beauty and the Brains," *Ms.* 9, no. 4 (1999): 73–76; Abiola Wendy Abrams, "Dear Monica," *Ms.* 9, no. 4 (1999): 80–81. See also Amelia Richards and Jennifer Baumgardner, "In Defense of Monica," *Nation*, December 21, 1998, 6–7. Abrams went on to launch a multiplatform career, including directing (as Venus Hottentot) the black feminist sex film *AfroDite Superstar*. See Mireille Miller-Young, *A Taste for Brown Sugar: Black Women in Pornography* (Durham, NC: Duke University Press, 2014), 275–76.

44. Lewinsky, "Shame and Survival," 45.

45. Lewinsky, "Price of Shame."

46. Monica Lewinsky, "Emerging from 'the House of Gaslight' in the Age of #MeToo," *Vanity Fair*, March 2018, www.vanityfair.com.

47. Lewinsky; Renee C. Romano, "Not Dead Yet: My Identity Crisis as a Historian of the Recent Past," in *Doing Recent History*, ed. Claire Bond Potter and Renee C. Romano (Athens: University of Georgia Press, 2012), 23–44; Joan W. Scott, "The Evidence of Experience," *Critical Inquiry* 17, no. 4 (1991): 773–97.

48. Lewinsky, "Emerging."

49. Lewinsky.

ACKNOWLEDGMENTS

Our deepest gratitude goes to all of the authors who contributed to this volume, whose scholarship made this book possible, and whose patience and good cheer made our editorial tasks tremendously rewarding. This book entered production nearly simultaneously with the issuance of statewide stay-at-home orders in response to Covid-19, presenting unprecedented challenges to our authors, who could not enter their departmental offices or visit libraries or archives to double-check their citations. These outstanding scholars persevered and, with the assistance of digital resources, dogged librarians, and shared resources, verified notes to the fullest extent possible. We are grateful for their perseverance, particularly as the national political crisis deepened and exacted an emotional toll. We are likewise indebted to Eric C. Zinner, Dolma Ombadykow, Alicia Nadkarni, Furqan Sayeed, and Alexia Traganas at New York University Press for shepherding this project through copyediting and production. Andrew Katz, copyeditor extraordinaire, earned praise and gratitude from this book's editors and authors for his scrupulous attention to detail, which clarified and improved each page. Thank you, Eric, for your initial interest and confidence in the project. Most especially, thank you for championing this project amid significant disruptions to the workplace; we truly appreciate the efforts that you and Dolma made to track down the permissions for the stunning image that graces this book's cover. We are additionally grateful to Ellen Chodosh, director of New York University Press, for her enthusiasm and support. Special thanks also to Sara Cohen, Regina Kunzel, Laura Doan, and Jonathan Ned Katz for their early encouragement and feedback. Important support also came from the anonymous readers of our book proposal, who conveyed that this project was worthwhile and provided critical feedback. We extend our additional thanks to the participants and attendees who joined a roundtable discussion, "Historicizing Heterosexualities in the United States," at the 2020 annual meeting of the

American Historical Association, especially Marc Stein, who organized the panel. Lastly, we also thank the participants in the "Circulating/ Constructing Heterosexuality" panel as well as the audience at the 2017 annual meeting of the Organization of American Historians; a special note of appreciation goes to Andrea Friedman, who stepped in to chair the session and read the comment when travel disruptions prevented both of us from actually reaching New Orleans.

Rebecca first thanks Michele for her steadfast and brilliant editing, intellectual companionship, and fortitude. Collaborating with her has been a gift; Michele's combination of vast historical knowledge, ethical rigor, and unflagging common sense ensured that this book was both ambitious and feasible. For seeing promise in this project when it was in its early stages, she also thanks Kimberly Blockett, Margot Canaday, Gillian Frank, Andrea Friedman, Richard Godbeer, Serena Mayeri, Joanne Meyerowitz, Bethany Moreton, Julia Ott, Gayle Rubin, and Judith Weisenfeld. More personally, Rebecca extends special thanks to Mark Hoffman, who never wavered in his enthusiasm for this book and who made the conditions of the work possible in every way.

Scholarship takes time—and many opportunities for feedback—for it to cohere. Rebecca thanks Peter Cryle and Elizabeth Stephens, two generous scholars who gathered a group of academics at an Italian mountaintop villa to discuss "normality" in the summer of 2018; Andrea Friedman, for inviting her to participate in a roundtable, "Critical Heterosexualities: Thinking about Heterosexuality as a Category of Historical Analysis," at the Seventeenth Berkshire Conference on the History of Women, Gender, and Sexualities in 2017; the organizers of the "Gay American History at 40" conference in 2016 to celebrate the work of Jonathan Ned Katz and copresenters and audience members for the "Inventing Heterosexual Histories" panel; fellow panelists and audience members at the "Women's Liberation and the Hetero/Homosexual Binary" panel at the 2014 conference "A Revolutionary Moment: Women's Liberation of the Late 1960s and Early 1970s"; and Samira Mehta for inviting her to present a paper titled "Heterosexuality/Homosexuality" at a panel on sexual binaries and religious histories at the annual meeting of the American Academy of Religion in 2013. She is grateful as well to the chairs of the Department of History at the University of Delaware— Arwen Mohun, James Brophy, and Alison Parker—who approved the multiple funding requests that enabled her to travel to these conferences. The Institute for Global Studies at the University of Delaware provided additional financial support for conference travel.

Michele would be remiss if she did not first thank Rebecca: not only did Rebecca extend the invitation to collaborate on this project, but Rebecca has also kept us on track throughout the years we have worked together—years that have had some unpredictable, difficult moments for Michele. Rebecca's extensive knowledge in histories of sexuality in the United States has been an inspiration; her kindness has been tremendously appreciated. Michele would additionally like to thank C. Joseph Genetin-Pilawa, Boyd Cothran, and Daniel Hart London for inviting her to participate in a forum on the "Second Gilded Age" for the *Journal of the Gilded Age and Progressive Era* (April 2020). More specifically, the opportunity to reflect on gender and sexuality for that forum enabled Michele to refine key points made within this book's introduction. And, with regard to her contribution to that forum ("Just the Status Quo?"), Michele is especially grateful to Linda Gordon for vital feedback on the initial draft of the essay. On another front, Michele thanks both Valerie Paley and Alice Kessler-Harris: by inviting her to serve as a scholarly advisor for the New-York Historical Society's Center for Women's History, Valerie and Alice—as well as fellow board members— have provided Michele with numerous opportunities to think anew and dynamically about the practice, writing, and presentation of histories of women, gender, and sexuality. Along similar lines, Michele wishes to thank Jon Butler for a similarly generative opportunity: the chance to serve on the editorial board of the *Oxford Research Encyclopedia of American History*, which is nothing less than a wonderful opportunity to deepen knowledge of American history and refine editorial skills. Lastly, Michele thanks her family and friends for ongoing support; she is especially grateful to Emilye Crosby, Anne Valk, and Naoko Shibusawa.

Rebecca and Michele are truly grateful for their respective students: students who push us to be better scholars and teachers, students whose own work and scholarly interests have helped inspire us as we have collaborated on this volume.

Rebecca L. Davis is the Miller Family Early Career Professor of History, with a joint appointment in the Department of Women and Gender Studies, at the University of Delaware. She specializes in the histories of sexuality, gender, and religion in the modern United States. She is the author of *More Perfect Unions: The American Search for Marital Bliss* (2010). Davis is currently at work on two books: *Public Confessions: The Religious Conversions That Changed American Politics* and *Sex in America*. She is a producer of the *Sexing History* podcast and a research associate for the Council on Contemporary Families.

Michele Mitchell is Associate Professor of History at New York University, where she teaches courses in gender history, the history of the United States, and histories of the African diaspora. She is the former North America editor of *Gender & History* and currently serves as Senior Editor for the *Oxford Research Encyclopedia of American History*. She is the author of *Righteous Propagation: African Americans and the Politics of Racial Destiny after Reconstruction* (2004). She coedited *Dialogues of Dispersal: Gender, Sexuality and African Diasporas* (2004) and *Gender, Imperialism and Global Exchanges* (2015). She is also a contributor to *Keywords in African American Studies* (NYU Press, 2018). Mitchell is currently working on a new book, *Idle Anxieties: Youth, Race, and Sexuality during the Great Depression*.

* * *

Sharon Block is Professor of History at the University of California, Irvine, working in colonial North American history, with specializations in the history of sexuality, race, and the body, as well as more broadly in digital humanities. She is the author of *Rape and Sexual Power in Early America* (2006) and *Colonial Complexions: Race and Bodies in Eighteenth-Century America* (2018). She is a coeditor of *Major*

Problems in American Women's History (2013) and a special issue of the *William and Mary Quarterly* on sexuality in early America (2003). An additional two dozen articles, essays, and multimedia publications have focused on the history of sexuality, gender, and race in colonial North America, as well as on data mining, digital humanities, and pedagogy.

Andrea Friedman is Professor of History and Women, Gender, & Sexuality Studies at Washington University in St. Louis. Her research focuses on gender, sexuality, and politics in the twentieth-century United States. She has authored two books: *Citizenship in Cold War America: The National Security State and the Possibilities of Dissent* (2014) and *Prurient Interests: Gender, Democracy, and Obscenity in New York City, 1909–1945* (2000). She is also codirector of *Mapping LGBTQ St. Louis, 1945–1992*, a historical GIS map that documents and analyzes multiple axes of urban segregation through a focus on the LGBTQ experience in the St. Louis metro region. She is currently at work on a history of lesbian feminism and racial politics in St. Louis.

Richard Godbeer is Charles W. Battey Distinguished Professor of History and Director of the Hall Center for the Humanities at the University of Kansas. His books include *The Devil's Dominion: Magic and Religion in Early New England* (1992), *Sexual Revolution in Early America* (2002), *Escaping Salem: The Other Witch Hunt of 1692* (2004), *The Overflowing of Friendship: Love between Men and the Creation of the American Republic* (2009), *The Salem Witch Hunt: A Brief History with Documents* (2011), and *World of Trouble: A Philadelphia Quaker Family's Journey through the American Revolution* (2019).

Zurisaday Gutiérrez Avila graduated in 2018 from Oberlin College, where she double majored in psychology and sociology. Growing up close to the Mexican border inspired her to pursue an honors project about the experiences of undocumented students. She also participated in organizations related to Latin American identity and immigration issues. Her career interests include social work and the law and advocacy on behalf of marginalized communities.

Rashauna Johnson is Associate Professor of History at the University of Chicago. She is interested in slavery and migration in the African diaspora, with attention to labor, space and place, and gender and sexuality in the Caribbean and southern United States. She is the author of the prize-winning *Slavery's Metropolis: Unfree Labor in New Orleans during the Age of Revolutions* (2016) and is currently at work on a book about slavery and emancipation in nineteenth-century Louisiana.

Carolyn Herbst Lewis is Associate Professor of History at Grinnell College. She is the author of *Prescription for Heterosexuality: Sexual Citizenship in Cold War America* (2010) and several articles that have appeared in the *Journal of Women's History, Social History of Medicine*, and various edited collections. Her research interests encompass constructions of norms, knowledge, and authority in the overlapping histories of gender, sexuality, and medicine.

Serena Mayeri is Professor of Law and History at the University of Pennsylvania Law School. Her first book, *Reasoning from Race: Feminism, Law, and the Civil Rights Revolution* (2011), received the Littleton-Griswold Prize from the American Historical Association and the Darlene Clark Hine Award from the Organization of American Historians. Her current book project, *The Status of Marriage: Marital Supremacy Challenged and Remade, 1960–2000*, examines the history of challenges to marriage's legal primacy. Mayeri received her JD and PhD (in history) from Yale. At Penn, she holds a secondary appointment in the History Department and serves on the executive committees of the Program on Gender, Sexuality, and Women's Studies and the Andrea Mitchell Center for the Study of Democracy.

Pablo Mitchell is Professor of History and Comparative American Studies at Oberlin College. He is the author of *West of Sex: Making Mexican America, 1900–1930* (2012) and *Coyote Nation: Sexuality, Race, and Conquest in Modernizing New Mexico, 1880–1920* (2005). A paperback edition of his Latina/o history textbook, *Understanding Latino History: Excavating the Past, Examining the Present*, was released in 2017. He is also the coeditor of *Beyond the Borders of the Law: Critical Legal Histories of the North American West* (2018).

Sarah Rodriguez is Senior Lecturer in Global Health Studies in the Weinberg College of Arts and Sciences, Lecturer in Medical Education in the Feinberg School of Medicine, and a faculty member in the Medical Humanities and Bioethics Graduate Program at Northwestern University in Evanston, Illinois. Her research is in the history of women's reproductive health and the practice of medicine, including in her books *Female Circumcision and Clitoridectomy in the United States: A History of a Medical Treatment* (2014) and *The Love Surgeon: A Story of Trust, Harm, and the Limitations of Medical Regulation* (2020).

Renee Romano is the Robert S. Danforth Professor of History and Professor of Comparative American Studies and Africana Studies at Oberlin College. A specialist in recent American cultural and political history and in the field of historical memory, she is the author of *Race Mixing: Black-White Marriage in Postwar America* (2003) and *Racial Reckoning: Reopening America's Civil Rights Trials* (2014). She has also coedited three volumes: *The Civil Rights Movement in American Memory* (2006), *Doing Recent History: On Privacy, Copyright, Video Games, Institutional Review Boards, Activist Scholarship, and History That Talks Back* (2012), and *Historians on "Hamilton": How a Blockbuster Musical Is Restaging America's Past* (2018). She has served as a historical consultant for several public history projects, including the "Mixed Heritage Families Project" at the Brooklyn Historical Society.

Marc Stein is the Jamie and Phyllis Pasker Professor of History at San Francisco State University. He is the author of *City of Sisterly and Brotherly Loves: Lesbian and Gay Philadelphia, 1945–1982* (2000), *Sexual Injustice: Supreme Court Decisions from* Griswold *to* Roe (2010), *Rethinking the Gay and Lesbian Movement* (2012), and *The Stonewall Riots: A Documentary History* (NYU Press, 2019). He also served as editor in chief of the *Encyclopedia of LGBT History in America* (2003) and guest editor of the "Homophile Internationalism" special issue of the *Journal of Homosexuality* (2017).

Nicholas L. Syrett is Professor and Chair of Women, Gender, and Sexuality Studies at the University of Kansas. He is a coeditor, with Corinne T. Field, of *Age in America: The Colonial Era to the Present* (NYU Press,

2015) and of the 2020 *American Historical Review* roundtable "Chronological Age: A Useful Category of Historical Analysis." He is the author of three books: *The Company He Keeps: A History of White College Fraternities* (2009), *American Child Bride: A History of Minors and Marriage in the United States* (2016), and the forthcoming *An Open Secret: The Family Story of Robert and John Gregg Allerton*. With Jen Manion, he is editing *The Cambridge History of Sexuality in the United States*.

Heather R. White is Visiting Assistant Professor at the University of Puget Sound, in Tacoma, Washington. She received the PhD in religious studies from Princeton University in 2007 and has also served as a visiting faculty at New College of Florida and Vassar College. She is a specialist in American religious history with a research focus on sexuality, gender, and twentieth-century social movements. She is the author of *Reforming Sodom: Protestants and the Rise of Gay Rights* (2015) and the coeditor (with Gillian Frank and Bethany Moreton) of *Devotions and Desires: Histories of Religion and Sexuality in the Twentieth Century United States* (2018).

Judy Tzu-Chun Wu is Professor in the Department of Asian American Studies and Director of the Humanities Center at the University of California, Irvine. She authored *Dr. Mom Chung of the Fair-Haired Bastards: the Life of a Wartime Celebrity* (2005) and *Radicals on the Road: Internationalism, Orientalism, and Feminism during the Vietnam Era* (2013). Her current book project, a collaboration with the political scientist Gwendolyn Mink, explores the political career of Patsy Takemoto Mink, the first woman of color US congressional representative and the cosponsor of Title IX. She also is working on a book that focuses on Asian American and Pacific Islander women who attended the 1977 National Women's Conference. Wu coedited *Women's America: Refocusing the Past*, 8th ed. (2015), *Gendering the Trans-Pacific World* (2017), and *Frontiers: A Journal of Women's Studies* (2012–17). She also coedits *Women and Social Movements in the United States, 1600–2000* and is the editor for *Amerasia Journal*.

INDEX

Page numbers in italics indicate figures.

America, 54, 148; family and, 274–75; gender and, 20; humiliation and, 363–64; intersectionality of, 76–77; Judeo-Christian sexuality and, 336–37; labor and, 20, 363–64; lesbianism and, 17–18; nation and, 75–83; in North America, 13; penal system and, 10–11; power and, 17; print culture, slavery, and, 153–54, 169–79; religion and, 336–37; respectability and, 10–11, 86–87; science and, 8; sexes and, 153–54; sexology and, 8; sexuality, heterosexuality, and, 2–3, 5, 19–20, 148; sexual revolution and, 126–27; as social construct, 13. *See also* interraciality; interracial marriage

racialized heteronormativity: Asian Americans and, 120–38; embracing and resisting, 133–37. *See also* interraciality

racialized heterosexuality, 2, 25n8, 31n61, 228–29; in antebellum period, 21, 28n32, 62n6, 169–86; in Broussais's *Self-Preservation*, 170–79, 187n9; in *Daily Orleanian*, 171, 179–86; homosexuality and, 171; in pseudoscience and medicine, 175–76, 188n10; slavery and, 170–79

racial liberalism, 123

racism: Asian Americans and, 122, 125, 128–29; homosexuality and, 171; lynching and, 232; racial "purity," whiteness, and, 72–73, 127; sexual, 70, 74, 84; structural or systemic, 6

Ramey, James, 266

rape, 177, 178. *See also* sexual abuse

Reconstruction, 75–76

Redbook, 256–57

Red Butterfly, 15

Reder, Francis, 315–16

"Red Scare," 131, 198

refugees, 136

regulation. See law

Reis, Elizabeth, 63n15

religion: abortion and, 286; Bible and, 334–35, 338, 342–43; birth control and, 349–50; body and, 47; Catholic Church and, 243, 335–36, 343–44; Christ and, 43–46, 50–52, 63n15; Christian Crusade and, 345; citizenship and, 336–37; culture and, 350–51; empirical studies of sex and, 337–41; evangelicalism and, 350–51; evolution and, 338–39; faith communities and, 334, 351–52; family and, 341–44; femininity in, 46–47; gender and, 42, 46–48; home and, 229; homosexuality and, 351; interfaith marriage and, 336–37; interfaith sexuality and, 344–48; Judeo-Christian morality and, 23, 331–34, 336–37, 348–52; Kinsey on, 339–41; love and, 37–39, 42–44, 50–52; marriage and, 25n9, 43–44, 243, 245–46, 336–37; marriage law and, 331–40, 351–52; medicine and, 339–41; Mexicans and, 243, 245–46; morality and, 23, 41, 331–37, 348–52; mother in, 46–47, 63n17; nation and, 341; pluralism and, 341–42, 344–48, 352; politics and, 350–51; popular culture and, 350–51; during Protestant Reformation, 335–36; psychology and, 339; Puritans and, 37–39, 42–43, 44, 46, 48–52; race and, 336–37; reproduction and, 46–47; same-sex marriage and, 332; science and, 339–41; sexual education and, 344–49; sexual liberalism and, 339–41, 352; sexual orientation, 62n7; in Southwest, 243

Religious Right, 348–52

reproduction, 4, 6; adoption and, 134–35; heterosexual privilege, culture, and, 18; homosexuality and, 196–97; interraciality and, 72–75, 177–79; religion and, 46–47; reproductive freedom and rights, 286–90; sexual abuse and, 177; sexual function, women, and, 23, 176; slavery and, 72–73, 172, 178. See also obstetrics

women (*cont.*)

Mexican, 227–28, 232, 244, 250n32; normality of vaginal intercourse and, 315–18; obstetrics and, 23, 303–21; oral sex and subordination of, 369–70, 375–76; orgasms and, 263, 265, 361; patriarchy and, 15, 32n62; perineum and sexual function, 303–21; policing of, 92n30; respectability of, 86–87, 283; sexual discrimination and, 274, 282–90, 362–63; sexual harassment and, 359, 362–66; sexual identity of, 74; VAWA and, 364, 383n15; virginity and, 304–5, 318, 320–21, 327n89; white supremacy and, 72–75. *See also* black women; lesbianism; mothers; prostitution; reproduction; sexual abuse

Wood, Leland Foster, 342–43, 355n36

Wood, Natalie, 255

Workingmen's Party of California, 122

workplace sex, 361–66, 383n13

World War II, 129, 133, 137, 333, 341–42; heteronormativity after, 195–96; mother and, 201

Wu, Ellen, 132

Wu, Judy Tzu-Chun, 21, 80

Wulf, Mel, 277

Wylie, Phillip, 201

xenophobic movements, 125, 128–29

"yellow peril," 121–22, 123, 128, 138

Young, Robert, 75

The Young Ladies and Gentlemen's Hymeneal Instructor (Caswall), 104

The Young Lady's Guide to the Harmonious Development of Christian Character (Newcomb), 105

Yuh, Ji-Yeon, 134

Zellerbach, Merla, 207